A Century of
English International
Football 1872-1972

A Century of English International Football
1872-1972

by
MORLEY FARROR
and
DOUGLAS LAMMING

Robert Hale and Company

ISBN 0 7091 3630 7

Robert Hale and Company
63 Old Brompton Road
London, S.W.7

PRINTED IN GREAT BRITAIN BY
BRISTOL TYPESETTING CO. LTD.
BARTON MANOR - ST. PHILIPS
BRISTOL

Contents

Illustrations

Preface

IT HAS often been said, and with some truth, that Association Football has not received the attention historically and statistically its popularity warrants. Other sports—particularly cricket—are cited as being much more favoured. Why should cricket, with moderate public support, a season little more than four months long and subject to the vagaries of English summer weather, be the subject of such a wealth of books?

The answer sometimes advanced—that cricket writers are catering for a more literate public—is only partly true, if true at all. Surely, out of soccer's enormous following, a potential readership exists for books treating the game more deeply. No, the answer is largely because Association Football does not have the corpus of reference works on its early decades; for example, it was not until 1907 that appearance lists for even the First Division were given in any annual. Until comparatively recently, too, works of a historical nature have generally dealt with administrative matters at the expense of the playing side—this is in direct contrast to cricket books and is a contributory cause of the summer sport's much greater readership. It is also one reason why our book is devoted entirely to players. The lack of early sources has been taken as a challenge and we have found satisfaction in the building-up of data, which has come from countless byways of reference.

We would like here to give thanks to friends and correspondents who have willingly given help on points of detail—in particular Maurice Golesworthy, Alex Wilson of Leicester, Paul de Jong of Wallasey, Bryan Horsnell of Reading and Keith Warsop of Nottingham. In the matter of illustrations acknowledgements are due to Messrs. D. C. Thomson & Co. Ltd., Barratt's Photo Press Ltd. and the Provincial Press Agency of Southport.

We hope the pages which follow prove acceptable to the game's followers. If further authentic information on any international player can be given by the reader we shall be grateful to receive it.

MORLEY FARROR
Great Bookham, Surrey

DOUGLAS LAMMING
North Ferriby, Yorkshire

1

Highlights of the Century

IT IS generally thought that International football emanated from a letter by Mr Charles W. Alcock, then secretary of the Football Association, to the *Glasgow Herald* dated 1 November 1870 notifying Scottish players that an England v Scotland match would take place on 19 November 1870, in London, and asking interested Scotsmen to contact A. F. Kinnaird or J. Kirkpatrick who were arranging the Scottish team. This match did take place on 19 November 1870, as arranged, but it was not the first such match.

Mr Alcock had written to *The Sportsman,* then the leading London newspaper dealing with football, and his letter was published on 5 February 1870:

From the Secretary of the Football Association

A match between the leading representatives of the Scotch and English sections will be played at The Oval on Saturday, 19 February, under the auspices of The Football Association. Players duly qualified and desirous of assisting either party must communicate with Mr A. F. Kinnaird of 2 Pall Mall East, S.W. or Mr J. Kirkpatrick, Admiralty, Somerset House, W.C. on behalf of the Scotch, or with Mr Charles W. Alcock, Boy Court, Ludgate Hill, E.C., or Mr R. G. Graham, 7 Finch Lane, E.C. on the part of the English.

(signed) Charles W. Alcock

As it transpired a severe frost on 19 February caused the cancellation of almost all football on that day. The match was rearranged to take place on 5 March 1870 and resulted in a 1-1 draw. The following report of the game appearing in *The Sportsman* of 8 March 1870:

ENGLAND v SCOTLAND

This match, which has for some weeks past occupied the attention of the numerous sections of players who follow the guidance of the Football Association, took place at Kennington Oval on Saturday in the presence of an assemblage of spectators such as has, in point of numbers, never been equalled, the entire limit of the ground being lined by an enthusiastic array of the supporters of the two sides. It will be remembered that the match was first fixed for Saturday 19

February but was postponed in consequence of severe frost until Saturday last, the postponement of the fixture fortunately being attended with such a favourable combination of weather as to leave no regret that the original date was cancelled. Both sides were well represented though the Scottish eleven were at the eleventh hour crippled by the unavoidable retirement of Lord Kilmarnock and R. N. Ferguson, both of whom were no mean members of the team. Soon after a quarter past three o'clock the English captain, having lost the toss for choice of goals and thereby placed the eleven under the great disadvantage of contending against an unusually strong wind, kicked off, the ground it may be added being rather too greasy for dribbling purposes. During the early portion of the game the Scottish team held a slight advantage, the opposition of the wind combined with the slippery state of the ground, preventing the Englishmen from making any impression on the ranks of their opponents. Gradually, however, warming to their work and becoming more accustomed to each other's game the Englishmen commenced to assail the quarters occupied by their rivals, and although, when three-quarters of an hour had elapsed, and a change of ends was necessitated, no event of moment had fallen to either side, it was apparent that the tide was steadily turning in favour of the English. At four o'clock positions were accordingly reversed, and from this time the English aided by the wind kept their opponents closely besieged, the excellent defence of Messrs W. H. Gladstone and A. Morten, the latter of whom proved a most efficient goalkeeper, alone frustrating the ceaseless attack of Baker, Crake and Vidal among the English forwards. This siege of the Scottish lines was never raised until a quarter of an hour before the time fixed for the cessation of the game when, owing to a reprehensible excess of confidence on the part of the English captain, the English goal, which had been left thoroughly unprotected, fell to a long and rather lucky kick by H. E. Crawford, this evidently unexpected success of the Scotchmen creating no little excitement among the partisans of the northern side. After the further change of ends the Englishmen awakened to the necessity of renewed exertions, played up with desperate energy, and their efforts were happily rewarded just as time was called by a most brilliant run on the part of A. Baker, who thus saved England from the odium of defeat, and left the question of the respective merits of the two countries on the football field as open a question as before the commencement of the match. The play on both sides was remarkable for the spirit and determination that actuated every member of the two sides, the Scottish eleven especially meriting the highest praise for the gallant stand they made throughout the game. It is only to be regretted that owing to unavoidable causes the chances of a return match are very remote during the present season, and the question of superiority must thus remain in abeyance until the commencement of another campaign. On the side of Scotland, W. H. Gladstone shone out conspicuously among his brethren, his kicking and back-play generally showing no lack of the skill for which he was so distinguished at Eton, and Crawford, Hamilton and Lindsay were also worthy of the highest commendation. For England, A. Baker was remarkable for the speed as well as the energy of his play, and E. Freeth and E. Lubbock were also very effective as backs. The sides were:

England: C. W. Alcock (Old Harrovians) captain, E. E. Bowen (Wanderers), A. Baker (NNs), W. C. Butler (Barnes Club), W. P. Crake (Harrow School), E. Freeth (Civil Service), E. Lubbock (Old Etonians), A. Nash (Clapham Rovers), J. C. Smith (Crusaders), A. H. Thornton (Old Harrovians) and R. W. Vidal (Westminster School).

Scotland: J. Kirkpatrick (Civil Service) captain, H. W. Crawford (Harrow School), W. H. Gladstone M.P. (Old Etonians), G. C. Gordon (NNs), C. R. B. Hamilton (Civil Service), W. A. B. Hamilton (Old Harrovians), A. F. Kinnaird (Crusaders), W. Lindsay (Old Wykehamists), J. W. Malcolm M.P. (London Scottish Rifles), A Morten (Crystal Palace) and K. Muir Mackenzie (Old Carthusians).

This, then, was the first " international match ". Further games between English and Scottish players were arranged by the Football Association and took place as stated on 19 November 1870, and also on 21 February and 18 November 1871, and on 24 February 1872, but these games are now regarded as unofficial internationals and pride of place as a full international is given to the match which took place on 30 November 1872 at Hamilton Crescent, Glasgow. As a matter of interest full details of the five unofficial internationals appear at the end of Chapter 5.

C. W. Alcock's letter of 1 November 1870 to the *Glasgow Herald* was not without response and the Queens Park Club nominated one of its members, Robert Smith, who had primarily resided in London since 1869, and played there with the South Norwood Club. Smith also played in the matches of February and November 1871.

The success of the matches in London prompted Queens Park to propose, during the summer of 1872, that one of the matches due to be played during the 1872-3 season should take place in Glasgow, and the Football Association finally agreed to send a team of Englishmen to Glasgow on 30 November 1872. The Scottish team was picked by the Queens Park captain, Robert Gardner, and the match resulted in a goalless draw. Reports of this match have been given in various books but just for the record this was the first full English international team:

W. J. Maynard (1st Surrey Rifles) goal; E. H. Greenhalgh (Notts) back; R. de C. Welch (Wanderers) and F. B. Maddison (Oxford University) half-backs; and R. Barker (Hertfordshire Rangers), J. Brockbank (Cambridge University), J. C. Clegg (Sheffield Wednesday), A. K. Smith (Oxford University), C. J. Ottaway (Oxford University) (captain), C. J. Chenery (Crystal Palace) and C. J. Morice (Barnes) forwards.

C. W. Alcock, M. P. Betts, A. Morten and T. C. Hooman, who were original choices, were unable to play.

A return game was played at The Oval on 8 March 1873, which England won 4-2. The Scottish team in this match was also chosen by Robert Gardner. The Scottish Football Association was formed on 13 March 1873, and in all subsequent international matches between the two countries that Association has arranged the Scottish team. Apart from the Victory internationals of 1919, and the matches during the Second World War, the games between England and Scotland have been on a home and away basis in alternate years.

In 1874 England visited Glasgow and the team included J. H. Edwards of Shropshire Wanderers who replaced an original choice, his clubmate, J. G. Wylie. Strangely, C. W. Alcock, in his *Football Annual* of that year, shows Wylie as having played although, being secretary of the F.A., he must have been aware that Edwards had played instead. More curious still, when the first list of international players was published in the *Football Annual* of 1892, Wylie is again listed instead of Edwards, although Alcock had in the intervening years referred to Edwards' participation in the match. Edwards was a Welshman and was the first Treasurer of the Football Association of Wales, on the formation of that body in 1876, and played for Wales v Scotland in that year and thus became the first of the few who have played for two countries, a fact which has strangely eluded historians to date.

Although Scotland commenced to play Wales in 1876, it was not until 1879 that England were, with some reluctance, prevailed upon to meet Wales and the first match took place on 18 January 1879, at The Oval, and resulted in a win for England by no more than 2-1. After another narrow victory in 1880, Wales scored her first win in 1881, at Blackburn, by a single goal, and in the following season, at Wrexham, got through by 5-3. The advent of professionalism, however, drained the Principality of many of its best players and the Football League Clubs being no more willing then than they are now to release their players, Wales had to wait a long time for the next victory, until 1920 in fact. Both England and Wales played Ireland for the first time in 1882, and when Scotland agreed to play Ireland in 1884 the Home International Championship competition was complete and has continued to be contested annually to this day, apart from the War years.

The next addition to the international fixture list was the match v Canada at The Oval, on 19 December 1891. This match is seldom now regarded as an international match but there is no doubt that at the time it was played it was in this category. The Canadian team had toured in 1888, when a match was played against Scotland, and the 1891 team played against Ireland, Wales and Scotland in turn before meeting England. The Canadian Football Association had not been formed at this time, and the tourists were privately organised, but this cannot be a good reason for relegating the status of the match in view of the fact that the first two Scottish teams were privately organised by the Queens Park Club prior to the formation of the Scottish Association. In this book, remember, the match has been treated as an unofficial international game to accord with the official view.

It is interesting to note that in 1890, 1891 and 1892 England played Wales and Ireland on the same day, a real indication of the gathering strength of English football, but as the margin in each match in 1892 was only 2-0 it was, no doubt, decided that the time had come to revert to different dates for the two matches. In actual fact, a completely amateur team was chosen for the Irish match in 1893 and a full professional team for the Welsh match, although the games were played on different dates. It is generally acknowledged that in 1894 and 1895, the Corinthians provided the whole of the England teams against Wales. While it is correct to say that all the players in these two teams were members of the Corinthians Club, the majority played more regularly for other Clubs at that particular time.

In November 1899, the first official tour abroad took place when the Football Association sent a team to Germany. It was a strong team, a mixture of amateur and professional players, most of whom were capped either before or after the tour. Four matches were played, three against teams labelled Germany and one against a combined Germany-Austria team. All the matches were won comfortably. Germany sent a team to England in September 1901, and two matches were played against England sides resulting in heavy losses for the Germans, but the English teams in these matches definitely played under the respective titles, England Amateurs and England Professionals and the games cannot be regarded as full international matches. Neither, of course, can the matches in Germany for they were played under the title of the Football Association.

The first mass football tragedy occurred in 1902 when, during the England v Scotland match at Ibrox Park, Glasgow, on 5 April, part of the terracing collapsed, twenty-five people being killed and many injured. To avoid panic among the spectators, most of whom were unaware of the happening, the match was played to a finish as a friendly match and was replayed at Villa Park, Birmingham, a month later when the proceeds were given to the Disaster Fund.

It was about this time that moves were on foot for the formation of F.I.F.A. and C. A. W. Hirschman, of Holland, and Robert Guerin, of France, made strong representations to the Football Association to lead the formation of this body. The Football Association, however, probably thinking that its power was in jeopardy, was very lukewarm in its interest and the F.I.F.A. was eventually formed in Paris, on 21 May 1904, without the co-operation of the Football Association. By April of 1905, the F.A. had decided to co-operate with the new body whilst remaining outside it, but in June 1906 they sent representatives to a meeting in Berne, at which it was decided to join the Federation and D. B. Woolfall of Blackburn was elected as President, a post which he occupied until his death in 1918. At this meeting it was also arranged that England should play amateur international matches, during the 1906-7 season, against France and Holland. These two matches duly took place and led the way to the intensive European competitions which we know today.

At the end of the following season, in June 1908, the first full England team went on tour, playing two international matches in Vienna against Austria, one in Budapest against Hungary and one in Prague against Bohemia (as Czechoslovakia was then called), all of which were won comfortably. The tour was repeated the following year when two matches were played one against Hungary and one against Austria with similar results.

The first Commonwealth tour was undertaken in the summer of 1910 when a fairly strong team was sent to South Africa. Three " Test " matches were played, all of which were won, as were the other 20 matches played.

From 1909 up to the First World War no further internationals were played against European opposition; these games were left to the England Amateur team who proved more than equal to the task by winning 21, drawing 2 and losing only 3 of the 26 matches played.

After the war difficulties immediately arose for England who, in common with the other British Associations and the Allied Football Associations, were not prepared to entertain the idea of playing against Austria, Germany and Hungary, and at a meeting in Brussels, in December 1919, further decided that they were not prepared to meet neutral countries who played against these former enemy countries. Subsequently, France and Belgium modified their attitudes in this respect but the British Associations stood firm and withdrew from F.I.F.A. on 23 April 1920. Nevertheless, England did not entirely fall out with the neutral countries and a match against Belgium in March 1921 was the first of a long run of games against this country up to the late 1920s. Of particular note was the fact that when Belgium visited Highbury, in March 1923, they became the first continental country to play in a full international match in England. By 1922 the F.A. had rescinded its earlier decision not to play against former neutral countries, which had been fraternising, with the result that, in May 1923, not only were France played in Paris but two matches were staged against Sweden.

Late in 1923 representations were made to the British Associations to rejoin F.I.F.A., which they did in June 1924, although it was clear that there were strong differences of opinion between the British Associations and the remainder of the F.I.F.A. countries on the question of broken time payments to amateurs, to which the British Associations were opposed.

This latter question turned out to be the cause of a further withdrawal of the British Associations from F.I.F.A. for, when discussions were proceeding prior to the 1928 Olympics in Amsterdam, F.I.F.A.'s interpretation of an amateur was found to be unacceptable although, strangely, the Olympic Games Committee found themselves able to accept it. The British Associations withdrew first from the Olympic Games and later from F.I.F.A.

Thus it was that England were missing from the first contest for the World Cup in 1930. The ambition to stage an International Cup competition had been voiced at the time of the formation of F.I.F.A. in 1904, but it was not until 1928, during the Olympic Games, that the proposal had come to fruition and resulted in Jules Rimet, President of F.I.F.A., presenting the trophy for the first competition which Uruguay, who had convincingly won the Olympic Games of 1928, were invited to stage. It was almost entirely an American competition as only France, Belgium, Yugoslavia and Rumania of the European countries took part. The host country were the victors. Italy was to win in 1934 and 1938, with the British Associations still absent.

Meanwhile, although not members of F.I.F.A., England retained a friendly individual relationship with its members and during the 1930s an increasingly varied number of European opponents were met both abroad and in England. It was in 1929 that England was first beaten by a European country, Spain winning 4-3 in Madrid, and in December 1932, at Stamford Bridge, Austria came near to being the first European country to lower England's colours at home, losing only 4-3. It was to be another twenty-two years before England's home record went.

In October 1938, F.I.F.A. provided a team under the title of "Rest of Europe" to play England in celebration of the F.A.'s 75th anniversary. The match ending in a comfortable 3-0 win for England. Perhaps a much more significant match had taken place earlier in that year in Berlin where England played Germany. The Germans, pursuing their quest for power, were very anxious to win this game but England put on a great display and won 6-3. There was considerable controversy over the pre-match preliminaries because the England officials had been persuaded to instruct the players to give the Nazi salute when lining up before the game.

International football came to an end so far as England was concerned with the outbreak of war in 1939, although a number of unofficial matches were played during the war against Scotland and Wales. Although Irish League football was probably strengthened by the presence of service players in Northern Ireland, Ireland did not attempt to put an international team in the field. England had a notable team during this period although, of course, it must be said that, with their greater number of players, they missed those who were not available, owing to service demands, rather less than Scotland and Wales. Wales, as it happened, had a rather better record than Scotland. Further, the looser defensive play which generally prevailed was greatly to the advantage of England's outstanding forwards for Matthews, Carter, Lawton, Hagan, Mannion, Welsh and Compton were in their heyday during this period.

In the autumn of 1945, a meeting of F.I.F.A. took place in Zurich to which the Football Association were invited, and as a result of the discussions which took place the British Associations again joined the Federation. To mark the occasion Great Britain played the Rest of Europe, at Glasgow, in May 1947, the match resulting in an emphatic 6-1 victory for Britain.

In 1946, Mr Walter Winterbottom had been elected Director of Coaching to the Football Association and his duties included the management of the England team, although the team itself was still being selected by a committee of amateur administrators whose long experience might have enabled them to become good judges of individual players but who were without experience of blending individuals into a team. At that time, too, the England team only met for a few hours before each international so that the opportunity of moulding the team in practice games did not exist either. In any event, Mr Winterbottom clearly considered that his duties stretched far beyond the running of the England international teams. His team management has, perhaps justly, been much criticised, but, in his capacity of Director of Coaching, he did notable work in establishing the intensive coaching which takes place today. This has undoubtedly enabled far more players to acquire the basic skill of the game, ball control.

England, of course, staged the Olympic Games of 1948 but could only finish fourth in the football competition. The return to F.I.F.A. membership, however, meant that the British Associations were eligible for the World Cup competition in 1950, the first since 1938. The latter event had taken place in Italy so that it fell to America's lot to stage the 1950 competition and it was allocated to Brazil. This posed climatic problems, which were not appreciated in advance so that the England team went to South America without proper preparation, but they had done well enough in European spheres to be regarded as second favourites after the host country. They started with a modest victory over Chile by 2-0, this being followed by the infamous defeat by United States of America at Belo Horizonte by one goal to nil. One would have thought that the shame of this defeat might have inspired the team to greater efforts in the concluding match of the qualifying competition, but another pathetic performance led to a similar defeat by Spain, and England had failed to qualify for the competition proper.

Following this, England had several years of success, with a mere couple of defeats, until the Hungarians came to Wembley in November of 1953 and gave a football lesson which was repeated in Hungary in the following May even more emphatically. This latter match was closely followed by the World Cup in Switzerland, in which England won its group and qualified for the quarter-finals where they succumbed to Uruguay.

After a not too successful season in 1955, a period of recovery commenced in 1956 and 1957 during which the only loss sustained was against Ireland at Wembley. The 1958 World Cup showed that the Irish were at this time reaching their peak. The years 1958 and 1959 were tragic ones, with Roger Byrne, Duncan Edwards and Tommy Taylor perishing at Munich and Jeff Hall dying of polio. Clearly, rebuilding was necessary and this could not, of course, be achieved before the 1958 World Cup in Sweden. England qualified for the competition proper, and in their group drew all their games, losing the play-off for second place to Russia.

The match against Scotland at Wembley on 11 April 1959 was notable as the occasion of Billy Wright's 100th appearance for England. He was the first player to achieve this distinction in international football for any country. He ended his career with 105 appearances, this figure having since been beaten by Bobby Charlton.

A disastrous tour of South America was made in the spring of 1959 when games against Brazil, Peru and Mexico were all lost,

B

and it was not until the latter end of 1960 that recovery started, sparked off by the goalscoring of Greaves and Smith aided by Haynes, Douglas and Charlton. Despite defeat by Scotland at Wembley in 1962, England went off to the World Cup in Brazil in good fettle but defeat in the first match by Hungary brought a return to realism. England won a place in the quarter-finals as runners-up in the group. That was the end, Brazil winning the quarter-final comfortably by 3-1.

There were other notable changes at this time for during the 1961–2 season Sir Stanley Rous announced his intention to retire from the secretaryship of the Football Association which he had held since 1934. It was largely expected that Walter Winterbottom would succeed, but the F.A. chose its treasurer, Denis Follows, and he took over in May 1962. Later in the year Winterbottom left the service of the F.A. to take over the leadership of the Central Council for Physical Recreation and the opportunity was taken to split the duties of Director of Coaching and the management of the England teams, the latter post falling to Alfred Ramsey who had enjoyed spectacular success in a short career as manager of Ipswich Town. Ramsey took up his duties at the end of the 1962–3 season.

The 1962–3 season saw the commencement of another venture, England's entry into the European Nations Cup. This competition had been started in the period 1958–60 for the Henri Delaunay Cup but England had not entered at that time. The first venture was not too successful, England being drawn against France in the first round and, after drawing at Sheffield 1-1, lost the second leg in Paris by the emphatic score of 5-2. The F.A. celebrated its centenary in October of 1963 with a match at Wembley against F.I.F.A. which resulted in a 2-1 win for England.

The next few years were devoted to building the side which was to contest the World Cup of 1966, which England were invited to stage, a re-building process carried on right to the final stages of the competition, for it was only then that Geoff Hurst and Martin Peters clinched their places.

England were fortunate to be grouped with Uruguay, Mexico and France and after a 0-0 draw in the initial game with Uruguay, the other two matches were won and England headed the group and passed into the quarter-finals. This was a bruising game against Argentine who were finally beaten 1-0. England were also fortunate to play Portugal in the semi-final at Wembley, whereas the previously announced arrangements indicated that the game should be played in the provinces. However, in the interest of finance, it was played at Wembley and a victory over Portugal took England into the Final. The dramatic victory by 4-2, after extra time, against

West Germany will be fresh in the memories of most readers but the team which accomplished this triumph is worthy of being placed on record: G. Banks, G. R. Cohen, R. Wilson, N. P. Stiles, J. Charlton, R. F. Moore (captain), A. J. Ball, R. Hunt, R. Charlton, G. C. Hurst and M. S. Peters.

There was no respite after this victory for the Home International Championships for 1966-7 and 1967-8 were the qualifiying competitions for the European Nations Cup of 1968. By winning at Wembley in 1967 Scotland took the lead, but they lost to Ireland in the 1968 competition so were in the position of having to beat England to qualify. In the event, the match at Hampden Park was drawn and England qualified for the final stages. In the quarter-finals Spain were beaten 2-1 but Yugoslavia gained a 1-0 victory in the semi-final and so England, although World Champions, were not European Champions.

The next event of note was, of course, the World Cup of 1970 which took place in Mexico. As holders England were given a place in the final stages without having to take part in the qualifying competition. By way of preparation, England undertook a tour of South America in the spring of 1969 which brought a draw against Mexico, a victory over Uruguay and defeat by Brazil, but it was felt that the lessons learned were worth the effort. England were in a difficult group which included Czechoslovakia, Rumania and Brazil. The latter country were the favourites, and the advantage of being in the same group was that in the event of England and Brazil being the qualifiers from the group they could not meet again until the final. Brazil won their match against England 1-0, but victories by England by similar scores against Rumania and Czechoslovakia put them into the quarter-finals where the opposition was provided by West Germany, eager to avenge the defeat in the Final in 1966. During the early part of the match England played their best football and took a deserved 2-0 lead, but after that they became overconfident, eased up and were unable to get into their full stride again. West Germany levelled the score in the second-half and got the winner in extra time. This match was Bobby Charlton's 106th (and at the moment last) game for England, beating Billy Wright's record.

For the 1972 European Nations Cup a different system of qualifying was adopted. The nations were placed in groups of four and they had to play each other home and away during the 1970-1 and 1971-2 seasons to qualify for the final stages in the spring of 1972. England were grouped with Malta, Greece and Switzerland, and with five wins and a draw headed the group and qualified to meet West Germany in the quarter final, losing the first leg 1-3 at

Wembley and drawing the second leg 0-0 to go out on aggregate 1-3.

As we write we find that these two competitions, the World Cup and the European Nations Cup being contested, one or the other, every two years, are tending to overshadow the Home International Championship which has now been played for annually since 1884. In fact, it is known that the Football League has been pressing for its abandonment in view of the demands made on its players by not only England but Scotland, Wales and Ireland. This is a somewhat narrow view to take for Wales and Ireland, in particular, and to a lesser extent, Scotland, are almost completely dependent on the revenue from these international matches, and their abandonment would be disastrous for them. In the long run it would be to the detriment of the Football League, for the slump of football in the other British countries would inevitably mean the drying up of one of the sources from which the League clubs draw their supply of players. Fortunately the Football Association appears to be making a determined stand for the retention of this tournament. After all, strong opposition from the other Home countries should automatically result in a stronger England. It is to be hoped that the F.A. will take firm action to ensure the release of players for the other Home countries. It would seem to be elementary sportsmanship for England to do its best to enable that other home countries should be fully represented in competitions in which they are opposed to England.

2

The Full Results

A COMPLETE RECORD of the full international matches played by England in chronological order including date, opponents, venue, score and scorers.

1	1872	Nov	30	Scotland	Glasgow	0-0
2	1873	Mar	8	Scotland	Oval	4-2 Chenery, Bonsor, Kenyon-Slaney 2
3	1874	Mar	7	Scotland	Glasgow	1-2 Kingsford
4	1875	Mar	6	Scotland	Oval	2-2 Alcock, Wollaston
5	1876	Mar	4	Scotland	Glasgow	0-3
6	1877	Mar	3	Scotland	Oval	1-3 Lyttelton
7	1878	Mar	2	Scotland	Glasgow	2-7 Wylie, Cursham
8	1879	Jan	18	Wales	Oval	2-1 Whitfeld, Corby
9		Apr	5	Scotland	Oval	5-4 Goodyer, Bailey, Mosforth, Bambridge 2
10	1880	Mar	13	Scotland	Glasgow	4-5 Mosforth, Bambridge 2, Sparks
11		Mar	15	Wales	Wrexham	3-2 Sparks 2, Brindle
12	1881	Feb	26	Wales	Blackburn	0-1
13		Mar	12	Scotland	Oval	1-6 Bambridge
14	1882	Feb	18	Ireland	Belfast	13-0 Vaughton 5, A. Brown 4, J. Brown 2, Cursham and Bambridge
15		Mar	11	Scotland	Glasgow	1-5 Vaughton
16		Mar	13	Wales	Wrexham	3-5 Mosforth, Parry, Cursham
17	1883	Feb	3	Wales	Oval	5-0 Mitchell 3, A. Cursham, E. Bambridge
18		Feb	24	Ireland	Liverpool	7-0 Cobbold 2, Dunn 2, Whately 2, Pawson
19		Mar	10	Scotland	Sheffield	2-3 Cobbold, Mitchell

20	1884	Feb	25	Ireland	Belfast	8-1	Johnson 2, E. Bambridge 2, Cursham 3 and A. Bambridge
21		Mar	15	Scotland	Glasgow	0-1	
22		Mar	17	Wales	Wrexham	4-0	Bromley-Davenport 2, Gunn, Bailey
23	1885	Feb	28	Ireland	Manchester	4-0	Bambridge, Spilsbury, Brown, Lofthouse
24		Mar	14	Wales	Blackburn	1-1	Mitchell
25		Mar	21	Scotland	Oval	1-1	Bambridge
26	1886	Mar	13	Ireland	Belfast	6-1	Spilsbury 4, Dewhurst, Lindley
27		Mar	27	Scotland	Glasgow	1-1	Lindley
28		Mar	29	Wales	Wrexham	3-1	Dewhurst, Bambridge, Lindley
29	1887	Feb	5	Ireland	Sheffield	7-0	Cobbold 2, Lindley 3, Dewhurst 2
30		Feb	26	Wales	Oval	4-0	Cobbold 2, Lindley 2
31		Mar	19	Scotland	Blackburn	2-3	Lindley, Dewhurst
32	1888	Feb	4	Wales	Crewe	5-1	Dewhurst 2, Woodhall, Lindley, Goodall
33		Mar	17	Scotland	Glasgow	5-0	Lindley, Hodgets, Dewhurst 2, Goodall
34		Mar	31	Ireland	Belfast	5-1	Dewhurst, Allen 3, Lindley
35	1889	Feb	23	Wales	Stoke	4-1	Bassett, Goodall, Southworth, Dewhurst
36		Mar	2	Ireland	Everton	6-1	Weir, Yates 3, Lofthouse, Brodie
37		Apr	13	Scotland	Oval	2-3	Bassett, Weir
38	1890	Mar	15	Wales	Wrexham	3-1	Currey 2, Lindley
39		Mar	15	Ireland	Belfast	9-1	Davenport 2, Townley 2, Geary 3, Lofthouse and Barton
40		Apr	5	Scotland	Glasgow	1-1	Wood
41	1891	Mar	7	Wales	Sunderland	4-1	Goodall, Southworth, Chadwick, Milward
42		Mar	7	Ireland	Wolverh'ton	6-1	Cotterill, Henfrey, Daft, Lindley 2 and Bassett
43		Apr	4	Scotland	Blackburn	2-1	Goodall, Chadwick

44	1892	Mar	5	Wales	Wrexham	2-0	Henfrey, Sandilands
45		Mar	5	Ireland	Belfast	2-0	Daft 2
46		Apr	2	Scotland	Glasgow	4-1	Southworth, Goodall 2, Chadwick
47	1893	Feb	25	Ireland	Birmingham	6-1	Sandilands, Winckworth, Gilliat 3, Smith
48		Mar	13	Wales	Stoke	6-0	Spiksley 2, Bassett, Goodall, Reynolds, Schofield
49		Apr	1	Scotland	Richmond	5-2	Gosling, Cotterill, Spiksley 2, Reynolds
50	1894	Mar	1	Ireland	Belfast	2-2	Devey, Spiksley
51		Mar	12	Wales	Wrexham	5-1	Veitch 3, Gosling and an opponent
52		Apr	7	Scotland	Glasgow	2-2	Goodall, Reynolds
53	1895	Mar	9	Ireland	Derby	9-0	Howell, Bassett, Bloomer 2, Goodall 2, Becton 2 and an opponent
54		Mar	18	Wales	Queens Club	1-1	Sandilands
55		Apr	6	Scotland	Everton	3-0	Bloomer, Smith and an opponent
56	1896	Mar	7	Ireland	Belfast	2-0	Bloomer, Smith
57		Mar	16	Wales	Cardiff	9-1	Bloomer 5, Smith 2, Goodall, Bassett
58		Apr	4	Scotland	Glasgow	1-2	Bassett
59	1897	Feb	20	Ireland	Nottingham	6-0	Bloomer 2, Wheldon 3, Athersmith
60		Mar	29	Wales	Sheffield	4-0	Needham, Bloomer, Milward 2
61		Apr	3	Scotland	Crystal Pal.	1-2	Bloomer
62	1898	Mar	5	Ireland	Belfast	3-2	Morren, Athersmith, Smith
63		Mar	28	Wales	Wrexham	3-0	Smith, Wheldon 2
64		Apr	2	Scotland	Glasgow	3-1	Bloomer 2, Wheldon
65	1899	Feb	18	Ireland	Sunderland	13-2	Frank Forman, Athersmith, Bloomer 2, Smith 4, Settle 3, Fred Forman 2
66		Mar	20	Wales	Bristol	4-0	Bloomer 2, Fred Forman, Needham

67		Apr	8	Scotland	Birmingham	2-1	Smith, Settle
68	1900	Mar	17	Ireland	Dublin	2-0	Johnson, Sagar
69		Mar	26	Wales	Cardiff	1-1	Wilson
70		Apr	7	Scotland	Glasgow	1-4	Bloomer
71	1901	Mar	9	Ireland	Southampt'n	3-0	Crawshaw, Foster 2
72		Mar	18	Wales	Newcastle	6-0	Bloomer 4, Needham, Foster
73		Mar	30	Scotland	Crystal Pal.	2-2	Blackburn, Bloomer
74	1902	Mar	3	Wales	Wrexham	0-0	
75		Mar	22	Ireland	Belfast	1-0	Settle
76		May	3	Scotland	Birmingham	2-2	Settle, Wilkes
77	1903	Feb	14	Ireland	Wolverh'ton	4-0	Woodward 2, Sharp, Davis
78		Mar	2	Wales	Portsmouth	2-1	Bache, Woodward
79		Apr	4	Scotland	Sheffield	1-2	Woodward
80	1904	Feb	29	Ireland	Wrexham	2-2	Common, Bache
81		Mar	12	Wales	Belfast	3-1	Common, Bache, Davis
82		Apr	9	Scotland	Glasgow	1-0	Bloomer
83	1905	Feb	25	Ireland	Middlesbro	1-1	Bloomer
84		Mar	27	Wales	Liverpool	3-1	Woodward 2, Harris
85		Apr	1	Scotland	Crystal Pal.	1-0	Bache
86	1906	Feb	17	Ireland	Belfast	5-0	Bond 2, Day, Brown, Harris
87		Mar	19	Wales	Cardiff	1-0	Day
88		Apr	7	Scotland	Glasgow	1-2	Shepherd
89	1907	Feb	16	Ireland	Everton	1-0	Hardman
90		Mar	18	Wales	Fulham	1-1	Stewart
91		Apr	6	Scotland	Newcastle	1-1	Bloomer
92	1908	Feb	15	Ireland	Belfast	3-1	Woodward, Hilsdon 2
93		Mar	16	Wales	Wrexham	7-1	Wedlock, Windridge, Woodward 3, Hilsdon 2
94		Apr	4	Scotland	Glasgow	1-1	Windridge
95		June	6	Austria	Vienna	6-1	Windridge 2, Hilsdon 2, Woodward, Bridgett
96		June	8	Austria	Vienna	11-1	Woodward 4, Bradshaw 3, Bridgett, Warren, Rutherford, Windridge
97		June	10	Hungary	Budapest	7-0	Hilsdon 4, Woodward, Windridge, Rutherford

98		June	13	Bohemia	Prague	4-0	Hilsdon 2, Windridge, Rutherford
99	1909	Feb	13	Ireland	Bradford	4-0	Hilsdon 2, Woodward 2
100		Mar	15	Wales	Nottingham	2-0	Holley, Freeman
101		Apr	3	Scotland	Crystal Pal.	2-0	Wall 2
102		May	29	Hungary	Budapest	4-2	Woodward 2, Fleming, Bridgett
103		May	31	Hungary	Budapest	8-2	Fleming 2, Woodward 4, Holley 2
104		June	1	Austria	Vienna	8-1	Warren, Halse 2, Woodward 3, Holley 2
105	1910	Feb	12	Ireland	Belfast	1-1	Fleming
106		Mar	14	Wales	Cardiff	1-0	Ducat
107		Apr	2	Scotland	Glasgow	0-2	
108	1911	Feb	11	Ireland	Derby	2-1	Shepherd, Evans
109		Mar	13	Wales	Millwall	3-0	Woodward 2, Webb
110		Apr	1	Scotland	Everton	1-1	Stewart
111	1912	Feb	10	Ireland	Dublin	6-1	Fleming 3, Holley, Freeman, Simpson
112		Mar	11	Wales	Wrexham	2-0	Holley, Freeman
113		Mar	23	Scotland	Glasgow	1-1	Holley
114	1913	Feb	15	Ireland	Belfast	1-2	Buchan
115		Mar	17	Wales	Bristol	4-3	Fleming, Latheron, McCall, Hampton
116		Apr	5	Scotland	Chelsea	1-0	Hampton
117	1914	Feb	14	Ireland	Middlesbro	0-3	
118		Mar	16	Wales	Cardiff	2-0	Smith, Wedlock
119		Apr	4	Scotland	Glasgow	1-3	Fleming
120	1919	Oct	25	Ireland	Belfast	1-1	Cock
121	1920	Mar	15	Wales	Arsenal	1-2	Buchan
122		Apr	10	Scotland	Sheffield	5-4	Kelly 2, Cock, Morris and Quantrill
123		Oct	23	Ireland	Sunderland	2-0	Kelly, Walker
124	1921	Mar	14	Wales	Cardiff	0-0	
125		Apr	9	Scotland	Glasgow	0-3	
126		May	21	Belgium	Brussels	2-0	Buchan, Chambers
127		Oct	22	Ireland	Belfast	1-1	Kirton
128	1922	Mar	13	Wales	Liverpool	1-0	Kelly
129		Apr	8	Scotland	Birmingham	0-1	
130		Oct	21	Ireland	West Brom.	2-0	Chambers 2
131	1923	Mar	5	Wales	Cardiff	2-2	Chambers, Watson
132		Mar	19	Belgium	Arsenal	6-1	Hegan 2, Chambers, Mercer, Seed, Bullock

133		Apr	14	Scotland	Glasgow	2-2 Kelly, Watson
134		May	10	France	Paris	4-1 Hegan 2, Buchan, Creek
135		May	21	Sweden	Stockholm	4-2 Walker 2, Moore, Thornewell
136		May	24	Sweden	Stockholm	3-1 Moore 2, Miller
137		Oct	20	Ireland	Belfast	1-2 Bradford
138		Nov	1	Belgium	Antwerp	2-2 Brown, Roberts
139	1924	Mar	3	Wales	Blackburn	1-2 Roberts
140		Apr	12	Scotland	Wembley	1-1 Walker
141		May	17	France	Paris	3-1 Gibbins 2, Storer
142		Oct	22	Ireland	Everton	3-1 Kelly, Bedford, Walker
143		Dec	8	Belgium	West Brom.	4-0 Bradford 2, Walker 2
144	1925	Feb	28	Wales	Swansea	2-1 Roberts 2
145		Apr	4	Scotland	Glasgow	0-2
146		May	21	France	Paris	3-2 Gibbins, Dorrell and an opponent
147		Oct	24	Ireland	Belfast	0-0
148	1926	Mar	1	Wales	Selhurst	1-3 Walker
149		Apr	17	Scotland	Manchester	0-1
150		May	24	Belgium	Antwerp	5-3 Osborne 3, Carter, Johnson
151		Oct	20	Ireland	Liverpool	3-3 Brown, Spence, Bullock
152	1927	Feb	12	Wales	Wrexham	3-3 Dean 2, Walker
153		Apr	2	Scotland	Glasgow	2-1 Dean 2
154		May	11	Belgium	Brussels	9-1 Brown 2, Dean 3, Rigby 2, Page, Hulme
155		May	21	Luxembourg	Luxembourg	5-2 Dean 3, Kelly, Bishop
156		May	26	France	Paris	6-0 Dean 2, Brown 2, Rigby and an opponent
157		Act	22	Ireland	Belfast	0-2
158		Nov	28	Wales	Burnley	1-2 An opponent
159	1928	Mar	31	Scotland	Wembley	1-5 Kelly
160		May	17	France	Paris	5-1 Jack, Stephenson 2, Dean 2
161		May	19	Belgium	Antwerp	3-1 Dean 2, Matthews
162		Oct	22	Ireland	Liverpool	2-1 Hulme, Dean
163		Nov	17	Wales	Swansea	3-2 Hulme 2, Hine
164	1929	Apr	13	Scotland	Glasgow	0-1
165		May	9	France	Paris	4-1 Kail 2, Camsell 2
166		May	11	Belgium	Brussels	5-1 Camsell 4, Carter
167		May	15	Spain	Madrid	3-4 Carter 2, Bradford
168		Oct	19	Ireland	Belfast	3-0 Camsell 2, Hine
169		Nov	20	Wales	Chelsea	6-0 Adcock, Camsell 3, Johnson 2

170	1930	Apr	5	Scotland	Wembley	5-2	Jack, Watson 2, Rimmer 2
171		May	10	Germany	Berlin	3-3	Bradford 2, Jack
172		May	14	Austria	Vienna	0-0	
173		Oct	20	Ireland	Sheffield	5-1	Crooks, Hampson, Burgess 2, Houghton
174		Nov	22	Wales	Wrexham	4-0	Hodgson, Hampson 2, Bradford
175	1931	Mar	28	Scotland	Glasgow	0-2	
176		May	14	France	Paris	2-5	Crooks, Waring
177		May	16	Belgium	Brussels	4-1	Burgess 2, Houghton, Roberts
178		Oct	17	Ireland	Belfast	6-2	Smith, Waring 2, Hine, Houghton 2
179		Nov	18	Wales	Liverpool	3-1	Smith, Crooks, Hine
180		Dec	9	Spain	Arsenal	7-1	Smith 2, Johnson 2, Crooks 2, Dean
181	1932	Apr	9	Scotland	Wembley	3-0	Waring, Barclay, Crooks
182		Oct	17	Ireland	Blackpool	1-0	Barclay
183		Nov	16	Wales	Wrexham	0-0	
184		Dec	7	Austria	Chelsea	4-3	Hampson 2, Houghton, Crooks
185	1933	Apr	1	Scotland	Glasgow	1-2	Hunt
186		May	13	Italy	Rome	1-1	Bastin
187		May	20	Switzerland	Berne	4-0	Bastin 2, J. R. Richardson 2
188		Oct	14	Ireland	Belfast	3-0	Brook, Grosvenor, Bowers
189		Nov	15	Wales	Newcastle	1-2	Brook
190		Dec	6	France	Tottenham	4-1	Camsell 2, Brook, Grosvenor
191	1934	Apr	14	Scotland	Wembley	3-0	Brook, Bastin, Bowers
192		May	10	Hungary	Budapest	1-2	Tilson
193		May	16	Czechoslovakia	Prague	1-2	Tilson
194		Sep	29	Wales	Cardiff	4-0	Tilson 2, Brook, Matthews
195		Nov	14	Italy	Arsenal	3-2	Brook 2, Drake
196	1935	Feb	6	Ireland	Everton	2-1	Bastin 2
197		Apr	6	Scotland	Glasgow	0-2	
198		May	18	Holland	Amsterdam	1-0	Worrall
199		Oct	19	Ireland	Belfast	3-1	Tilson 2, Brook
200		Dec	4	Germany	Tottenham	3-0	Camsell 2, Bastin
201	1936	Feb	5	Wales	Wolverh'ton	1-2	Bowden
202		Apr	4	Scotland	Wembley	1-1	Camsell
203		May	6	Austria	Vienna	1-2	Camsell
204		May	9	Belgium	Brussels	2-3	Camsell, Hobbis
205		Oct	17	Wales	Cardiff	1-2	Bastin

206		Nov 18	Ireland	Stoke	3-1	Carter, Bastin, Worrall
207		Dec 2	Hungary	Arsenal	6-2	Brook, Drake 3, Britton, Carter
208	1937	Apr 17	Scotland	Glasgow	1-3	Steele
209		May 14	Norway	Oslo	6-0	Kirchen, Galley, Steele 2, Goulden and an opponent
210		May 17	Sweden	Stockholm	4-0	Steele 3, Johnson
211		May 20	Finland	Helsinki	8-0	Kirchen, Payne 2, Johnson, Steele 2 Willingham, Robinson
212		Oct 23	Ireland	Belfast	5-1	Mills 3, Hall, Brook
213		Nov 17	Wales	Middlesbro	2-1	Matthews, Hall
214		Dec 1	Czechoslovakia	Tottenham	5-4	Crayston, Morton, Matthews 3
215	1938	Apr 9	Scotland	Wembley	0-1	
216		May 14	Germany	Berlin	6-3	Bastin, Robinson 2, Broome, Matthews, Goulden
217		May 21	Switzerland	Zurich	1-2	Bastin,
218		May 26	France	Paris	4-2	Drake 2, Broome, Bastin
219		Oct 22	Wales	Cardiff	2-4	Lawton, Matthews
220		Oct 26	F.I.F.A.	Arsenal	3-0	Hall, Lawton, Goulden
221		Nov 9	Norway	Newcastle	4-0	Smith 2, Dix, Lawton
222		Nov 16	Ireland	Manchester	7-0	Lawton, Hall 5, Matthews
223	1939	Apr 15	Scotland	Glasgow	2-1	Beasley, Lawton
224		May 13	Italy	Milan	2-2	Lawton, Hall
225		May 18	Yugoslavia	Belgrade	1-2	Broome
226		May 24	Rumania	Bucharest	2-0	Goulden, Welsh
227	1946	Sep 28	Ireland	Belfast	7-2	Carter, Mannion 3, Finney, Lawton, Langton
228		Sep 30	Eire	Dublin	1-0	Finney
229		Nov 13	Wales	Manchester	3-0	Mannion 2, Lawton
230		Nov 27	Holland	Huddersf'd	8-2	Lawton 4, Carter 2, Mannion, Finney
231	1947	Apr 12	Scotland	Wembley	1-1	Carter
232		May 3	France	Arsenal	3-0	Finney, Mannion, Carter
233		May 18	Switzerland	Zurich	0-1	

234		May	25	Portugal	Lisbon	10-0	Mortensen 4, Lawton 4, Matthews and Finney
235		Sep	21	Belgium	Brussels	5-2	Lawton 2, Mortensen, Finney 2
236		Oct	18	Wales	Cardiff	3-0	Finney, Mortensen, Lawton
237		Nov	5	Ireland	Everton	2-2	Mannion, Lawton
238		Nov	19	Sweden	Arsenal	4-2	Mortensen 3, Lawton
239	1948	Apr	10	Scotland	Glasgow	2-0	Finney, Mortensen
240		May	16	Italy	Turin	4-0	Mortensen, Lawton, Finney 2
241		Sep	26	Denmark	Copenhagen	0-0	
242		Oct	9	Ireland	Belfast	6-2	Matthews, Milburn, Mortensen 3, Pearson
243		Nov	10	Wales	Birmingham	1-0	Finney
244		Dec	2	Switzerland	Arsenal	6-0	Haines 2, Hancocks 2, Rowley, Milburn
245	1949	Apr	9	Scotland	Wembley	1-3	Milburn
246		May	13	Sweden	Stockholm	1-3	Finney
247		May	18	Norway	Oslo	4-1	Mullen, Finney, Morris and an opponent
248		May	22	France	Paris	3-1	Morris 2, Wright
249		Sep	21	Eire	Everton	0-2	
250		Oct	15	Wales	Cardiff	4-1	Mortensen, Milburn 3
251		Nov	16	Ireland	Manchester	9-2	Rowley 4, Froggatt, Pearson 2, Mortensen 2
252		Nov	30	Italy	Tottenham	2-0	Rowley, Wright
253	1950	Apr	15	Scotland	Glasgow	1-0	Bentley
254		May	14	Portugal	Lisbon	5-3	Finney 4, Mannion
255		May	18	Belgium	Brussels	4-1	Mullen, Mortensen, Mannion, Bentley
256		June	25	Chile	Rio de Janeiro	2-0	Mortensen, Mannion
257		June	29	U.S.A.	B. Horizonte	0-1	
258		July	2	Spain	Rio de Jan.	0-1	
259		Oct	7	Ireland	Belfast	4-1	Baily 2, Lee, Wright
260		Nov	15	Wales	Sunderland	4-2	Baily 2, Mannion, Milburn

261		Nov	22	Yugoslavia	Arsenal	2-2	Lofthouse 2
262	1951	Apr	14	Scotland	Wembley	2-3	Hassall, Finney
263		May	9	Argentine	Wembley	2-1	Mortensen, Milburn
264		May	19	Portugal	Everton	5-2	Nicholson, Milburn 2, Finney, Hassall
265		Oct	3	France	Arsenal	2-2	Medley and an opponent
266		Oct	20	Wales	Cardiff	1-1	Baily
267		Nov	14	Ireland	Birmingham	2-0	Lofthouse 2
268		Nov	28	Austria	Wembley	2-2	Ramsey, Lofthouse
269	1952	Apr	5	Scotland	Glasgow	2-1	Pearson 2
270		May	18	Italy	Florence	1-1	Broadis
271		May	25	Austria	Vienna	3-2	Sewell, Lofthouse 2
272		May	28	Switzerland	Zurich	3-0	Lofthouse 2, Sewell
273		Oct	4	Ireland	Belfast	2-2	Lofthouse, Elliott
274		Nov	12	Wales	Wembley	5-2	Finney, Lofthouse 2, J. Froggatt, Bentley
275		Nov	26	Belgium	Wembley	5-0	Elliott 2, Lofthouse 2, R. Froggatt
276	1953	Apr	18	Scotland	Wembley	2-2	Broadis 2
277		May	17	Argentine	Buenos Aires	0-0	
278		May	24	Chile	Santiago	2-1	Taylor, Lofthouse
279		May	31	Uruguay	Montevideo	1-2	Taylor
280		June	8	U.S.A.	New York	6-3	Broadis, Finney 2, Lofthouse 2, R. Froggatt
281		Oct	10	Wales	Cardiff	4-1	Wilshaw 2, Lofthouse 2
282		Oct	21	F.I.F.A.	Wembley	4-4	Mortensen, Mullen 2, Ramsey
283		Nov	11	Ireland	Liverpool	3-1	Hassall 2, Lofthouse
284		Nov	25	Hungary	Wembley	3-6	Sewell, Mortensen, Ramsey
285	1954	Apr	3	Scotland	Glasgow	4-2	Broadis, Nicholls, Allen, Mullen
286		May	16	Yugoslavia	Belgrade	0-1	
287		May	23	Hungary	Budapest	1-7	Broadis
288		June	17	Belgium	Basle	4-4	Broadis 2, Lofthouse 2
289		June	20	Switzerland	Berne	2-0	Mullen, Wilshaw

290		June 26 Uruguay	Basle	2-4	Lofthouse, Finney
291		Oct 2 Ireland	Belfast	2-0	Haynes, Revie
292		Nov 10 Wales	Wembley	3-2	Bentley 3
293		Dec 1 West Germany	Wembley	3-1	Bentley, Allen, Shackleton
294	1955	Apr 2 Scotland	Wembley	7-2	Wilshaw 4, Lofthouse 2, Revie
295		May 15 France	Paris	0-1	
296		May 18 Spain	Madrid	1-1	Bentley
297		May 22 Portugal	Oporto	1-3	Bentley
298		Oct 2 Denmark	Copenhagen	5-1	Revie 2, Lofthouse 2, Bradford
299		Oct 22 Wales	Cardiff	1-2	An opponent
300		Nov 2 Ireland	Wembley	3-0	Wilshaw 2, Finney
301		Nov 30 Spain	Wembley	4-1	Atyeo, Perry 2, Finney
302	1956	Apr 14 Scotland	Glasgow	1-1	Haynes
303		May 9 Brazil	Wembley	4-2	Taylor 2, Grainger 2
304		May 16 Sweden	Stockholm	0-0	
305		May 20 Finland	Helsinki	5-1	Wilshaw, Haynes, Astall, Lofthouse 2
306		May 26 West Germany	Berlin	3-1	Edwards, Grainger, Haynes
307		Oct 6 Ireland	Belfast	1-1	Matthews
308		Nov 14 Wales	Wembley	3-1	Haynes, Brooks, Finney
309		Nov 28 Yugoslavia	Wembley	3-0	Brooks, Taylor 2
310		Dec 5 Denmark	Wolverh'ton	5-2	Taylor 3, Edwards 2
311	1957	Apr 6 Scotland	Wembley	2-1	Kevan, Edwards
312		May 8 Eire	Wembley	5-1	Taylor 3, Atyeo 2
313		May 15 Denmark	Copenhagen	4-1	Haynes, Atyeo, Taylor 2
314		May 19 Eire	Dublin	1-1	Atyeo
315		Oct 19 Wales	Cardiff	4-0	Haynes 2, Finney and an opponent
316		Nov 6 Ireland	Wembley	2-3	A'Court, Edwards
317		Nov 27 France	Wembley	4-0	Taylor 2, Robson 2
318	1958	Apr 19 Scotland	Glasgow	4-0	Douglas, Kevan 2, Charlton
319		May 7 Portugal	Wembley	2-1	Charlton 2
320		May 11 Yugoslavia	Belgrade	0-5	
321		May 18 Russia	Moscow	1-1	Kevan
322		June 8 Russia	Gothenberg	2-2	Kevan, Finney
323		June 11 Brazil	Gothenberg	0-0	

324		June	15	Austria	Boras	2-2	Haynes, Kevan
325		June	17	Russia	Gothenberg	0-1	
326		Oct	4	Ireland	Belfast	3-3	Charlton 2, Finney
327		Oct	22	Russia	Wembley	5-0	Haynes 3, Charlton, Lofthouse
328		Nov	26	Wales	Birmingham	2-2	Broadbent 2
329	1959	Apr	11	Scotland	Wembley	1-0	Charlton
330		May	6	Italy	Wembley	2-2	Bradley, Charlton
331		May	13	Brazil	Rio de Jan.	0-2	
332		May	17	Peru	Lima	1-4	Greaves
333		May	24	Mexico	Mexico City	1-2	Kevan
334		May	28	U.S.A.	Los Angeles	8-1	Bradley, Flowers 2, Kevan, Charlton 3, Haynes
335		Oct	17	Wales	Cardiff	1-1	Greaves
336		Oct	28	Sweden	Wembley	2-3	Connelly, Charlton
337		Nov	18	Ireland	Wembley	2-1	Baker, Parry
338	1960	Apr	9	Scotland	Glasgow	1-1	Charlton
339		May	11	Yugoslavia	Wembley	3-3	Douglas, Greaves, Haynes
340		May	15	Spain	Madrid	0-3	
341		May	22	Hungary	Budapest	0-2	
342		Oct	8	Ireland	Belfast	5-2	Greaves 2, Smith, Douglas, Charlton
343		Oct	19	Luxembourg	Luxembourg	9-0	Greaves 3, Charlton 3, Smith 2, Haynes
344		Oct	26	Spain	Wembley	4-2	Greaves, Douglas, Smith 2
345		Nov	23	Wales	Wembley	5-1	Greaves 2, Haynes, Charlton, Smith
346	1961	Apr	15	Scotland	Wembley	9-3	Robson, Greaves 3, Douglas, Haynes 2, Smith 2
347		May	10	Mexico	Wembley	8-0	Charlton 3, Hitchens, Robson, Douglas 2, Flowers
348		May	21	Portugal	Lisbon	1-1	Flowers
349		May	24	Italy	Rome	3-2	Hitchens 2, Greaves
350		May	27	Austria	Vienna	1-3	Greaves
351		Sep	28	Luxembourg	Arsenal	4-1	Pointer, Viollet, Charlton 2
352		Oct	14	Wales	Cardiff	1-1	Douglas

353		Oct	25	Portugal	Wembley	2-0	Connelly, Pointer
354		Nov	22	Ireland	Wembley	1-1	Charlton
355	1962	Apr	4	Austria	Wembley	3-1	Crawford, Flowers, Hunt
356		Apr	14	Scotland	Glasgow	0-2	
357		May	9	Switzerland	Wembley	3-1	Flowers, Hitchens, Connelly
358		May	20	Peru	Lima	4-0	Flowers, Greaves 3
359		May	31	Hungary	Rancagua	1-2	Flowers
360		June	2	Argentine	Rancagua	3-1	Flowers, Charlton, Greaves
361		June	7	Bulgaria	Rancagua	0-0	
362		June	10	Brazil	Vina del Mar	1-3	Hitchens
363		Oct	3	France	Sheffield	1-1	Flowers
364		Oct	20	Ireland	Belfast	3-1	Greaves, O'Grady 2
365		Nov	21	Wales	Wembley	4-0	Connelly, Peacock 2, Greaves
366	1963	Feb	27	France	Paris	2-5	Smith, Tambling
367		Apr	6	Scotland	Wembley	1-2	Douglas
368		May	8	Brazil	Wembley	1-1	Douglas
369		May	29	Czechoslovakia	Bratislau	4-2	Greaves 2, Smith, Charlton
370		June	2	East Germany	Leipzig	2-1	Hunt, Charlton
371		June	5	Switzerland	Basle	8-1	Charlton 3, Byrne 2, Douglas, Kay and Melia
372		Oct	12	Wales	Cardiff	4-0	Smith 2, Greaves, Charlton
373		Oct	23	F.I.F.A.	Wembley	2-1	Paine, Greaves
374		Nov	20	Ireland	Wembley	8-3	Greaves 4, Paine 3, Smith
375	1964	Apr	11	Scotland	Glasgow	0-1	
376		May	6	Uruguay	Wembley	2-1	Byrne 2
377		May	17	Portugal	Lisbon	4-3	Charlton, Byrne 3
378		May	24	Eire	Dublin	3-1	Eastham, Byrne, Greaves
379		May	27	U.S.A.	New York	10-0	Hunt 4, Pickering 3, Paine 2 and Charlton
380		May	30	Brazil	Rio de Jan.	1-5	Greaves
381		June	4	Portugal	San Paulo	1-1	Hunt
382		June	6	Argentine	Rio de Jan.	0-1	
383		Oct	3	Ireland	Belfast	4-3	Pickering, Greaves 3
384		Oct	21	Belgium	Wembley	2-2	Pickering and an opponent
385		Nov	18	Wales	Wembley	2-1	Wignall 2

c

386		Dec	9	Holland	Amsterdam	1-1	Greaves
387	1965	Apr	10	Scotland	Wembley	2-2	R. Charlton, Greaves
388		May	5	Hungary	Wembley	1-0	Greaves
389		May	9	Yugoslavia	Belgrade	1-1	Bridges
390		May	12	West Germany	Nuremburg	1-0	Paine
391		May	16	Sweden	Gothenberg	2-1	Ball, Connelly
392		Oct	2	Wales	Cardiff	0-0	
393		Oct	20	Austria	Wembley	2-3	R. Charlton, Connelly
394		Nov	10	Ireland	Wembley	2-1	Baker, Peacock
395		Dec	8	Spain	Madrid	2-0	Baker, Hunt
396	1966	Jan	5	Poland	Everton	1-1	Moore
397		Feb	23	West Germany	Wembley	1-0	Stiles
398		Apr	2	Scotland	Glasgow	4-3	Hurst, Hunt 2, R. Charlton
399		May	4	Yugoslavia	Wembley	2-0	Greaves, R. Charlton
400		June	26	Finland	Helsinki	3-0	Peters, Hunt, J. Charlton
401		June	29	Norway	Oslo	6-1	Greaves 4, Connelly, Moore
402		July	3	Denmark	Copenhagen	2-0	J. Charlton, Eastham
403		July	5	Poland	Katowicz	1-0	Hunt
404		July	11	Uruquay	Wembley	0-0	
405		July	16	Mexico	Wembley	2-0	R. Charlton, Hunt
406		July	20	France	Wembley	2-0	Hunt 2
407		July	23	Argentine	Wembley	1-0	Hurst
408		July	26	Portugal	Wembley	2-1	R. Charlton 2
409		July	30	West Germany	Wembley	4-2	Hurst 3, Peters
410		Oct	22	Ireland	Belfast	2-0	Hunt, Peters
411		Nov	2	Czechoslovakia	Wembley	0-0	
412		Nov	16	Wales	Wembley	5-1	Hurst 2, R. and J. Charlton and an opponent
413	1967	Apr	15	Scotland	Wembley	2-3	J. Charlton, Hurst
414		May	24	Spain	Wembley	2-0	Greaves, Hunt
415		May	27	Austria	Vienna	1-0	Ball
416		Oct	21	Wales	Cardiff	3-0	Peters, R. Charlton, Ball
417		Nov	22	Ireland	Wembley	2-0	Hurst, R. Charlton
418		Dec	6	Russia	Wembley	2-2	Ball, Peters
419	1968	Feb	24	Scotland	Glasgow	1-1	Peters
420		Apr	3	Spain	Wembley	1-0	R. Charlton
421		May	8	Spain	Madrid	2-1	Peters, Hunter
422		May	22	Sweden	Wembley	3-1	Peters, R. Charlton, Hunt
423		June	1	West Germany	Hanover	0-1	
424		June	5	Yugoslavia	Florence	0-1	

425		June	8	Russia	Rome	2-0	R. Charlton, Hurst
426		Nov	6	Rumania	Bucharest	0-0	
427		Dec	11	Bulgaria	Wembley	1-1	Hurst
428	1969	Jan	15	Rumania	Wembley	1-1	J. Charlton
429		Mar	12	France	Wembley	5-0	O'Grady, Hurst 3, Lee
430		May	3	Ireland	Belfast	3-1	Peters, Lee, Hurst
431		May	7	Wales	Wembley	2-1	R. Charlton, Lee
432		May	10	Scotland	Wembley	4-1	Hurst 2, Peters 2
433		June	1	Mexico	Mexico City	0-0	
434		June	8	Uruguay	Montevideo	2-1	Lee, Hurst
435		June	12	Brazil	Rio de Jan.	1-2	Bell
436		Nov	5	Holland	Amsterdam	1-0	Bell
437		Dec	10	Portugal	Wembley	1-0	J. Charlton
438	1970	Jan	14	Holland	Wembley	0-0	
439		Feb	25	Belgium	Brussels	3-1	Ball 2, Hurst
440		Apr	18	Wales	Cardiff	1-1	Lee
441		Apr	21	Ireland	Wembley	3-1	Peters, Hurst, R. Charlton
442		Apr	25	Scotland	Glasgow	0-0	
443		May	20	Columbia	Bogota	4-0	Peters 2, R. Charlton, Ball
444		May	24	Ecuador	Quito	2-0	Lee, Kidd
445		June	2	Rumania	Guadalajara	1-0	Hurst
446		June	7	Brazil	Guadalajara	0-1	
447		June	11	Czechoslovakia	Guadalajara	1-0	Clarke
448		June	14	West Germany	Leon	2-3	Mullery, Peters
449		Nov	25	East Germany	Wembley	3-1	Lee, Peters, Clarke
450	1971	Feb	3	Malta	Valetta	1-0	Peters
451		Apr	21	Greece	Wembley	3-0	Chivers, Hurst, Lee
452		May	12	Malta	Wembley	5-0	Chivers 2, Lee, Clarke, Lawler
453		May	15	Ireland	Belfast	1-0	Clarke
454		May	19	Wales	Wembley	0-0	
455		May	22	Scotland	Wembley	3-1	Peters, Chivers 2
456		Oct	13	Switzerland	Basle	3-2	Hurst, Chivers and an opponent
457		Nov	10	Switzerland	Wembley	1-1	Summerbee
458		Dec	1	Greece	Athens	2-0	Hurst, Chivers
459	1972	Apr	29	West Germany	Wembley	1-3	Lee
460		May	13	West Germany	Berlin	0-0	
461		May	20	Wales	Cardiff	3-0	Hughes, Marsh, Bell
462		May	23	Ireland	Wembley	0-1	
463		May	27	Scotland	Glasgow	1-0	Ball

SUMMARY OF RESULTS 1872–1972

Opponents	P	W	D	L	F	A
Argentine	5	3	1	1	6	3
Austria	13	7	3	3	44	21
Belgium	16	12	3	1	65	23
Bohemia	1	1	0	0	4	0
Brazil	8	1	2	5	8	16
Bulgaria	2	0	2	0	1	1
Chile	2	2	0	0	4	1
Columbia	1	1	0	0	4	0
Czechoslovakia	5	3	1	1	11	8
Denmark	5	4	1	0	16	4
Ecuador	1	1	0	0	2	0
Eire	5	3	1	1	10	5
Finland	3	3	0	0	16	1
France	18	13	2	3	57	24
Germany	3	2	1	0	12	6
East Germany	2	2	0	0	5	2
West Germany	9	5	1	3	15	11
Greece	2	2	0	0	5	0
Holland	5	3	2	0	11	3
Hungary	10	5	0	5	32	25
Ireland	79	61	12	6	286	76
Italy	8	4	4	0	18	10
Luxembourg	3	3	0	0	18	3
Malta	2	2	0	0	6	0
Mexico	4	2	1	1	11	2
Norway	4	4	0	0	20	2
Peru	2	1	0	1	5	4
Poland	2	1	1	0	2	1
Portugal	11	8	2	1	34	15
Rumania	4	2	2	0	4	1
Russia	6	2	3	1	12	6
Scotland	89	32	22	35	160	156
Spain	11	7	1	3	26	14
Sweden	9	6	1	2	23	13
Switzerland	10	7	1	2	31	8
United States	4	3	0	1	24	5
Uruguay	5	2	1	2	7	8
Wales	82	54	17	11	220	78
Yugoslavia	9	2	3	4	12	15
F.I.F.A.	3	2	1	0	9	5
	463	278	92	93	1256	576

INDEX OF OPPONENTS

[*As games against Scotland, Wales and Ireland have been played annually they are not included.*]

Opponents	Match numbers
Argentine	263-277-360-382-407
Austria	95-96-104-172-184-203-268-271-324-350-355 393-415
Belgium	126-132-138-143-150-154-161-166-177-204-235 255-275-288-384-439
Bohemia	98
Brazil	303-323-331-362-368-380-435-446
Bulgaria	361-427
Chile	256-278
Columbia	443
Czechoslovakia	193-214-369-411-447
Denmark	241-298-310-313-402
Ecuador	444
Eire	228-249-312-314-378
Finland	211-305-400
France	134-141-146-156-160-165-176-190-218-232-248 265-295-317-363-366-406-429
Germany	171-200-216
East Germany	370-449
West Germany	293-306-390-397-409-423-448-459-460
Greece	451-458
Holland	198-230-386-436-438
Hungary	97-102-103-192-207-284-287-341-359-388
Italy	186-195-224-240-252-270-330-349
Luxembourg	155-343-351
Malta	450-252
Mexico	333-347-405-433
Norway	209-221-247-401
Peru	332-358
Poland	396-403
Portugal	234-254-264-297-319-348-353-377-381-408-437
Rumania	226-426-428-445
Russia	321-322-325-327-418-425
Spain	167-180-258-296-301-340-344-395-414-420-421
Sweden	135-136-210-238-246-304-336-391-422
Switzerland	187-217-233-244-272-289-357-371-456-457
United States	257-280-334-379
Uruguay	279-290-376-404-434
Yugoslavia	225-261-286-309-320-339-389-399-424
F.I.F.A.	220-282-373

3

England International Players 1873-1972

THIS IS A complete list of players' appearances in recognised "full" internationals. The figure in front of the player's name indicates the number of appearances. Where the player was a substitute the appearance is marked (s) and is included in the total. The year represents the second half of the season in which the match was played with the exception that the first match v Scotland in November 1872 is shown as 1872 to distinguish it from the match played in March 1873. Players' appearances are in chronological order.

Abbreviations

Ar	Argentina	G	Germany	Pol	Poland
Au	Austria	EG	East Germany	Por	Portugal
Be	Belgium	WG	West Germany	Rum	Rumania
Bo	Bohemia	Gr	Greece	Rus	Russia
Br	Brazil	Ho	Holland	S	Scotland
Bu	Bulgaria	Hu	Hungary	(s)	substitute
Ch	Chile	I	Northern Ireland	Sp	Spain
Co	Columbia	It	Italy	Swe	Sweden
Cz	Czechoslovakia	L	Luxembourg	Swi	Switzerland
D	Denmark	Ma	Malta	U	Uruguay
Ec	Ecuador	Me	Mexico	US	United States
Ei	Irish Republic	N	Norway	W	Wales
Fi	Finland	Pe	Peru	Y	Yugoslavia
Fr	France				

1 W. Abbott (Everton) v W 1902
5 A. A'Court (Liverpool) v I Br Au Rus 1958 v W 1959
5 H. Adcock (Leicester City) v Fr Be Sp 1929 v I W 1930
1 C. W. Alcock (Wanderers) v S 1875
1 J. T. Alderson (Crystal Palace) v Fr 1923
2 A. Aldridge (West Bromwich Albion) v I 1888 (Walsall Town Swifts) v I 1889
1 A. Allen (Aston Villa) v I 1888
3 A. Allen (Stoke City) v W Swe I 1960
5 H. Allen (Wolverhampton Wanderers) v W S I 1888 v S 1889-90
2 J. P. Allen (Portsmouth) v I W 1934
5 R. Allen (West Bromwich Albion) v Swi 1952 v S Y 1954 v W WG 1955

1 W. J. Alsford (Tottenham Hotspur) v S 1935
2 A. Amos (Cambridge University) v S 1885 v W 1886
1 R. D. Anderson (Old Etonians) v W 1879
2 S. Anderson (Sunderland) v Au S 1962
1 J. Angus (Burnley) v Au 1961
43 J. C. Armfield (Blackpool) v Br Pe Me US 1959 v S Y Sp Hu 1960 v I L Sp W S Me Por It Au 1961 v L W Por I Au S Swi Pe Hu Ar Bu Br 1962 v Fr I W Fr S Br EG Swi 1963 v W FIFA I S 1964 v Y Fi 1966
1 G. H. Armitage (Charlton Athletic) v I 1926
1 K. Armstrong (Chelsea) v S 1955
1 J. Arnold (Fulham) v S 1933
7 J. W. H. Arthur (Blackburn Rovers) v I W S 1885 v S W 1886 v I W 1887
3 J. Ashcroft (Woolwich Arsenal) v I W S 1906
1 G. S. Ashmore (West Bromwich Albion) v Be 1926
1 C. T. Ashton (Corinthians) v I 1926
5 W. Ashurst (Notts County) v Swe(2) 1923 v Be W S 1925
2 G. Astall (Birmingham City) v Fi WG 1956
5 J. Astle (West Bromwich Albion) v W 1969 v Por S Br(s) Cz 1970
17 J. Aston (Manchester United) v D W Swi S Swe N Fr 1949 v Ei W I It S Por Be Ch US 1950 v I 1951
12 W. C. Athersmith (Aston Villa) v I 1892 v I W S 1897-8-9 v W S 1900
6 P. J. W. Atyeo (Bristol City) v Sp Br Swe 1956 v Ei D Ei 1957
1 S. W. Austin (Manchester City) v I 1926

1 P. Bach (Sunderland) v I 1899
7 J. W. Bache (Aston Villa) v W 1903 v W I 1904 v S 1905 v I 1907-10 v S 1911
5 T. Baddeley (Wolverhampton Wanderers) v I S 1903 v W I S 1904
1 J. J. Bagshaw (Derby County) v I 1920
5 H. P. Bailey (Leicester Fosse) v W Au(2) Hu Bo 1908
2 M. A. Bailey (Charlton Athletic) v US 1964 v W 1965
19 N. C. Bailey (Clapham Rovers) v S 1878 v W S 1879 v S 1880-1 v S W 1882 v W S 1883 v I S W 1884 v I W S 1885 v S W 1886 v W S 1887
9 E. F. Baily (Tottenham Hotspur) v Sp 1950 v I W Y 1951 v W Au(2) Swi 1952 v I 1953
1 J. Bain (Oxford University) v S 1877
1 A. Baker (Arsenal) v W 1928
2 B. H. Baker (Everton) v Be 1921 (Chelsea) v I 1926
8 J. H. Baker (Hibernian) v I S Y Sp Hu 1960 (Arsenal) v I Sp Pol 1966
56 A. J. Ball (Blackpool) v Y WG Swe 1965 v Sp Pol WG S Fi D Pol U Ar Por WG 1966 (Everton) v I Cz W S Sp Au 1967 v W Rus S Sp(2) WG Y 1968 v Rum(2) I W S Me U Br 1969 v Por Be W S Co Ec Rum Br Cz(s) WG 1970 v EG Ma Gr Ma(s) I S 1971 v Swi Gr 1972 (Arsenal) v WG(2) S 1972
1 J. Ball (Bury) v I 1928
1 W. Balmer (Everton) v I 1905
1 J. Bamber (Liverpool) v W 1921
3 A. L. Bambridge (Swifts) v W 1881-3 v I 1884

18 E. C. Bambridge (Swifts) v S 1879-80-1 v I S W 1882 v W
 1883 v I S W 1884 v I W S 1185 v S W 1886 v I W S 1887
1 E. H. Bambridge (Swifts) v S 1876
73 G. Banks (Leicester City) v S Br Cz EG 1963 v W FIFA I S
 U Por US Por Ar 1964 v I S Hu Y WG Swe 1965 v I Sp Pol
 WG S Y Fi Pol U Me Fr Ar Por WG 1966 v I Cz W S 1967
 (Stoke City) v W I Rus S Sp WG Y Rus 1968 v Rum(2) Fr
 I S U Br 1969 v Ho Be W I S Co Ec Rum Br Cz 1970 v
 Ma Gr Ma I S 1971 v Swi Gr WG(2) W S 1972
1 H. E. Banks (Millwall Athletic) v I 1901
6 T. Banks (Bolton Wanderers) v Rus(2) Br Au Rus 1958 v I 1959
2 W. Bannister (Burnley) v W 1901 (Bolton Wanderers) v I 1902
3 R. Barclay (Sheffield United) v S 1932 v I 1933 v S 1936
5 S. Barkas (Manchester City) v Be 1936 v S 1937 v I W Cz 1938
11 J. W. Barker (Derby County) v W It I S Ho 1935 v I G W S
 Au 1936 v W 1937
1 R. Barker (Hertfordshire Rangers) v S 1872
1 R. R. Barker (Casuals) v W 1895
1 R. J. Barlow (West Bromwich Albion) v I 1955
1 H. H. Barnet (Royal Engineers) v I 1882
3 M. W. Barrass (Bolton Wanderers) v W I 1952 v S 1953
1 A. F. Barrett (Fulham) v 1930
1 J. W. Barrett (West Ham United) v I 1929
5 L. J. Barry (Leicester City) v Fr Be 1928 v Fr Be Sp 1929
1 F. Barson (Aston Villa) v W 1920
1 J. Barton (Blackburn Rovers) v I 1890
7 P. H. Barton (Birmingham) v Be 1921 v I 1922 v Fr 1923 v Be
 W S 1924 v I 1925
16 W. I. Bassett (West Bromwich Albion) v I 1888 v W S 1889-90
 v I S 1891 v S 1892 v W S 1893 v S 1894 v I S 1895 v I W
 S 1896
1 S. R. Bastard (Upton Park) v S 1880
21 C. S. Bastin (Arsenal) v W 1932 v It Swi 1933 v I W S Hu Cz
 1934 v It I S 1935 v G W S Au 1936 v W I 1937 v S G Swi
 Fr 1938
2 R. Baugh (Stafford Road) v I 1886 (Wolverhampton Wanderers)
 v I 1890
1 A. E. J. M. Bayliss (West Bromwich Albion) v I 1891
3 R. L. Baynham (Luton Town) v D I Sp 1956
1 A. Beasley (Huddersfield Town) v S 1939
2 W. E. Beats (Wolverhampton Wanderers) v W 1901 v S 1902
2 F. Becton (Preston North End) v I 1895 (Liverpool) v W 1897
2 H. Bedford (Derby County) v Swe 1923 v I 1925
20 C. Bell (Manchester City) v Swe WG 1968 v Bu Fr W U Br
 1969 v Ho Por Ho I(s) Br(s) Cz WG(s) 1970 v Gr WG(2) W
 I S 1972
2 W. Bennett (Sheffield United) v W S 1901
1 R. W. Benson (Sheffield United) v I 1913
12 R. T. F. Bentley (Chelsea) v Swe 1949 v S Por Be Ch US 1950
 v W Be 1953 v W WG Sp Por 1955
1 J. Beresford (Aston Villa) v Cz 1934
1 A. Berry (Oxford University) v I 1909
4 J. J. Berry (Manchester United) v Ar Ch U 1953 v Swe 1956
1 J. G. Bestall (Grimsby Town) v I 1935

1   H. A. Betmead (Grimsby Town) v Fi 1937
1   M. P. Betts (Old Harrovians) v S 1877
1   W. Betts (Sheffield Wednesday) v W 1889
3   J. Beverley (Blackburn Rovers) v I S W 1884
1   R. H. Birkett (Clapham Rovers) v S 1879
1   R. J. E. Birkett (Middlesbrough) v I 1936
2   F. H. Birley (Oxford University) v S 1874 (Wanderers) v S 1875
4   S. M. Bishop (Leicester City) v S Be L Fr 1927
3   F. Blackburn (Blackburn Rovers) v S 1901 v I 1902 v S 1904
1   G. F. Blackburn (Aston Villa) v Fr 1924
26 E. Blenkinsop (Sheffield Wednesday) v Fr Be 1928 v I W S Fr Be Sp 1929 v I W S G Au 1930 v I W S Fr Be 1931 v I W Sp S 1932 v I W Au S 1933
1   H. Bliss (Tottenham Hotspur) v S 1921
23 Bloomer (Derby County) v I S 1895 v I W 1896 v I W S 1897 v S 1898 v I W S 1899 v S 1900 v I S 1901 v W I S 1902 v S 1904 v I W S 1905 (Middlesbrough) v W S 1907
5   F. Blunstone (Chelsea) v W S Fr Por 1955 v Y 1957
8   R. Bond (Preston North End) v I W 1905 v I W S 1906 (Bradford City) v I W S 1910
7   P. P. Bonetti (Chelsea) v D 1966 v Sp Au 1967 v Sp 1968 v Ho Por WG 1970
2   A. G. Bonsor (Wanderers) v S 1873-5
1   F. Booth (Manchester City) v I 1905
2   T. Booth (Blackburn Rovers) v W 1898 (Everton) v S 1903
6   E. R. Bowden (Arsenal) v W It 1935 v I W Au 1936 v Hu 1937
5   A. G. Bower (Corinthians) v I Be 1924 v Be W 1925 v W 1927
3   J. W. Bowers (Derby County) v I W S 1934
1   S. Bowser (West Bromwich Albion) v I 1920
3   W. E. Boyes (West Bromwich Albion) v Ho 1935 (Everton) v W FIFA 1939
1   T. W. Boyle (Burnley) v I 1913
3   P. Brabrook (Chelsea) v Rus 1958 v I 1959 v Sp 1960
1   G. R. W. Bradford (Bristol Rovers) v D 1956
12 J. Bradford (Birmingham) v I 1924 v Be 1925 v S 1928 v I W Fr Sp 1929 v I S G Au 1930 v W 1931
3   W. Bradley (Manchester United) v It Me(s) US 1959
1   F. Bradshaw (Sheffield Wednesday) v Au 1908
1   T. H. Bradshaw (Liverpool) v I 1897
4   W. Bradshaw (Blackburn Rovers) v I W 1910 v I 1912 v W 1913
3   G. Brann (Swifts) v S W 1886 v W 1891
2   W. F. Brawn (Aston Villa) v W I 1904
6   J. Bray (Manchester City) v W 1935 v I G W S 1936 v S 1937
1   E. Brayshaw (Sheffield Wednesday) v I 1887
4   B. J. Bridges (Chelsea) v S Hu Y 1965 v Au 1966
11 A. Bridgett (Sunderland) v S 1905 v S Au(2) Hu Bo 1908 v I W Hu(2) Au 1909
2   T. Brindle (Darwen) v S W 1880
5   J. T. Brittleton (Sheffield Wednesday) v I W S 1912 v S 1913 v W 1914
9   C. S. Britton (Everton) v W It I S 1935 v I Hu S N Swe 1937
7   P. F. Broadbent (Wolverhampton Wanderers) v Rus 1958 v I W S It Br 1959 v S 1960
14 I. A. Broadis (Manchester City) v Au S It 1952 v S Ar Ch U US

1953 (Newcastle United) v S Y HU Be Swi U 1954

1   J. Brockbank (Cambridge University) v S 1872

3   J. B. Brodie (Wolverhampton Wanderers) v I S 1889 v I 1891

5   T. G. Bromilow (Liverpool) v W 1921 v W S 1922 v Be 1923 v I 1926

2   W. E. Bromley-Davenport (Oxford University) v S W 1884

18 E. F. Brook (Manchester City) v I 1930 v Swi 1933 v I W Fr S Hu Cz 1934 v W It I S 1935 v I W S 1936 v Hu 1937 v I W 1938

3   J. Brooks (Tottenham Hotspur) v W Y D 1957

7   F. H. Broome (Aston Villa) v G Swi Fr 1938 v N It Y Rum 1939

3   A. Brown (Aston Villa) v I S W 1882

1   A. Brown (West Bromwich Albion) v W 1971

2   A. S. Brown (Sheffield United) v W 1904 v I 1906

9   G. Brown (Huddersfield Town) v I W S Be L Fr 1927 v W 1928 v S 1929 (Aston Villa) v W 1933

5   J. Brown (Blackburn Rovers) v W 1881 v I 1882 v I W S 1885

6   J. H. Brown (Sheffield Wednesday) v W S Be L Fr 1927 v I 1930

1   K. Brown (West Ham United) v I 1960

1   W. Brown (West Ham United) v Be 1924

3   J. Bruton (Burnley) v Fr Be 1928 v S 1929

1   W. I. Bryant (Clapton) v Fr 1925

6   C. M. Buchan (Sunderland) v I 1913 v W 1920 v W Be 1921 v Fr 1923 v S 1924

1   W. S. Buchanan (Clapham Rovers) v S 1876

1   F. C. Buckley (Derby County) v I 1914

1   F. E. Bullock (Huddersfield Town) v I 1921

3   N. Bullock (Bury) v Be 1923 v W 1926 v I 1927

4   H. Burgess (Manchester City) v W I S 1904 v S 1906

4   H. Burgess (Sheffield Wednesday) v I S Fr Be 1931

1   C. J. Burnup (Cambridge University) v S 1896

3   H. Burrows (Sheffield Wednesday) v Hu Cz 1934 v Ho 1935

1   F. E. Burton (Nottingham Forest) v I 1889

2   L. Bury (Cambridge University) v S 1877 v W 1879

1   J. D. Butler (Arsenal) v Be 1925

1   W. Butler (Bolton Wanderers) v S 1924

2   G. Byrne (Liverpool) v S 1963 v N 1966

11 J. J. Byrne (Crystal Palace) v I 1962 (West Ham United) v Swi 1963 v S U Por Ei Br Por Arg 1964 v W S 1965

33 R. W. Byrne (Manchester United) v S Y Hu Be Swi U 1954 v I W WG S Fr Sp Por 1955 v D W I Sp S Br Swe Fi WG 1956 v I W Y D S Ei D Ei 1957 v W I Fr 1958

2   I. R. Callaghan (Liverpool) v Fi Fr 1966

1   J. Calvey (Nottingham Forest) v I 1902

8   A. F. Campbell (Blackburn Rovers) v I W 1929 (Huddersfield Town) v I W S 1931 v I W Sp 1932

9   G. H. Camsell (Middlesbrough) v Fr Be 1929 v I W 1930 v Fr 1934 v G S Au Be 1936

1   A. J. Capes (Stoke) v S 1903

2   J. Carr (Newcastle United) v I 1905-7

2   J. Carr (Middlesbrough) v I 1920 v W 1923

1   W. H. Carr (Owlerton, Sheffield) v S 1875
13   H. S. Carter (Sunderland) v S Hu 1934 v G 1936 v I Hu S 1937 (Derby County) v I Ei W Ho S Fr Swi 1947
3   J. H. Carter (West Bromwich Albion) v Be 1926 v Be Sp 1929
5   A. E. Catlin (Sheffield Wednesday) v W I Hu N Swe 1937
2   A. Chadwick (Southampton) v W S 1900
7   E. Chadwick (Everton) v W S 1891 v S 1892-3-4 v I 1896 v S 1897
8   H. Chambers (Liverpool) v W S Be 1921 v I W Be S 1923 v I 1924
35   J. Charlton (Leeds United) v S Hu Y WG Swe 1965 v W Au I Sp Pol WG S Y Fi D Pol U Me Fr Ar Por WG 1966 v I Cz W S 1967 v W Sp 1968 v Rum Fr W 1969 v Ho Por Ho Cz 1970
106   R. Charlton (Manchester United) v S Por Y 1958 v I Rus W S It Br Pe Me US 1959 v W Swe S Y Sp Hu 1960 v I L Sp W S Me Por It Au 1961 v L W Por I Au S Swi Pe Hu Ar Bu Br 1962 v Fr S Br Cz EG Swi 1963 v W FIFA I S U Por Ei US(s) Br Ar 1964 v I Ho S 1965 v W Au I Sp WG S Y Fi N Pol U Me Fr Ar Por WG 1966 v I Cz W S 1967 v W I Rus S Sp(2) Swe Y Rus 1968 v Rum Bu Rum I W S Me Br 1969 v Ho Por Ho W I Co Ec Rum Br Cz WG 1970
1   R. O. Charnley (Burnley) v Fr 1963
1   C. C. Charsley (Small Heath) v I 1893
8   S. Chedgzoy (Everton) v W 1920 v I W S 1921 v I 1922 v S 1923 v W 1924 v I 1925
3   C. J. Chenery (Crystal Palace) v S 1872-3-4
2   A. Chilton (Manchester United) v I 1951 v Fr 1952
1   H. Chippendale (Blackburn Rovers) v I 1894
12   M. H. Chivers (Tottenham Hotspur) v Ma Gr Ma I S 1971 v Swi Swi(s) Gr WG(2) I(s) S 1972
1   E. Christian (Old Etonians) v S 1879
4   E. Clamp (Wolverhampton Wanderers) v Rus(2) Br Au 1958
1   D. R. Clapton (Arsenal) v W 1959
4   T. Clare (Stoke) v I 1889-92 v W 1893 v S 1894
6   A. J. Clarke (Leeds United) v Cz 1970 v EG Ma I W(s) S(s) 1971
1   H. A. Clarke (Tottenham Hotspur) v S 1954
4   T. Clay (Tottenham Hotspur) v W 1920 v I W S 1922
35   R. Clayton (Blackburn Rovers) v I Sp Br Swe Fi WG 1956 v I W Y D S Ei D Ei 1957 v I Fr S Por Y Rus 1958 v I Rus W S It Br Pe Me US 1959 v W Swe I S Y 1960
1   J. C. Clegg (Sheffield Wednesday) v S 1872
2   W. E. Clegg (Sheffield Wednesday) v S 1873 (Sheffield Albion) v W 1879
2   B. H. Clough (Middlesbrough) v W Swe 1960
4   R. Coates (Burnley) v I 1970 v Gr(s) 1971 (Tottenham Hotspur) v Ma W 1971
9   W. N. Cobbold (Cambridge University) v I S 1883-5 v S W 1886 (Old Carthusians) v I W S 1887
2   J. G. Cock (Huddersfield Town) v I 1920 (Chelsea) v S 1920
13   H. Cockburn (Manchester United) v I Ei W 1947 v S It 1948 v D I Swi S Swe 1949 v Arg Por 1951 v Fr 1952
37   G. R. Cohen (Fulham) v U Por Ei US Br 1964 v I Be W Ho S Hu Y WG Swe 1965 v W Au I Sp Pol WG S N D Pol U Me Fr Ar Por WG 1966 v I Cz W S Sp 1967 v W I 1968

1 H. Colclough (Crystal Palace) v W 1914
1 E. H. Coleman (Dulwich Hamlet) v W 1921
1 J. G. Coleman (Woolwich Arsenal) v I 1907
3 A. Common (Sheffield United) v W I 1904 (Middlesbrough) v W 1906
2 L. H. Compton (Arsenal) v W Y 1951
1 J. Conlin (Bradford City) v S 1906
20 J. M. Connelly (Burnley) v W Swe I S 1960 v W Por Au Swi 1962 v W Fr 1963 (Manchester United) v Hu Y Swe 1965 v W Au I S N D U 1966
1 T. E. R. Cook (Brighton & Hove Albion) v W 1925
1 N. C. Cooper (Cambridge University) v I 1893
19 T. Cooper (Derby County) v I 1928 v I W S Fr Be Sp 1929 v Fr 1931 v W Sp 1932 v S 1933 v S Hu Cz 1934 v W 1935
17 T. Cooper (Leeds United) v Fr W S Me 1969 v Ho Be Co Ec Rum Br Cz WG 1970 v EG Ma I W S 1971 v Swi(2) 1972
20 W. Copping (Leeds United) v It Swi 1933 v I W Fr S 1934 v Rum 1939 (Arsenal) v It I 1935 v Au Be 1936 v N Swe Fi 1937 v I W Cz S 1938 v W FIFA 1939
1 B. O. Corbett (Corinthians) v W 1901
1 R. Corbett (Old Malvernians) v W 1903
3 W. S. Corbett (Birmingham) v Au Hu Bo 1908
4 G. H. Cotterill (Cambridge University) v I 1891 (Old Brightonians) v W 1892 v I S 1893
1 J. R. Cottle (Bristol City) v I 1909
3 S. Cowan (Manchester City) v Be 1926 v Au 1930 v Be 1931
1 A. Cowell (Blackburn Rovers) v I 1910
3 J. Cox (Liverpool) v I 1901 v S 1902-3
1 J. D. Cox (Derby County) v I 1892
14 J. W. Crabtree (Burnley) v I 1894 v I S 1895 (Aston Villa) v I W S 1896-9-1900 v W 1901-2
1 J. F. Crawford (Chelsea) v S 1931
2 R. Crawford (Ipswich Town) v I Au 1962
10 T. H. Crawshaw (Sheffield Wednesday) v I 1895 v I W S 1896-7 v I 1901 v W I 1904
8 W. J. Crayston (Arsenal) v G W S Au Be 1936 v I W Cz 1938
1 F. N. S. Creek (Corinthians) v Fr 1923
7 W. Cresswell (South Shields) v W 1921 (Sunderland) v Fr 1923 v Be 1924 v I 1925 v W 1926 v I 1927 (Everton) v I 1930
41 R. Crompton (Blackburn Rovers) v W I S 1902 v W S 1903 v W I S 1904 v I W S 1906-7 v I W S Au(2) Hu Bo 1908 v I W S Hu(2) Au 1909 v W S 1910 v I W S 1911-12-13-14
26 S. D. Crooks (Derby County) v S G Au 1930 v I W S Fr Be 1931 v I W Sp S 1932 v I W Au 1933 v I W Fr S Hu Cz 1934 v I 1935 v W S 1936 v W Hu 1937
1 C. Crowe (Wolverhampton Wanderers) v Fr 1963
2 F. Cuggy (Sunderland) v I 1913-14
12 S. Cullis (Wolverhampton Wanderers) v I W Cz S Fr 1938 v FIFA N I S It Y Rum 1939
2 A. Cunliffe (Blackburn Rovers) v I W 1933
1 D. Cunliffe (Portsmouth) v I 1900
1 J. N. Cunliffe (Everton) v Be 1936
2 E. S. Currey (Oxford University) v W S 1890
1 A. W. Currie (Sheffield United) v I 1972

6   A. W. Cursham (Notts County) v S 1876-7-8 v W 1879 v W S 1883

8   H. A. Cursham (Notts County) v W 1880 v I S W 1882 v W I S 1883 v I 1884

5   H. B. Daft (Notts County) v I 1889 v W S 1890 v I 1891-2

1   T. Danks (Nottingham Forest) v S 1885

2   J. K. Davenport (Bolton Wanderers) v W 1885 v I 1890

2   G. Davis (Derby County) v W I 1904

3   H. Davis (Sheffield Wednesday) v I W S 1903

1   J. E. Davison (Sheffield Wednesday) v W 1922

2   J. Dawson (Burnley) v I S 1922

3   S. H. Day (Old Malvernians) v I W S 1906

16   W. R. Dean (Everton) v W S Be L Fr 1927 v I W S Fr Be 1928 v I W S 1929 v S 1931 v Sp 1932 v I 1933

2   N. V. Deeley (Wolverhampton Wanderers) v Br Pe 1959

2   J. H. G. Devey (Aston Villa) v I 1892-4

9   F. Dewhurst (Preston North End) v I W 1886 v I W S 1887 v W S I 1888 v W 1889

1   G. P. Dewhurst (Liverpool Ramblers) v W 1895

48   J. W. Dickinson (Portsmouth) v N Fr 1949 v Ei W S Por Be Ch US Sp 1950 v I W Y 1951 v W I Au S It Au Swi 1952 v I W Be S Ar Ch U US 1953 v W FIFA I Hu S Y Hu Be Swi U 1954 v Sp Por 1955 v D W I Sp S 1956 v W Y D 1957

3   J. H. Dimmock (Tottenham Hotspur) v S 1921 v W Be 1926

6   E. G. Ditchburn (Tottenham Hotspur) v Swi Swe 1949 v US 1953 v W Y D 1957

1   R. W. Dix (Derby County) v N 1939

1   J. A. Dixon (Notts County) v 1885

4   A. T. C. Dobson (Notts County) v I 1882 v I S W 1884

1   C. F. Dobson (Notts County) v I 1886

1   A. G. Doggart (Corinthians) v Be 1924

4   A. R. Dorrell (Aston Villa) v Be W Fr 1925 v I 1926

36   B. Douglas (Blackburn Rovers) v W I Fr S Por Y Rus(2) Br Au 1958 v Rus S 1959 v Y Hu 1960 v I L Sp W S Me Por It Au 1961 v L W Por I S Pe Hu Ar Bu Br 1962 v S Br Swi 1963

1   R. W. Downs (Everton) v I 1921

5   E. J. Drake (Arsenal) v It I 1935 v W 1936 v Hu 1937 v Fr 1938

6   A. Ducat (Woolwich Arsenal) v I W S 1910 (Aston Villa) v W S 1920 v I 1921

4   A. T. B. Dunn (Cambridge University) v I 1883-4 (Old Etonians) v W S 1892

2   S. G. J. Earle (Clapton) v Fr 1924 (West Ham United) v I 1928

19   G. E. Eastham (Arsenal) v Br Cz EG 1963 v W FIFA I S U Por Ei US Br Ar 1964 v Hu WG Swe 1965 v Sp Pol D 1966

1   G. R. Eastham (Bolton Wanderers) v Ho 1935

17   W. Eckersley (Blackburn Rovers) v Sp 1950 v Y S Ar Por 1951 v Au(2) Swi 1952 v I Ar Ch U US 1953 v W FIFA I Hu 1954

18   D. Edwards (Manchester United) v S Fr Sp Por 1955 v S Br Swe Fr WG 1956 v I D S Ei D Ei 1957 v W I Fr 1958

1   J. H. Edwards (Shropshire Wanderers) v S 1874

16   W. Edwards (Leeds United) v W S 1926 v I W S Be L Fr 1927 v S Fr Be 1928 v I W S 1929 v I W 1930

2 W. Ellerington (Southampton) v N Fr 1949
3 G. W. Elliott (Middlesbrough) v I 1913-14 v W 1920
5 W. H. Elliott (Burnley) v It Au 1952 v I W Be 1953
4 R. E. Evans (Sheffield United) v I W S 1911 v W 1912
2 F. H. Ewer (Casuals) v Fr 1924 v Be 1925

1 P. Fairclough (Old Foresters) v S 1878
1 D. L. Fairhurst (Newcastle United) v Fr 1934
1 J. Fantham (Sheffield Wednesday) v L 1962
1 W. Felton (Sheffield Wednesday) v Fr 1925
1 M. Fenton (Middlesbrough) v S 1938
2 E. Field (Clapham Rovers) v S 1876-81
76 T. Finney (Preston North End) v I Ei W Ho Fr Por 1947 v Be
     W I Swe S It 1948 v I W S Swe N Fr 1949 v Ei W I It S
     Por Be Ch US Sp 1950 v W S Ar Por 1951 v Fr W I S It Au
     Swi 1952 v I W Be S Ar Ch U US 1953 v W S Y Hu Be Swi
     U 1954 v WG 1955 v D I W Sp S 1956 v W Y D S Ei D Ei
     1957 v W Fr S Por Y Rus(2) 1958 v I Rus 1959
11 H. J. Fleming (Swindon Town) v S Hu(2) 1909 v I W 1910-11 v
     I 1912 v W S 1913 v S 1914
2 A. Fletcher (Wolverphampton Wanderers) v W 1889-90
49 R. Flowers (Wolverhampton Wanderers) v Fr 1955 v W S It Br
     Pe Me(s) US 1959 v W Swe I S Y Sp Hu 1960 v I L Sp W S
     Me Por It Au 1961 v L W Por I Au S Swi Pe Hu Ar Bu Br
     1962 v Fr I W Fr S Swi 1963 v Ei US Por 1964 v W Ho WG
     1965 v N 1966
9 Frank Forman (Nottingham Forest) v I S 1898 v I W S 1899 v
     S 1901 v I S 1902 v W 1903
3 F. R. Forman (Nottingham Forest) v I W S 1899
11 J. H. Forrest (Blackburn Rovers) v W 1884 v I W S 1885 v S W
     1886 v I W S 1887 v S 1889 v I 1890
1 J. Fort (Millwall Athletic) v Be 1921
5 R. E. Foster (Oxford University) v W 1900 (Corinthians) v
     I W S 1901 v W 1902
1 W. J. Foulke (Sheffield United) v W 1897
1 W. A. Foulkes (Manchester United) v I 1955
1 F. S. Fox (Millwall Athletic) v Fr 1925
27 C. F. Franklin (Stoke City) v I Ei W Ho S Fr Swi Por 1947
     v Be W I Swe S It 1948 v D I W Swi S Swe N Fr 1949 v Ei W
     I It S 1950
5 B. C. Freeman (Everton) v W S 1909 (Burnley) v I W S 1912
13 J. Froggatt (Portsmouth) v I It 1950 v S 1951 v Au S It Au Swi
     1952 v I W Be S US 1953
4 R. Froggatt (Sheffield Wednesday) v W Be S US 1953
1 C. B. Fry (Southampton) v I 1901
1 W. I. Furness (Leeds United) v It 1933

2 T. Galley (Wolverhampton Wanderers) v N Swe 1937
2 T. Gardner (Aston Villa) v Cz 1934 v Ho 1935
1 B. Garfield (West Bromwich Albion) v I 1898
1 W. Garratty (Aston Villa) v W 1903
3 T. Garrett (Blackpool) v S It 1952 v W 1954
3 L. H. Gay (Cambridge University) v S 1893 (Old Brightonians)
     v W S 1894

2   F. Geary (Everton) v I 1890 v S 1891
1   R. L. Geaves (Clapham Rovers) v S 1875
3   C. W. Gee (Everton) v W Sp 1932 v I 1937
4   A. Geldard (Everton) v It Swi 1933 v S 1935 v I 1938
3   W. George (Aston Villa) v W I S 1902
2   W. V. T. Gibbins (Clapton) v Fr 1924-5
1   W. E. Gilliat (Old Carthusians) v I 1893
25 F. R. Goodall (Huddersfield Town) v S 1926 v S Be L Fr 1927
    v W S Fr Be 1928 v S G Au 1930 v I W S Be 1931 v I 1932
    v I W Au It Swi 1933 v I W Fr 1934
14 J. Goodall (Preston North End) v W S 1888-9 (Derby County)
    v W S 1891 v S 1892 v W 1893 v S 1894 v I S 1895 v W S
    1896 v W 1898
3   H. C. Goodhart (Old Etonians) v W I S 1883
1   A. G. Goodwyn (Royal Engineers) v S 1873
1   A. C. Goodyer (Nottingham Forest) v S 1879
5   R. C. Gosling (Old Etonians) v W 1892 v S 1893 v W 1894 v
    W S 1895
1   A. A. Gosnell (Newcastle United) v I 1906
1   H. Gough (Sheffield United) v S 1921
14 L. A. Goulden (West Ham United) v N Swe 1937 v I W Cz G
    Swi Fr 1938 v W FIFA S It Y Rum 1939
2   L. Graham (Millwall Athletic) v W S 1925
2   T. Graham (Nottingham Forest) v Fr 1931 v I 1932
7   C. Grainger (Sheffield United) v Br Swe Fi WG 1956 v I W
    1957 (Sunderland) v S 1957
57 J. P. Greaves (Chelsea) v Pe Me US 1959 v W Swe Y Sp 1960
    v I L Sp W S Por It Au 1961 (Tottenham Hotspur) v S Swi
    Pe Hu Ar Bu Br 1962 v Fr I W Fr S Br Cz Swi 1963 v W
    FIFA I U Por Ei Br Por Ar 1964 v I Be Ho S Hu Y 1965
    v W Au Y N D Pol U Me Fr 1966 v S Sp Au 1967
1   F. T. Green (Wanderers) v S 1876
8   G. H. Green (Sheffield United) v Fr 1925 v W S Be 1926 v I W
    1927 v Fr Be 1928
2   E. H. Greenhalgh (Notts County) v S 1872-3
2   D. H. Greenwood (Blackburn Rovers) v I S 1882
6   A. Grimsdell (Tottenham Hotspur) v W S 1920 v I S 1921 v I
    W 1923
3   A. T. Grosvenor (Birmingham) v I W Fr 1934
2   W. Gunn (Notts County) v S W 1884
1   R. Gurney (Sunderland) v 1935

3   J. Hacking (Oldham Athletic) v I W S 1929
1   H. Hadley (West Bromwich Albion) v I 1903
1   J. Hagan (Sheffield United) v D 1949
1   J. T. W. Haines (West Bromwich Albion) v Swi 1949
1   A. E. Hall (Aston Villa) v I 1910
10 G. W. Hall (Tottenham Hotspur) v Fr 1934 v I W Cz S 1938 v
    FIFA I S It Y 1939
17 J. J. Hall (Birmingham City) v D W I Sp S Br Swe Fi WG 1956
    v I W Y D S Ei D Ei 1957
1   H. J. Halse (Manchester United) v Au 1909
1   H. E. D. Hammond (Oxford University) v S 1889
3   J. Hampson (Blackpool) v I W 1931 v Au 1933

 4 H. Hampton (Aston Villa) v W S 1913-14
 3 J. Hancocks (Wolverhampton Wanderers) v Swi 1949 v W 1950 v Y 1951
30 E. A. Hapgood (Arsenal) v It Swi 1933 v I W S Hu Cz 1934 v W It I S Ho 1935 v I G W S Au Be 1936 v Fi 1937 v S G Swi Fr 1938 v W FIFA N I S It Y 1939
 1 H. T. W. Hardinge (Sheffield United) v S 1910
 4 H. P. Hardman (Everton) v W 1905 v I S 1907 v W 1908
13 G. F. M. Hardwick (Middlesbrough) v I Ei W Ho S Fr Swi Por 1947 v Be W I Swe S 1948
 1 H. Hardy (Stockport County) v Be 1925
21 S. Hardy (Liverpool) v I W S 1907 v S 1908 v I W S Hu(2) Au 1909 v I W S 1910 v I 1912 (Aston Villa) v S 1913 v I W S 1914-20
 3 F. W. Hargreaves (Blackburn Rovers) v W 1880-1 v I 1882
 2 J. Hargreaves (Blackburn Rovers) v W S 1881
 1 E. C. Harper (Blackburn Rovers) v S 1926
 1 G. Harris (Burnley) v Pol 1966
 2 P. P. Harris (Portsmouth) v Ei 1950 v Hu 1954
 6 S. S. Harris (Cambridge University) v S 1904 (Old Westminsters) v I W 1905 v I W S 1906
 2 A. H. Harrison (Old Westminsters) v I S 1893
 2 G. Harrison (Everton) v Be 1921 v I 1922
 2 J. H. Harrow (Chelsea) v I Swe 1923
 8 E. A. Hart (Leeds United) v W 1929 v I W 1930 v Au S 1933 v S Hu Cz 1934
 1 F. Hartley (Oxford City) v Fr 1923
 1 A. Harvey (Wednesbury Strollers) v W 1881
 1 J. C. Harvey (Everton) v Malta 1971
 5 H. W. Hassall (Huddersfield Town) v S Ar Por 1951 v Fr 1952 (Bolton Wanderers) v I 1954
 5 R. M. Hawkes (Luton Town) v I 1907 v Au(2) Hu Bo 1908
 5 G. Haworth (Accrington) v I W S 1887 v S 1888 v S 1890
 2 J. P. Hawtrey (Old Etonians) v W S 1881
 1 E. B. Haygarth (Swifts) v S 1875
56 J. N. Haynes (Fulham) v I 1955 v I Sp S Br Swe Fi WG 1956 v W Y Ei D Ei 1957 v W I Fr S Por Y Rus(2) Br Au Rus 1958 v I Rus S It Br Pe Me US 1959 v I Y Sp Hu 1960 v I L Sp W S Me Por It Au 1961 v W Por I Au S Swi Pe Hu Ar Bu Br 1962
 2 H. Healless (Blackburn Rovers) v I 1925 v S 1928
 1 G. A. Hedley (Sheffield United) v I 1901
 4 K. E. Hegan (Corinthians) v Be Fr 1923 v I Be 1924
 2 M. S. Hellawell (Birmingham City) v Fr I 1963
 5 A. G. Henfrey (Cambridge University) v I 1891 (Corinthians) v W 1892-5 v W S 1896
 1 R. P. Henry (Tottenham Hotspur) v Fr 1963
 1 F. Heron (Wanderers) v S 1876
 5 G. H. H. Heron (Uxbridge) v S 1873-4 (Wanderers) v S 1875-6-8
 1 W. Hibbert (Bury) v S 1910
25 H. E. Hibbs (Birmingham) v W S G Au 1930 v I W S 1931 v I W Sp 1932 v I W Au S It Swi 1933 v I W Fr 1934 v W I S Ho 1935 v G W 1936
 2 F. Hill (Bolton Wanderers) v I W 1963

11 J. H. Hill (Burnley) v W 1925 v S 1926 v I S Be Fr 1927 v I W 1928 (Newcastle United) v Fr Be Sp 1929
1 R. H. Hill (Millwall Athletic) v Be 1926
1 J. Hillman (Burnley) v I 1899
1 A. F. Hills (Old Harrovians) v S 1879
8 G. R. Hilsdon (Chelsea) v I 1907 v I W S Au Hu Bo 1908 v I 1909
6 E. W. Hine (Leicester City) v I W 1929-30-2
3 A. T. Hinton (Wolverhampton Wanderers) v Fr 1963 (Nottingham Forest) v Be W 1965
7 G. A. Hitchens (Aston Villa) v Me It Au 1961 (Internazionale Milan) v Swi Pe Hu Br 1962
2 H. H. F. Hobbis (Charlton Athletic) v Au Be 1936
6 D. Hodgetts (Aston Villa) v W S I 1888 v I S 1892 v I 1894
5 A. Hodgkinson (Sheffield United) v S Ei D Ei 1957 v W 1961
3 G. Hodgson (Liverpool) v I W S 1931
3 J. Hodkinson (Blackburn Rovers) v W S 1913 v I 1920
3 W. Hogg (Sunderland) v W I S 1902
2 G. H. Holdcroft (Preston North End) v W I 1937
5 A. D. Holden (Bolton Wanderers) v S It Br Pe Me 1959
4 G. H. Holden (Wednesbury Old Athletic) v S 1881 v I S W 1884
2 C. H. Holden-White (Corinthians) v W S 1888
1 T. Holford (Stoke) v I 1903
10 G. H. Holley (Sunderland) v W S Hu(2) Au 1909 v W 1910 v I W S 1912 v S 1913
3 E. Holliday (Middlesbrough) v W Swe I 1960
1 J. W. Hollins (Chelsea) v Sp 1967
7 R. Holmes (Preston North End) v I 1888 v S 1891-2 v W S 1893 v I 1894-5
10 J. Holt (Everton) v W 1890 v W S 1891 v I S 1892 v S 1893 v I S 1894 v S 1895 (Reading) v I 1900
14 E. Hopkinson (Bolton Wanderers) v W I Fr S Por Y 1958 v S It Br Pe Me US 1959 v W Swe 1960
2 A. H. Hossack (Corinthians) v W 1892-4
7 W. E. Houghton (Aston Villa) v I W Fr Be 1931 v I S 1932 v Au 1933
5 A. E. Houlker (Blackburn Rovers) v S 1902 (Portsmouth) v W S 1903 (Southampton) v I W 1906
5 R. H. Howarth (Preston North End) v I 1887 v W S 1888 v S 1891 (Everton) v I 1894
23 D. Howe (West Bromwich Albion) v W I Fr S Por Y Rus(2) Br Au Rus 1958 v I Rus W S It Br Pe Me US 1959 v W Swe I 1960
3 J. R. Howe (Derby County) v It 1948 v I S 1949
1 L. S. Howell (Wanderers) v S 1873
2 R. Howell (Sheffield United) v 1895 (Liverpool) v S 1899
1 J. Hudson (Sheffield Wednesday) v I 1883
1 F. C. Hudspeth (Newcastle United) v I 1926
6 A. E. Hufton (West Ham United) v Be 1924 v I S 1928 v Fr Be Sp 1929
18 E. W. Hughes (Liverpool) v Ho Por Be W I S 1970 v EG Ma Gr Ma W 1971 v Swi Gr WG(2) W I S 1972
3 L. Hughes (Liverpool) v Ch US Sp 1950
9 J. H. A. Hulme (Arsenal) v S Be Fr 1927 v I W S 1928 v I W

D

1929 v S 1933

1 P. Humphreys (Notts County) v S 1903

3 G. S. Hunt (Tottenham Hotspur) v S It Swi 1933

2 K. R. G. Hunt (Leyton) v W S 1911

34 R. Hunt (Liverpool) v Au 1962 v EG 1963 v S US Por 1964 v W 1965 v Sp Pol WG S Fi N Pol U Me Fr Ar Por WG 1966 v I Cz W Sp Au 1967 v W I Rus Sp(2) Swe Y Rus 1968 Rum(2) 1969

7 J. Hunter (Sheffield Heeley) v S 1878 v S W 1880 v W S 1881 v S W 1882

20 N. Hunter (Leeds United) v Sp(s) WG Y Fi 1966 v Au 1967 v Sp Swe WG Y Rus 1968 v Rum W 1969 v Ho WG(s) 1970 v Ma 1971 v WG(2) W I S 1972

49 G. C. Hurst (West Ham United) v WG S Y Fi D Ar Por WG 1966 v I Cz W S Sp Au 1967 v W I Rus S Swe(s) WG Rus 1968 v Rum Bu Rum Fr I S Me U Br 1969 v Ho Ho(s) Be W I S Co Ec Rum Br WG 1970 v EG Gr W S 1971 v Swi(2) Gr WG 1972

2 J. Iremonger (Nottingham Forest) v S 1901 v I 1902

9 D. B. N. Jack (Bolton Wanderers) v W S 1924 v Fr Be 1928 (Arsenal) v S G Au 1930 v W Au 1933

1 E. Jackson (Oxford University) v W 1891

3 B. G. Jarrett (Cambridge University) v S 1876-7-8

2 F. Jefferis (Everton) v W S 1912

2 B. A. G. Jezzard (Fulham) v Hu 1954 v I 1956

2 E. Johnson (Saltley College) v W 1880 (Stoke) v I 1884

5 J. A. Johnson (Stoke City) v I S N Swe Fi 1937

5 T. C. F. Johnson (Manchester City) v Be 1926 v W 1930 (Everton) v Sp S 1932 v I 1933

6 W. H. Johnson (Sheffield United) v I W S 1900-3

10 H. Johnston (Blackpool) v Ho S 1947 v S 1951 v Ar Ch U US 1953 v W I Ho 1954

3 A. Jones (Walsall Town Swifts) v S W 1882 (Great Lever) v S 1883

1 H. Jones (Nottingham Forest) v Fr 1923

6 H. Jones (Blackburn Rovers) v S Be L Fr 1927 v I S 1928

3 M. D. Jones (Sheffield United) v WG Swe 1965 (Leeds United) v Ho 1970

1 W. Jones (Bristol City) v I 1901

2 W. H. Jones (Liverpool) v Por Be 1950

1 B. Joy (Casuals) v Be 1936

3 E. I. L. Kail (Dulwich Hamlet) v Fr Be Sp 1929

1 A. H. Kay (Everton) v Swi 1963

9 F. W. Kean (Sheffield Wednesday) v Be S 1923 v W 1924 v I 1925 v I Be 1926 v L 1927 (Bolton Wanderers) v Fr Sp 1929

4 E. R. L. Keen (Derby County) v Au 1933 v W I Hu 1937

14 R. Kelly (Burnley) v S 1920 v I W S 1921 v W S 1922 v S 1923 v I 1924 v I W S 1925 (Sunderland) v W 1926 (Huddersfield Town) v L 1927 v S 1928

1 W. S. Kenyon-Slaney (Wanderers) v S 1873

14 D. T. Kevan (West Bromwich Albion) v S 1957 v W I S Por Y Rus(2) Br Au Rus 1958 v Me US 1959 v Me 1961

2   B. Kidd (Manchester United) v I Ec(s) 1970
1   R. S. King (Oxford University) v I 1882
1   R. K. Kingsford (Wanderers) v S 1874
1   M. Kingsley (Newcastle United) v W 1901
4   G. Kinsey (Wolverhampton Wanderers) v W 1892 v S 1893 (Derby County) v I W 1896
3   A. J. Kirchen (Arsenal) v N Swe Fi 1937
1   W. J. Kirton (Aston Villa) v I 1922
1   A. E. Knight (Portsmouth) v I 1920
4   C. B. Knowles (Tottenham Hotspur) v Rus Sp Swe WG 1968

26   B. L. Labone (Everton) v I W Fr 1963 v Sp Au 1967 v S Sp Swe WG Y Rus 1968 v Rum Bu I S Me U Br 1969 v Be W S Co Ec Rum Br WG 1970
3   E. J. Langley (Fulham) v S Por Y 1958
11   R. Langton (Blackburn Rovers) v I Ei W Ho Fr Swi 1947 v Swe 1948 (Preston North End) v D Swe 1949 (Bolton Wanderers) v S 1950 v I 1951
2   E. G. Latheron (Blackburn Rovers) v W 1913 v I 1914
4   C. Lawler (Liverpool) v Ma W S 1971 v Swi 1972
23   T. Lawton (Everton) v W FIFA N I S It Y Rum 1939 (Chelsea) v I Ei W Ho S Fr Swi Por 1947 v Be W I 1948 (Notts County) v Swe S It 1948 v D 1949
2   T. Leach (Sheffield Wednesday) v I W 1931
5   A. Leake (Aston Villa) v I S 1904 v I W S 1905
1   E. A. Lee (Southampton) v W 1904
27   F. H. Lee (Manchester City) v Bu Fr I W S Me U 1969 v Ho Por Ho Be W Co Ec Rum Br WG 1970 v EG Gr Ma I W S 1971 v Swi(2) Gr WG 1972
1   J. Lee (Derby County) v I 1951
1   J. E. Leighton (Nottingham Forest) v I 1886
1   H. E. Lilley (Sheffield United) v W 1892
2   J. H. Linacre (Nottingham Forest) v W S 1905
13   T. Lindley (Cambridge University) v I S W 1886 v I W S 1887 v W S I 1888 (Nottingham Forest) v S 1889 v W S 1890 v

1   W. Lindsay (Wanderers) v S 1877
7   E. H. Lintott (Queens Park Rangers) v I W S 1908 (Bradford City) v I S Hu(2) 1909
1   H. B. Lipsham (Sheffield United) v W 1902
3   L. V. Lloyd (Liverpool) v W 1971 v Swi I 1972
1   A. Lockett (Stoke) v I 1903
5   L. V. Lodge (Cambridge University) v W 1894 v W S 1895 (Corinthians) v I S 1896
7   J. M. Lofthouse (Blackburn Rovers) v I W S 1885 v W S 1887 (Accrington) v I 1889 (Blackburn Rovers) v I 1890
33   N. Lofthouse (Bolton Wanderers) v Y 1951 v W I Au S It Au Swi 1952 v I W Be S Ar Ch U US 1953 v W FIFA I Be U 1954 v I S Fr Sp Por 1955 v D W Sp S Fi(s) 1956 v Rus W 1959
5   E. Longworth (Liverpool) v S 1920 v Be 1921 v W Be S 1923
1   A. Lowder (Wolverhampton Wanderers) v W 1889
3   E. Lowe (Aston Villa) v Fr Swi Por 1947
3   T. Lucas (Liverpool) v I 1922 v Fr 1924 v Be 1926

 2 E. Luntley (Nottingham Forest) v S W 1880
 1 Hon. A. Lyttelton (Cambridge University) v S 1877
 1 Hon. E. Lyttelton (Cambridge University) v S 1878

 1 R. H. Macaulay (Cambridge University) v S 1881
 3 M. Macdonald (Newcastle United) v W I S(s) 1972
 5 J. McCall (Preston North End) v W S 1913 v S 1914-20 v I 1921
 8 C. A. McDonald (Burnley) v Rus(2) Br Au Rus 1958 v I Rus W 1959
10 R. L. McFarland (Derby County) v Ma Gr Ma I S 1971 v Swi Gr WG W S 1972
 4 W. H. McGarry (Huddersfield Town) v Swi U 1954 v D W 1956
 2 W. McGuinness (Manchester United) v I Me 1959
 1 A. McInroy (Sunderland) v I 1927
 4 R. McNab (Arsenal) v Rum(s) Bu Rum I 1969
 2 R. McNeal (West Bromwich Albion) v W S 1914
 9 M. McNeil (Middlesbrough) v I L Sp W S Me Por It 1961 v L 1962
 5 S. Macrae (Notts County) v W I S 1883 v I S 1884
 1 F. B. Maddison (Oxford University) v S 1872
 8 P. E. Madeley (Leeds United) v I 1971 v Swi(2) Gr WG(2) W S 1972
 5 T. P. Magee (West Bromwich Albion) v W Swe 1923 v Be S Fr 1925
 4 H. Makepeace (Everton) v S 1906-10 v W S 1912
19 C. G. Male (Arsenal) v It I S Ho 1935 v I G W S Au Be 1936 v I Hu S N Swe Fi 1937 v It Y Rum 1939
26 W. J. Mannion (Middlesbrough) v I Ei W Ho S Fr Swi Por 1947 v Be W I Swe It 1948 v N Fr 1949 v Ei S Por Be Ch US 1950 v I W Y S 1951 v Fr 1952
 1 J. T. Marsden (Darwen) v I 1891
 3 W. Marsden (Sheffield Wednesday) v W S G 1930
 6 R. W. Marsh (Queens Park Rangers) v Swi(s) 1972 (Manchester City) v WG(s) WG W I S 1972
 2 T. Marshall (Darwen) v W 1880-1
 1 H. Martin (Sunderland) v I 1914
 1 H. M. Maskrey (Derby County) v 1908
 3 C. Mason (Wolverhampton Wanderers) v I 1887 v W 1888 v I 1890
 5 R. D. Matthews (Coventry City) v S Br Swe WG 1956 v I 1957
54 S. Matthews (Stoke City) v W It 1935 v G 1936 v S 1937 v W Cz S G Swi Fr 1938 v W FIFA N I S It Y 1939 v S 1947 (Blackpool) v Swi Por 1947 v Be W I S It 1948 v D I W Swi S 1949 v Sp 1950 v I S 1951 v FIFA I Hu Be U 1954 v I W WG S Fr Sp Por 1955 v W Be 1956 v I W Y D S Ei D 1957
 2 V. Matthews (Sheffield United) v Fr Be 1928
 2 W. J. Maynard (1st Surrey Rifles) v S 1872-6
 1 J. Meadows (Manchester City) v S 1955
 6 L. D. Medley (Tottenham Hotspur) v W Y 1951 v Fr W I Au 1952
 1 T. Meehan (Chelsea) v I 1924
 2 J. Melia (Liverpool) v S Swi 1963
 2 D. W. Mercer (Sheffield United) v I Be 1923
 5 J. Mercer (Everton) v I S It Y Rum 1939

23 G. H. Merrick (Birmingham City) v I Au S It Au Swi 1952 v I
   W Be S Ar Ch U 1953 v W FIFA I Hu S Y Hu Be Swi U 1954
2 V. Metcalfe (Huddersfield Town) v Ar Por 1951
1 J. W. Mew (Manchester United) v I 1921
1 B. Middleditch (Corinthians) v I 1897
13 J. E. T. Milburn (Newcastle United) v I W Swi S 1949 v W
   Por Be Sp 1950 v W Ar Por 1951 v Fr 1952 v D 1956
1 B. G. Miller (Burnley) v Au 1961
1 H. S. Miller (Charlton Athletic) v Swe 1923
3 G. R. Mills (Chelsea) v I W Cz 1938
14 G. Milne (Liverpool) v Br Cz EG 1963 v W FIFA I S U Por
   Ei Br Ar 1964 v I Be 1965
1 C. A. Milton (Arsenal) v Au 1952
4 A. Milward (Everton) v W S 1891-7
5 C. Mitchell (Upton Park) v W 1880 v S 1881 v W S 1883 v
   W 1885
1 J. F. Mitchell (Manchester City) v I 1925
1 H. Moffat (Oldham Athletic) v W 1913
4 G. Molyneux (Southampton) v S 1902 v I W S 1903
7 W. R. Moon (Old Westminsters) v W S 1888-9-90 v S 1891
2 H. T. Moore (Notts County) v I 1883 v W 1885
1 J. Moore (Derby County) v Swe 1923
96 R. F. Moore (West Ham United) v Pe Hu Ar Bu Br 1962 v Fr
   I W Fr S Br Cz EG Swi 1963 v W FIFA I S U Por
   Ei Br Por Ar 1964 v I Be S Hu Y WG Swe 1965 v W Au I Sp
   Pol WG S N D Pol U Me Fr Ar Por WG 1966 v I Cz W S
   Sp Au 1967 v W I Rus S Sp(2) Swe WG Y Rus 1968 v Rum
   Bu Fr I W S Me U Br 1969 v Ho Por Be W I S Co Ec Rum
   Br Cz WG 1970 v EG Gr Ma I S 1971 v Swi(2) Gr WG(2)
   W S 1972
1 W. G. B. Moore (West Ham United) v Swe 1923
2 J. Mordue (Sunderland) v I 1912-13
1 C. J. Morice (Barnes) v S 1872
1 H. Morley (Notts County) v I 1910
1 T. Morren (Sheffield United) v I 1898
2 F. Morris (West Bromwich Albion) v S 1920 v I 1921
3 J. Morris (Derby County) v N Fr 1949 v Ei 1950
3 W. W. Morris (Wolverhampton Wanderers) v I S Rum 1939
1 H. Morse (Notts County) v S 1879
3 T. Mort (Aston Villa) v W Fr 1924 v S 1926
1 A. Morten (Crystal Palace) v S 1873
25 S. H. Mortensen (Blackpool) v Por 1947 v Be W I Swe S It 1948
   v I W S Swe N 1949 v W I It S Por Be Ch US Sp 1950 v S
   Ar 1951 v FIFA Hu 1954
1 J. R. Morton (West Ham United) v Cz 1938
9 W. Mosforth (Sheffield Wednesday) v S 1877 (Sheffield Albion)
   v S 1878 v W S 1879 v S W 1880 (Sheffield Wednesday) v
   W 1881 v S W 1882
5 F. Moss (Aston Villa) v I S 1922 v I 1923 v Be S 1924
4 F. Moss (Arsenal) v S Hu Cz 1934 v It 1935
2 E. Mosscrop (Burnley) v W S 1914
3 B. Mozley (Derby County) v Ei W I 1950
12 J. Mullen (Wolverhampton Wanderers) v S 1947 v N Fr 1949
   v Be(s) Ch US 1950 v W FIFA I S Y Swi 1954

35 A. P. Mullery (Tottenham Hotspur) v Ho 1965 v Sp Au 1967
v W I Rus S Sp(2) Swe Y 1968 v Rum Bu Fr I S Me U Br
1969 v Ho Por Ho(s) W I S(s) Co Ec Rum Br Cz WG 1970
v EG Ma Gr 1971 v Swi 1972

16 E. Needham (Sheffield United) v S 1894-5 v I W S 1897 v W S
1898 v I W S 1899 v I S 1900 v I W S 1901 v W 1902

27 K. R. Newton (Blackburn Rovers) v WG S 1966 v Sp Au 1967
v W S Sp Swe WG Y 1968 v Rum Bu Fr I W S Me U Br
1969 (Everton) v Ho I S Co Ec Rum Cz WG 1970

2 J. Nicholls (West Bromwich Albion) v S Y 1954

1 W. E. Nicholson (Tottenham Hotspur) v Por 1951

23 M. Norman (Tottenham Hotspur) v Pe Hu Ar Bu Br 1962 v
Fr S Br Cz EG 1963 v W FIFA I S U Por US Br Por Ar 1964
v I Be Ho 1965

3 H. Nuttall (Bolton Wanderers) v I W 1928 v S 1929

16 W. J. Oakley (Oxford University) v W 1895 v I W S 1896 (Corinthians) v I W S 1897-8-1900-1

3 J. P. O'Dowd (Chelsea) v S 1932 v I Swi 1933

1 R. A. M. M. Ogilvie (Clapham Rovers) v S 1874

2 M. O'Grady (Huddersfield Town) v I 1963 (Leeds United) v Fr
1969

1 L. F. Oliver (Fulham) v Be 1929

2 B. A. Olney (Aston Villa) v Fr Be 1928

4 F. R. Osborne (Fulham) v I Fr 1923 (Tottenham Hotspur) v Be
1925-6

1 R. Osborne (Leicester City) v W 1928

3 P. L. Osgood (Chelsea) v Be Rum(s) Cz(s) 1970

2 C. J. Ottaway (Oxford University) v S 1872-4

1 J. R. B. Owen (Sheffield F.C.) v S 1874

3 S. W. Owen (Luton Town) v Y Hu Be 1954

7 L. A. Page (Burnley) v W S Be L Fr 1927 v I W 1928

19 T. L. Paine (Southampton) v Cz EG 1963 v W FIFA I S U US
Por 1964 v I Hu Y WG Swe 1965 v W Au Y N Me 1966

1 H. H. Pantling (Sheffield United) v I 1924

3 P. J. de Paravicini (Cambridge University) v W I S 1883

1 T. R. Parker (Southampton) v Fr 1925

2 J. Parkinson (Liverpool) v W S 1910

1 P. C. Parr (Oxford University) v W 1882

3 E. H. Parry (Old Carthusians) v W 1879 v S W 1882

2 R. A. Parry (Bolton Wanderers) v I S 1960

2 B. C. A. Patchitt (Corinthians) v Swe(2) 1923

2 F. W. Pawson (Cambridge University) v I 1883 (Swifts) v I 1885

1 J. Payne (Luton Town) v Fi 1937

6 A. Peacock (Middlesbrough) v Ar Bu 1962 v I W 1963 (Leeds
United) v W I 1966

3 J. Peacock (Middlesbrough) v Fr Be Sp 1929

1 H. F. Pearson (West Bromwich Albion) v S 1932

1 J. H. Pearson (Crewe Alexandra) v I 1892

8 S. C. Pearson (Manchester United) v S 1948 v I S 1949 v I It
1950 v Por 1951 v I It 1952

1 W. H. Pease (Middlesbrough) v W 1927

1   D. Pegg (Manchester United) v Ei 1957
3   F. R. Pelly (Old Foresters) v I 1893 v W S 1894
25 J. Pennington (West Bromwich Albion) v W S 1907 v I W S Au
    1908 v W S Hu(2) Au 1909 v W S 1910 v I W S 1911-12 v
    W S 1913 v I S 1914 v W S 1920
5   F. B. Pentland (Middlesbrough) v W S Hu(2) Au 1909
3   C. Perry (West Bromwich Albion) v I 1890-1 v W 1893
1   T. Perry (West Bromwich Albion) v W 1898
3   W. Perry (Blackpool) v I Sp S 1956
54 M. S. Peters (West Ham United) v Y Fi Pol Me Fr Ar Por WG
    1966 v I Cz W S 1967 v W I Rus S Sp(2) Swe Y Rus 1968
    v Rum Bu Fr I S Me U Br 1969 v Ho Por(s) Ho Be 1970
    (Tottenham Hotspur) v W I S Co Ec Rum Br Cz WG 1970
    v EG Ma Gr Ma I W S 1971 v Swi Gr WG WG(s) I(s) 1972
3   L. H. Phillips (Portsmouth) v I 1952 v W WG 1955
3   F. Pickering (Everton) v US 1964 v I Be 1965
1   J. Pickering (Sheffield United) v S 1933
1   T. M. Pike (Cambridge University) v I 1886
1   B. Pilkington (Burnley) v I 1955
1   J. Plant (Bury) v S 1900
1   S. L. Plum (Charlton Athletic) v Fr 1923
3   R. Pointer (Burnley) v L W Por 1962
1   T. S. Porteous (Sunderland) v W 1891
1   A. E. Priest (Sheffield United) v I 1900
1   J. F. M. Prinsep (Clapham Rovers) v S 1879
2   S. C. Puddefoot (Blackburn Rovers) v I S 1926
1   J. Pye (Wolverhampton Wanderers) v Ei 1950
3   R. H. Pym (Bolton Wanderers) v W S 1925 v W 1926

4   A. E. Quantrill (Derby County) v W S 1920 v I W 1921
5   A. Quixall (Sheffield Wednesday) v W FIFA I 1954 v Sp Por(s)
    1955

2   J. Radford (Arsenal) v Rum 1969 v Swi(s) 1972
4   G. B. Raikes (Oxford University) v W 1895 v I W S 1896
32 A. E. Ramsey (Southampton) v Swi 1949 (Tottenham Hotspur)
    v It S Por Be Ch US Sp 1950 v I W Y S Ar Por 1951 v Fr
    W I Au S It Au Swi 1952 v I W Be S Ar Ch U US 1953 v
    FIFA Hu 1954
1   A. Rawlings (Preston North End) v Be 1921
2   W. E. Rawlings (Southampton) v W S 1922
1   J. F. P. Rawlinson (Cambridge University) v I 1882
1   H. E. Rawson (Royal Engineers) v S 1875
2   W. S. Rawson (Oxford University) v S 1875-7
1   A. Read (Tufnell Park) v Be 1921
1   J. Reader (West Bromwich Albion) v I 1894
3   P. Reaney (Leeds United) v Bu(s) 1969 v Por 1970 v Ma 1971
6   D. G. Revie (Manchester City) v I S Fr 1955 v D W 1956 v
    I 1957
8   J. Reynolds (West Bromwich Albion) v S 1892 v W S 1893
    (Aston Villa) v I S 1894 v S 1895 v W S 1897
1   C. H. Richards (Nottingham Forest) v I 1898
1   G. H. Richards (Derby County) v Au 1909
2   J. R. Richardson (Newcastle United) v It Swi 1933

1   W. "G." Richardson (West Bromwich Albion) v Ho 1935
1   S. Rickaby (West Bromwich Albion) v I 1954
5   A. Rigby (Blackburn Rovers) v S Be L Fr 1927 v W 1928
4   E. J. Rimmer (Sheffield Wednesday) v S G Au 1930 v Sp 1932
1   G. Robb (Tottenham Hotspur) v· Hu 1954
3   C. Roberts (Manchester United) v I W S 1905
4   F. Roberts (Manchester City) v Be W S Fr 1925
1   H. Roberts (Arsenal) v S 1931
1   H. Roberts (Millwall) v Be 1931
3   R. Roberts (West Bromwich Albion) v S 1887 v I 1888-90
2   W. T. Roberts (Preston North End) v Be W 1924
4   J. Robinson (Sheffield Wednesday) v Fi 1937 v G Swi 1938 v W 1939
11   J. W. Robinson (Derby County) v I S 1897 (New Brighton Tower) v I W S 1898 (Southampton) v W S 1899 v I W S 1900 v I 1901
20   R. W. Robson (West Bromwich Albion) v Fr Rus(2) Br Au 1958 v Sp Hu 1960 v I L Sp W S Me Por It 1961 v L W Por I Swi 1962
5   W. C. Rose (Swifts) v I S W 1884 (Preston North End) v I 1886 (Wolverhampton Wanderers) v I 1891
2   T. Rostron (Darwen) v W S 1881
1   A. S. Rowe (Tottenham Hotspur) v Fr 1934
6   J. F. Rowley (Manchester United) v Swi Swe Fr 1949 v I It 1950 v S 1952
2   W. Rowley (Stoke) v I 1889-92
1   J. Royle (Everton) v Ma 1971
3   H. Ruddlesdin (Sheffield Wednesday) v W I 1904 v S 1905
6   J. W. Ruffell (West Ham United) v S 1926 v I 1927 v I W S 1929 v W 1930
1   B. B. Russell (Royal Engineers) v W 1883
11   J. Rutherford (Newcastle United) v S 1904 v I W S 1907-8 v Au(2) Hu Bo 1908

4   D. Sadler (Manchester United) v I Rus 1968 v Ec(s) 1970 v EG 1971
2   C. Sagar (Bury) v I 1900 v W 1902
4   E. Sagar (Everton) v I S Au Be 1936
1   E. A. Sandford (West Bromwich Albion) v W 1933
5   R. R. Sandilands (Old Westminsters) v W 1892 v I 1893 v W 1894-5-6
1   J. Sands (Nottingham Forest) v W 1880
1   F. E. Saunders (Swifts) v W 1888
1   A. H. Savage (Crystal Palace) v S 1876
1   J. Sayer (Stoke) v I 1887
1   E. Scattergood (Derby County) v W 1913
3   J. A. Schofield (Stoke) v W 1892-3 v I 1895
17   L. Scott (Arsenal) v I Ei W Ho S Fr Swi Por 1947 v Be W I Swe S It 1948 v D I W 1949
1   W. R. Scott (Brentford) v W 1937
6   J. Seddon (Bolton Wanderers) v Fr Swe(2) 1923 v Be 1924 v W 1927 v S 1929
5   J. M. Seed (Tottenham Hotspur) v Be 1921 v I W Be 1923 v S1925

6 J. Settle (Bury) v I W S 1899 (Everton) v I S 1902 v I 1903
6 J. Sewell (Sheffield Wednesday) v I Au Swi 1952 v I 1953 v Hu(2) 1954
1 W. R. Sewell (Blackburn Rovers) v W 1924
5 L. F. Shackleton (Sunderland) v D W 1949 v W 1950 v W WG 1955
2 J. Sharp (Everton) v I 1903 v S 1905
1 G. E. Shaw (West Bromwich Albion) v S 1932
5 G. L. Shaw (Sheffield United) v Rus W S It 1959 v W 1963
2 D. Shea (Blackburn Rovers) v I W 1914
1 K. J. Shellito (Chelsea) v Cz 1963
6 A. Shelton (Notts County) v I 1889 v W S 1890-1 v S 1892
1 C. Shelton (Notts Rangers) v I 1888
2 A. Shepherd (Bolton Wanderers) v S 1906 (Newcastle United) v I 1911
4 P. L. Shilton (Leicester City) v EG W 1971 v Swi I 1972
1 E. Shimwell (Blackpool) v Swe 1949
1 G. Shutt (Stoke) v I 1886
3 J. Silcock (Manchester United) v W S 1921 v Swe 1923
3 R. P. Sillett (Chelsea) v Fr Sp Por 1955
1 E. Simms (Luton Town) v I 1922
8 J. Simpson (Blackburn Rovers) v I W S 1911-12 v S 1913 v W 1914
12 W. J. Slater (Wolverhampton Wanderers) v W WG 1955 v S Por Y Rus(2) Br Au Rus 1958 v Rus 1959 v S 1960
1 T. Smalley (Wolverhampton Wanderers) v W 1937
5 T. Smart (Aston Villa) v S 1921 v W S 1924 v I 1926 v W 1930
3 A. Smith (Nottingham Forest) v W S 1891 v I 1893
1 A. K. Smith (Oxford University) v S 1872
2 B. Smith (Tottenham Hotspur) v S 1921 v W 1922
1 C. E. Smith (Crystal Palace) v S 1876
20 G. O. Smith (Oxford University) v I 1893 v W S 1894 v W 1895 v I W S 1896 (Old Carthusians) v IWS 1897-8 (Corinthians) v I W S 1899-1900 v S 1901
4 H. Smith (Reading) v W S 1905 v I W 1906
5 J. Smith (Bolton Wanderers) v I 1913 v W S 1914 v I W 1920
2 J. Smith (West Bromwich Albion) v I 1920-3
2 J. C. R. Smith (Millwall) v N I 1939
3 J. W. Smith (Portsmouth) v I W Sp 1932
6 L. Smith (Arsenal) v W 1951 v W I 1952 v W Be S 1953
1 L. G. F. Smith (Brentford) v Rum 1939
15 R. A. Smith (Tottenham Hotspur) v I L Sp W S Por 1961 v S 1962 v Fr S Br Cz EG 1963 v W FIFA I 1964
1 S. Smith (Aston Villa) v S 1895
1 S. C. Smith (Leicester City) v I 1936
2 T. Smith (Birmingham City) v W Swe 1960
1 T. Smith (Liverpool) v W 1971
3 W. H. Smith (Huddersfield Town) v W S 1922 v S 1928
1 T. H. Sorby (Thursday Wanderers, Sheffield) v W 1879
3 John Southworth (Blackburn Rovers) v W 1889-91 v S 1892
3 F. J. Sparks (Hertfordshire Rangers) v S 1879 (Clapham Rovers) v S W 1880
2 J. W. Spence (Manchester United) v Be 1926 v I 1927
2 R. Spence (Chelsea) v Au Be 1936

2 C. W. Spencer (Newcastle United) v S 1924 v W 1925

6 H. Spencer (Aston Villa) v W S 1897 v W 1900 v I 1903 v W S 1905

7 F. Spiksley (Sheffield Wednesday) v W S 1893 v I S 1894 v I 1896 v W S 1898

3 B. W. Spilsbury (Cambridge University) v I 1885 v I S 1886

1 W. A. Spouncer (Nottingham Forest) v W 1900

33 R. D. G. Springett (Sheffield Wednesday) v I S Y Sp Hu 1960 v I L Sp S Me Por It Au 1961 v L W Por I Au S Swi Pe Hu Ar Bu Br 1962 v Fr I W Fr Swi 1963 v W Au N 1966

11 B. Sproston (Leeds United) v W 1937 v I W Cz S G Swi Fr 1938 (Tottenham Hotspur) v W FIFA 1939 (Manchester City) v N 1939

3 R. T. Squire (Cambridge University) v I S W 1886

1 M. H. Stanbrough (Old Carthusians) v W 1895

8 R. Staniforth (Huddersfield Town) v S Y Hu Be Swi U 1954 v W WG 1955

2 R. W. Starling (Sheffield Wednesday) v S 1933 (Aston Villa) v S 1937

6 F. C. Steele (Stoke City) v W I S N Swe Fi 1937

1 C. Stephenson (Huddersfield Town) v W 1924

3 G. T. Stephenson (Derby County) v Fr Be 1928 (Sheffield Wednesday) v Fr 1931

2 J. E. Stephenson (Leeds United) v S 1938 v I 1939

1 A. C. Stepney (Manchester United) v Swe 1968

3 J. Stewart (Sheffield Wednesday) v W S 1907 (Newcastle United) v S 1911

28 N. P. Stiles (Manchester United) v S Hu Y Swe 1965 v W Au I Sp Pol WG S N D Pol U Me Fr Ar Por WG 1966 v I Cz W S 1967 v Rus 1968 v Rum 1969 v I S 1970

3 L. Stoker (Birmingham) v W 1933 v S Hu 1934

2 H. Storer (Derby County) v Fr 1924 v I 1928

8 P. E. Storey (Arsenal) v Gr I S 1971 v Swi WG W I S 1972

1 I Storey-Moore (Nottingham Forest) v Ho 1970

20 A. H. Strange (Sheffield Wednesday) v S G Au 1930 v I W S Fr Be 1931 v I W Sp S 1932 v I Au S It Swi 1933 v I W Fr 1934

1 A. H. Stratford (Wanderers) v S 1874

1 B. R. Streten (Luton Town) v I 1950

2 A. Sturgess (Sheffield United) v I 1911 v S 1914

7 M. G. Summerbee (Manchester City) v S Sp WG 1968 v Swi WG(s) W I 1972

5 J. W. Sutcliffe (Bolton Wanderers) v W 1893 v I S 1895 v S 1901 (Millwall Athletic) v W 1903

19 P. Swan (Sheffield Wednesday) v Y Sp Hu 1960 v I L Sp W S Me Por It Au 1961 v L W Por I Au S Swi 1962

6 H. A. Swepstone (Pilgrims) v S 1880 v S W 1882 v W I S 1883

19 F. V. Swift (Manchester City) v I Ei W Ho S Fr Swi Por 1947 v Be W I Swe S It 1948 v D I W S N 1949

1 G. Tait (Birmingham Excelsior) v W 1881

3 R. V. Tambling (Chelsea) v W Fr 1963 v Y 1966

3 J. T. Tate (Aston Villa) v Fr Be 1931 v W 1933

1 E. Taylor (Blackpool) v Hu 1954

8 E. H. Taylor (Huddersfield Town) v I W Be S 1923 v I S Fr
1924 v S 1926

2 J. G. Taylor (Fulham) v Por Ar 1951

3 P. H. Taylor (Liverpool) v W I Swe 1948

19 T. Taylor (Manchester United) v Ar Ch U 1953 v Be Swi 1954
v S Br Swe Fi WG 1956 v I Y(s) D Ei D Ei 1957 v W I Fr 1958

1 D. W. Temple (Everton) v WG 1965

2 H. Thickett (Sheffield United) v W S 1899

16 P. Thompson (Liverpool) v Por Ei US Br Por Ar 1964 v I Be
W Ho S 1965 v I 1966 v I WG 1968 v Ho(s) S 1970

2 T. Thompson (Aston Villa) v W 1952 (Preston North End) v
S 1957

8 R. A. Thomson (Wolverhampton Wanderers) v I US Por Ar
1964 v I Be W Ho 1965

4 G. Thornewell (Derby County) v Swe(2) 1923 v Fr 1924-5

1 I. Thornley (Manchester City) v W 1907

4 S. F. Tilson (Manchester City) v Hu Cz 1934 v W 1935 v I 1936

2 F. Titmuss (Southampton) v W 1922-3

1 C. Todd (Derby County) v I 1972

2 G. Toone (Notts County) v W S 1892

1 A. G. Topham (Casuals) v W 1894

2 R. Topham (Wolverhampton Wanderers) v I 1893 (Casuals) v
W 1894

2 W. J. Townley (Blackburn Rovers) v W 1889 v I 1890

2 J. E. Townrow (Clapton Orient) v S 1925 v W 1926

1 D. R. Tremelling (Birmingham) v W 1928

2 J. Tresadern (West Ham United) v S Swe 1923

7 F. E. Tunstall (Sheffield United) v S 1923 v I W S Fr 1924 v
I S 1925

1 R. J. Turnbull (Bradford) v I 1920

2 A. Turner (Southampton) v I 1900-1

2 H. Turner (Huddersfield Town) v Fr Be 1931

3 J. A. Turner (Bolton Wanderers) v W 1893 (Stoke) v I 1895
(Derby County) v I 1898

1 G. J. Tweedy (Grimsby Town) v Hu 1937

1 D. G. Ufton (Charlton Athletic) v FIFA 1954

2 A. Underwood (Stoke) v I 1891-2

4 T. Urwin (Middlesbrough) v Swe(2) 1923 v Be 1924 (Newcastle
United) v W 1926

1 G. Utley (Barnsley) v I 1913

5 O. H. Vaughton (Aston Villa) v I S W 1882 v S W 1884

6 C. C. M. Veitch (Newcastle United) v I W S 1906 v W S 1907
v W 1909

1 J. G. Veitch (Old Westminsters) v W 1894

2 T. F. Venables (Chelsea) v Be Ho 1965

1 R. W. S. Vidal (Oxford University) v S 1873

2 D. S. Viollet (Manchester United) v Hu 1960 v L 1962

2 P. G. Von Donop (Royal Engineers) v D 1873-5

3 H. Wace (Wanderers) v S 1878 v W S 1879

9 S. J. Wadsworth (Huddersfield Town) v S 1922 v Be S 1923
v I S 1924-5 v W 1926 v I 1927

1   W. R. Wainscoat (Leeds United) v S 1929
5   A. K. Waiters (Blackpool) v Ei Br 1964 v Be W Ho 1965
2   F. I. Walden (Tottenham Hotspur) v S 1914 v W 1922
18 W. H. Walker (Aston Villa) v I 1921 v I W S 1922 v Swe(2) 1923
      v S 1924 v I Be W S Fr 1925 v I W S 1926 v I W 1927 v
      Au 1933
7   G. Wall (Manchester United) v W 1907 v I 1908 v S 1909 v W S
      1910 v S 1912 v I 1913
3   C. W. Wallace (Aston Villa) v W 1913 v I 1914 v S 1920
9   A. M. Walters (Cambridge University) v I S 1885 v S 1886 v
      W S 1887 (Old Carthusians) v W S 1889-90
13 P. M. Walters (Oxford University) v I S 1885 (Old Carthusians)
      v I S W 1886 v W S 1887 v S I 1888 v W S 1889-90
1   N. Walton (Blackburn Rovers) v I 1890
1   J. T. Ward (Blackburn Olympic) v W 1885
2   T. V. Ward (Derby County) v Be 1948 v W 1949
5   T. Waring (Aston Villa) v Fr Be 1931 v I W S 1932
1   C. Warner (Upton Park) v S 1878
22 B. Warren (Derby County) v I W S 1906-7-8 v Au(2) Hu Bo 1908
      (Chelsea) v I W S Hu(2) Au 1909 v I W S 1911
1   G. S. Waterfield (Burnley) v W 1927
5   V. M Watson (West Ham United) v W S 1923 v S G Au 1930
3   W. Watson (Burnley) v S 1913 v I 1914-20
4   W. Watson (Sunderland) v I It 1950 v W Y 1951
3   S. Weaver (Newcastle United) v S 1932 v I S 1933
2   G. W. Webb (West Ham United) v W S 1911
3   M. Webster (Middlesbrough) v S G Au 1930
26 W. J. Wedlock (Bristol City) v I W S 1907-8 v Au(2) Hu Bo
      1908 v I W S Hu(2) Au 1909 v I W S 1910-11-12 v W 1914
2   D. Weir (Bolton Wanderers) v S I 1889
2   R. de C. Welch (Wanderers) v S 1872 (Harrow Chequers) v S
      1874
3   D. Welsh (Charlton Athletic) v G Swi 1938 v Rum 1939
3   G. West (Everton) v Bu W Me 1969
6   R. W. Westwood (Bolton Wanderers) v W S Ho 1935 v I G 1936
      v W 1937
2   O. Whateley (Aston Villa) v I S 1883
1   J. E. Wheeler (Bolton Wanderers) v I 1955
4   G. F. Wheldon (Aston Villa) v I 1897 v I W S 1898
1   T. A. White (Everton) v It 1933
2   J. Whitehead (Accrington) v W 1893 (Blackburn Rovers) v I 1894
1   H. Whitfeld (Cambridge University) v W 1879
1   M. Whitham (Sheffield United) v I 1892
1   S. W. Widdowson (Nottingham Forest) v S 1880
2   F. Wignall (Nottingham Forest) v W Ho 1965
5   A. Wilkes (Aston Villa) v W S 1901 v W I S 1902
1   B. Wilkinson (Sheffield United) v S 1904
1   L. R. Wilkinson (Oxford University) v W 1891
24 B. F. Williams (Wolverhampton Wanderers) v Fr 1949 v Ei W It
      S Por Be Ch US Sp 1950 v I W Y S Ar Por 1951 v Fr W 1952
      v WG S Fr Sp Por 1955 v W 1956
2   O. Williams (Clapton Orient) v I W 1923
6   W. Williams (West Bromwich Albion) v I 1897 v I W S 1898
      v I W 1899

2 E. C. Williamson (Arsenal) v Swe(2) 1923
7 R. G. Williamson (Middlesbrough) v I 1905 v I W S 1911 v W S 1912 v I 1913
12 C. K. Willingham (Huddersfield Town) v Fi 1937 v S G Swi Fr 1938 v W FIFA N I S It Y 1939
1 A. Willis (Tottenham Hotspur) v Fr 1952
12 D. J. Wilshaw (Wolverhampton Wanderers) v W Swi U 1954 v S Fr Sp Por 1955 v W I Fi WG 1956 v I 1957
2 C. P. Wilson (Hendon) v S W 1884
2 C. W. Wilson (Oxford University) v W 1879 v S 1881
12 G. Wilson (Sheffield Wednesday) v W S Be 1921 v I S 1922 v I W Be S 1923 v I W Fr 1924
2 G. P. Wilson (Corinthians) v W S 1900
63 R. Wilson (Huddersfield Town) v S Y Sp Hu 1960 v W Por I Au S Swi Pe Hu Ar Bu Br 1962 v Fr I Br Cz EG Swi 1963 v W FIFA S U Por Ei Br Por Ar 1964 (Everton) v S Hu Y WG Swe 1965 v W Au I Sp Pol WG(s) Y Fi D Pol U Me Fr Ar Por WG 1966 v I Cz W S Au 1967 v I Rus S Sp(2) Y Rus 1968
1 T. Wilson (Huddersfield Town) v S 1928
2 W. N. Winckworth (Old Westminsters) v W 1892 v I 1893
8 J. E. Windridge (Chelsea) v I W S Au(2) Hu Bo 1908 v I 1909
1 C. V. Wingfield-Stratford (Royal Engineers) v S 1877
4 C. H. R. Wollaston (Wanderers) v S 1874-5-7-80
3 S. Wolstenholme (Everton) v S 1904 (Blackburn Rovers) v I W 1905
3 H. Wood (Wolverhampton Wanderers) v W S 1890 v S 1896
3 R. E. Wood (Manchester United) v I W 1955 v Fi 1956
1 G. Woodger (Oldham Athletic) v I 1911
2 G. Woodhall (West Bromwich Albion) v W S 1888
19 V. R. Woodley (Chelsea) v S N Swe Fi 1937 v I W Cz S G Swi Fr 1938 v W FIFA N I S It Y Rum 1939
23 V. J. Woodward (Tottenham Hotspur) v I W S 1903 v I S 1904 v I W S 1905 v S 1907 v I W S Au(2) Hu Bo 1908 v I W Hu(2) Au 1909 (Chelsea) v I 1910 v W 1911
1 M. Woosnam (Manchester City) v W 1922
2 F. Worrall (Portsmouth) v Ho 1935 v I 1937
4 C. Wreford-Brown (Oxford University) v I 1889 (Old Carthusians) v W 1894-5 v S 1898
1 E. G. D. Wright (Cambridge University) v W 1906
1 J. D. Wright (Newcastle United) v N 1939
11 T. J. Wright (Everton) v Rus 1968 v Rum(2) Me(s) U Br 1969 v Ho Be W Rum(s) Br 1970
105 W. A. Wright (Wolverhampton Wanderers) v I Ei W Ho S Fr Swi Por 1947 v Be W I Swe S It 1948 v D I W Swi S Swe N Fr 1949 v Ei W I It S Por Be Ch US Sp 1950 v I S Ar 1951 v W F W I Au S It Au Swi 1952 v I W Be S Ar Ch U US 1953 v W FIFA I Hu S Y Hu Be Swi U 1954 v I W WG S Fr Sp Por 1955 v D W I Sp S Br Swe Fi WG 1956 v I W Y D S Ei D Ei 1957 v W I Fr S Por Y Rus(2) Br Au Rus 1958 v I Rus W S It Br Pe Me US 1959
1 J. G. Wylie (Wanderers) v S 1878

1 J. Yates (Burnley) v I 1889
2 R. E. York (Aston Villa) v S 1922-6

9   A. Young (Huddersfield Town) v W 1933 v Hu S N Swe 1937
    v G Swi Fr 1938 v W 1939
1   G. M. Young (Sheffield Wednesday) v W 1965

HOW THE PLAYERS WERE PROVIDED

The following table shows the number of international players provided by each Club and the number of appearances made by those players. In the case of amateur players, they are included in the record of the Club of which they were primarily a playing member at the time of the international appearance. The first column shows the appearances and the second column the number of players.

Club	App.	Players	Club	App.	Players
Accrington	7	3	Hertfordshire Rangers	2	2
Arsenal	204	29	Hibernian	5	1
Aston Villa	172	43	Huddersfield Town	138	21
Barnes	1	1	Internazionale, Milan	4	1
Barnsley	1	1	Ipswich Town	2	1
Birmingham	101	13	Leeds United	138	16
Birmingham Excelsior	1	1	Leicester City	68	9
Blackburn Olympic	1	1	Leyton	2	1
Blackburn Rovers	251	38	Liverpool	156	27
Blackpool	144	11	Liverpool Ramblers	1	1
Bolton Wanderers	111	25	Luton Town	14	6
Bradford	1	1	Manchester City	145	22
Bradford City	8	3	Manchester United	300	27
Brentford	2	2	Middlesbrough	98	19
Brighton & Hove Albion	1	1	Millwall	10	8
Bristol City	34	4	New Brighton Tower	3	1
Bristol Rovers	1	1	Newcastle United	59	18
Burnley	80	24	Nottingham Forest	42	21
Bury	11	6	Notts County	56	17
Cambridge University	56	26	Notts Rangers	1	1
Casuals	6	5	Old Brightonians	5	2
Charlton Athletic	11	7	Old Carthusians	32	8
Chelsea	131	27	Old Etonians	14	6
Clapham Rovers	28	8	Old Foresters	4	2
Clapton	4	3	Oldham Athletic	5	3
Clapton Orient	4	2	Old Harrovians	3	3
Corinthians	51	16	Old Malvernians	4	2
Coventry City	5	1	Old Westminsters	22	6
Crewe Alexandra	1	1	Owlerton	1	1
Crystal Palace (original)	6	4	Oxford City	1	1
Crystal Palace (present)	3	3	Oxford University	40	22
Darwen	7	4	Pilgrims	6	1
Derby County	162	33	Portsmouth	77	10
Dulwich Hamlet	4	2	Preston North End	120	14
Everton	240	42	Queens Park Rangers	4	2
Fulham	105	9	Reading	5	2
Great Lever	1	1	Royal Engineers	7	6
Grimsby Town	3	2	Saltley College	1	1
Harrow Chequers see			Sheffield Club	1	1
Old Harrovians			Sheffield Albion	6	2
Hendon	2	1	Sheffield Heeley	7	1

Sheffield United	92	33	Tottenham Hotspur	277	32
Sheffield Wednesday	209	36	Tufnell Park	1	1
Shropshire Wanderers	1	1	Upton Park	7	3
Southampton	45	13	Uxbridge	2	1
South Shields	1	1	Walsall	3	2
Stafford Road	1	1	Wanderers	23	15
Stockport County	1	1	Wednesbury Old Athletic	4	1
Stoke City	113	17	Wednesbury Strollers	1	1
Sunderland	63	18	West Bromwich Albion	158	35
1st Surrey Rifles	2	1	West Ham United	229	16
Swifts	31	8	Wolverhampton		
Swindon Town	11	1	Wanderers	288	30
Thursday Wanderers	1	1			

It will thus be seen that Manchester United have won the most caps, 300 and that Aston Villa have produced the most players, 43. Blackburn Rovers and Everton have the best "all-round" records with Tottenham Hotspur and Wolverhampton Wanderers not far behind. West Ham United whose 16 internationals have won an average of more than 14 caps apiece have the highest average.

DOUBLE INTERNATIONALS

Soccer and rugby: R. H. Birkett, C. P. Wilson and J. W. Sutcliffe.
Soccer and cricket: J. Arnold, A. Ducat, R. E. Foster, C. B. Fry, L. H. Gay, W. Gunn, H. T. W. Hardinge, Hon. A. Lyttelton, H. Makepeace, C. A. Milton, J. Sharp and W. Watson.
E. H. Hendren and D. C. S. Compton are frequently stated to be double internationals but neither played in a full soccer international.

TWO COUNTRIES

England and Wales: J. H. Edwards and R. E. Evans.
England and Ireland: J. Reynolds.
Evans and Reynolds were both discovered to have been born in England after playing for Wales and Ireland respectively. Edwards seems to have been sent to Glasgow to deputise at the last minute for J. G. Wylie against Scotland in 1874. Both lived in Shrewsbury at the time. Edwards subsequently played for Wales and was the first Treasurer of the F.A. of Wales, on its formation in 1876.

FULL INTERNATIONALS WHO WERE SCHOOLBOY
INTERNATIONALS

S. Anderson,	C. Crowe,	J. Hagan,
J. H. Baker,	W. Cresswell,	J. N. Haynes,
A. F. Barrett,	N. V. Deeley,	E. I. L. Kail,
J. W. Barrett,	R. W. Dix,	C. Lawler,
C. S. Bastin,	S. G. J. Earle,	W. McGuinness,
B. J. Bridges,	D. Edwards,	S. Matthews,
H. S. Carter,	W. Ellerington,	L. D. Medley,
H. Chambers,	A. Geldard,	J. Melia,
R. Charlton,	L. A. Goulden,	J. Mullen,
E. Clamp,	A. Grimsdell,	R. A. Parry,

D. Pegg,	S. C. Smith,	P. Thompson,
M. S. Peters,	N. P. Stiles,	J. E. Townrow,
A. Quixall,	P. E. Storey,	T. F. Venables,
J. R. Richardson,	R. V. Tambling,	D. S. Viollet,
L. F. Shackleton,	P. H. Taylor,	R. E. York.
P. L. Shilton,	D. W. Temple,	

J. H. Baker and C. Crowe, although born in England, both attended schools in Scotland and played for Scotland Boys.

T. F. Venables played for England at five levels: School, Youth, Amateur, Under-23 and Full.

RELATIONSHIPS

Father and son: there is only one instance of father and son playing for England, that of G. R. and G. E. Eastham.

Brothers: there is one instance of three brothers playing. A. L., E. C. and E. H. Bambridge.

There are eighteen instances of two brothers playing: J. and R. Charlton, J. C. and W. E. Clegg, B. O. and R. Corbett, A. W. and H. A. Cursham, A. T. C. and C. F. Dobson, Frank and F. R. Forman, F. W. and J. Hargreaves, F. and G. H. H. Heron, A. and E. Lyttelton, F. R. and R. Osborne, C. and T. Perry, H. E. and W. S. Rawson, A. and C. Shelton, J. W. and S. C. Smith, C. and G. T. Stephenson, A. G. and R. Topham, A. M. and P. M. Walters, C. P. and G. P. Wilson.

THE UNLUCKY ONES

Quite a number of players have been selected for England but have been unable to play, and have not been subsequently selected:

T. C. Hooman (Wanderers) v Scotland 1872 and 1873
E. Lubbock (Old Etonians) v Scotland 1875
R. S. Hedley (Royal Engineers) v Scotland 1878 and 1879
Rev. W. Blackmore (Remnants) v Wales 1879
G. B. Childs (Oxford University) v Scotland 1879
C. D. Learoyd (Royal Engineers) v Wales 1880
C. J. Clerke (Old Etonians) v Wales 1880
E. J. Wilson (Old Carthusians) v Ireland 1882
W. S. Vidal (Royal Engineers) v Wales 1883
T. Dewhurst (Blackburn Olympic) v Ireland 1884
K. P. Wilson (Cambridge University) v Ireland 1884
G. S. S. Vidal (Oxford University) v Wales 1885
F. M. Ingram (Old Westminsters) v Wales 1886
W. S. Tattersall (Accrington) v Ireland 1891
J. Haydock (Blackburn Rovers) v Ireland 1895
G. C. Vassall (Oxford University) v Ireland 1899
H. P. Pearson (West Bromwich Albion) v France 1923
A. Finney (Bolton Wanderers) v France 1924
H. W. Cope (Notts County) v Ireland 1926
G. H. Ashall (Wolverhampton Wanderers) v Czechoslovakia 1938
F. P. Kippax (Burnley) v France 1947
V. J. Mobley (Sheffield Wednesday) v Holland 1965.

Ingram, Tattersall, Cope, Ashall and Mobley were not original choices but had been selected to replace other players unable to play. The list is unlikely to be added to under the present system of selecting the team at a late stage from a squad of players.

4

All the Players

A SHORT BIOGRAPHICAL note on each English international player. To save space and to avoid saying " transfer " in several different ways, verbiage has been cut out in the career section of these notes. In the case of professional players, each move or club is separated by a comma and in the absence of a full stop or " later ", or other such word, the moves can be taken as consecutive. In the case of amateur players, where there is considerable overlapping of clubs, the clubs are separated by semi-colons. Only the universally known abbreviations are used but it should be mentioned that " cs " stands for close season—that diminishing period between the end of one season and the start of another. The figures in the top right-hand corner of the note show for quick reference the dates of the first and last appearance for England and the figure in brackets the total appearances. In the club honours, the year always represents the second half of the season in which the honour was achieved.

ABBOTT, Walter   1902(1)
b Birmingham 1878 ; d 1 February 1941.
Career: Rosewood Victoria, Small Heath, Everton cs 1899, Burnley cs 1908, Birmingham cs 1910 briefly. Later worked in the motor component industry in Birmingham
Club Honours: Everton—F.A. Cup winners 1906, finalists 1907
An inside-forward before and after his playing peak at Everton, where he gained reputation and honours at left-half. Industrious and efficient his half-back play was characterised by storming long range shooting.

A'COURT, Alan   1958-9(5)
b Rainhill, Lancs 30 September 1934.
Career: Prescot Grammar School, Prescot Celtic, Liverpool September 1952, Tranmere Rovers October 1964, Norwich City as player coach July 1966, Chester assistant manager early 1969 thence Crewe Alexandra assistant manager to September 1969, Stoke City coaching staff later in 1969-70 season
Club Honour: Liverpool—Second Division Champions 1962
An elusive outside-left well known for speed off the mark and strikingly accurate with his centres.

ADCOCK, Hugh   1929-30(5)
b Coalville, Leics 10 April 1903.
Career: Coalville All Saints School, Coalville Town, Loughborough Corinthians April 1921,

Leicester City March 1923, Bristol Rovers July 1935, Folkestone September 1936. After retirement was a licensee at Sileby, Leics before moving back to Coalville where he worked as a maintenance engineer. Part time manager at times of Coalville Town and Whitwick Colliery. Cousin of J. Bradford

Club Honour: Leicester City— Second Division Champions 1925 Entranced crowds home and away with his dazzling performances on the right-wing. Quick witted, fast and plucky and liable to turn up in unexpected places.

ALCOCK, Charles William 1875(1) b Sunderland 2 December 1842; d 26 Feburuary 1907.
Career: Forest School; Harrow School; Wanderers; Surrey. F.A. Committee 1866-9, Hon. Secretary 1870-86, Hon. Treasurer 1877, Secretary 1887-95, Vice-President 1896-1907. F.A. Cup Final referee 1875 and 1879. Secretary of Surrey County Cricket Club from February 1872 until his death and was also a journalist connected with a number of sporting newspapers and compiler of the first Football Annual in 1868.
Club Honour: Wanderers—F.A. Cup winners 1872
Was a hard-working forward consistently on target with his shooting.

ALDERSON, John Thomas 1923(1) b Crook, Co. Durham 1893.
Career: Crook Town, Middlesbrough amateur cs 1912, Newcastle United mid 1912-13, Crystal Palace cs 1919, Pontrypridd cs 1924, Sheffield United May 1925, Exeter City May 1929 retired injury cs 1930
Club Honour: Crystal Palace— Third Division Champions 1921
Big and heavy, Alderson was a competent goalkeeper of splendid consistency. When with Crystal Palace accomplished a rare record in saving eleven penalties out of twelve, including two in one game.

ALDRIDGE, Alfred 1888-9(2) d prior to 1931.
Career: Walsall Town Swifts, West Bromwich Albion cs 1886, Walsall Town Swifts cs 1888, Aston Villa cs 1889 to 1890.
Club Honours: West Bromwich Albion—F.A. Cup finalists 1887, winners 1888.
Played in both fullback positions during his first class career, presenting a formidable barrier: hardy, resolute and unyielding.

ALLEN, Albert 1888(1) b 1867; d 13 October 1899
Career: Aston junior football, Aston Villa retiring owing to ill-health 1891. Worked locally until illhealth, which resulted in his early death, compelled him to give up.
When with Aston Villa had rapport with his partner, Dennis Hodgetts, blending to initiate many an attack with that great winger. Allen was an inside-left who had scoring capability besides —in his one international he scored three times.

ALLEN, Anthony 1960(3) b Stoke-on-Trent November 1939
Career: Broom Street School Stoke and Wellington Road School Hanley, Stoke Boy's Brigade, Stoke City professional circa 1957 (England Youth international 1958), Bury October 1970 to November 1971 when he became a licensee in Stoke. Joined Hellenic of Cape Town in February 1972.
Club Honours: Stoke City— Second Division Champions 1963, F.L. Cup finalists 1964
Left-back stylist, accurate alike in

kicking and tackling. Was considered by some judges to have been adversely affected by receiving England recognition too early. Has played at left-half in recent seasons.

ALLEN, Harry   1888-90(5)
b Walsall 1866; d 23 February 1895.
Career: Walsall Town Swifts, Wolverhampton Wanderers 1886 to late 1894 thence briefly a coal dealer and licensee in Wolverhampton until shortly before his death
Club Honours: Wolverhampton Wanderers—F.A. Cup winners 1893, finalists 1889
A little imprudent sometimes but, in the main, a splendid pivot and captain. Was quite unflagging and especially good at heading and passing.

ALLEN, James Phillips   1934(2)
b Poole, Dorset 16 October 1909.
Career: Longfleet St Mary's School, Poole Central, Poole Town 1927, Portsmouth February 1930, Aston Villa June 1934, retired during the War. After being a Sports and Welfare officer with a Birmingham firm he was manager of Colchester United from July 1948 to April 1953 when he left football and became a licensee at Southsea
Club Honours: Portsmouth—F.A. Cup finalists 1934, Aston Villa— Second Division Champions 1938
A thoroughly sporting player and a centre-half largely of defensive bent. He was a big, tall man ideally built for the " stopper " duties dictated by the tactics of his time.

ALLEN, Ronald   1952-5(5)
b Fenton, Staffs 15 January 1929.
Career: Hanley High School (where he was in the rugby fifteen), Wellington Scouts, Northwood Mission, Port Vale amateur

March 1944, professional January 1946, West Bromwich Albion March 1950, Crystal Palace May 1961, player coach 1964, Wolverhampton Wanderers coach March 1965, acting manager January 1966, appointed manager July 1966, resigned November 1968, Atletico Bilbao manager from February 1969 to November 1971, Sporting Lisbon manager April 1972
Club Honour: West Bromwich Albion—F.A. Cup winners 1954
An attractive player who, though slight, could perform in any forward position. Had a strong attacking inclination and shot with both feet.

ALSFORD, Walter John   1935(1)
b Tottenham 6 November 1911; d 3 June 1968
Career: Tottenham Schools Cheshunt, Northfleet, Tottenham Hotspur amateur May 1929, professional August 1930, Nottingham Forest January 1937, retired owing to injury May 1938. After retirement was a licensee at Nottingham and Brighton and, from 1963, at Bedford
A stylish left-half with a football brain, distributing sagaciously and defending with commendable steadiness.

AMOS, Andrew   1885-6(2)
b 20 September 1863; d 2 October 1931.
Career: Charterhouse School (XI 1882); Clare College Cambridge (Blue 1884-5-6); Old Carthusians; Hitchin Town; Corinthians 1885-90; Herts: Ordained in 1887 he was in the Ministry in South East London from 1889 being Rector of Rotherhithe from 1922 until his death. Served as an Alderman on the Bermondsey Borough Council
A useful half-back mainly notable for his headwork and the excellent service he gave to his forwards.

ANDERSON, Rupert Darnley
1879(1)
b 29 April 1859 ; d 23 December 1944.
Career: Eton College (XI 1878) ; Trinity Hall, Cambridge (no Blue) ; Old Etonians. An orange planter in Florida for some time he later lived in Staffordshire and at Waverley Abbey Farnham, Surrey. Awarded O.B.E. for his services to the Territorial Army and Royal Air Force in the 1914-18 war
Played in goal in his solitary international appearance but was generally regarded as a zealous attacking forward. Missed the 1879 Cup Final owing to injury.

ANDERSON, Stanley   1962(2)
b Horden, Co. Durham 12 December 1933.
Career: Horden Schools (England v Scotland and Wales Schools 1949), Horden Colliery Welfare, Sunderland February 1951, Newcastle United November 1963, Middlesbrough as player coach November 1965, team manager April 1966
Club Honour: Newcastle United —Second Division Champions 1965
His play seemed to have a craggy North Eastern aura, especially in the tackle which was among the strongest of his time. A clever, wholehearted right-half.

ANGUS, John   1961(1)

b Amble, Northumberland 2 September 1938.
Career: Amble Boys Club, Burnley amateur 1954, professional 1956 (England Youth international 1957-8)
Club Honours: Burnley—F.L. Champions 1960, F.A. Cup finalists 1962
The bulk of a sizeable career has been spent at right-back with some senior appearances on the

left in recent times. Like so many modern defenders Angus is an adventurous spirit loving to attack, and polished withal.

ARMFIELD, James Christopher
1959-66(43)
b Denton, Lancs 21 September 1935.
Career: Revoe School and Arnold Grammar School Blackpool (where he was in the rugby XV), St Peters Youth Club Blackpool, Highfield Youth Club, Blackpool amateur 1951, professional 1955, player coach February 1971, Bolton Wanderers player manager May 1971
Could stake a claim to being the innovator of the modern overlap ploy, doing it so often from the right-back position, his weight and speed making such incursions dangerous. In defence exhibited a good hard tackle.

ARMITAGE, George Henry 1926(1)
b Stoke Newington 1898 ; d 29 August 1936.
Career: Wordsworth Road School Hackney, Wimbledon, Charlton Athletic (as an amateur) March 1924 to March 1931, Leyton from January 1931. Won 5 England amateur international caps 1923-6
Club Honour: Charlton Athletic —Third Division South Champions 1929
An outstanding amateur centre-half. Could control the centre of the field, tackling and passing judiciously, without losing any poise.

ARMSTRONG, Kenneth   1955(1)
b Bradford 3 June 1924
Career: Bradford Rovers, Chelsea December 1946, emigrated to New Zealand May 1957 where he played for Eastern Union, North Shore United and Gisborne and played for New Zealand on a number of occasions between 1958-64. He later became Chief

coach to the New Zealand F.A.
Club Honour: Chelsea—F.L.
Champions 1955
A right-half who played with evident enjoyment, tenacity, magnificent consistency and constructiveness. Eventually became an excellent Chelsea captain.

ARNOLD, John 1933(1)
b Cowley, Oxon 30 November 1907.
Career: Oxford Schools and Junior football, Oxford City, Southampton, Fulham February 1933 retired during the War. Also an England Test cricketer v New Zealand 1931, playing for Oxfordshire and then for Hampshire until 1950 when he had to retire owing to ill health. 21,831 runs in first class cricket including 37 centuries. Appointed a first class umpire in 1961 and still stands.
Had impressive goal tallies for a left-winger with both his League clubs. Of stocky build, mobile and assertive.

ARTHUR, John William Herbert
(more commonly called H. J. Arthur)
1885-7(7)
b Blackburn 14 February 1863 ; d 27 November 1930.
Career: Lower Bank Academy Blackburn, King's Own, Blackburn Rovers (initially as a right-half) 1880, Southport Central cs 1890. He always played as an amateur and was by profession a commercial traveller
Club Honours: Blackburn Rovers —F.A. Cup winners 1884-5-6
A goalkeeper of quality, cool in action and quick to clear his lines.

ASHCROFT, James 1906(3)
b Liverpool 12 September 1878 ; d 9 April 1943.
Career: Garston Copper Works Liverpool, Gravesend United cs 1899, Woolwich Arsenal May 1900, Blackburn Rovers May 1908, Tranmere Rovers cs 1913

One of those goalkeepers whose anticipation was such that difficult saves were made to look simple. Equally adept with high and low shots.

ASHMORE, George Samuel 1926(1)
b Plymouth 1898.
Career: Nineveh Wesley (Handsworth League), West Bromwich Albion 1920, to cs 1931, Chesterfield October 1931 retired cs 1933
An agile and daring 'keeper expert at positioning himself. Was also quick in movement and commendably alert.

ASHTON, Claude Thesiger 1926(1)
b Calcutta 19 February 1901 ; d 31 October 1942.
Career: Winchester College (XI 1918-20 captain 1920) ; Trinity College Cambridge (Blue 1921-2 but unable to play v Oxford in 1923 when captain) ; Corinthians from 1920 ; Old Wykehamists ; 12 England amateur international appearances 1922-32. Also a blue for cricket 1921-2-3 (captain in 1923) and a hockey blue 1922-3. Played cricket for Essex. When he retired from soccer in 1933 he joined Beckenham Hockey Club and played in England trials. A Chartered Accountant by profession he was later on the Stock Exchange. Killed in a flying accident whilst serving with R.A.F.
His "full" England appearance was made at centre-forward but he played in almost every position for the Corinthians and it was considered that he was best at wing-half. Strong in dribbling, tackling and shooting his sole blemish was in headwork.

ASHURST, William 1923-5(5)
b Willington, Co. Durham 1894 ; d 26 January 1947.
Career: Durham City, Leeds City cs 1919, Lincoln City October 1919, Notts County June 1920, West Bromwich Albion Novem-

ber 1926, Newark Town August 1928 retired cs 1929
Club Honour: Notts County—Second Division Champions 1923
Dour, crisp tackling right-back. A thought slow sometimes but fearless and able to place his powerful clearances with discernment.

ASTALL, Gordon 1956(2)
b Horwich, Lancs 22 September 1927.
Career: Horwich Schools, one trial match with Bolton Wanderers reserves before joining Royal Marines. Whilst serving with Royal Marines signed an amateur form for Southampton but did not play for them and signed amateur forms for Plymouth Argyle in 1947 and as a professional shortly after his demobilisation later in the same year, Birmingham City October 1953, Torquay United May 1961 retired cs 1963. Since his retirement he has worked for an insurance company in the Torquay area and until pressure of work caused his resignation coached Upton Vale, a South Devon League club.
Club Honours: Plymouth Argyle —Third Division South Champions 1952, Birmingham City—Second Division Champions 1955, F.A. Cup finalists 1956
Sturdily built outside-right and sometimes outside-left, orthodox in type. Became more valuable when his considerable shooting powers were fully utilised.

ASTLE, Jeffrey 1969-70(5)
b Eastwood, Notts 13 May 1942.
Career: West Notts Schools, Notts County amateur 1958, professional October 1959, West Bromwich Albion September 1964.
Club Honours: West Bromwich Albion—F.L. Cup winners 1966, finalists 1967, 70, F.A. Cup winners 1968

His fine headwork was remarked upon in his first senior season and is still an outstanding asset a decade later. A brainy inside-right or centre-forward useful on the ground also.

ASTON, John 1949-51(17)
b Manchester 3 September 1921.
Career: Clayton Methodists, Manchester United juniors, Manchester United amateur May 1939, professional 1946, retired owing to illness June 1955 when he joined the Manchester United staff being appointed Chief Scout August 1970
Club Honours: Manchester United—F.A. Cup winners 1948, F.L. Champions 1952
Adept with both feet and so able to occupy either full-back berth. Appeared at centre-forward on occasion for Manchester United where his qualities of speed, headwork and whole-hearted endeavour were valuable also.

ATHERSMITH, William Charles 1892-1900(12)
b 1872; d 18 September 1910.
Career: Bloxwich Strollers, Unity Gas Works (Saltley), Aston Villa February 1891, Small Heath September 1901 later Grimsby Town trainer June 1907 to cs 1909
Club Honours: Aston Villa—F.A. Cup winners 1895, 7, finalists 1892, F.L. Champions 1894-6-7-9-1900
Made full use of his great pace, wonderfully consistent and always able to rise to the big occasion. A superb outside-right.

ATYEO, Peter John W. 1956-7(6)
b Westbury, Wilts 7 February 1932.
Career: Dilton School, Trowbridge High School, Westbury United, Portsmouth amateur (England Youth 1950), Bristol City professional June 1951 retired May 1966. Qualified as a teacher and continued to teach at War-

minster after his retirement from
the game
Club Honour: Bristol City—Third
Division South Champions 1955
Goal scoring inside-right or
centre-forward. Quick to pounce
on the ball and hard to dispossess not least because of an en-
viable physique.

AUSTIN, Sidney William   1926(1)
b Arnold, Notts circa 1899.
Career: Arnold junior football,
Arnold United, Norwich City
October 1920, Manchester City
May 1924, Chesterfield December
1931
Club Honours: Manchester City
—F.A. Cup finalists 1926, Second
Division Champions 1928
Good ball control and speed
marked this outside-right's dis-
plays. His accurate centres paved
the way to many goals and he had
a fair haul himself.

BACH, Philip   1899(1)
b Shropshire 1873; d 30 Decem-
ber 1937.
Career: Middlesbrough juniors,
Middlesbrough, Reading cs 1895,
Sunderland cs 1897, Bristol City
cs 1900 retired 1904 and was reinstated as an amateur. Elected a
Middlesbrough director February
1911, Chairman July 1911 resigning in 1925. Reappointed Chairman 1931 finally resigning in
1935. F.A. Councillor 1925-37,
F.A. Selection Committee from
October 1929, F.L. Management
Committee from June 1929. Proprietor of Empire Hotel, Middlesbrough
Useful full-back and a model of
consistency, sound rather than
brilliant.

BACHE, Joseph William 1903-11(7)
b Stourbridge 8 February 1880;
d 10 November 1960.
Career: Bewdley Victoria, Stourbridge, Aston Villa December
1900, Mid Rhondda June 1919,

Grimsby Town cs 1920, later a
coach in Germany and from
August 1927 of Aston Villa. Later
a licensee in Aston
Club Honours: Aston Villa—F.A.
Cup winners 1905, 13, F.L. Champions 1910
This cultured inside-left had few
equals at dribbling, at which art
he was brilliant. He displayed also
masterly generalship in midfield.

BADDELEY, Thomas   1903-4(5)
b Bycars near Burslem 1874; d
24 September 1946.
Career: Burslem Swifts, Burslem
Port Vale 1892, Wolverhampton
Wanderers 1896, Bradford cs
1907, Stoke briefly 1910
Only of middling height (5 foot 9
inches) as goalkeepers go but bore
comparison with the best in every
other respect. Had outstanding
agility and brilliantly capable of
dealing with any type of shot.

BAGSHAW, John James   1920(1)
b Derby 1886; d August 1966.
Career: Graham Street Primitives
(Derby), Derby County October
1906, Notts County February
1920, Watford May 1921, Ilkeston
United cs 1922
Club Honour: Derby County—
Second Division Champions 1912
and 1915
Cool and calculating right-half
able to fill the other intermediate
line positions. Efficient in tackling
and placing, a quick mover and
ever reliable.

BAILEY, Horace Peter   1908(5)
b Derby 1881; d 1 August 1960.
Career: Derby County reserves
1899-1902, Ripley Athletic 1903-5,
Leicester Imperial, Leicester
Fosse cs 1906, Derby County mid
1909-10, Birmingham cs 1910 to
1913. Eight England amateur
international appearances 1908-13.
A railway rating official by profession

Rather below the average height associated with goalkeepers. This did not, however, affect this gifted amateur who could deal capably, and often brilliantly, with all manner of shots.

BAILEY, Michael Alfred 1964-5(2)
b Wisbech, Cambs 27 February 1942
Career: Alderman Leach School Gorleston, Gorleston Juniors, Charlton Athletic ground staff June 1958, professional March 1959, Wolverhampton Wanderers February 1966
Club Honour: Wolverhampton Wanderers—UEFA Cup finalists 1972
His gifts of driving leadership are much in evidence as Wolves captain. Is a fine right-half besides—forceful, hard tackling and tireless.

BAILEY, Norman Coles 1878-87(19)
b Streatham 23 July 1857; d 13 January 1923.
Career: Westminster School (XI 1874); Old Westminsters; Clapham Rovers; Corinthians 1886-9; Wanderers; Swifts; Surrey: F.A. Committee 1882-4, Vice President 1887-90. Admitted a solicitor in 1880 he practised in London with the still existent firm of Baileys, Shaw & Gillett.
Club Honours: Clapham Rovers —F.A. Cup finalists 1879, winners 1880
Strong in all facets of half-back play: safe, difficult to pass and a fine feeder of the attack.

BAILY, Edward Francis 1950-3(9)
b Clapton, 6 August 1926.
Career: Hackney Schools, Finchley, Tottenham Hotspur as an amateur during the War, professional 1946, Port Vale January 1956, Nottingham Forest October 1956, Leyton Orient December 1958 retired and became Club coach cs 1961, Tottenham Hotspur assistant manager October 1963

Club Honours: Tottenham Hotspur—Second Division Champions 1950, F.L. Champions 1951
When a player commentators often referred to him as football's " Cheeky Chappie ". Certainly a tincture of Cockney pertness seemed present in his inside-forward play, which had panache and was to the obvious enjoyment of Baily himself.

BAIN, John 1877(1)
b 15 July 1854; d 7 August 1929.
Career: Sherborne School; Winchester College; New College Oxford (Blue 1876): Called to the Bar at Lincoln's Inn 1880. Master Marlborough College from 1879-83 and from 1886-1913 when he retired
Club Honour: Oxford University —F.A. Cup finalists 1877
The speedy forward was a good team man who always loved to be involved in the action.

BAKER, Alfred 1928(1)
b Ilkeston 1899.
Career: Chaucer Street School, Ilkeston, Cossall St Catherines, Long Eaton, Eastwood Rangers, Chesterfield (once only during the 1914-18 War), Crystal Palace (also during the 1914-18 War), Huddersfield Town, Arsenal May 1919 retired May 1931. After retirement he was for some time a Sports Club groundsman in South London
Club Honours: Arsenal—F.A. Cup finalists 1927, winners 1930
Gave Arsenal excellent service at right-back and right-half. He had a grand tackle and it was said that, if his distribution had been on a par with this, he would have gained more represent. honours.

BAKER, Benjamin Howard 1921-6(2)
b Liverpool February 1892
Career: Marlborough Old Boys; Northern Nomads (playing for Blackburn Rovers reserves and

having an England amateur trial as a centre-half) ; Everton ; Chelsea ; Oldham Athletic ; Lancashire County (as a centre-half) ; Corinthians from 1920 ; 10 England Amateur international appearances between 1921-9. Was the Amateur Athletic Association High Jump Champion in 1910-12-13-19-20-21 and holder of the British record jump of 6 foot 5 inches for some time, jumped at Huddersfield on 5 June 1921

Club Honour: Northern Nomads —Welsh Amateur Cup winners 1921

Popular, colourful character whose goalkeeping acrobatics were made possible by his athletic prowess. Exceptional too in his prodigious kicking.

BAKER, Joseph Henry   1960-6(8)
b Liverpool 17 July 1940
Career: St Joseph's School Motherwell (Scotland Schools v England and Wales 1955), Coltness United, Armadale Thistle, Hibernian June 1956, Turin May 1961, Arsenal July 1962, Nottingham Forest February 1966, Sunderland July 1969, Hibernian January 1971, Raith Rovers June 1972

Not surprisingly a centre-forward typically Scots in craft. Has endurance, resolution, shooting power and a distinctive short-stepped gait.

BALL, Alan James   1965-72(56)
b Farnworth, Lancs 5 May 1945
Career: Farnworth Grammar School, Bolton Wanderers amateur, Blackpool amateur September 1961, professional cs 1962, Everton August 1966, Arsenal December 1971. A member of the England World Cup winning team of 1966

Club Honours: Everton—F.A. Cup finalists 1968, F.L. Champions 1970, Arsenal—F.A. Cup finalists 1972

Veritable little dynamo of inside-forward energy buzzing around for the whole of the game. Has the competitive spirit associated with redheads, is brave and played on England right wing in earlier internationals.

BALL, John   1928(1)
b Hazel Grove, Stockport 29 September 1899.
Career: Silverwood, Sheffield United cs 1919, Bristol Rovers May 1921, Wath Athletic cs 1922, Bury May 1923, West Ham United cs 1929, Coventry City May 1930

His peak was at Bury in the mid-twenties when his power and thrust at inside-left produced many goals. There, too, he formed an excellent link between Norman Bullock and Amos.

BALMER, William   1905(1)
b Liverpool 1877 ; d
Career: Aintree Church, South Shore, Everton 1896, Croydon Common cs 1908. From cs 1921 was for a time coach of Huddersfield Town

Club Honours: Everton—F.A. Cup winners 1906, finalists 1907

Was a lusty right-back typical of his time. Could not be faulted in the matter of resolution, tackling and clearing his lines in fine style.

BAMBER, John   1921(1)
b Peasley Cross near St Helens, Lancs 1895.
Career: St Helens, Liverpool December 1915, Leicester City February 1924, Tranmere Rovers cs 1927, Prescot Cables August 1930

Club Honour: Leicester City—Second Division Champions 1925

Played at right-half for Liverpool, left-half at Leicester and pivot with Tranmere Rovers. Strongly built, crisp tackling and accurate in distribution.

BAMBRIDGE, Arthur Leopold
1881-4(3)
b 16 June 1861 ; d 27 November 1923.
Career: St Mark's School Windsor (XI 1877) ; Swifts ; Clapham Rovers ; Berkshire ; Corinthians : Retired injury 1884 and went abroad to study art. Brother of E.C. and E.H.
Valuable and perceptive player at both back and half-back and an awkward one to pass. His last appearance for England was at outside-right and in this position showed speed and the ability to centre well.

BAMBRIDGE, Edward Charles
1879-87(18)
b Windsor 30 July 1858 ; d 8 November 1935.
Career: St Marks School Windsor ; Windsor Home Park ; Swifts ; Streatham ; Berkshire ; Upton Park ; Clapham Rovers ; Corinthians 1886-9 : F.A. Committee 1883-6. Honorary secretary of Corinthians 1923-32
The greatest outside-left of his day, very fast with outstanding ball control. His left-foot shooting was devastating.

BAMBRIDGE, Ernest Henry
1876(1)
b 16 May 1848 ; d 16 October 1917.
Career: Swifts ; Windsor Home Park ; East Sheen ; Berkshire ; Corinthians (a member of the original committee 1882) ; F.A. Committee 1876-82. A Stock Exchange clerk
Thrived on hard work and a difficult man to dispossess. Delighted in scoring goals from his forward position.

BANKS, Gordon   1965-72(73)
b Sheffield 30 December 1937.
Career: Sheffield Schools, Millspaugh Steelworks FC (Sheffield), Rawmarsh Welfare, Chesterfield October 1955, Leicester City May

1959, Stoke City April 1967. A member of the World Cup winning team of 1966. Awarded O.B.E. June 1970 for his services to the game.
Club Honours: Chesterfield— F.A. Youth Cup finalists 1956, Leicester City—F.A. Cup finalists 1961, 3, F.L. Cup winners 1964, finalists 1965, Stoke City—F.L. Cup winners 1972
A 'keeper to rank with the greatest the game has produced. Superb in handling and marvellous in reflex action. The only blemish the most exacting critics have found is in his kicking, but one doubts whether even this is proven.

BANKS, Herbert E.   1901(1)
Career: Army football, Everton 1897, Third Lanark cs 1897, Millwall Athletic cs 1898, Aston Villa April 1901, Bristol City November 1901, Watford cs 1903. Later with a Birmingham engineering firm
Shortish, heavily built inside-left of the bustling type with a telling shot.

BANKS, Thomas   1958-9(6)
b Farnworth, Lancs 10 November 1929.
Career: Farnworth Boys Club, Prestwich's XI, Bolton Wanderers 1947, Altrincham cs 1961, Bangor City early 1963. Later was a building contractor in Bolton
Club Honours: Bolton Wanderers —F.A. Cup winners 1958, Bangor City—Welsh Cup finalists 1964
Short, thickset left-back. He was a player of natural ability quick to tackle and eminently solid in defence.

BANNISTER, William   1901-2(2)
b Burnley 1879 ; d 26 March 1942.
Career: Earley, Burnley mid 1899-1900, Bolton Wanderers November 1901, Woolwich Arsenal Janu-

ary 1903, Leicester Fosse May
1904, Burnley cs 1910 retired cs
1911 thence a licensee in Burnley
and Leicester.
Competent in all aspects of a
centre-half's duties, specially in
defence. Hardly the most polished
of performers being something of
a plodder.

BARCLAY, Robert   1932-6(3)
b Scotswood 27 October 1907.
Career: Scotswood United
Church, Bell's Close Juniors,
Allendale, Scotswood, Derby
County February 1927, Sheffield
United June 1931, Huddersfield
Town March 1937 retiring during
the War
Club Honours: Sheffield United
—F.A. Cup finalists 1936, Hud-
dersfield Town—F.A. Cup final-
ists 1938
Neat little inside-forward, with an
Alex James-like style: construc-
tive and deft in footwork. Had
good firing power which he per-
haps used too sparingly.

BARKAS, Samuel   1936-8(5)
b Tyne Dock, South Shields 29
December 1909.
Career: Middle Dock, Bradford
City 1928, Manchester City April
1934, Workington manager May
1947 later Wigan Athletic mana-
ber briefly from April to September 1957 thence a scout for Manchester City and Leeds United. In
1965 joined Bradford City staff to
run the pools scheme
Club Honours: Bradford City—
Third Division North Champions
1929, Manchester City—F.L.
Champions 1937, Second Division
Champions 1947
An eminently consistent left-back
Barkas had also appeared at right-
half for Bradford City. Clever
and stylish he loved to engage in
an occasional upfield attacking
foray.

BARKER, John William 1935-7(11)
b Denaby 27 February 1907.
Career: Denaby Rovers, Denaby
United, Derby County April
1928, Bradford City manager
briefly from May 1946, Dundalk
manager January 1947 following
which he worked in Derby at
Rolls Royce. Had a short spell as
Oldham Athletic trainer coach
November 1948 to January 1949
and was later Derby County
manager November 1953 to May
1955
A player with an attacking flair
rare in the centre-halves of his
time. Was excellent in defence
too, and certainly among the best
of the inter-war pivots.

BARKER, Robert   1873(1)
b Rickmansworth, Herts 19 June
1847; d 11 November 1915.
Career: Marlborough College
(where he played rugby); Hertfordshire Rangers; Middlesex;
Kent: A civil Engineer in the
Engineers Department of the
South Eastern and London Chatham and Dover Railways
Robust forward who used his
weight well. His deficiency in
pace was not such a handicap
when he played in his other position of full-back.

BARKER, Richard Raine 1895(1)
b 29 May 1869; d 1 September
1940.
Career: Repton School (XI
1887); Casuals; Corinthians
1894-7: Was by profession an
engineer and one time manager
of Bromley Electric Light Co.
Club Honour: Casuals—F.A.
Amateur Cup finalists 1894
A capable wing-half in many
ways, his kicking and passing
being first-rate. However, he suffered from a deficiency in speed
—as a contemporary bluntly put
it "much too slow for an international".

BARLOW, Raymond John 1955(1)
b Swindon 8 August 1926.
Career: Sandford Street School
Swindon, Garrard's F.C. (Swindon), West Bromwich Albion
amateur June 1944 professional
November 1944, Birmingham
City August 1960 retired March
1961 but joined Stourbridge as a
permit player July 1961. A newsagent in Stourbridge
Club Honour: West Bromwich
Albion—F.A. Cup winners 1954
A skilful player—fast, wholehearted and enthusiastic. From
inside-left he moved back to lefthalf where he developed a singularly sound tackle.

BARNET, Horace Hutton 1882(1)
b 1855 ; d 29 March 1941.
Career: Royal Engineers ; Corinthians: Served in the Royal Engineers retiring circa 1905 with the
rank of Colonel
Club Honour: Royal Engineers
—F.A. Cup finalists 1878
Fast and clever outside-right
whose performances were marred
by indifferent centring and
shooting.

BARRASS, Malcolm Williamson
1952-3(3)
b Blackpool.
Career: Fords Motor Works
Toolshop F.C. (Manchester), Bolton Wanderers early 1944, Sheffield United September 1956,
Wigan Athletic as player manager
July 1958 to January 1959,
Nuneaton 1959-60, Pwllheli early
1961, Hyde United trainer cs
1962
Club Honours: Bolton Wanderers—F.L. North Cup winners
1945, F.A. Cup finalists 1953
Had spells at inside-left and lefthalf, after which his pivotal
displays earned him "full"
caps. A fine physique was of
great value in the latter role, his
headwork, mobility and dominance generally being notable.

BARRETT, Albert Frank 1930(1)
b West Ham 11 November 1903.
Career: Park School West Ham
(England v Scotland Schools
1917), Fairbairn House, Leytonstone, Essex, West Ham United
amateur 1923-4, Southampton
amateur 1924-5, Fulham June
1925 retired cs 1937. Made four
England amateur international
appearances 1923-5. Post-War
was secretary of a wholesale
firm in Romford Market
Club Honour: Fulham—Third
Division South Champions 1932
Easily picked out on the field by
his blond, almost white, hair.
A real stylist at left-half, cool
and unruffled, attacking and
passing with nice judgment. Late
in his career played at left-back.

BARRETT, James William 1929(1)
b Stratford, East London, 19 January 1907 ; d 26 November 1970.
Career: Park School West Ham
(England Schools v Wales and
Scotland 1921), Fairbairn House,
West Ham United 1923 retired
during the War and was later
on the West Ham staff
Revealed an amazing versatiliy
—playing in every position including goal—before settling
down at centre-half. Big and
weighty with a fine defensive flair
and a mighty kick.

BARRY, Leonard James 1928-9(5)
b Sneinton, Notts 27 October
1901 ; d 17 April 1970.
Career: Sneinton Boys School,
Mundella Grammar School (a
rugby school), returned to Sneinton School so that he could
return to playing soccer, R.A.F.
Cranwell as a boy, Notts County
amateur 1921, professional late
1923 shortly after playing for
England amateur v Ireland,
Leicester City September 1927,
Nottingham Forest cs 1933 to cs
1934 when he retired from the
game. Later worked on transport
at R.A.F. Chilwell and at Lan-

gar and Newton Aerodromes
An accomplished left-winger with control, speed and centring capability. Was wont to cut in and try a shot on his own account.

BARSON, Frank 1920(1)

b Sheffield 10 April 1891; d 13 September 1968.
Career: Grimethorpe School, Albion F.C. (Sheffield), Cammell Laird F.C. (Sheffield), Barnsley 1911, Aston Villa October 1919, Manchester United August 1922, Watford May 1928, Hartlepools United May 1929, Wigan Borough July 1930, Rhyl Athletic player manager mid 1930-1 to cs 1935, Stourbridge manager July 1935, Aston Villa coach October 1935 up to the War. Swansea Town trainer cs 1947 to cs 1954, Lye Town trainer September 1954
Club Honour: Aston Villa—F.A. Cup winners 1920
Despite his several brushes with authority Barson was a great centre-half. Perfectly proportioned, a hard tackler, a tactician and dominant in the air.

BARTON, John 1890(1)
b Blackburn 1866; d 22 April 1910.
Career: Witton, Blackburn West End, Blackburn Rovers 1887, retired owing to injury received at Birmingham in September 1891. Later had a spell as trainer to Preston North End and was then a licensee in Blackburn
Club Honours: Blackburn Rovers —F.A. Cup winners 1890 and 1891
Right-half who modelled his play on that of his wing-half colleague, the great James Forrest. He accordingly acquired a neat style, passing with commendable precision.

BARTON, Percival Harry 1921-5(7)
b Edmonton 1895.

Career: Montague Road School Edmonton, Tottenham Thursday, Metropolitan Sunday School football, Birmingham 1913 retired cs 1929
Club Honour: Birmingham— Second Division Champions 1921
Thickset left-half who, towards the end of his career, appeared at left-back. A dour, industrious player clever at breaking up attacks and plying his forwards with seductive passes.

BASSETT, William Isaiah
1888-96(16)
b West Bromwich 27 January 1869; d 8 April 1937.
Career: West Bromwich Strollers, West Bromwich Albion 1887 retired cs 1899. Was elected a director of West Bromwich Albion in March 1905 and was Chairman from September 1908 until his death. Member of the F.A. Council 1930-7
Club Honours: West Bromwich Albion—F.A. Cup winners 1888, 92, finalists 1895
One of the greatest outside-rights of all time. Of slight physique but fast and tricky, had fine judgment and was dangerous in front of goal.

BASTARD, Segar Richard 1880(1)
b 1853; d 20 March 1921.
Career: Upton Park; Corinthians; Essex: F.A. Committee 1877-82, F.A. Cup final referee 1878. Later was a racehorse owner
Was a strong winger with a fair turn of speed.

BASTIN, Clifford Sydney 1932-8(21)
b Exeter 14 March 1912.
Career: Ladysmith Road School Exeter (England v Wales Schools 1926), St Marks Exeter, St James Exeter, Exeter City amateur 1926, professional October 1928, Arsenal May 1929 retired cs 1947 since when he has been a licensee

in Devon and is now such at Heavitree

Club Honours: Arsenal—F.A. Cup winners 1930, 6, finalists 1932, F.L. Champions 1931-3-4-5-8, F.L. Cup finalists 1941, F.L. South Cup winners 1943

As a mere stripling made a great name at outside-left and subsequently proved an able performer at inside-forward and wing-half. He had a natural body swerve and a deadly left foot shot but his outstanding characteristic was an ice-cool temperament.

BAUGH, Richard 1886-90(2)
b 1864 ; d 14 August 1929.

Career: St Luke's School Blakenhall (Wolverhampton), Rose Villa, Wolverhampton Rangers, Stafford Road, Wolverhampton Wanderers cs 1886, Walsall September 1896 retired 1897

Club Honours: Wolverhampton Wanderers—F.A. Cup finalists 1889, 96, winners 1893

A redoubtable defender at right-back: dour, zealous and quick to clear. A good and loyal club man, too.

BAYLISS, Albert Edward
James Matthias 1891(1)
b Dudley, Worcestershire 1863 ; d 19 August 1933.

Career: Tipton Providence, Wednesbury Old Athletic, West Bromwich Albion mid 1884-5 retired cs 1892. Elected a West Bromwich Albion director during his playing career, he was later Chairman until his resignation in 1905 when he was elected a Life member. Was on the staff of Guest, Keen & Nettlefold for many years

Club Honours: West Bromwich Albion—F.A. Cup finalists 1886, 7, winners 1888

For most of his first-class career a powerful and prolific scoring centre-forward. In 1890-1 successfully made the transition to wing-half, in which position he won his cap and exhibited splendid qualities in the tackle.

BAYNHAM, Ronald Leslie. 1956(3)
b Birmingham 10 June 1929.

Career: Erdington Rovers 1946, Bromford Amateurs, Worcester City, Luton Town November 1951 to cs 1965. Now an interior decorator in Bedfordshire

Club Honour: Luton Town—F.A. Cup finalists 1959

Quickly developed on joining a League club and displaced Streten. an England goalkeeper. Baynham's judgment and all-round efficiency were aided by height and litheness.

BEASLEY, Albert ("Pat") 1939(1)
b Stourbridge 27 July 1912.

Career: Brierley Hill Schools, Cookesley, Stourbridge, Arsenal May 1931, Huddersfield Town October 1936, Fulham December 1945, Bristol City July 1950 as player manager retired as a player May 1952 and resigned as manager January 1958, Birmingham City joint manager February 1958, sole manager September 1958 Team manager January 1959 resigned May 1960, Dover manager cs 1960 to cs 1964

Club Honours: Arsenal—F.L. Champions 1934, 5, Huddersfield Town—F.A. Cup finalists 1938, Fulham—Second Division Champions 1949

Won international recognition at outside-left and his direct, forceful wing play was at that time often seen on the right flank also. After the War he usually appeared as a sage and thoughtful left-half.

BEATS, William Edwin 1901-2(2)
b Wolstanton, Staffs 13 November 1871 ; d 6 April 1939.

Career: Porthill, Port Vale Rovers 1889, Burslem Port Vale, Wolverhampton Wanderers cs 1895, Bristol Rovers May 1903, Burslem Port Vale May 1906, Reading cs 1907 becoming trainer on giving up playing, Bristol Rovers

trainer cs 1911, Reading trainer 1914. Retired during the 1914-18 War and became a licensee being at The Truro, Castle Street, Reading until his retirement in 1936
Club Honours: Wolverhampton Wanderers—F.A. Cup finalists 1896, Bristol Rovers—Southern League Champions 1905
Quiet and unassuming, Beats was a valuable centre-forward usually in the right place at the right time and always showed commendable unselfishness.

BECTON, Francis   1895-7(2)
b Preston, Lancs 1873 ; d 6 November 1909.
Career: Preston junior football, Fishwick Ramblers, Preston North End, Liverpool March 1895, Sheffield United October 1898, Bedminster cs 1899, Preston North End cs 1900, Swindon Town cs 1901, Ashton Town cs 1903, New Brighton Tower for a year or so before retiring owing to illhealth.
Club Honour: Liverpool—Second Division Champions 1896
Clever, scheming inside-forward whose creative gifts brought the best out of a variety of partners, notably so in his association with Harry Bradshaw at Liverpool.

BEDFORD, Henry   1923-5(2)
b Calow near Chesterfield 1899.
Career: Grassmoor Ivanhoe, Nottingham Forest August 1919, Blackpool March 1921, Derby County September 1925, Newcastle United December 1930, Sunderland January 1932, Bradford May 1932, Chesterfield cs 1933, Heanor Town player coach late 1934. In 1937-8 season was coaching with Newcastle United. In 1938-9 he was a licensee in Derby and was a part time member of the Derby County staff. Lived in Heanor after the War and had a brief spell as manager of Heanor Town.
Any lack of ball finesse was more

than atoned for by his dashing, fearless, fine shooting play, which brought a rich goal harvest at centre-forward and inside-right.

BELL, Colin   1968-72(20)
b Heselden, Co. Durham 26 February 1946.
Career: Horden Schools, Horden Colliery, Bury August 1963, Manchester City March 1966
Club Honours: Manchester City —F.L. Champions 1968, F.A. Cup winners 1969, F.L. Cup winners and European Cup Winners Cup winners 1970
Numbered among the most potent attacking forces in the game today. A great all-round inside-right full of running, always working and foraging, always likely to notch a spectacular goal.

BENNETT, Walter   1901(2)
b Mexborough, Yorks 1874 ; d 6 April 1908.
Career: Mexborough, Sheffield United February 1896, Bristol City mid 1904-5, Denaby United cs 1907. Was killed in a mining accident at Denaby
Club Honours: Sheffield United— F.L. Champions 1898, F.A. Cup winners 1899, 1902, finalists 1901, Bristol City—Second Division Champions 1906
Short but heavy outside-right, aggressive and able to centre from any angle. On his day was England's best, on other occasions he was temperamental.

BENSON, Robert William 1913(1)
b Swalwell 1882 ; d 19 February 1916.
Career: Newcastle United 1903, Southampton cs 1904, Sheffield United cs 1905, Arsenal early 1913-14. Died in the dressing-room at Highbury after collapsing whilst playing in a war-time match. He had been engaged in munitions work, had not played for some time and was playing as a late substitute.

Finely built back equally adept on either flank. Famous for his method of taking penalties: the ball was placed on the spot for him and he ran the full length of the field from his full-back position to kick it.

BENTLEY, Roy Thomas Frank 1949-55(12)
b Bristol 17 May 1923.
Career: Portway School Bristol, Bristol Rovers (amateur), Bristol City ground staff 1938, professional August 1941, Newcastle United June 1946, Chelsea January 1948, Fulham September 1956, Queens Park Rangers May 1961, Reading manager January 1963 to February 1969, Bradford City scout March 1969, Swansea City manager August 1969
Club Honour: Chelsea—F.L. Champions 1955
Unorthodox and one of the first roving centre-forwards. Fine at heading and equally valuable on the right-wing and at inside-forward. Later became a centre-half (at Fulham) and a right-back (at Loftus Road).

BERESFORD, Joseph 1934(1)
b Chesterfield circa 1905.
Career: Askern Road Working Men's Club Doncaster, Bentley Colliery, Mexborough Athletic, Mansfield Town May 1926, Aston Villa May 1927, Preston North End September 1935, Swansea Town December 1937. After the War had a fish business in Kingstanding.
Club Honours: Preston North End—F.A. Cup finalists 1937, Swansea Town—Welsh Cup finalists 1938
Inside-forward more often found on the right. Stocky in build, he was a fine forager and packed a terrific shot.

BERRY, Arthur 1909(1)
b Liverpool 3 January 1888.

F

Career: Denstone School (where he was in the rugby XV 1904-5 captain 1905); Wadham College Oxford (Blue 1908-9); Liverpool; Fulham; Everton; Wrexham; Oxford City. Made 32 England amateur international appearances 1908-13. His father was a Liverpool director and Chairman of the club from 1904-9 who practised as a solicitor in Liverpool. Berry himself was called to the Bar at Gray's Inn in 1913 and then retired from the game
Club Honour: Oxford City— F.A. Amateur Cup finalists 1913
One of the most brilliant amateurs of his day and an outside-right with thought and precision. A contemporary summed up his direct style as "a complete art without tinsel or gaudiness".

BERRY, John J. 1953-6(4)
b Aldershot circa 1926.
Career: Aldershot schools, Army football, Birmingham City December 1944, Manchester United August 1951 retired 1958 through injuries received in the Munich air crash
Club Honours: Manchester United—F.L. Champions 1952-6-7, F.A. Cup finalists 1957
Plucky little wingman, fleet of foot and able to operate on either flank. His overriding skill was in the dribble, at which he was brilliant.

BESTALL, John Gilbert 1935(1)
b Sheffield 24 June 1900.
Career: Crookesmoor School Sheffield, Beighton Miners Welfare, Rotherham United, Grimsby Town November 1926, Birmingham coach June 1938, Doncaster Rovers manager March 1946 to April 1949, Blackburn Rovers manager June 1949 to May 1953, Nelson manager cs 1953 to November 1954. Later Doncaster Rovers chief scout August 1958 (manager March 1959 to August

1960 then reverting to chief scout).
Club Honour: Grimsby Town—
Second Division Champions 1934
A grand little player who vied
with Alex James as being the
smallest inside-forward of the
time. His footwork was intricate,
his feeding of his fellow forwards
subtle and his service to Grimsby
Town outstanding.

BETMEAD, Harry A.   1937(1)
b Grimsby 11 April 1912.
Career: Grimsby Sunday schools
football, Hay Cross, Grimsby
Town October 1930 retired December 1947. Played cricket for
Lincolnshire
Club Honour: Grimsby Town—
Second Division Champions 1934
Like several of his Grimsby contemporaries gave long anl loyal
service to the Club. Admirably
built for his centre-half role, Betmead was dominant in the air
and strong in the tackle.

BETTS, Morton Peto   1877(1)
b London 30 August 1847 ; d 19
April 1914.
Career: Harrow School ; Wanderers ; Old Harrovians ; Kent:
F.A. Committee 1870-2 and 1881-
90, Vice-President 1890-1. Played
cricket for Kent and Middlesex
in 1872 and was secretary of
Essex C.C.C. from 1887-90
Club Honour: Wanderers—F.A.
Cup winenrs 1872
One of the earliest utility players,
useful in any position but played
mainly at back or in the forward
line. In the vanguard he excelled
as a dribbler and at full-back was
vigorous in his charging.

BETTS, William   1889(1)
b Sheffield 1864 ; d 8 August 1941.
Career: Sheffield Wednesday
1883, Lockwood Bros late 1883
to 1885, Sheffield Wednesday
from 1885. Later the Sheffield
Wednesday groundsman and at

times, assistant trainer
Club Honour: Sheffield Wednesday—F.A. Cup finalists 1890
A centre-half of parts. Although
small he could break up the move-
ments of big forwards, tackling
when least expected. Fine, too,
with his head.

BEVERLEY, Joseph   1884(3)
b Blackpool 1857 ; d 21 May
1897.
Career: St John's School Blackburn, Blackburn Olympic (founder
member 1876), Blackburn Rovers
October 1882, Blackburn Olympic
cs 1884 but had a second spell
with Blackburn Rovers commenc-
ing late 1887. Later worked at the
Albion Mill in Blackburn and
whilst working there on 15 May
1897 sustained injuries from which
he died
Club Honour: Blackburn Rovers
—F.A. Cup winners 1884
Useful utility player who played
at back (where he appeared for
England), half and forward. Swift
moving and judicious.

BIRKETT, Reginald Halsey 1879(1)
b 28 March 1849 ; d 30 June 1898.
Career: Lancing College (XI
1866-7) ; Lancing Old Boys ; Clapham Rovers ; Surrey: He was
also a rugby international playing
v Scotland in 1871-5-6 and v
Ireland in 1877 being a member
of the Clapham Rovers club which
played both codes. Member of the
original committee of the Rugby
Union in 1871. His brother, L.
and his son J.G.G. were both also
rugby internationals. A hide and
skin broker in the City of London,
he died following an accident sustained whilst suffering from
delirium during an attack of
typhoid fever
Club Honours: Clapham Rovers
—F.A. Cup finalists 1879, winners
1880
Fearless and with a sure kick he

played well in all positions from goalkeeper to forward.

BIRKETT, Ralph James E. 1936(1)
b Ashford, Middlesex 9 January 1912.
Career: Woodthorpe School Ashford, Dartmouth United, Torquay United 1929, Arsenal April 1933, Middlesbrough March 1935, Newcastle United July 1938 retired during the War.
Club Honour: Arsenal—F.L. Champions 1934
Regular scorer from the extreme right-wing where he combined powerful shooting with pace and craft.

BIRLEY, Francis Hornby 1874-5(2)
b 14 March 1850; d 1 August 1910.
Career: Winchester College; University College, Oxford (Blue 1874); Wanderers; Middlesex: Athletics blue 1872. Played cricket for Lancashire and Surrey. Barrister, Inner Temple, January 1876.
Club Honours: Oxford University —F.A. Cup finalists 1873, winners 1874, Wanderers—F.A. Cup winners 1876, 7
An accomplished two-footed half, difficult to beat who played the game with unbounded enthusiasm.

BISHOP, Sidney Macdonald
1927(4)
b Stepney, East London 1900; d 5 April 1949.
Career: Lexford School, Ilford, R.A.F. football during the 1914-18 War, Crystal Palace, West Ham United May 1920, Leicester City November 1926, Chelsea June 1928 retired May 1933
Club Honour: West Ham United —F.A. Cup finalists 1923
Ball control and an unflurried demeanour graced his game. Was clever in the air also and altogether a fine wing-half.

BLACKBURN, Frederick 1901-4(3)
b Mellor, Lancs September 1879;
Career: Mellor, Blackburn Rovers 1897, West Ham United May 1905 retired cs 1913. Later a seafarer but was living in East London in 1931 being appointed Barking Town coach cs 1931
Reverted successfully from the inside to the extreme left-wing position. Good ball control and centring ability and difficult to dispossess, he was erratic in shooting.

BLACKBURN, George Frederick
1924(1)
b Willesden Green 8 March 1899.
Career: Pound Lane School Willesden, London Schools, Willesden Juniors, Army football, Hampstead Town, Aston Villa amateur December 1920, professional January 1921, Cardiff City cs 1926, Mansfield Town June 1931, Cheltenham Town player coach July 1932, Moor Green coach cs 1934, Birmingham trainer 1937-46 thence coach
Club Honours: Aston Villa— F.A. Cup finalists 1924, Cardiff City—Welsh Cup winners 1927, 30, finalists 1929
A most useful left-half—tireless tenacious and whole-hearted. A contemporary writer referred to him as one of the most persistent workers in football.

BLENKINSOP, Ernest 1928-33(26)
b Cudworth, Yorks 20 April 1900; d 24 April 1969.
Career: Cudworth United Methodists, Hull City October 1921, Sheffield Wednesday January 1923, Liverpool March 1934, Cardiff City November 1937, Buxton August 1939, Hurst during the War after which he retired and was a licensee in Sheffield.
Club Honours: Sheffield Wednesday—Second Division Champions 1926, F.L. Champions 1929 and

1930
England has invariably been well served at left-back and seldom better than by Blenkinsop. He had a polished style, was judicious in tackling, cool and placed his clearances with unfailing accuracy.

BLISS, Herbert 1921(1)
b Willenhall, Staffs 29 March 1890 ; d 14 June 1968:
Career: Willenhall Swifts, Tottenham Hotspur April 1912, Clapton Orient December 1922, Bournemouth & Boscombe Athletic July 1925 retired cs 1926
Club Honours: Tottenham Hotspur—Second Division Champions 1920, F.A. Cup winners 1921
Was renowned for his shooting—when on target his shots were almost unstoppable—and quite without fear. A terror of an inside-left for his size.

BLOOMER, Stephen 1895-1907(23)
b Cradley Heath, Worcs 20 January 1874 ; d 16 April 1938
Career: Derby Schools, Derby Swifts, Derby County 1892, Middlesbrough March 1906, Derby County September 1910 retired January 1914. Coach in Germany July 1914 and was interned during the 1914-18 War later a coach in Rotterdam, Canada briefly in 1922, Derby County from August 1922 thence to Spain in 1924. Scored 352 goals in Football League matches and 5 for England v Wales at Cardiff in 1896. Father-in-law of A. E. Quantrill.
Club Honours: Derby County—F.A. Cup finalists 1898 and 1899, Second Division Champions 1912. Missed the 1903 Cup final owing to injury
A legendary inside-right of genius. Pale of face and slight but with an unquenchable thirst for goals. Constant practice enabled him to shoot without hesitation from any angle.

BLUNSTONE, Frank 1955-7(5)
b Crewe 17 October 1934.
Career: Bedford Street School Crewe (England schools reserve 1950), Crewe Alexandra amateur 1951 professional January 1952 (England Youth international 1951), Chelsea February 1953 retired injury and joined the Club coaching staff October 1964, Brentford manager December 1969.
Club Honour: Chelsea—F.L. Champions 1955
In his early playing days was hailed as a new Bastin, his left-wing displays being precociously cool, clever and mature. Subsequently he revealed a deal of courage besides, twice coming back after breaking a leg.

BOND, Richard 1905-10(8)
b Garstang 14 December 1883 ; d 25 April 1955.
Career: Royal Artillery football, Preston North End professional August 1902, Bradford City May 1909, Blackburn Rovers May 1922, Lancaster Town August 1923, retired 1924 but in 1926-7 was playing with Garstang where he had a fried fish business.
Club Honour: Preston North End —Second Division Champions 1904
A superficial observer might find it strange that this outside-right's small frame could withstand over 20 years in the top flight. Bond, however, was wiry and his slippery cleverness stood him in good stead.

BONETTI, Peter Phillip 1966-70(7)
b Putney 27 September 1941.
Career: St Mary's School Worthing, Worthing Roman Catholic Youth Club, Chelsea amateur cs 1958, professional April 1959
Club Honours: Chelsea—F.A. Youth Cup winners 1960, F.L. Cup winners 1965, F.A. Cup finalists 1967, winners 1970, European

Cup Winners Cup winners 1971, F.L. Cup finalists 1972
A goalkeeper astounding at times in the quickness of his reflexes. Spectacularly agile, his actions are usually perfectly timed.

BONSOR, Alexander George
1873-5(2)
d 17 August 1907.
Career: Eton College; Old Etonians; Wanderers; Surrey: A Brewer with Combe & Delafield now incorporated in Watneys.
Club Honours: Wanderers—F.A. Cup winners 1872, 3, Old Etonians —F.A. Cup finalists 1875, 6
Made directly for goal using his hefty weight allied with pace. A close dribbler and altogether an effective forward.

BOOTH, Frank 1905(1)
b Hyde, Lancs 1882; d 22 June 1919.
Career: Hyde, Glossop, Stockport County, Manchester City, Bury January 1907, Clyde June 1909, Manchester City July 1911 to cs 1912
Club Honour: Manchester City— F.A. Cup winners 1904
A slim and lively outside-left generally playing an orthodox game, keeping to the touchline and putting over precise, accurate centres.

BOOTH, Thomas 1898-1903(2)
b Pin Mill Brow, Ardwick 25 April 1874; d
Career: Hooley Hill, Ashton North End 1892, Blackburn Rovers May 1896, Everton April 1900 to cs 1908. Carlisle United November 1908. Missed 1906 Cup Final owing to injury
An unspectacular but worthy and consistent pivot fine in defence. In essence a first-rate club man.

BOWDEN, Edwin Raymond
1935-7(6)
b Looe, Cornwall 13 September 1909
Career: Liskeard Secondary School, Looe, Plymouth Argyle cs 1926, Arsenal March 1933, Newcastle United November 1937 retired during the War. Later a sports outfitter in Plymouth but now retired
Club Honours: Plymouth Argyle —Third Division South Champions 1930, Arsenal—F.L. Champions 1934, 5, F.A. Cup winners 1936
Inside or centre-forward of style and grace. Notched a useful tally of goals despite his career being punctuated with ankle injuries.

BOWER, Alfred George 1924-7(5)
b Bromley, Kent 10 November 1895; d
Career: Charterhouse School (not in XI); Old Carthusians; Chelsea; Casuals; Corinthians: 13 England amateur international appearances between 1921-8. F.A. Council 1928-33. Later a member of the Stock Exchange
Tall, strong right or left-back particularly good in tackling and heading. Could inspire his comrades with his unruffled confidence but often below par when worried by captaincy cares.

BOWERS, John William 1934(3)
b Santon near Scunthorpe 22 February 1908.
Career: Appleby Works, Scunthorpe & Lindsey United mid 1927-8, Derby County May 1928, Leicester City November 1936 retired and appointed to coach Notts County colts August 1943, later Derby County assistant-trainer for a time
Club Honour: Leicester City— Second Division Champions 1937
Opportunist centre-forward forever worrying the opposing defence. His unerring marksmanship made him a consistent scorer and he kept his line moving smoothly.

BOWSER, Sidney 1920(1)
b Handsworth 1893 ; d 25 February 1961.
Career: Wattville Road School Handsworth, Asbury Richmond, West Bromwich Albion August 1908, Distillery cs 1913 (played for Irish League v Football League 1914), West Bromwich Albion mid 1913-14, Walsall August 1924 retired cs 1925. Became a licensee in Dudley on retirement, was for many years licensee of The Crown, Wolverhampton Street, Dudley and at the time of his death was manager of an off license at Acocks Green.
Club Honours: West Bromwich Albion—Second Division Champions 1911, F.A. Cup finalists 1912, F.L. Champions 1920
Divided his considerable talents between two diverse positions—centre-half and inside-right. In both he was resilient, tenacious and hard-working.

BOYES, Walter E. 1935-9(3)
b Sheffield 5 January 1913 ; d 16 September 1960.
Career: Sheffield Schools, Woodhouse Mills United, West Bromwich Albion January 1931, Everton February 1938, Notts County player coach cs 1949, Scunthorpe United August 1950 later Retford Town player manager, Hyde United manager April 1958, Swansea Town trainer 1959 retiring owing to illness June 1960
Club Honours: West Bromwich Albion—F.A. Cup finalists 1935, Everton—F.L. Champions 1939
A splendid little player, perhaps best known as an outside-left although he was equally effective on the inside and at left-half. An adroit schemer who could score goals.

BOYLE, Thomas W. 1913(1)
b Hoyland near Barnsley, Yorks 1889 ; d 5 January 1940.
Career: Hoyland Star, Elsecar,

Barnsley May 1906, Burney September 1911 player coach cs 1922, Wrexham cs 1923, coach in Germany cs 1924
Club Honours: Barnsley—F.A. Cup finalists 1910, Burnley—F.A. Cup winners 1914, F.L. Champions 1921
Fine pivot very much in the tough Barnsley mould. Strong physically and strong in all phases of half-back play he was especially good with his head.

BRABROOK, Peter 1958-60(3)
b Greenwich 8 November 1937.
Career: Windsor and Napier Schools East Ham, Chelsea ground staff March 1953 professional March 1955 (England Youth international 1955-57), West Ham United October 1962, Orient July 1968, Romford August 1971, probably Woodford Town cs 1972
Club Honours: West Ham United—F.A. Cup winners 1964, F.L. Cup finalists 1966, Orient—Third Division Champions 1970
Played on both wings in his League period, mostly on the right. Exceptional acceleration and a searing shot though somewhat uneven in performance.

BRADFORD, Geoffrey R. W.
1956(1)
b Frenchay, Bristol 18 July 1928.
Career: Soundwell School, Soundwell, Bristol Rovers June 1949 to cs 1964 when he left football and has since worked for an oil company at Avonmouth
Club Honour: Bristol Rovers—Third Division South Champions 1953
A forcible inside-forward and the brains behind the Bristol Rovers attack for many seasons. He was a sharp-shooter and serious leg injuries did not seem to affect this potency unduly.

BRADFORD, Joseph 1924-31(12)
b Peggs Green, Leics 22 January

1901.
Career: Peggs Green Victoria
1913, Birmingham February 1920,
Bristol City May 1935 retired cs
1936. Cousin of H. Adcock. After
retiring from the game was at one
time a licensee in Birmingham
and Stourbridge and later ran a
sports shop in Sutton Coldfield.
Became President of Sutton Town
F.C.
Club Honour: Birmingham—F.A.
Cup finalists 1931
Very sporting type of player.
Revealed dash, marksmanship and
shooting power at centre-forward
before later becoming equally successful in the inside-left position.

BRADLEY, Warren 1959(3)
b Hyde 20 June 1933.
Career: Hyde Grammar School,
Durham University, Durham City
(Bolton Wanderers amateur),
Bishop Auckland 1955, Nottingham Forest amateur February
1958 but released to join Manchester United in the same month
as an amateur, professional November 1958, Bury March 1962,
Northwich Victoria July 1963,
Macclesfield November 1963, Bangor City cs 1964 to cs 1965. Did
not play again until April 1966
when he joined Macclesfield again.
11 England amateur international
appearances 1957-9. A schoolmaster by profession he became
headmaster of a Manchester comprehensive school in 1970
Club Honours: Bishop Auckland
—F.A. Amateur Cup winners 1956
and 1957
A shrewd little right winger who
quickly adapted to the professional game. Had confidence, ball
control and few could better his
quickness off the mark.

BRADSHAW, Frank 1908(1)
b Sheffield 31 May 1884.
Career: Sheffield Schools 1895-7,
Oxford Street Sunday School
Sheffield, Sheffield Wednesday

amateur early 1904, professional
cs 1904, Northampton Town cs
1910, Everton November 1911,
Arsenal cs 1914 retired May 1923,
manager Aberdare Athletic until
cs 1924
Club Honour: Sheffield Wednesday—F.A. Cup winners 1907
Early, when in form, was a magnificent inside-left—potent, brainy
and dangerous—and then unluck-
ily sustained serious knee injuries.
With Arsenal successfully made
the transition first to wing-half
and later to back.

BRADSHAW, Thomas Henry
1897(1)
b Liverpool 1873 ; d 25 December
1899.
Career: Northwich Victoria,
Liverpool, Tottenham Hotspur cs
1898, Thames Ironworks cs 1899
Club Honours: Liverpool—
Second Division Champions 1894
and 1896
An ingenious and fleet outside-
left. Responded best to a ball-
playing partner, hence his notable
association at Anfield with
Becton.

BRADSHAW, William 1910-13(4)
b Padiham, Lancs circa 1885.
Career: Padiham, Accrington
Stanley, Blackburn Rovers May
1903, Rochdale player manager
April 1920 to September 1920
Club Honours: Blackburn Rovers
—F.L. Champions 1912 and 1914
A most attractive left-half with
his intricate footwork and quiet
but subtle prompting of his forwards. An expert at penalty
taking.

BRANN, George 1886-91(3)
b Eastbourne 23 April 1865 ; d
14 June 1954.
Career: Ardingly College (XI
1885) ; Swifts ; Slough ; Corinthians 1886-93. Played cricket for
Sussex from 1885-1905 scoring
over 11,000 runs including 24 cen-

turies. A fine golfer he was secretary of Home Park Golf Club, Surbiton for 20 years
A leading player of his day appearing at either outside or inside-right. Strong and fast and a sure shot.

BRAWN, William Frederick 1904(2)
b Wellingborough 1 August 1878 ; d 18 August 1932.
Career: Wellingborough Schools, Wellingborough, Northampton Town, Sheffield United January 1900, Aston Villa December 1901, Middlesbrough March 1906, Chelsea late 1907, Brentford cs 1911 retired 1913 and was thereafter until his death licensee of Kings Arms, Boston Road, Brentford. From July 1919 was for a time advisory manager of Brentford
Club Honour: Aston Villa—F.A. Cup winners 1905
Few players have been so appropriately named—he exceeded 6 foot in height and 13 stones in weight. Such a physique has seldom been found in right-wingers and helped to make Brawn a particularly dangerous one when in form.

BRAY, John 1935-7(6)
b Oswaldtwistle, Lancs 22 April 1909.
Career: St Andrews School Oswaldtwistle, Clayton Olympia, Manchester Central 1928, Manchester City cs 1929 retired during the War. Watford manager February 1947 to February 1948 and thence coach to Nelson until September 1948 when he left football
Club Honours: Manchester City —F.A. Cup finalists 1933, winners 1934, F.L. Champions 1937
Brought a degree of constructiveness to his performance at lefthalf. Had all-round ability perhaps being at his best in attack.

BRAYSHAW, Edward 1887(1)
b 1863 ; d 20 November 1908.
Career: All Saints, Walkley, Sheffield Wednesday mid 1884-5 retired injury 1891. Thence a licensee in the Sheffield area until he had to retire owing to illness in 1907
Club Honour: Sheffield Wednesday—F.A. Cup finalists 1890.
A fine right-back typical of his period: robust, brave and resilient. A club historian looking back some 40 years later said Brayshaw was one of the finest defenders the Wednesday ever had.

BRIDGES, Barry John 1965-6(4)
b Horsford near Norwich 29 April 1941.
Career: Norwich Schools (England Schools v Ireland 1955 v Scotland (2) Germany Wales and Eire 1956), Chelsea ground staff July 1956, professional May 1958 (England Youth international 1957-8), Birmingham City May 1966, Queens Park Rangers August 1968, Millwall September 1970
Club Honours: Chelsea—F.A. Youth Cup finalists 1958, F.L. Cup winners 1965
The most striking thing about this player, whether at outside-right or centre-forward, is his prodigious fleetness of foot. Has good control, too, and is a dangerous shot.

BRIDGETT, Arthur 1905-9(11)
b Forsbrook near Stoke 1884.
Career: Stoke St Peters School, Burslem Park, Trentham, Stoke, Sunderland January 1903, South Shields manager July 1912 later North Shields manager. Thence in retirement for some years until resuming playing with Port Vale during 1923-4 season
A fleet and markedly unselfish outside-left. In the vicinity of goal was outstandingly quick and dangerous.

BRINDLE, Thomas 1880(2)
b Darwen, Lancs; d ——
Career: Darwen principally but
had a spell with Blackburn Olympic in 1886-7
Strong kicking, powerful left-back
with a noteworthy capacity for
work.

BRITTLETON, James Thomas
1912-14(5)
b Winsford, Cheshire April 1879;
d
Career: Winsford Juniors 1896,
Winsford Celtic, Winsford United,
Winsford, Stockport County, Sheffield Wednesday September 1904,
Stoke May 1920, Winsford United
player coach March 1925 thus
leaving the Football League within weeks of his 46th birthday
Club Honour: Sheffield Wednesday—F.A. Cup winners 1907
Right-half. In the course of an
exceptionally long first-class
career developed a remarkably
lengthy throw. Indefatigable and
possessed of a formidable tackle.

BRITTON, Clifford Samuel
1935-7(9)
b Hanham, Bristol 27 August
1909.
Career: Hanham Athletic, Hanham United Methodists, Bristol
St George, Bristol Rovers 1926,
professional cs 1928, Everton June
1930, retired October 1945 when
he became Burnley manager,
Everton manager September 1948
to February 1956, Preston North
End manager August 1956 resigning April 1961, Hull City manager
July 1961, general manager November 1969. Retired October
1971
Club Honour: Everton—F.A.
Cup winners 1933
Was a right-half of great style and
polish. He liked to have a full
share of the ball and to join in an
attack with his forwards.

BROADBENT, Peter F. 1958-60(7)
b Elvington, Kent 1933.
Career: Deal County Modern
School, Dover, Brentford cs 1950,
Wolverhampton Wanderers February 1951, Shrewsbury Town
January 1965, Aston Villa October 1966, Stockport County October 1969, Bromsgrove Rovers
November 1970 retired November
1971. Now has a children's wear
shop in Halesowen.
Club Honours: Wolverhampton
Wanderers — F.L. Champions
1954-8-9, F.A. Cup winners 1960
Throughout a long career this
brainy and thoughtful inside-
forward excelled in providing
openings for his attacking
partners.

BROADIS, Ivan A. 1952-4(14)
b Isle of Dogs, East London 18
December 1922.
Career: Glengall Road School
Isle of Dogs, Coopers' Company
School Bow (a rugby school),
Finchley, Northfleet, Finchley
(playing as an amateur for Tottenham Hotspur and Millwall in
War-time football), Carlisle
United player manager August
1946, Sunderland January 1949,
Manchester City October 1951,
Newcastle United October 1953,
Carlisle United July 1955, Queen
of the South June 1959 retired
1960. After his retirement he became a sports journalist in Car-
lisle which he still is.
Put a deal of creative thought into
his inside-forward performance in
which speed and hard shooting
were prominent features.

BROCKBANK, John 1873(1)
b Whitehaven, Cumberland 22
August 1848; d 29 January 1904.
Career: Shrewsbury School;
Trinity College, Cambridge (Blue
1874-5); An actor by profession.
A useful club cricketer
He was a fleet forward, quick on

the turn and a good dribbler despite a suspect knee.

BRODIE, John Brant   1889-91(3)
b Wolverhampton 1863 ; d 16 February 1925.
Career: St Luke's School Blakenhall ; Saltley College 1880-2 ; Founder member Wolverhampton Wanderers 1877 retired cs 1891. Became a referee in 1892. On leaving Saltley College became a pupil teacher at St Luke's School. Elected a Wolverhampton Wanderers director in June 1913
Club Honour: Wolverhampton Wanderers—F.A. Cup finalists 1889
Was a penetrative forward who gave the Wolves eminent service on and off the field. Very popular during his playing days and afterwards because of his gentlemanly deportment.

BROMILOW, Thomas George
1921-6(5)
b Liverpool 7 October 1894 ; d 4 March 1959.
Career: United West Dingle Presbyterian Club, Liverpool 1919 retiring May 1930, Amsterdam coach cs 1931, Burnley manager October 1932, Crystal Palace manager July 1935 to June 1936, re-appointed December 1936, Leicester City manager July 1939 to May 1945, Newport County manager May 1946 resigned January 1950, Leicester City scout from July 1950 until his death.
Club Honours: Liverpool—F.L. Champions 1922 and 1923
Carried out his duties at left-half with style and artistry being especially notable for his anticipation and attacking flair.

BROMLEY-DAVENPORT,
 General Sir William   1884(2)
b 21 January 1863 ; d 6 February 1949.
Career: Eton College (XI 1881) ; Balliol College, Oxford (Blue 1884) ; Old Etonians: M.P. for Macclesfield 1886-1906, Financial Secretary to War Office 1903-5. Lord Lieutenant of Cheshire 1920-49. Served in Staffordshire Yeomanry in South Africa winning D.S.O. 1900, Brigadier in Command 22nd Mounted Brigade, Egypt 1916, Assistant Director of Labour in France 1917. K.C.B. 1924.
A centre-forward whose chief attributes were speed and a penchant for clever dribbling.

BROOK, Eric Fred   1930-8(18)
b Mexborough, Yorks 27 November 1907 ; d 29 March 1965.
Career: Dolcliffe Road School Mexborough, Oxford Road Y.M.C.A., Swinton Primitives, Mexborough, Wath Athletic, Barnsley February 1926, Manchester City March 1928, retired during the War. After retirement he lived in Manchester and worked as a crane driver.
Club Honours: Manchester City—F.A. Cup finalists 1933, winners 1934, F.L. Champions 1937.
Ostensibly an outside-left but likely to bob up anywhere in the attack. An ebullient character with a rocket shot.

BROOKS, John   1957(3)
b Reading 1932.
Career: Coley Boys Club, Reading amateur February 1949, professional April 1949, Tottenham Hotspur February 1953, Chelsea December 1959, Brentford September 1961, Crystal Palace January 1964, Stevenage Town October 1964. Had a spell in Canadian football and now plays for Knebworth and works as an Exchange broker's messenger in the City of London
Club Honour: Brentford—Fourth Division Champions 1963
In his heyday was a cogent inside-forward who zestfully plied his fellow forwards with scoring

chances and displayed clever ball control.

BROOME, Frank Henry 1938-9(7)
b Berkhamsted, Herts 11 June 1915.
Career: Berkhamsted Victoria Church of England School, Boxmoor United Juniors and Seniors, Berkhamsted Town, Aston Villa November 1934, Derby County September 1946, Notts County October 1949, Brentford July 1953, Crewe Alexandra October 1953, Shelbourne February 1955, Notts County assistant trainer cs 1955, acting manager January to May 1957 thence assistant manager to December 1957, Exeter City manager January 1958, Southend United manager May 1960 to December 1960, Bankstown (New South Wales) manager coach July 1961 to October 1962, Corinthians (Sydney) manager coach 1962 later Exeter City manager May 1967 to February 1969. Then after briefly coaching in the Middle East he left the game and lives and works near Exeter
Club Honours: Aston Villa—Second Division Champions 1938, F.L. North Cup winners 1944, Wolverhampton Wanderers—F.L. Cup winners 1942 as a guest, Notts County—Third Division South Champions 1950
Played for England in four different positions—both wings, inside-right and centre—though he usually appeared as leader or outside-right in club games. Despite being small and frail Broome was extremely dangerous with his remarkable speed and marksmanship.

BROWN, Arthur 1882(3)
b 1859; d 1 July 1909.
Career: Florence F.C. (Aston), Aston Unity, Aston Villa 1881, Birmingham St George briefly late 1884 and at the same time briefly associated with Excelsior before

returning to Aston Villa October 1884. He retained his interest in Aston Villa after giving up playing.
An opportunist inside-right of short and sturdy build with a deadly shot. Curiously had the habit of keeping clean on the muddiest of pitches.

BROWN, Anthony 1971(1)
b Oldham, Lancs 3 October 1945.
Career: Manchester Schools, West Bromwich Albion apprentice 1961, professional October 1963
Club Honours: West Bromwich Albion—F.A. Cup winners 1968, F.L. Cup winners 1966, finalists 1967, 70
Has considerable striking power, being able to run to the right position instinctively and possessing strong marksmanship. Earlier played outside-right and since has been at right-half and (generally) inside-right.

BROWN, Arthur Samuel 1904-6(2)
b Gainsborough, Lincs 6 April 1885; d 27 June 1944.
Career: Gainsborough Church Lads Brigade, Gainsborough Trinity early 1902, Sheffield United cs 1902, Sunderland June 1908, Fulham late 1910, Middlesbrough cs 1912
A centre-forward chiefly notable for his opportunism which was outstanding. He was usually on target with his shooting.

BROWN, George 1927-33(9)
b Mickley, Northumberland circa 1903; d 10 June 1948.
Career: Mickley Colliery, Huddersfield Town May 1921, Aston Villa August 1929, Burnley October 1934, Leeds United September 1935, Darlington as player manager October 1936 resigned October 1938. He then left the game and became a licensee in Aston. A cousin of J. W. Spence.
Club Honours: Huddersfield

Town—F.L. Champions 1924-5-6,
F.A. Cup finalists 1928
Played at inside-right or centre-forward and had all the qualities
the positions demanded. A skilful
dribbler, a hard shot and a good
eye for an opening.

BROWN, James   1881-5(5)
b Blackburn 1862; d 4 July 1922.
Career: St John's School Black-burn, Mintholme College, Black-burn Rovers 1879 to 1889. After
leaving Blackburn Rovers played
no further football and became a
solicitor's managing clerk.
Club Honours: Blackburn Rovers
—F.A. Cup finalists 1882, winners
1884-5-6
Not ideally built for a centre-forward, being small and light,
but he was extremely fast and
elusive and carried a good shot.
Also played at outside-left.

BROWN, John H.   1927-30(6)
b Worksop, Notts 19 March 1899;
d 10 April 1962.
Career: Manton Colliery, Work-sop Town 1919, Sheffield Wednes-day February 1923, Hartlepools
United September 1937 but re-leased after a fortnight
Club Honours: Sheffield Wednes-day—Second Division Champions
1926, F.L. Champions 1929, 30,
F.A. Cup winners 1935
Broad-shouldered, hefty goal-keeper whose usefulness was not
confined to the goal line—he
would advance to avert danger
but without taking foolish risks.
Efficient, sound and dependable.

BROWN, Kenneth   1960(1)
b Forest Gate, Essex 16 February
1934.
Career: Lymington Secondary
Modern School, Neville United,
West Ham United October 1951,
Torquay United May 1967, Here-ford United cs 1969, Bourne-mouth & Boscombe Athletic
trainer coach May 1970

Club Honours: West Ham United
—Second Division Champions
1958, F.A. Cup winners 1964,
European Cup Winners Cup win-ners 1965, F.L. Cup finalists 1966
Quiet, competent centre-half both
creative and firm. Seldom drawn
out of position.

BROWN, William   1924(1)
b Hetton, Co. Durham.
Career: Hetton, West Ham
United 1922, Chelsea February
1924, Fulham cs 1929 briefly
Club Honour: West Ham United
—F.A. Cup finalists 1923
An inside-right whose first-class
career was comparatively short (he
aggregated 116 League games
only.) His play was distinguished
mainly for skilful ball control and
accurate shooting.

BRUTON, John   1928-9(3)
b Westhoughton, Lancs 21 Nov-ember 1903.
Career: Westhoughton Sunday
School football, Hindley Green
(having trials with Bolton Wan-derers and Wigan Borough), Hor-wich R.M.I. 1924-5, Burnley
March 1925, Blackburn Rovers
December 1929. Retired during
the War and was appointed
Rovers assistant secretary Septem-ber 1947, manager December 1947
resigning May 1949. Bournemouth
& Boscombe Athletic manager
from March 1950 to March 1956.
He then left football and lived at
Bournemouth acting at various
times as part time coach and
scout for Portsmouth, Bourne-mouth and Blackburn Rovers.
His easy running action deluded
many opposing defenders for he
was, in fact, outstandingly fast.
An outside-right with ball control
and artistry.

BRYANT, William Ingram 1925(1)
b Ghent, Belgium 1 March 1899.
Career: St Olave's Grammar

School, Chelmsford, Clapton, Millwall Athletic cs 1925, Clapton May 1931 retired cs 1933. Seven England amateur international appearances between 1925 and 1928. Later was a director of a wholesale seed company and is now living in retirement at Witham in Essex

Club Honours: Clapton—F.A. Amateur Cup winners 1924 and 1925, Millwall—Third Division South Champions 1928

One of three from the great Clapton amateur team of 1923-5 to gain full international honours (the others were Earle and Gibbins and, like the latter, Bryant never turned professional). He was an astute centre-half especially good in the air thanks to a height of 6 ft I in.

BUCHAN, Charles Murray
1913-24(6)
b Plumstead 22 September 1891 ; d 25 June 1960.
Career: Bloomfield Road School Woolwich, High Street School Plumstead, Woolwich Polytechnic, Plumstead St Nicholas Church, Plumstead F.C., Woolwich Arsenal amateur December 1908, Northfleet November 1909, Leyton March 1910, Sunderland March 1911, Arsenal July 1925 retiring May 1928. On his retirement he became a football journalist with the *Daily News* later the *News Chronicle*. Played cricket on occasion for Durham county, 1920

Club Honours: Sunderland—F.L. Champions and F.A. Cup finalists 1913, Arsenal—F.A. Cup finalists 1927

A marvellous inside-right (and occasional centre-forward) whose subtleties were said to bewilder his team-mates as well as the opposition. Whether true or not Buchan had mastered every trick aided by unusual length of limb, his glancing headers being especi-ally brilliant.

BUCHANAN, W. S. 1876(1)
Career: Clapham Rovers ; Surrey. Suffered from the disadvantage of being too light and a tendency to over-run the ball. Nevertheless a fast forward and a fair dribbler.

BUCKLEY, Franklin Charles
1914(1)
b Urmston, Manchester 9 November 1883 ; d 22 December 1964.
Career: Aston Villa, Brighton & Hove Albion cs 1905, Manchester United cs 1906, Manchester City cs 1907, Birmingham July 1909, Derby County cs 1911, Bradford City cs 1914 retiring during the 1914-18 War when he served in the Footballers Battalion and became its Commanding Officer. Norwich City manager March 1919 to 1920 thence a commercial traveller in London until Blackpool manager July 1923, Wolverhampton Wanderers manager May 1927, Notts County manager March 1944, Hull City manager May 1946, Leeds United manager May 1948, Walsall manager April 1953 retiring June 1955

Club Honour: Derby County—Second Division Champions 1912

Won more fame, of course, as a manager but earlier was a vigorous attacking centre-half, skilled in tackling and a glutton for work.

BULLOCK, Frederick Edwin
1921(1)
b Hounslow 1886 ; d 15 November 1922.
Career: Isleworth Schools, Hounslow Town, Ilford cs 1909, Huddersfield Town, December 1910 to cs 1922. England amateur international in 1911. After retirement was for a brief period up to his death licensee of the Slubbers Arms, Huddersfield

Club Honour: Huddersfield Town—F.A. Cup finalists 1920

A left-back sound in tackling and kicking. His reliability and all-round strength had not a little to do with Huddersfield's emergence as a major force around 1920.

BULLOCK, Norman 1923-7(3)
b Monton Green, Lancs 8 September 1900.
Career: Sedgley Park, Bury as a professional February 1921, player manager cs 1934, retired cs 1935 and continued as manager until June 1938, Chesterfield manager June 1938, Bury manager July 1945 to December 1949, Leicester City manager December 1949 resigning February 1955
A great club servant who early showed speed, staying power and shooting ability at centre-forward. Later in his playing career showed unusual versatility by playing at inside-right, centre and right-half.

BURGESS, Herbert 1904-6(4)
b Openshaw, Manchester 1883.
Career: Openshaw United, Glossop, Manchester City cs 1903, Manchester United 1 January 1907 to 1910. Later coached in Hungary, Spain and Italy
Club Honours: Manchester City —F.A. Cup winners 1904, Manchester United—F.L. Champions 1908
Marvellous left-back for his size —5 ft 5 in. Had the gift of anticipation, a stout tackle and placed his clearances beautifully. Played on the right flank sometimes as well.

BURGESS, Harry 1931(4)
b Alderley Edge, Cheshire 20 August 1904.
Career: Alderley Edge, Stockport County, Sandbach Ramblers (on loan), Stockport County 1926, Sheffield Wednesday June 1929, Chelsea March 1935 retired during the War
Club Honour: Sheffield Wednesday—F.L. Champions 1930
Solid, stocky inside-forward clever in dribbling. With all his League clubs played penetratively and scored with clockwork regularity.

BURNUP, Cuthbert James 1896(1)
b Blackheath, Kent 21 November 1875; d 5 April 1960.
Career: Malvern College (XI 1893); Clare College Cambridge (Blue 1895-6-7-8 captain 1897); Old Malvernians; Corinthians 1895-1901. Also a cricket blue for Cambridge 1896-7-8 and played for Kent 1896-1907 being captain in 1903. Scored over 13,000 runs in first class cricket including 26 centuries. At one time a stockbrocker he was later engaged in commerce in the City of London. Whole-hearted outside-left who varied his game judiciously. A good dribbler and shot and had a useful turn of speed.

BURROWS, Horace 1934-5(3)
b Sutton-in-Ashfield, Notts 1910; d 23 January 1969.
Career: Notts Schools, Sutton Junction, Coventry City February 1930, Mansfield Town cs 1930, Sheffield Wednesday May 1931 retired during the War. Subsequently a sports outfitter in Sutton-in-Ashfield
Club Honour: Sheffield Wednesday—F.A. Cup winners 1935
A wing-half usually found on the left flank. He had a cogent tackle, good powers of distribution and maintained a consistent level of performance in his service with Sheffield Wednesday.

BURTON, Frank Ernest 1889(1)
b 18 March 1865; d 10 February 1948.
Career: Nottingham High School; Notts County October 1886 to October 1887; Nottingham Forest November 1887 to November 1891. Later in turn manager, managing director and finally Chairman of the family firm of Joseph Burton & Sons Ltd., owners of a chain of grocery stores founded by his father. High Sheriff of Nottinghamshire 1938-9. One of the more prominent of the

several Forest men to play for England in the early days. He played a keen game at inside-right carrying raids to enemy territory with dash and verve and also frequently played on the right-wing.

BURY, Lindsay   1877-9(2)
b Withington, Manchester 9 July 1857; d 30 October 1935.
Career: Eton College (XI 1875-6); Trinity College, Cambridge (Blue 1877-8 but was not chosen in 1879 and 1880 as he preferred to play for Old Etonians in the F.A. Cup); Old Etonians: Athletics Blue 1878-9-80. Cricket Blue 1877 and also played for Hampshire. F.A. Committee 1878.
One-time orange planter in Florida he later lived in Wiltshire
Club Honour: Old Etonians— F.A. Cup winners 1879
Reputed to be the strongest back of his period. His sure kicking had an admirable length.

BUTLER, John Dennis   1925(1)
b Colombo, Ceylon 14 August 1894; d 5 January 1961.
Career: West London Schools, Fulham (amateur) 1913, Dartford mid 1913-14, Arsenal May 1914, Torquay United May 1930, coach to Daring F.C. Brussels 1932-9, Leicester City coach October 1940, Copenhagen coach briefly in 1946, Torquay United manager June 1946, Crystal Palace manager cs 1947, Daring F.C. manager May 1949 later Colchester United manager June 1953 to January 1955
Club Honour: Arsenal—F.A. Cup finalists 1927
A centre-half of willowy build whose height gave him command in the air. Cool in action and capable of precise distribution.

BUTLER, William   1924(1)
b Atherton, Lancs 27 March 1900; d 11 July 1966.
Career: Howe Bridge F.C., Atherton Colliery, Bolton Wanderers

May 1921, Reading June 1933 appointed manager August 1935 until February 1939, Guildford City manager June 1939, Torquay United manager cs 1945 to May 1946 when he emigrated to South Africa where he managed Johannesburg Rangers and coached for Pietermaritzburg and District F.A. and subsequently in Rhodesia for the Rhodesian F.A.
Club Honours: Bolton Wanderers —F.A. Cup winners 1923-6-9
An outside-right possessing a fine turn of speed and expertise at dribbling.

BYRNE, Gerald   1963-6(2)
b Liverpool 1938.
Career: Liverpool Schools, Liverpool professional August 1955 retired through injury December 1969
Club Honours: Liverpool—Second Division Champions 1962, F.L. Champions 1964 and 1966, F.A. Cup winners 1965, European Cup Winners Cup finalists 1966
Was a thoughtful right or left-back always seeking to part with the ball to the best advantage. Will long be remembered for his courage in playing through practically the whole of the 1965 Cup Final with a broken shoulder.

BYRNE, John J.   1962-5(11)
b West Horsley, Surrey May 1939.
Career: Effingham School, Epsom Town, Guildford City Youth (England Youth 1956), Crystal Palace July 1956, West Ham United March 1962, Crystal Palace February 1967, Fulham March 1968, Durban City May 1969, manager cs 1972
Club Honours: West Ham United —F.A. Cup winners 1964, F.L. Cup finalists 1966
Inside-right or centre-forward and a dangerous man in the vicinity of goal. Could bore a way through skilfully, requiring little space in which to manoeuvre.

BYRNE, Roger William 1954-8(33)
b Manchester late 1929 ; d 6 February 1958.
Career: Burnage Grammar School Manchester, Ryder Brow Boys Club Gorton, Manchester United 1949. Killed in the Munich air crash
Club Honours: Manchester United—F.L. Champions 1952-6-7, F.A. Cup finalists 1957.
His left-back play was renowned for exceptional speed, an asset developed in earlier days on the left wing. Became an excellent club skipper and was also a reliable penalty taker.

CALLAGHAN, Ian Robert 1966(2)
b Liverpool 10 April 1942.
Career: St Patrick's Roman Catholic School Liverpool, Liverpool ground staff cs 1958, professional March 1960
Club Honours: Liverpool— Second Division Champions 1962, F.L. Champions 1964 and 1966, F.A. Cup winners 1965, European Cup Winners Cup finalists 1966, F.A. Cup finalists 1971
Has always put maximum effort into his performance. When honoured was an outside-right of the direct kind able to centre beautifully. Has lately had a more aggressive midfield role and finds the opportunity to shoot more often.

CALVEY, John   1902(1)
b South Bank, Middlesbrough 23 August 1876 ; d
Career: South Bank, Millwall Athletic, Nottingham Forest cs 1899, Millwall Athletic cs 1904
Had a somewhat uneven career and his Forest spell was disappointing. Even so, when in form, he was a sterling goal scoring centre-forward who could carve a way through aided by a weighty frame.

CAMPBELL, Austin Fenwick
                          1929-32(8)
b Hamsterley, Co. Durham 5 May 1901.
Career: Coventry City mid 1919-20, Leadgate Park June 1921, Blackburn Rovers February 1923, Huddersfield Town September 1929, Hull City November 1935 to cs 1936
Club Honours: Blackburn Rovers —F.A. Cup winners 1928, Huddersfield Town—F.A. Cup finalists 1930
Uncommonly fast for a left-half gathering the ball and passing to set up an attack in almost one movement. Trenchant in the tackle and stylish in all that he did.

CAMSELL, George Henry
                          1929-36(9)
b Framwellgate Moor, Co. Durham 27 November 1902 ; d 7 March 1966.
Career: Durham Chapel club 1921, Tow Law Town, Esh Winning, Durham City June 1924, Middlesbrough October 1925 retired during the War and became chief scout, coach and, in October 1956, assistant secretary of the Club from which post he retired owing to illness December 1963.
Scored 59 League goals in 1927, at the time a record total. It was beaten by Dean with 60 in 1928 and that still remains the record for a League season. In League matches for Durham City and Middlesbrough scored a total of 344 goals.
Club Honours: Middlesbrough— Second Division Champions 1927 and 1929
Famed sharp-shooting centre who amassed a formidable goals total. A real driving force his enthusiasm for the game was infectious.

CAPES, Arthur John   1903(1)
b Burton 1875 ; d
Career: Burton Wanderers, Not-

tingham Forest cs 1896, Stoke cs 1902, Bristol City May 1904, Swindon Town cs 1905 to 1906
Club Honour: Nottingham Forest—F.A. Cup winners 1898
Not the most polished of inside-lefts but was workmanlike and combined excellently with the other forwards. Was a fair marksman too.

CARR, John   1905-7(2)
b Seaton Burn, Northumberland 1876; d 17 March 1948.
Career: Seaton Burn, Newcastle United mid 1895-6, Newcastle United training staff on retirement, Blackburn Rovers team manager February 1922, secretary manager September 1925 resigned December 1926
Club Honours: Newcastle United —F.L. Champions 1905, 7, F.A. Cup Winners 1910, finalists 1905, 6
Originally a half-back, Carr became a monumental left-back. Was well-built and used his physical advantages with brilliant judgment.

CARR, Jack   1920-3(2)
b South Bank, Middlesbrough 1891; d 10 May 1942.
Career: South Bank, Middlesbrough February 1911, Blackpool May 1930, Hartlepools United player-coach July 1931 manager April 1932 to April 1935, Tranmere Rovers manager July 1935, Darlington manager October 1938
Club Honours: South Bank— F.A. Amateur Cup finalists 1910, Middlesbrough—Second Division Champions 1927 and 1929
A forward of consequence whether at outside-right or inside-forward. Not a great scorer himself but a subtle schemer and provider-in-chief over many years to a succession of noted Middlesbrough marksmen.

CARR, William Henry   1875(1)
b 1850; d 22 February 1924.

G

Career: Walkley; Owlerton; Sheffield Wednesday; Sheffield F.A.
Although a competent outfield player his fame rested on his gifts as a goalkeeper. In this he was aided by tremendous height and qualities of coolness and judgment.

CARTER, Horatio Stratton ("Raich")   1934-7(13)
b Sunderland 21 December 1913.
Career: Hendon School Sunderland (England Schools v Scotland and Wales 1927 and 1928), Whitburn St Mary, Sunderland Forge, Esh Winning September 1931, Sunderland November 1931, Derby County December 1945, Hull City March 1948 as player-assistant-manager, full player manager May 1948, resigned as manager September 1951 and after a short period resumed as a player until April 1952. Came out of retirement to sign for Cork Athletic January 1953 finally retiring in May 1953. Manager of Leeds United May 1953 to June 1958, left football for a period until becoming Mansfield Town manager February 1960, Middlesbrough manager January 1963 to February 1966 when he left football. Later lived in Hull first as a Sports Shop manager and later as a confectioner. Played cricket on two occasions for Derbyshire in 1946 and also played minor county cricket for Durham
Club Honours: Sunderland—F.L. Champions 1936, F.A. Cup winners 1937, F.L. War Cup finalists 1942, Derby County—F.A. Cup winners 1946, Hull City—Third Division North Champions 1949, Cork Athletic—F.A. of Ireland Cup winners 1953
The perfect inside-forward possessing superb ball control and a powerful and accurate shot but his forte was probably his tactical genius.

CARTER, Joseph Henry 1926-9(3) b Aston, Birmingham 16 April 1901.
Career: Westbourne Celtic, West Bromwich Albion April 1921, Sheffield Wednesday February 1936 but the transfer was cancelled owing to an accident at home, Tranmere Rovers June 1936, Walsall November 1936 retired cs 1937
Club Honours: West Bromwich Albion—F.A. Cup winners 1931, finalists 1935
Gave West Bromwich Albion 15 years magnificent service at inside-right. Hard and wiry with a fine body swerve and a good shot.

CATLIN, Arthur Edward 1937(5) b South Bank, Middlesbrough 11 January 1911
Career: Middlesbrough Schools, South Bank, Sheffield Wednesday October 1930 retired during the War owing to injury
Club Honours: Sheffield Wednesday—F.A. Cup winners 1935, F.L. North Cup finalists 1943
Always thoughtful and composed, this left-back positioned himself skilfully and placed his clearances with immaculate judgment. Was rarely guilty of an ill-timed tackle.

CHADWICK, Arthur 1900(2) b Church, Lancs, 1866; d 21 March 1936.
Career: Church, Accrington, Burton Swifts, Southampton cs 1897, Portsmouth cs 1901, Northampton Town cs 1904, Accrington cs 1906, Exeter City cs 1908, Exeter City manager cs 1910 to December 1922, Reading manager January 1923 to October 1925, Southampton manager October 1925 to April 1931. After leaving Southampton lived in retirement at Exeter and died in the stand whilst watching a match at St James Park
Club Honours: Southampton—Southern League Champions 1898-9-1901, F.A. Cup finalists 1900,

Portsmouth—Southern League Champions 1902
Powerful centre-half at his best at the turn of the century. Not always at ease with intricate dribbling but mostly efficient in attack and defence.

CHADWICK, Edgar 1891-7(7) b Blackburn 1869; d 14 February 1942.
Career: Blackburn Olympic, Blackburn Rovers cs 1887, Everton cs 1888, Burnley cs 1899, Southampton August 1900, Liverpool cs 1902, Blackpool May 1904, Glossop cs 1905, Darwen cs 1906 retired 1908. Coached for a time in Germany and Holland and then pursued his trade of a baker in Blackburn
Club Honours: Everton—F.L. Champions 1891, F.A. Cup finalists 1893, 7. Southampton—Southern League Champions 1901, F.A. Cup finalists 1902
An inside-left of enormous talent; quick, cunning, distributor of excellent passes and a forceful shot.

CHAMBERS, Henry 1921-4(8) b Willington Quay, Northumberland 1896; d 29 June 1949.
Career: Percy Main School, Tynemouth (England Schools v Wales and Scotland 1911), Willington United Methodists, North Shields Athletic, Liverpool April 1915, West Bromwich Albion March 1928, Oakengates Town July 1929 becoming manager of the club and remaining with it until the War. From 1939 until his death he worked with Sankeys at Hadley.
Club Honours: Glentoran—Irish Cup finalists 1919 (as a guest), Liverpool—F.L. Champions 1922 and 1923
Brainy and thoughtful centre-forward or inside-left. Had a hard, accurate shot with the left foot which he could swerve markedly

at will. At West Bromwich performed successfully as a pivot.

CHARLTON, John   1965-70(35)
b Ashington, Northumberland 8 May 1936.
Career: Hirst Park Modern School Ashington, Ashington Y.M.C.A., Ashington Welfare, Leeds United amateur 1950, professional May 1952. Brother of Bobby and, like him, a member of the England World Cup winning team 1966
Club Honours: Leeds United—Second Division Champions 1964, F.A. Cup finalists 1965, 70, winners 1972, F.L. Champions 1969, F.L. Cup winners 1968, Fairs Cup finalists 1967, winners 1968 and 1971
Great height has enabled this centre-half to win dominance in the air and cause apprehension to opponents when advancing to their goal-line for his side's corners. Effective on the ground, too, with a telling tackle.

CHARLTON, Robert   1958-70(106)
b Ashington, Northumberland 11 October 1937.
Career: Bealington Grammar School Ashington (England v Wales (2) Eire and Scotland Schools 1953), Manchester United amateur August 1953, professional October 1954 (England Youth international 1954). A member of the England World Cup winning team 1966. His 106 appearances for England is a record. Awarded O.B.E. June 1969.
Club Honours: Manchester United—F.A. Youth Cup winners 1954-5-6, F.L. Champions 1957-65-7, F.A. Cup finalists 1957 and 1958, winners 1963, European Cup winners 1968
Perhaps the best liked footballer in Britain over the past decade and certainly one who has given memorable service to club and country at centre, inside-forward

and outside-left. Lately has played as a deep centre, splaying out immaculate passes and occasionally indulging his explosive shooting power.

CHARNLEY, Raymond O.   1963(1)
b Lancaster 29 May 1935.
Career: Bolton-le-Sands (Preston North End amateur), Morecombe, Blackpool May 1957, Preston North End December 1967, Wrexham July 1968, Bradford January 1969, Morecambe cs 1970
Had an ideal build for leading the attack, which he did with speed and thrust. Was a consistent scorer all through his League career.

CHARSLEY, Charles Christopher
1893(1)
b Leicester 1865 ; d 10 January 1945.
Career: Stafford Rangers, Small Heath retiring cs 1893 but played in the Test matches of 1894. Joined Birmingham City Police 1884, Chief Constable of Coventry August 1899 retiring in 1918. Lived in retirement at Weston-super-Mare and was on the Borough Council 1933-45, deputy Mayor 1939-40
Club Honour: Small Heath—Second Division Champions 1893
Chronologically the first in line of Birmingham's several England goalkeepers. A fine amateur, sound, and sometimes brilliant, in dealing with all manner of shots and an excellent club man.

CHEDGZOY, Samuel   1920-5(8)
b Ellesmere Port, Cheshire 27 January 1890 ; d 15 January 1967.
Career: Birnell's Ironworks (Ellesmere Port), Everton December 1910, New Bedford U.S.A. May 1926 to 1930 thence for Carsteel F.C. Montreal until 1940. Remained in Canada after his retirement from the game
Club Honour: Everton—F.L. Champions 1915

A resourceful and swift right-winger with a good shot who did not use robust tactics. Started the practice of dribbling corner kicks —a loophole in the laws soon amended.

CHENERY, Charles John 1873-4(3)
b Lambourn, Berks 1 January 1850 ; d
Career : Crystal Palace (the original club) ; Surrey to 1975 ; Wanderers : Played cricket for Surrey in 1872 and 1873
An admirable forward, a dribbling artist and one who played at full stretch until the last minute.

CHILTON, Allenby 1951-2(2)
b South Hylton, Co. Durham 16 September 1918.
Career : Ford School Sunderland (Sunderland — England Schools Shield winners 1933), Seaham Colliery, Manchester United November 1938, Grimsby Town as player manager March 1955, retiring as a player October 1956 and as manager April 1959, Wigan Athletic manager May 1960, Hartlepools United scout 1961-2, manager July 1962 to May 1963
Club Honours : Charlton Athletic —F.L. South Cup winners (as a guest) 1944, Manchester United— F.L. North Cup finalists 1945, F.A. Cup winners 1948, F.L. Champions 1952, Grimsby Town —Third Division North Champions 1956
A key defensive figure at centre-half, his height being especially valuable in headwork. Was accurate and creative in ground passing.

CHIPPENDALE, Harry 1894(1)
b Blackburn 1870 ; d 29 September 1952.
Career : Nelson, Blackburn Rovers cs 1891 to cs 1897. Worked for some years at Hornby's Brookhouse Mill in Blackburn and later became a mill manager with that firm. Retained his interest in Blackburn Rovers until his death. At one time a Football League linesman
Tall, well built outside-right of the forceful type. His speedy dashes down the wing were rounded off with accurate centres and shots.

CHIVERS, Martin Harcourt
1971-2(12)
b Southampton 27 April 1945.
Career : Taunton School Southampton, Southampton junior football, Southampton amateur early 1962, professional September 1962, Tottenham Hotspur January 1968
Club Honours : Tottenham Hotspur—F.L. Cup winners 1971, UEFA Cup winners 1972
Astonishingly nimble for a big man and difficult to dispossess when boring his way through a defence. A fine centre-forward who played at inside-right for much of his Southampton spell.

CHRISTIAN, Edward 1879(1)
b Malvern, Worcs 14 September 1858 ; d 3 April 1934.
Career : Eton College ; Trinity College Cambridge (No Blue) ; Old Etonians
Club Honour : Old Etonians— F.A. Cup winners 1879
An excellent full-back equally adept with either foot. In Ceylon from 1881-1904 and his playing career, therefore, closed on his leaving Cambridge.

CLAMP, Edwin 1958(4)
b Coalville, Leicestershire 1934.
Career : Coalville Schools (England Schools v Ireland 1949, v Scotland (2) Wales and Eire 1950), Wolverhampton Wanderers amateur cs 1950, professional April 1952, Arsenal November 1961, Stoke City September 1962, Peterborough United Ocotber 1964,

Worcester City August 1965 to cs 1966, thence out of football until he joined Lower Gornal in September 1967

Club Honours: Wolverhampton Wanderers—F.L. Champions 1958 and 1959, F.A. Youth Cup finalists 1953, F.A. Cup winners 1960, Stoke City—Second Division Champions 1963

First achieved senior status at left-half, subsequently and permanently moving to the other flank. Was a forceful half, biting in the tackle and vigorous throughout.

CLAPTON, Daniel Robert
1959(1)
b Stepney 22 July 1934.

Career: Hackney Schools, Leytonstone, Arsenal August 1953, Luton Town September 1962 to cs 1963. Went to Australia late 1964 and joined Corinthians F.C., Sydney

An outside-right with a dashing style. Had tricks in abundance and kept up his pace throughout.

CLARE, Thomas   1889-94(4)
b Congleton 1865 ; d 27 December 1929.

Career: Talke, Goldenhill Wanderers, Stoke 1883, Burslem Port Vale cs 1897 as coach later manager. Emigrated to Canada prior to the 1914-18 War and died there at Ladysmith in Vancouver.

A right-back of thoughtful bent, also being quick and resolute. A good header of the ball in a period when this art was comparatively rare.

CLARKE, Allan John   1970-1(6)
b Shortheath, Willenhall, Staffs 31 July 1946.

Career: Birmingham Schools, Walsall apprentice 1961, professional August 1963, Fulham March 1966, Leicester City June 1968, Leeds United June 1969

Club Honours: Leicester City— F.A. Cup finalists 1969, Leeds

United—F.A. Cup finalists 1970, winners 1972, Fairs Cup winners 1971

Slimly built inside-right with some experience in leading the attack. Unsurpassed at taking difficult scoring chances with lightning speed in the vicinity of the enemy goal.

CLARKE, Henry Alfred   1954(1)
b Woodford Green, Essex 23 February 1923.

Career: Ray Lodge School Woodford Bridge 1933-7, Lovells Athletic, Tottenham Hotspur March 1949, Llanelly player manager February 1959, Romford manager from March 1962

Club Honours: Tottenham Hotspur—Second Division Champions 1950, F.L. Champions 1951

Very tall, lanky pivot usually master in the air. He was perceptive in the tackle and distributed the ball with studied foresight.

CLAY, Thomas   1920-2(4)
b Leicester 19 November 1892 ; d 21 February 1949.

Career: Belvoir Street Sunday School Leicester, Leicester Fosse cs 1911, Tottenham Hotspur January 1914, Northfleet player coach cs 1929, St Albans coach cs 1931. Later worked in the building trade in the Southend area.

Club Honours: Tottenham Hotspur—Second Division Champions 1920, F.A. Cup winners 1921

A right-back strategist who more than balanced any deficiency in speed by an innate positional sense. Often cleared his lines by a low, skimming pass which invariably found its man.

CLAYTON, Ronald   1956-60(35)
b Preston 5 August 1934.

Career: Ribbleton Avenue Methodist and Fishwick Secondary Modern Schools Preston, Blackburn Rovers amateur July 1949,

professional August 1951, Morecambe player manager July 1969 to August 1970, Great Harwood late 1970. A newsagent in Blackburn for some years he is now a company representative.
Club Honour: Blackburn Rovers —F.A. Cup finalists 1960
A classic right-half of all-round ability. Made his senior debut when 17 and for the next 18 years or so exhibited a constructiveness (and eventually leadership) of the highest order.

CLEGG, Sir John Charles 1873(1)
b Sheffield 15 June 1850; d 26 June 1937.
Career: Sheffield Wednesday; Sheffield F.C.; Norfolk F.C.; Perseverance; Sheffield F.A. Refereed the F.A. Cup final of 1882 and 1892 also the England v Scotland match 1886. F.A. Committee 1885, Chairman 1889, Vice-President 1889-1923, President 1923 to his death. At times Chairman of both Sheffield Wednesday and Sheffield United. A noted sprinter in his young days he was by profession a solicitor practising in Sheffield with Clegg and Sons. Knighted in June 1927 for his services to football he was brother of W.E.
His forward play was remarkable for its speed in dribbling. Was also an unerring shot and showed great judgment in the distribution of passes.

CLEGG, Sir William Edwin
1873-9(2)
b 21 April 1852; d 22 August 1932.
Career: Sheffield Wednesday; Sheffield F.C.; Perseverance; Sheffield Albion; Norfolk F.C.; Sheffield F.A.: retired owing to injury in January 1880. Later like his brother a director of both Sheffield Wednesday and Sheffield United. Admitted a solicitor in 1874 he, too, practised in the family firm of Clegg & Sons in

Sheffield. Lord Mayor of Sheffield from 1893-99 he was knighted in 1906. Awarded O.B.E. 1918 for his work on Sheffield Munitions Tribunal. He was also a noted sprinter in his young days.
Mostly played half-back where he was a safe and reliable performer discerning in his passing of the ball.

CLOUGH, Brian H. 1960(2)
b Middlesbrough 21 March 1935.
Career: Great Broughton (Yorks), Middlesbrough amateur November 1951, professional May 1952, Sunderland July 1961, retired injury November 1964 and joined Sunderland coaching staff until cs 1965, Hartlepools United manager October 1965, Derby County manager June 1967
In his day had few equals and no superiors at snapping up scoring chances. A dynamic, straight-for-goal centre-forward.

COATES, Ralph 1970-1(4)
b Hetton-le-Hole, Co. Durham 26 April 1946.
Career: Hetton Schools, Hetton Juniors, Burnley amateur October 1961, professional April 1963, Tottenham Hotspur May 1971
Club Honour: Tottenham—UE F.A. Cup winners 1972
Has no claims to greatness in heading or goal-getting but second to none in foraging and distribution skills. Plays anywhere in the attack except centre-forward.

COBBOLD, William Nevill
1883-7(9)
b Long Melford, Suffolk 4 February 1863; d 8 April 1922.
Career: Cranbrook School; Charterhouse School (XI 1881-2); Jesus College Cambridge (Blue 1883-4-5-6 captain 1885-6); Old Carthusians; Wratting Park; Corinthians 1885-8. Played cricket once for Kent in 1887. Cambridge Lawn Tennis Blue 1885-6. By

profession a private tutor.
Arguably the most brilliant forward of the eighties. Combined his magnificent dribbling with great pace and fine shooting.

COCK, John Gilbert   1920(2)
b Hayle, Cornwall 14 November 1893 ; d 19 April 1966.
Career: West Kensington United 1908, Forest Gate, Old Kingstonian (Brentford amateur March 1914), Huddersfield Town cs 1914, Chelsea October 1919, Everton January 1923, Plymouth Argyle March 1925, Millwall November 1927, Folkestone July 1931, Walton F.C. (Surrey) as a permit player October 1932. Returned to football as Millwall manager November 1944 to August 1948 and on his retirement became a licensee at New Cross. Won M.M. in the 1914-18 War.
Club Honour: Millwall—Third Division South Champions 1928.
Perfectly proportioned physically for his job at centre-forward Cock was a fine athlete. He was fast, had command of the ball and could score with head and both feet.

COCKBURN, Henry   1947-52(13)
b Ashton-under-Lyme, Lancs 1923.
Career: Gosling's F.C. (Manchester), Manchester United August 1944, Bury October 1954, Peterborough United July 1956, Corby Town July 1959, Sankeys cs 1960 to December 1960, Oldham Athletic assistant trainer February 1961, Huddersfield Town assistant trainer coach September 1964 later becoming the senior coach
Club Honours: Manchester United—F.L. Cup winners 1948, F.L. Champions 1952
A mighty atom of a wing-half. Though small he could, thanks to assiduous practice, leap high to the ball, and he used to dominate on the ground with terrier-like tackles.

COHEN, George Reginald
                    1964-8(37)
b Kensington 22 October 1939.
Career: Hammersmith schoolboy football, Fulham amateur 1955, professional October 1956 retired injury March 1969. Fulham Youth team manager January 1970 to June 1971 and for a time also ran a sports shop. A member of England's World Cup winning team of 1966.
Was among the earliest players in his position (right-back) to exploit the overlap gambit, which he did most successfully being fast and intelligent. In defence speed was evident in his tackling too.

COLCLOUGH, H.   1914(1)
Career: Crewe Alexandra, Crystal Palace cs 1912, retired owing to injury during the 1914-18 War.
His peace-time first-class experience was limited to two seasons so it can be said he did well to obtain a full cap—the more so as Pennington's tenure at left-back was then not ended. Colclough was a solid defender, kicking and tackling well.

COLEMAN, Ernest Herbert 1921(1)
b Steyning, Sussex 19 October 1889 ; d 15 June 1958.
Career: Croydon Amateurs, Dulwich Hamlet from 1912 and served on the Club committee after his retirement as a player. 4 England amateur international appearances between 1920-2. An accountant by profession
Club Honour: Dulwich Hamlet— F.A. Amateur Cup winners 1920
Prominent inter-war amateur personality. Made a study of the goalkeeping art and became a fine, and often brilliant, exponent in all its phases.

COLEMAN, John George ("Tim")
                    1907(1)
b Kettering 1881 ; d 20 November 1940.

Career: Kettering, Northampton Town cs 1901, Woolwich Arsenal May 1902, Everton February 1908, Sunderland cs 1910, Fulham May 1911, Nottingham Forest cs 1914, retired during 1914-18 War but was with Tunbridge Wells Rangers in September 1920

An inside-forward usually found on the right. His craft was designed to bring the best out of his team-mates and his ball control was deft.

COMMON, Alfred   1904-6(3)
b Sunderland 1880; d 3 April 1946.
Career: South Hylton Juniors, Jarrow 1897, Sunderland, Sheffield United November 1901, Sunderland cs 1904, Middlesbrough February 1905, Woolwich Arsenal cs 1910, Preston North End December 1912 to cs 1914 when he left football and went to live at Darlington. He was a licensee there for many yars including 11 years at Alma Hotel, Cockerton until his retirement in 1943.
Club Honours: Sheffield United —F.A. Cup winners 1902, Preston North End—Second Division Champions 1913
A jovial, loquacious character able to play equally well at centre and inside-forward. Possessed an aggressive and powerful style and was an ever-present threat to his opponents' goal.

COMPTON, Leslie Harry   1951(2)
b Woodford, 12 September 1912.
Career: Bell Lane School Hendon, Bell Lane Old Boys, Hampstead Town, Arsenal February 1932 retired July 1953 and was on Arsenal coaching staff until February 1956. He was a licensee for some time and is now a representative for a wine company. Also played cricket for Middlesex for a long spell helping to win the County Championship in 1947
Club Honours: Arsenal—F.L.

War Cup finalists 1941, F.L. South Cup winners 1943, F.L. Champions 1948, F.A. Cup winners 1950
Big strong pivot cool in demeanour and almost unbeatable in the air. Before the War had been an efficient deputy at back for both Male and Hapgood and he appeared in Wartime internationals at centre-forward.

CONLIN, James   1906(1)
b Durham 6 July 1881; d 23 June 1917.
Career: Capt. Colt's Rovers Cambuslang, Hibernian, Falkirk, Albion Rovers, Bradford City cs 1904, Manchester City cs 1906, Birmingham September 1911, Airdrieonians cs 1912. Killed in action whilst serving with 15th Highland Light Infantry in Flanders.
Club Honour: Manchester City— Second Division Champions 1910. Diminutive outside-left often roughly treated by opposing defenders. Was a born footballer, though, and a clever one whose expertise at centring led to many goals.

CONNELLY, John Michael
                          1960-6(20)
b St Helens, Lancs 18 July 1938.
Career: St Teresa's School St Helens, St Teresa's Old Boys, Southport juniors, St Helens Town, Burnley November 1956, Manchester United April 1964, Blackburn Rovers September 1966, Bury June 1970
Club Honours: Burnley—F.L. Champions 1960, F.A. Cup finalists 1962, Manchester United— F.L. Champions 1965
It is immaterial which flank this winger occupies, he being notably two-footed. Direct in style and always seeking to have a crack at goal.

COOK, Thomas Edwin Reed
1925(1)
b Cuckfield, Sussex 5 February
1901 ; d 15 January 1950.
Career: Brighton Municipal
School, Cuckfield, Brighton &
Hove Albion 1921 to cs 1929,
coached cricket in South Africa
1929-30, Northfleet September
1930, Bristol Rovers October 1931
retired cs 1933
Played cricket for Sussex from
1922-37 scoring 20,206 runs including 31 centuries. Went to
South Africa as a coach in Cape
Town in 1937 remaining there
serving with the South African
forces during the War. Returned
to England after the War and was
manager of Brighton & Hove
Albion 1946-7
An outstanding centre-forward
in Third Division football—as he
had to be to achieve full England
recognition. Efficient, constructive,
a sure shot and capable of inspiring his less able club colleagues.

COOPER, Norman Charles
1893(1)
b Norbiton, Surrey 12 July 1870 ;
d 30 July 1920.
Career: Brighton College (XI
1887-8-9 captain 1889) ; Jesus College Cambridge (Blue 1891-2-3
captain 1893) ; Corinthians 1891-
5; Old Brightonians ; Sussex.
Played cricket for Cambridge University (no blue) and Sussex on
occasion 1888-93
Neat, stylish wing-half, clever at
timing his tackles and shrewd in
passing to unmarked colleagues.

COOPER, Thomas   1928-35(15)
b Fenton, Staffs 1904 ; d 25 June
1940.
Career: Trentham, Port Vale
August 1924, Derby County
March 1926, Liverpool December
1934. Killed in a motor cycle accident.
Magnificently accurate tackling
distinguished his displays at right-
back and, although his kicking

was strong, he was said by a
writer in 1929 to feed his forwards
as well as a half-back.

COOPER, Terence   1969-72(19)
b Castelford, Yorks 12 July 1945.
Career: Brotherton School, Ferry-
bridge Amateurs (Wolverhampton
Wanderers trial 1961), Leeds
United apprentice May 1961 professional July 1962
Club Honours: Leeds United—
Fairs Cup finalists 1967, winners
1968, 71. F.L. Cup winners 1968,
F.L. Champions 1969, F.A. Cup
finalists 1970
Frequently seems to be more a
forward than a left-back, dribbling
through with great skill. This is
not surprising as he served his
apprenticeship on the left wing
and has the speed to get back
smartly to a defensive position if
necessary.

COPPING, Wilfred   1933-9(20)
b Barnsley, 17 August 1909.
Career: Houghton Council School,
Dearne Valley Old Boys, Middle-
cliffe Rovers, Leeds United 1930,
Arsenal June 1934, Leeds United
March 1939, retired during the
War, coached in Belgium 1945-6,
Southend United trainer cs 1946,
Bristol City trainer July 1954,
Coventry City trainer November
1956 to May 1959
Club Honours: Arsenal—F.L.
Champions 1935, 8, F.A. Cup win-
ners 1936
Left-half of grim mien famed for
his hard tackling. Gave his for-
wards splendid service and was a
full ninety minutes player.

CORBETT, Bertie Oswald   1901(1)
b Thame, Oxon 13 May 1875 ; d
30 November 1967.
Career: Thame Grammar School;
Oriel College Oxford (Blue 1896-
7); Corinthians 1897-1906 (secretary 1902-4); Reading; Slough:
Cricket once for Derbyshire in
1910. Editor of " Annals of the

Corinthian Football Club " published in 1906. A schoolmaster he had a spell at Brighton College and then taught in Derbyshire before becoming proprietor of a preparatory school in Dorset. Brother of Reginald

Extremely fast outside-left who played in the typical Corinthian attacking style. His expert dribbling was enhanced by a fine natural swerve.

CORBETT, Reginald   1903(1)
b Thame, Oxon 1879 ; d 2 September 1967.
Career: Malvern College (XI 1898); Old Malvernians; Corinthians 1902-5 : A schoolmaster at first in Derbyshire and later for many years in Dorset like his brother
Club Honour: Old Malvernians —F.A. Amateur Cup winners 1902
Played inside or outside-left, being best known in the latter berth. A little erratic he was capable of turning in a magnificent performance and had a good goal-scoring record.

CORBETT, Walter S.   1908(3)
b Birmingham.
Career: King Edward Grammar School Birmingham, Asbury Richmond, Bournbrook, Aston Villa, Birmingham cs 1907 to 1911, Queens Park Rangers once in September 1907, Wellington Town April 1909 : 18 England amateur international appearances 1907-11
In the years leading up to the 1914-18 War was one of the best amateurs. He played at full-back, showing infinite resource and splendid speed.

COTTERILL, George Huth
1891-3(4)
b Brighton 4 April 1868; d 1 October 1950.
Career: Brighton College (XI 1882-6 captain 1884-6); Trinity College Cambridge (Blue 1888-9-

90-1 captain 1890); Old Brightonians; Weybridge; Burgess Hill; Surrey; Sussex; Corinthians 1887-98 : Played cricket for Cambridge University (no blue) and Sussex (from 1886-90) and rugby for Richmond and Surrey
A great centre-forward of immense physique—he was over 6 ft 3 in in height. A strong, astute dribbler and a good shot who combined well with his fellow attackers.

COTTLE, Joseph Richard 1909(1)
b Bedminster 1886; d 3 February 1958.
Career: Eclipse, Dolphin F.C. (Bristol), Bristol City cs 1904, retired cs 1911. After retirement was a licensee in Bristol until his death
Club Honours: Bristol City— Second Division Champions 1906, F.A. Cup finalists 1909
A driving, dashing left-back. He knew no fear and no defender in his time played with more gusto.

COWAN, Samuel   1926-31(3)
b Chesterfield 10 May 1901; d 4 October 1964.
Career: Ardwick Juniors, Bullcroft Colliery, Denaby United, Doncaster Rovers cs 1923, Manchester City December 1924, Bradford City October 1935, Mossley July 1937, Brighton & Hove Albion coach June 1938, Manchester City manager November 1946 to June 1947. After leaving the game he was a physiotherapist in Brighton and masseur to the Sussex County Cricket Club and to Australian tour of M.C.C. in 1962-3 and other touring teams. Died whilst refereeing a Charity match at Haywards Heath
Club Honours: Manchester City —F.A. Cup finalists 1926, 33 winners 1934, Second Division Champions 1928
Hefty pivot who was happiest in an attacking role. For much of

his career a club captain, in which position the qualities of resource and enthusiasm were given full scope.

COWELL, Arthur 1910(1)
b Blackburn 1886; d 12 February 1959.
Career: Blackburn St Peters (a Sunday school team), Nelson, Blackburn Rovers May 1905 retired cs 1920, trainer circa 1920 to May 1937, Wrexham trainer cs 1937, team manager August 1938 to early 1939 following which he was a newsagent at Kirkham and Darwen. Cousin of A. E. Houlker.
Club Honours: Blackburn Rovers —F.L. Champions 1912 and 1914
At left-back an excellent foil to the celebrated Crompton. A lack of inches was more than discounted by his persistence, polish, judgment and the ability to manoeuvre in the smallest space.

COX, John 1901-3(3)
b Blackpool 1877; d
Career: South Shore Standard, South Shore, Blackpool cs 1897, Liverpool early 1898, Blackpool player manager cs 1909 retired cs 1911
Club Honours: Liverpool—F.L. Champions 1901 and 1906, Second Division Champions 1905
Mercurial outside-left, fast and able to centre in splendid style when in the mood. Unfortunately liked to beat an opponent twice to the detriment of teamwork.

COX, John Davies 1892(1)
b Spondon, Derbyshire circa 1870; d
Career: Spondon, Long Eaton Rangers, Derby County cs 1891 to 1900
Club Honours: Derby County— F.A. Cup finalists 1898 and 1899.
From his position of right-half revealed skill in giving the ball to his forwards at the most advantageous moment.

CRABTREE, James William
1894-1902(14)
b Burnley 23 December 1871; d 18 June 1908.
Career: Burnley Royal Swifts 1885, Burnley reserves, Rossendale cs 1890, Heywood Central cs 1891, Burnley cs 1892, Aston Villa August 1895, Plymouth Argyle for a short spell from January 1904
Club Honours: Aston Villa—F.L. Champions 1896-7-9-1900, F.A. Cup winners 1897
Naturally gifted, versatile player he appeared mainly at left-half with Aston Villa at the peak of his career. His pattern-weaving could be overdone but, for all that, he was a master. Reputed to be very sensitive to criticism.

CRAWFORD, John F. 1931(1)
b South Shields.
Career: Jarrow Celtic, Palmers F.C. (Jarrow), Hull City March 1920, Chelsea May 1923, Queens Park Rangers May 1934 retired cs 1937 and became Queens Park Rangers coach. Worked in a factory in Essex during the War and remained there after the War and was part time coach of Maldon Town
After over a decade in the first class game at outside-right became an outside-left to accommodate Alex Jackson and received his only cap there. A diminutive winger, full of tricks and skilled at middling the ball.

CRAWFORD, Raymond 1962(2)
b Portsmouth 13 July 1936.
Career: Portsmouth juniors, Portsmouth amateur June 1954, professional December 1954, Ipswich Town September 1958, Wolverhampton Wanderers September 1963, West Bromwich Albion February 1965, Ipswich Town March 1966, Charlton Athletic March 1969 to October 1969, Kettering Town later October 1969, Colchester United June

1970, Durban City August 1971. Returned to U.K. October 1971 and signed on a month's trial for Brighton & Hove Albion November 1971, now club coach
Club Honours: Ipswich Town—F.L. Champions 1962, Second Division Champions 1961 and 1968
In this case zest for the game has been carried to the veteran stage. Earned a reputation as a prolific scoring, thrustful, opportunist centre-forward, later appearing at inside-right with his opportunism undiminished.

CRAWSHAW, Thomas Henry
                    1895-1904 (10)
b Sheffield 1872; d 25 November 1960.
Career: Park Grange, Attercliffe, Heywood Central for one season, Sheffield Wednesday 1894, Chesterfield cs 1908 later secretary of Glossop briefly just before the 1914-18 War. After the First War was a licensee in Sheffield
Club Honours: Sheffield Wednesday—F.A. Cup winners 1896, 1907, Second Division Champions 1900, F.L. Champions 1903 and 1904
In his prime the best centre-half in the country. A thoroughly hard worker, clever in heading and tackling, and unselfish to a marked degree.

CRAYSTON, William John
                    1936-8(8)
b Grange-over-Sands, Lancs 9 October 1910.
Career: Barrow Schools football, Ulverston Town, Barrow 1928, Bradford cs 1930, Arsenal May 1934 retired injury 1943 becoming first assistant manager then team manager from November 1956 to May 1958, Doncaster Rovers manager June 1958, secretary manager March 1959 until June 1961. After leaving the game he went into business in Birmingham

Club Honours: Arsenal—F.L. Champions 1935, 8, F.A. Cup winners 1936, F.L. War Cup finalists 1941, F.L. South Cup winners 1943
Graceful and methodical right-half whose height enabled him to dominate in the air. He could throw a ball a prodigious length and, at Barrow and Bradford, had experience at centre-half.

CREEK, Frederick Norman Smith
                    1923(1)
b 12 January 1898.
Career: Darlington Grammar School (Capt. of XI); Trinity College Cambridge (Blue 1920 and 1922 unfit 1921); Corinthians from 1920; Darlington as an amateur early 1922; 5 England amateur international appearances 1922-32. Played cricket for Wiltshire. Master at Dauntsey's School for many years until December 1953 when he joined the F.A. Staff retiring in October 1963. Author of " A History of the Corinthian Football Club " published in 1933. Won M.C. whilst serving with the Royal Flying Corps in 1914-18 War and M.B.E. in 1943.
His slight frame received rough treatment at centre-forward and he moved to inside-right. In both positions he showed a degree of keenness and penetration. A prolific goal scorer.

CRESSWELL, Warneford 1921-30(7)
b South Shields 5 November 1894.
Career: Stanhope Road School South Shields (England v Wales schools 1911), South Shields junior football, Hearts and Hibernian in Scottish League football during the first War, South Shields cs 1919, Sunderland March 1922, Everton February 1927, Port Vale coach May 1936 later manager until cs 1937, Northampton Town manager April 1937 to September 1939. After the War a licensee
Club Honours: Everton—F.L.

Champions 1928 and 1932, F.A. Cup winners 1933, Second Division Champions 1931

Appeared completely unhurried because of his innate sense of positioning and anticipation. Kicked an immaculate length, placing the ball perfectly. On either flank a full-back of stature.

CROMPTON, Robert 1902-14(41)
b Blackburn 26 September 1879; d 16 March 1941.
Career: Moss Street School Blackburn, Rose & Thistle, Blackburn Trinity, Blackburn Rovers September 1896 retired May 1920, team manager December 1926 to February 1931, director June 1921 to March 1931 Bournemouth & Boscombe Athletic manager June 1935 to February 1936, Blackburn Rovers honorary manager from April 1938 to his death. Director of a contracting firm in Blackburn. Club Honours: Blackburn Rovers —F.L. Champions 1912 and 1914
One of the greatest names in the annals of English international football. A superbly equipped right-back, robust but scrupulously fair and notably quick in recovery.

CROOKS, Samuel D. 1930-7(26)
b Bearpark, Co. Durham 16 January 1909.
Career: Bearpark Colliery, Brandon Juniors, Tow Law Town, Durham City mid 1926-7, Derby County April 1927 retired cs 1947 and became Club coach until August 1949. Retford Town player manager December 1949, Shrewsbury Town player manager May 1950 until June 1954. On leaving Shrewsbury he returned to his Derby sports outfitting business and managed in turn, Gresley Rovers (two spells), Burton Albion and Heanor Town. From 1960 until May 1967 was Derby County's chief scout.
Sprightly, long-serving right-winger. Direct in style, skilful and

quick with the ability to centre perfectly.

CROWE, Christopher 1963(1)
b Newcastle-upon-Tyne 11 June 1939.
Career: Edinburgh Schools (Scotland v Wales and England Schools 1954), Edinburgh juniors, Leeds United amateur October 1954 professional June 1956 (England Youth international 1956), Blackburn Rovers March 1960, Wolverhampton Wanderers January 1962, Nottingham Forest August 1964, Bristol City January 1967, Auburn (Sydney) May 1969, Walsall September 1969. Retired cs 1970 and became a licensee in Leeds and later a newsagent in Bristol. Came out of retirement to join Bath City in February 1971
One of those adroit, if lightly built, forwards who achieve prominence in every age. Crowe played in both right wing positions, his thoughtful passing resulting in many goals.

CUGGY, Francis 1913-14(2)
b Walker, Northumberland 1889; d 27 March 1965.
Career: Willington Athletic, Sunderland 1909, Wallsend as player manager cs 1921 to cs 1922. Later coach in Spain for some years and was then a shipyard worker
Club Honours: Sunderland—F.A. Cup finalists and F.L.Champions 1913
At right-half the apex of the celebrated Sunderland triangle of Cuggy, Mordue and Buchan. A tireless player always unruffled and precise without any hint of robustness.

CULLIS, Stanley 1938-9(12)
b Ellesmere Port 25 October 1915.
Career: Cambridge Road School Ellesmere Port, Ellesmere Port Wednesday, Wolverhampton Wanderers February 1934, assistant manager August 1947, manager June 1948 to September 1964,

Birmingham City manager December 1965 to March 1970. After leaving the game he worked for a travel agency
Club Honour: Wolverhampton Wanderers—F.A. Cup finalists 1939
Unquestionably among the greatest of England centre-halves. Fine in defence, supreme in the air and master of the through pass.

CUNLIFFE, Arthur   1933(2)
b Blackrod, Lancs 5 February 1909.
Career: Adlington, Chorley 1927, Blackburn Rovers early 1928, Aston Villa May 1933, Middlesbrough December 1935, Burnley April 1937, Hull City June 1938, Rochdale cs 1946, trainer July 1947, Bournemouth & Boscombe Athletic trainer July 1950. Cousin of J.N.
Early regarded as a right-winger but made his reputation at outside-left. Astonishingly fast, able to control and manoeuvre the ball at high speed and in a small space and a regular scorer.

CUNLIFFE, Daniel   1900(1)
b Bolton 1875; d 28 December 1937.
Career: Little Lever, Middleton Borough, Oldham County, Liverpool cs 1897, New Brighton Tower cs 1898, Portsmouth cs 1899, New Brighton Tower cs 1900, Portsmouth cs 1901, New Brompton May 1906, Millwall Athletic cs 1907, Heywood September 1909 to April 1912, Rochdale cs 1912 retired during the War.
Club Honour: Portsmouth— Southern League Champions 1902
Inside-right of stocky, sturdy build, hard to knock off the ball. Admirably persistent and a frequent scorer.

CUNLIFFE, James Nathaniel
    1936(1)
b Blackrod, Lancs.

Career: Adlington, Everton May 1930, Rochdale September 1946 briefly.
Usually found in the forefront of an attack where he was a dangerous inside-forward because of quickness in going through. Striking power gave him a good goal tally.

CURREY, Edward Samuel 1890(2)
b 28 January 1868; d 12 March 1920.
Career: Charterhouse School (XI 1885-6); Magdalen College, Oxford (Blue 1888-9-90 captain 1890); Old Carthusians; Corinthians 1888-91; Sussex. Admitted a solicitor 1895 and practised in London
Performed at centre or inside-forward with equal facility—indeed he led the attack in one of his England appearances and was at inside-right in the other. Like many Carthusian forwards he was aggressive and had a real attacking flair.

CURRIE, Anthony William 1972(1)
b Edgware, Middlesex 1st January 1950.
Career: Hendon Schools, Watford amateur September 1965, apprentice February 1966, full professional May 1967, Sheffield United February 1968 (England Youth international 1968)
A left wing forward playing inside for his club. He is a spirited yet composed player with good ball control.

CURSHAM, Arthur William
    1876-83(6)
b Wilford, Notts 14 March 1853; d 24 December 1884.
Career: Oakham School, Notts County from 1875; Sheffield F.C.; Nottingham Law Club. Played cricket for Notts (1876-8) and Derbyshire (1879-80). A Colliery proprietor he emigrated to Florida in 1884 and died there shortly

afterwards of yellow fever. Brother of H. A. Cursham. An energetic outside-right who was adroit and swift also.

CURSHAM, Henry Alfred 1880-4(8)
b Wilford, Notts 27 November 1859; d 6 August 1941.
Career: Repton School; Notts County; Corinthians 1882-6 (a member of the original committee) Grantham; Thursday Wanderers (Sheffield); retired from playing 1886. Played cricket once for Notts in 1880 and once in 1904. An insurance broker he was associated with the Union Insurance Society from 1889 to 1939.
A winger who built up the reputation of being a very good dribbler.

DAFT, Harry Butler 1889-92(5)
b Radcliffe-on-Trent, Notts 5 April 1866; d 12 January 1945.
Career: Trent College; Notts County; Nottingham Forest; Newark; Corinthians 1887-90. F.A. Committee 1884-5. Played cricket for Notts 1885-99 helping to win the County Championship 1885-6-9. Scored 4,415 runs in his first class career and was later connected with Oxford University cricket up to 1914
Club Honours: Notts County— F.A. Cup finalists 1891, winners 1894
Apt to be inconsistent but nonetheless a very fast outside-left, brilliant on occasion. Specialised in goal-creating passes.

DANKS, Thomas 1885(1)
b 1863; d 27 April 1908.
Career: Nottingham Forest December 1882 to February 1889. Also had spells with Notts County late 1884 and Burslem Port Vale September 1888. An ironmonger in Nottingham
In club games an excellent, industrious and unselfish inside-right, he was somewhat outclassed in his sole international match.

DAVENPORT, J. Kenneth 1885-90(2)
b Bolton 1863; d
Career: Gilnow Rangers (Bolton), Bolton Wanderers 1883, Southport Central mid 1892-3
Played in a variety of positions for Bolton Wanderers and proved an admirable servant. Usually to be found in the forward line and early in his career won the reputation of being one of the fastest players in the North.

DAVIS, George 1904(2)
b Alfreton 1881.
Career: Alfreton, Derby County to 1908, Calgary Hillhurst F.C. (Canada). In 1954 was still living in Canada but in 1967 was reported to be living in retirement in the Nottingham district.
Club Honours: Derby County— F.A. Cup finalists 1903, Calgary Hillhurst—Canadian Cup winners 1922
Came to the selectors' notice when partnering G. H. Richards, his virile, progressive play at outside-left then being at its zenith. Was a model player and trained diligently although unlucky with injuries.

DAVIS, Harry 1903(3)
b Barnsley.
Career: Barnsley, Sheffield Wednesday January 1900, broke a leg during 1906-7 season and rarely played again. Became assistant trainer
Club Honours Sheffield Wednesday—Second Division Champions 1900, F.L. Champions 1903 and 1904
The smallest player in the First Division of his day, standing only 5 foot 4 inches. He was extremely solid, however, at around 12 stones and brought to his play at outside-right a lethal shot and speed in short bursts.

DAVISON, John Edward 1922(1)
b Gateshead 2 September 1887.

Career: Gateshead St Chads, Sheffield Wednesday April 1908 retired cs 1926, Mansfield Town player manager June 1926, Chesterfield manager December 1927, Sheffield United manager June 1932, Chesterfield manager August 1952 retired May 1958 and became chief scout.

Considered to be the shortest man ever to keep goal for England and this made his brilliant saves appear even more brilliant. Both acrobatic and plucky, Davison had greater muscular strength than was imagined.

DAWSON, Jeremiah   1922(2)
b Holme near Burnley, Lancs 18 March 1888; d August 1970.
Career: Portsmouth Rovers (Todmorden), Holme, Burnley February 1907, retired cs 1929
Club Honours: Burnley—F.L. Champions 1921. Missed the 1914 F.A. Cup Final owing to injury
A great goalkeeper unlucky in that his playing days largely coincided with those of Sam Hardy. An impeccable performer over a generation his judgment being remarkably unfaltering.

DAY, Samuel Hulme   1906(3)
b Peckham 29 December 1878 ; d 20 February 1950.
Career: Malvern College (XI 1896-7-8 captain 1898); Queens College Cambridge (Blue 1901); Corinthians 1902-12 (secretary for a short spell); Old Malvernians; England amateurs v France 1907. Had a notable cricket career playing for Kent from 1897 to 1919 scoring a century in his first first class match in 1897 whilst still at school. A Cambridge Blue in 1899-1900-1-2 he scored 117 not out v Oxford in the latter year and was captain in 1901. Scored 7,722 runs in first class cricket including 7 centuries. A schoolmaster at Westminster School 1902-13 thence Headmaster of Heatherdown Preparatory School, Ascot

Club Honour: Old Malvernians—F.A. Amateur Cup winners 1902
An inside-forward in the grand Corinthian tradition, quick moving and possessor of a sure shot. His comparative lightness was offset by neatness and speed.

DEAN, William Ralph (" Dixie ")
                              1927-33(16)
b Birkenhead 22 January 1907.
Career: Laird Street School Birkenhead, Moreton Bible Class, Heswall, Pensby United, Tranmere Rovers November 1923, Everton March 1925, Notts County March 1938, Sligo Rovers January 1939, Hurst cs 1939, retired during the War. Became a licensee in Chester but had to give up in 1962 owing to ill-health thence worked for Littlewood Pools in Liverpool until his retirement in January 1972
Club Honours: Everton—F.L. Champions 1928 and 1932, Second Division Champions 1931, F.A. Cup winners 1933, Sligo Rovers—F.A. of Ireland Cup finalists 1939
A football immortal. A centreforward with unsurpassed goalscoring capability—strong, dashing, a powerful shot and, above all, one of the greatest exponents of headwork the game has seen. Scored 379 goals in Football League matches including 60 in 1928 which is still the record.

DEELEY, Norman Victor 1959(2)
b Wednesbury, Staffs 30 November 1933.
Career: Holyhead Road School Wednesbury (England Schools v Wales 1948), Wolverhampton Wanderers amateur cs 1948 professional November 1950, Leyton Orient February 1962, Worcester City July 1964, Bromsgrove Rovers cs 1967, Darlaston August 1971
Club Honours: Wolverhampton Wanderers—F.L. Champions 1958 and 1959, F.A. Cup winners 1960
His innate footballing skill triumphantly overcame the disadvan-

tage of being very small. Had success at right-half and inside-forward before settling at outside-right and in each berth was shrewd and plucky.

DEVEY, John Henry George
1892-4(2)
b Birmingham 26 December 1866; d 13 October 1940.
Career: Excelsior, Aston Unity, Mitchells St George (later known as Birmingham St George), Aston Villa March 1891 to April 1902. Appointed a director of Aston Villa later in 1902 resigning in September 1934. A sports outfitter in Lozells, he played cricket for Warwickshire from 1888-1907 scoring over 6,500 runs including 8 centuries
Club Honours: Aston Villa—F.L. Champions 1894-6-7-9-1900, F.A. Cup winners 1895, 7, finalists 1892
An inside-right or centre-forward who relied on skill rather than strength. Had the trick of suddenly pivoting on his heel and shooting.

DEWHURST, Frederick 1886-9(9)
b Preston 1863; d 21 April 1895.
Career: Preston junior football; Preston North End from 1882; Corinthians 1886-9. A schoolmaster at Preston Catholic Grammar School
Club Honours Preston North End —F.A. Cup finalists 1888, F.L. Champions and F.A. Cup winners 1889
Inside-forward commendable in diligence, footwork and the art of passing.

DEWHURST, Gerald Powys
1895(1)
b London 14 February 1872; d 29 March 1956.
Career: Repton School (XI 1889-90); Trinity College, Cambridge (Blue 1892-3-4); Liverpool Ramblers; Corinthians 1892-5. By profession a cotton merchant in

H

Liverpool
Liable to keep the ball too long at times otherwise an excellent inside-forward. Had a strong shot and was fast for a man of heavy build.

DICKINSON, James William
1949-57(48)
b Alton, Hants 24 April 1925.
Career: Alton Secondary Modern School, Alton Youth Club, Portsmouth January 1944 retired cs 1965 and became Public Relations Officer and Scout until July 1968 when he was appointed as the Club secretary. Awarded M.B.E. June 1964. Holder of the record number of Football League appearances—764 all for one club
Club Honours: Portsmouth—F.L. Champions 1949 and 1950, Third Division Champions 1962
The club servant par excellence whose quiet, super efficient skills were often called upon by his country too. He mostly appeared at left-half although he played for England on the other flank and for Portsmouth latterly at centre-half and left-back.

DIMMOCK, James Henry 1921-6(3)
b Edmonton 5 December 1900.
Career: Montague Road School Edmonton, Park Avenue, Gothic Works, Clapton Orient amateur during 1914-18, Edmonton Ramblers, Tottenham Hotspur May 1919, Thames August 1931, Clapton Orient September 1932, Ashford March 1934 retired cs 1934. After his retirement from the game was in the road haulage business
Club Honours Tottenham Hotspur—Second Division Champions 1920, F.A. Cup winners 1921
Gifted outside-left with a physique to withstand a heavy charge. His chief assets were elusiveness and brilliant ball control.

DITCHBURN, Edwin George
                        1949-57(6)
b Gillingham, Kent 24 October
1921.
Career: Lawn Road School Northfleet, Northfleet Paper Mills,
Northfleet 1938, Tottenham Hotspur early 1939, Romford April
1959, player manager July 1959,
resigned as manager March 1962
but remained as a player until cs
1965, Brentwood August 1965.
Has been a sports outfitter in
Romford for some years
Club Honours Tottenham Hotspur—Second Division Champions
1950, F.L. Champions 1951
Not only a tremendously acrobatic
goalkeeper but also a remarkably
consistent one, once having a run
of 247 consecutive League appearances. His speciality saves were
from high balls directed to the
top corner.

DIX, Ronald W.   **1939(1)**
b Bristol 5 September 1912.
Career: South Central School
Bristol (England Schools v Wales
and Scotland 1927), Bristol Rovers
1927, Blackburn Rovers May
1932, Aston Villa May 1933,
Derby County February 1937,
Tottenham Hotspur June 1939,
Reading November 1947 retired
cs 1949
Club Honours: Blackpool—F.L.
North Cup winners 1943, finalists
1944 whilst guesting for that Club
Earned a mammoth reputation as
a schoolboy and developed subsequently into a stocky, cleverly
constructive inside-forward of
high consistency.

DIXON, John Auger   1885(1)
b Grantham, Lincs 27 May 1861 ;
d 8 June 1931.
Career: Grantham Grammar
School; Nottingham High School;
Chigwell School; Notts County
(from mid 1884-5) ; Corinthians.

Played cricket for Notts from
1882-1905 (captain from 1889-99)
scoring 9,544 runs in first class
cricket including 11 centuries. A
Test selector in 1905. A director
of Dixon & Parke Ltd, manufac-
turing clothiers in Nottingham.
Left-wing forward and an earnest
and hard worker throughout any
game.

DOBSON, Alfred Thomas Carrick
                         1882-4(4)
b 1859 ; d 22 October 1932.
Career: Downside School ; Notts
County ; Corinthians. Brother of
C. F. Dobson he was connected
with the family fabric business in
Nottingham
Energetic, plucky and safe full-
back with a useful tackle handi-
capped a little by poor eyesight.

DOBSON, Charles Frederick
                          1886(1)
b Basford, Notts 1862 ; d 18 May
1939.
Career: Notts County, Corinthians 1885-6. Like his brother,
A. T. C., he was connected with
the family fabric business
Could be uncertain at times but
generally a handy half-back giving good service to his forwards.

DOGGART, Alexander Graham
                          1924(1)
b Bishop Auckland 2 June 1897 ;
d 7 June 1963 after collapsing at
the F.A. Annual meeting on that
day.
Career: Darlington Grammar
School ; Bishop's Stortford School
(XI 1912-16) ; Kings College Cambridge (Blue 1921-2) ; Corinthians
from 1921 ; Darlington ; Bishop
Auckland. 4 England amateur
inetrnational appearances between
1921-9. F.A. Council 1932-50,
Vice President 1950-61 thence
Chairman from 5 May 1961 after
acting for a year during Mr
Arthur Drewery's illness. Cricket
Blue 1921-2 and also played for

Durham County and Middlesex, served on the M.C.C. Committee and the Sussex County Committee at various times. A Chartered Accountant by profession

Close dribbling inside-left with excellent ball control. Was consistently on target with lethal left foot shooting, so much so he easily heads the Corinthian goal-scoring list for all time. He also scored 5 goals in his two Football League appearances for Darlington in April 1922.

DORRELL, Arthur Reginald
1925-6(4)
b Small Heath, Birmingham 30 March 1898; d 14 September 1942.
Career: Belper Road School Leicester, Carey Hall F.C. (Leicester), Army service, Aston Villa May 1919, Port Vale June 1931 retired cs 1932
Club Honours: Aston Villa—F.A. Cup winners 1920, finalists 1924
Fast and often brilliant outside-left who formed a famous wing with Billy Walker. Among the most unemotional of players and ice-cool in any situation.

DOUGLAS, Bryan   1958-63(36)
b Blackburn 1935.
Career: St Bartholomew's and Blakey Moor Secondary Modern Schools Blackburn, Lower Darwen Youth Club, Blackburn Rovers April 1952, Great Harwood June 1969
Club Honour: Blackburn Rovers —F.A. Cup finalists 1960
No finer ball artist has emerged in the post-war period. Douglas was a great little forward (outside-right and inside-forward) unorthodox in his wanderings.

DOWNS, Richard W.   1921(1)
b Midridge, Co. Durham 1886; d 24 March 1949.
Career: Crook, Shildon Athletic, Barnsley cs 1908, Everton March 1920, Brighton & Hove Albion August 1924 retired injury mid

1924-5. After his retirement as a player he was for some years a coach in Europe
Club Honours: Barnsley—F.A. Cup finalists 1910, winners 1912
Something of a cartoonist's delight with his bowed, heavily muscled legs and he had some unusual traits in his play at right-back. These included the sliding tackle—of which he was an early practitioner—fly-kick volleys and the flying tackle.

DRAKE, Edward Joseph 1935-8(5)
b Southampton 16 August 1912
Career: Southampton Schools, Winchester City, Southampton November 1931, Arsenal March 1934 retired injury 1945. Manager of Hendon for a time, Reading manager June 1947, Chelsea manager June 1952 to September 1961 thence a bookmaker until becoming Barcelona assistant manager from January to June 1970, thence a commercial salesman in London. Played cricket for Hampshire 1931-6
Club Honours: Arsenal—F.L. Champions 1935, 8, F.A. Cup winners 1936, F.L. War Cup finalists 1941, F.L. South Cup winners 1943
Centre-forwards do not come any braver than Drake whose courage was a byword. He was speedy as well, had ball control and a sharp-shooter of the highest order. His most notable achievement was to score seven goals v Aston Villa for Arsenal on 14 December 1935 at Villa Park.

DUCAT, Andrew   1910-21(6)
b Brixton 16 February 1886; d 23 July 1942.
Career: Brewery Road School and Compton House School Southend, Westcliff Athletic, Southend Athletic, Woolwich Arsenal February 1905, Aston Villa June 1912, Fulham May 1921 retired cs 1924. Fulham

manager May 1924 to May 1926. Was then reinstated as an amateur and signed for Casuals cs 1926. Sports outfitter in Birmingham during his Aston Villa days. Cricket for Surrey 1906-31 and one Test appearance v Australia in 1921. Scored over 23,000 runs in first class cricket including 52 centuries. After leaving football management in addition to his county cricket career he coached cricket at Eton and was a part time journalist and later in life a licensee. Died whilst batting in a cricket match at Lords.
Club Honour: Aston Villa—F.A. Cup winners 1920
From centre-forward moved to right-half where he became an outstanding performer of the unflurried academic type. A master of positional play and especially good in the air.

DUNN, Arthur Tempest Blakiston
1883-92(4)
b Whitby, Yorks 12 August 1860; d 20 February 1902.
Career: Eton College; Trinity College, Cambridge (Blue 1883-4); Old Etonians; Granta; Corinthians 1886-90; Cambridgeshire. Schoolmaster by profession and Founder of Ludgrove School in 1892
Club Honours: Old Etonians— F.A. Cup winners 1882, finalists 1883
Remarkably quick centre-forward with an ability for dribbling and marksmanship. His last international appearance in 1892 was made at right-back.

EARLE, Stanley George J.
1924-8(2)
b Stratford, East London 6 September 1897.
Career: Goodwin Road School West Ham (England v Wales Schools 1912), Clapton (England amateur v Ireland 1923 and 1924). Signed amateur forms for Arsenal for which club he made Football

League appearances in 1922-3-4, West Ham United August 1924, Clapton Orient May 1932 retired cs 1933. Later had spells as Walthamstow Avenue coach and Leyton manager
Club Honour: Clapton—F.A. Amateur Cup winners 1924
Successfully made the transition from top amateur to First Division football. A well-built insideright playing an attractive game of the keen attacking Corinthian type.

EASTHAM, George Edward
1963-6(19)
b Blackpool 23 September 1936.
Career: Ards amateur, professional May 1956, Newcastle United May 1956, Arsenal November 1960, Stoke City August 1966, Hellenic F.C. of Cape Town as player manager February to October 1971, when he returned to Stoke City
Club Honour: Stoke City—F.L. Cup winners 1972
A real chip off the old block, George junior having many footballing affinities with his father, he also being a graceful ball playing inside-forward and a provider. In addition he is a stickler when in possession.

EASTHAM, George Richard
1935(1)
b Blackpool 13 September 1914.
Career: Cambridge Juniors (Blackpool), South Shore Wednesday, Bolton Wanderers 1932, Brentford June 1937, Blackpool November 1938, Swansea Town August 1947, Rochdale June 1948, Lincoln City December 1948, Hyde United cs 1950, Ards player manager July 1953 retiring as a player 1955 but continuing as manager until October 1958, Accrington Stanley manager October 1958 to June 1959, Distillery manager June 1959 to March 1964, Ards manager late 1964 to March 1970. Later on Stoke City scouting staff, but late

1971 went to South Africa to manage Hellenic F.C.

Crafty inside-forward and a past-master of the close dribble and the delayed pass. Not a prolific scorer himself he laid on chances and schemed for others.

ECKERSLEY, William 1950-4(17)
b Southport 16 July 1926.
Career: High Park (Southport), Blackburn Rovers November 1947 retired injury February 1961. He is now a private car driver in Blackburn

Though of slight build a grand left-back. He was always calm, excelling in tackling and clearance placing.

EDWARDS, Duncan 1955-8(18)
b Dudley 1 October 1936; d 21 February 1958 as a result of injuries sustained in the Munich air disaster.
Career: Wolverhampton Street Secondary Modern School Dudley (England Schools v Ireland 1950 v Wales (2) Scotland Ireland 1951 v Scotland (2) Wales Eire 1952), Manchester United amateur May 1952 professional October 1953 (England Youth international 1955)

Club Honours: Manchester United —F.A. Youth Cup winners 1953-4-5, F.L. Champions 1956 and 1957, F.A. Cup finalists 1957

The game has never sustained a greater individual loss than was caused by Duncan Edwards' untimely end. Even so at 21 he had made an indelible impression as the complete left-half, brave, immensely skilled in the use and distribution of the ball and astonishingly mature. There is no knowing what pinnacle this great player would have reached. There are two stained glass windows to his memory in St Francis Church, Dudley.

EDWARDS, John Hawley 1874(1)
b 1850; d 14 January 1893.
Career: Shropshire Wanderers; Wanderers; Shrewsbury. A Welshman he played as a late substitute for J. G. Wylie v Scotland in 1874. He later played for Wales v Scotland in 1876 and was Treasurer of the F.A. of Wales on its formation in 1876. Admitted a solicitor in September 1871, he was Clerk to the Shrewsbury magistrates for 19 years up to his death

Club Honour: Wanderers—F.A. Cup winners 1876

An industrious, unselfish forward. Could dribble strongly but apt to over-run the ball.

EDWARDS, Willis 1926-30(16)
b Newton, near Alfreton 28 April 1903.
Career: Newton Rangers, Chesterfield cs 1922, Leeds United March 1925, retired during the War and became Club trainer, team manager May 1947 to April 1948 thence reverting to trainer until June 1960

A right-half for the connoisseur and arguably the best man in the position between the Wars. Superb at trapping and distribution and a delight to watch.

ELLERINGTON, William 1949(2)
b Southampton 1923.
Career: Barnes School Sunderland, Sunderland Junior Technical School (England Schools v Scotland Wales and Ireland 1937), Fatfield Juniors (Sunderland amateur), Southampton amateur 1940, professional 1945 retired cs 1961. Continued to live in Southampton after his retirement and looked after Southampton's Colts team.

Not wholly dependent on height and weight, though these natural factors were useful to him at right-back. In addition he had solidity and proficiency in tackling and positioning.

ELLIOTT, George Washington
                            1913-20(3)
b Middlesbrough early 1889; d
27 November 1948.
Career: Middlesbrough High
School, Redcar Crusaders, South
Bank, Middlesbrough May 1909
retired August 1925. He was a
cargo superintendent in Middlesbrough Docks where his family
had been engaged in shipping for
generations
Cultured inside or centre-forward.
Was highly skilled in ball manipulation and his goal scoring record
was impressive.

ELLIOTT, William Henry 1952-3(5)
b Bradford 20 March 1925.
Career: Thornbury Boys and
Lapage Street Schools Bradford,
Bradford junior football, Bradford amateur 1939, professional
March 1942, Burnley August 1951,
Sunderland June 1953, Wisbech
Town July 1959, Libya National
coach October 1961 to 1963. Sheffield Wednesday scout 1963-4,
Coach to U.S. Forces in Germany
1964-6, Daring F.C. (Brussels)
trainer manager July 1966 to January 1968, Sunderland trainer
coach from January 1968
Attained prominence in the first
place as a brisk, penetrative, dangerous outside-left. Afterwards he
moved to left-half and left-back
in turn, where his crisp tackling
was invaluable.

EVANS, Robert Ernest   1911-12(4)
b Chester 21 November 1885.
Career: Saltley Ferry, Wrexham
cs 1905, Aston Villa early 1906,
Sheffield United mid 1908-9 retired during the 1914-18 War. Later
worked and played for Shell Mex,
Ellesmere Port.
Club Honour: Sheffield United—
F.A. Cup winners 1915
Unusually tall—approaching 6
foot—for an outside left. Covered
his wing with a long, raking stride
and was a noted shot. Prior to

playing for England he had played
10 times for Wales between 1906-
10 before it was discovered that
he was born on the England side
of the border.

EWER, Frederick Harold 1924-5(2)
b West Ham 30 September 1898;
d 27 January 1971.
Career: Casuals; Corinthians from
1923. 14 England amateur international appearances 1924-30.
Later a member of the Stock Exchange
Suffered many injuries but always
came up smiling. A wing-half full
of grit and determination who
never knew when he was beaten.

FAIRCLOUGH, Percy   1878(1)
b 1 February 1858 ; d 22 June
1947.
Career: Forest School (XI 1876-
7); Old Foresters; Corinthians;
Essex. Member of the Stock Exchange for 40 years with the firm
of Fairclough, Dodd and Jones.
Died as a result of a road accident
A forward possessing a powerful
if erratic kick and the knack of
charging well but was a shade
ponderous.

FAIRHURST, David Liddle 1934(1)
b Blyth, Northumberland 20 July
1907.
Career: New Delaval Villa, Blyth
Spartans, Walsall June 1927, Newcastle United March 1929 retired
May 1946. Birmingham City
trainer for a spell from July 1946
Club Honour: Newcastle United
—F.A. Cup winners 1932
Reliable and competent left-back
who nicely complemented the
better-known Jimmy Nelson at
Newcastle. He was heavy in build
and possessed a good kick.

FANTHAM, John   1962(1)
b Sheffield 6 February 1939.
Career: Doncaster schoolboy football, Sheffield Y.M.C.A., Sheffield

Wednesday amateur 1954 professional October 1956, Rotherham United October 1969, Macclesfield cs 1971

Club Honours: Sheffield Wednesday—Second Division Champions 1959, F.A. Cup finalists 1966

Foraging, penetrative, tenacious inside-forward. His fame as a goal snatcher rests on a capacity to be on the right spot at the right time.

FELTON, William 1925(1)
b Wardley Colliery, Co. Durham 1902.

Career: Wardley Colliery, Jarrow, Grimsby Town January 1921, Sheffield Wednesday January 1923, Manchester City March 1929, Tottenham Hotspur March 1932, Altrincham cs 1935

Club Honour: Sheffield Wednesday—Second Division Champions 1926

Lusty right-back quick in tackling and recovery. Made many appearances at left-back also.

FENTON, Michael 1938(1)
b South Bank, Yorks 30 October 1913.

Career: Stockton Schools, South Bank East End, Middlesbrough March 1933 retired cs 1951 and remained on the Club staff until cs 1966. Since then has been a newsagent in Stockton

Amazingly fast whether from a standing start or when in flight and equally effective at inside or centre-forward. Shot well with either foot and strong enough to withstand hard knocks.

FIELD, Edgar 1876-81(2)
b 29 July 1854 ; d 11 January 1934.

Career: Lancing College (XI 1870-1); Clapham Rovers; Reading; Berks and Bucks. A Chartered Accountant by profession

Club Honours: Clapham Rovers —F.A. Cup finalists 1879, winners 1880.

Robust full-back kicking strongly,

if rather erratically and charging to some effect. On the slow side.

FINNEY, Thomas 1947-59(76)
b Preston 5 April 1922.

Career: Deepdale Council and Modern Schools Preston, Holme Slack, Preston North End amateur 1937, professional January 1940 retired cs 1960. Came out of retirement to play in a European Cup match for Distillery v Benfica September 1963. Awarded O.B.E. June 1961 for his services to the game. Now head of a plumbing and electrical contracting business in Preston.

Club Honours: Preston North End—F.L. War Cup winners 1941, Second Division Champions 1951, F.A. Cup finalists 1954

A measure of his greatness was that the English selectors preferred him to Stanley Matthews on a number of occasions. Finney was an outside-right of genius slightly built but able to ride through a defence to smash home a shot. He also had substantial and successful runs on the left wing and at centre-forward.

FLEMING, Harold John
1909-14(11)
b Downton near Salisbury 30 April 1887 ; d 23 August 1955.

Career: Swindon junior football, Swindon Town October 1907 retired August 1924. Continued to live in Swindon until his death. Played cricket for Wiltshire on occasion

Club Honours: Swindon Town— Southern League Champions 1911 and 1914.

An unorthodox roaming player possessed of marvellous ball control and a masterly trick of suddenly changing direction. A great club servant and a very great inside-right indeed.

FLETCHER, Albert 1889-90(2)
b 1867; d

Career: Willenhall Pickwick, Wolverhampton Wanderers 1885,
retired owing to injury cs 1891
and became assistant trainer until
cs 1896 when he was appointed
first team trainer. Remained in
that capacity until his retirement
in cs 1920
Club Honour: Wolverhampton
Wanderers—F.A. Cup finalists
1889
Brought physical advantages to
bear in the carrying out of his
right-half duties and was a hard
worker. Rather marred his performance at times by rashness.

FLOWERS, Ronald   1955-66(49)
b Edlington near Doncaster 28
July 1934.
Career: Edlington Secondary
Modern School, Doncaster Rovers
juniors, Wath Wanderers, Wolverhampton Wanderers July 1952,
Northampton Town September
1967, player manager May 1968
resigned May 1969, Telford United
player coach July 1969 resigned
October 1971
Club Honours: Wolverhampton
Wanderers—F.L. Champions
1954-8-9, F.A. Cup winners 1960
An industrious wing-half who
preferred the attacking game
where he could indulge his hard
shooting. Tenacious in the tackle
and enormous in stamina.

FORMAN, Frank   1898-1903(9)
b Aston-on-Trent, Derbyshire
1875 ; d 4 December 1961.
Career: Aston-on-Trent, Beeston
Town, Derby County, Nottingham
Forest December 1894 retired cs
1905. Nottingham Forest committee 1903-61. After retirement was
engaged in business as a Building
Contractor in West Bridgford
with his brother-in-law, J. H.
Linacre. Brother of F. R. Forman
Club Honour: Nottingham Forest
—F.A. Cup winners 1898
A born leader whether at right or
centre-half whose generalship
and tactical know-how were of

the highest order. Calm and unflurried in the tightest of corners.

FORMAN, Frederick Ralph 1899(3)
b Aston-on-Trent 1874; d 14 June
1910.
Career: Beeston Town, Derby
County, Nottingham Forest cs
1894 to cs 1903, when he retired
from the game. A railway
draughtsman by profession
A player of some versatility—
half-back, inside-forward and outside-left—as well as competency.
A little lethargic on occasion.

FORREST, James Henry
                        1884-90(11)
b Blackburn 24 June 1864; d 30
December 1925.
Career: Imperial United, Witton
1880, King's Own Blackburn,
Blackburn Rovers January 1883
retired cs 1895 but joined Darwen
October 1895. Appointed a director of Blackburn Rovers 1906 remaining on the Board until his
death
Club Honours: Blackburn Rovers
—F.A. Cup winners 1884-5-6-90-1
being one of the three men to win
five Cup winners medals
Had no superior as a left-half in
the eighties. Rather light in build
but elusive and admirably precise
in his kicking. A great player.

FORT, John   1921(1)
b Leigh, Lancs 1889 ; d 23 November 1965.
Career: St Andrews Mission 1904,
Atherton July 1907, Exeter City
cs 1911, Millwall Athletic cs 1914,
retired cs 1930 and remained with
the Club as coach, trainer, scout
and groundsman at various times
only leaving shortly before his
death
Club Honour: Millwall—Third
Division South Champions 1928
Stocky right-back with excellent
positional sense and a formidable
tackle. A grand club man.

FOSTER, Reginald Erskine
1900-2(5)
b Malvern 16 April 1878 ; d 13 May 1914.
Career: Malvern College (XI 1896) ; University College Oxford (Blue 1898-9) ; Old Malverians ; Corinthians 1899-1902. Also a Test cricketer playing 8 Tests between 1903-7 scoring 287 in his first Test v Australia at Sydney in 1903. Played for Worcestershire and was an Oxford cricket blue 1897-8-9-1900 scoring 171 v Cambridge in his last year when captain. Altogether in his first-class career lasting from 1897 to 1912 he scored 9,037 runs including 22 centuries. Also a Rackets blue 1897-8 and a Golf blue 1897-9. A Stockbroker by profession.
Club Honour: Old Malverians—F.A. Amateur Cup winners 1902
Long limbed, crafty player with wonderful ball control and a powerful shot whose infinite resource appeared almost cheeky. A richly gifted inside-forward.

FOULKE, William J. 1897(1)
b Blackwell, Derbyshire 12 April 1874 ; d 1 May 1916.
Career: Alfreton, Blackwell Colliery, Sheffield United cs 1894, Chelsea May 1905, Bradford City April 1906 retired November 1907. Derbyshire cricket on four occasions in 1900. Later was in a penny a shot sideshow at Blackpool
Club Honours: Sheffield United—F.L. Champions 1898, F.A. Cup winners 1899, 1902, finalists 1901
The Colossus among goalkeepers (in 1901 his dimensions were 6 foot 2½ inches in height and 21 stones in weight). His clearance kicks were made with tremendous force and he could fist a ball further than many players could kick it.

FOULKES, William Anthony
1955(1)
b St Helens, Lancs 5 January 1932.
Career: St Helens Schools, Whiston Boys Club (St Helens), Manchester United amateur 1949, professional 1952 retired cs 1970 and joined the Club coaching staff, assistant trainer coach July 1971
Club Honours: Manchester United—F.L. Champions 1956-7-65-7, F.A. Cup finalists 1957 and 1958, winners 1963, European Cup winners 1968
Rendered long and splendid service to Manchester United at right-back and centre-half—strong, steady and ever reliable.

FOX, Frederick S. 1925(1)
b Swindon.
Career: Swindon Town (during the first World War), Abertillery, Preston North End cs 1921, Gillingham cs 1922, Millwall Athletic May 1925, Halifax Town June 1927, Brentford March 1928
Became an international proposition at Gillingham, a rather unlikely habitat for such eminence. Fox, however, was a brilliant goalkeeper, with a sure pair of hands and keen anticipation. Selected for England whilst with Gillingham, he had been transferred to Millwall by the time the match was played.

FRANKLIN, Cornelius F.
(" Neil ") 1947-50(27)
b Stoke-on-Trent 24 January 1922.
Career: Stoke Schools, Stoke Old Boys, Stoke City amateur 1936, professional January 1939, Santa Fe (Bogota) May 1950 returning to England later 1950 and was suspended until 31 January 1951, Hull City February 1951, Crewe Alexandra February 1956, Stockport County October 1957, Wellington Town player coach July 1959, Sankeys July 1960, player manager cs 1961 reverted to player only cs 1961 shortly after accepting the managership and retired

December 1962. Coach to Appoel Nicosia February to November 1963, Colchester United manager November 1963 to May 1968. Became a licensee in Oswaldtwistle January 1969

At his peak a brilliant stubborn centre-half relying entirely on skill. He marshalled a defence like a general and was magnificent in heading and positioning.

FREEMAN, Bertram Clewley
1909-12(5)
b Birmingham October 1885 ; d 11 August 1955.
Career: Gower Street School Aston, Gower Street Old Boys, Aston Manor, Aston Villa April 1904, Woolwich Arsenal late 1905, Everton late 1907, Burnley April 1911, Wigan Borough September 1921 to cs 1922. Signed for Kettering Town in 1923-4 and finally retired cs 1924
Club Honour: Burnley—F.A. Cup winners 1914
Differed from many of his contemporaries in not being a centre-forward addicted to robust tactics. He placed rather than blasted the ball, was graceful and schemed to good effect. Had a formidable goal tally.

FROGGATT, Jack   1950-3(13)
b Sheffield 17 November 1922.
Career: R.A.F. football, Portsmouth amateur 1945 professional September 1945, Leicester City March 1954, Kettering Town player coach November 1957 player manager January 1958 to September 1961 when he reverted to player only. Retired cs 1962 since when he has been a licensee in the Portsmouth area. Cousin of Redfern Froggatt
Club Honours: Portsmouth—F.L. Champions 1949 and 1950, Leicester City—Second Division Champions 1957
Successful in two such disparate positions as centre-half and out-

side-left. As a pivot he utilised a grand tackle, on the wing a surging vitality and in both, strength and enthusiasm.

FROGGATT, Redfern   1953(4)
b Sheffield 23 August 1923.
Career: Sheffield Y.M.C.A., Sheffield Wednesday professional July 1942, Stalybridge Celtic May 1962
Club Honours: Sheffield Wednesday—Second Division Champions 1952-6-9
This finely built inside-forward was the motivating force behind the Wednesday attack for many seasons. He had constructive ability of a high order and excelled in the crossfield pass.

FRY, Charles Burgess   1901(1)
b Croydon 25 April 1872; d 7 September 1956.
Career : Repton School (XI 1888-91 captain 1891) ; Wadham College, Oxford (Blue 1892-3-4-5 captain 1894); Old Reptonians ; Southampton ; Portsmouth; Corinthians 1892-1903. A cricket blue 1892-3-4-5, captain 1894, he played 26 Tests between 1899-1912. Played for Surrey 1891-3, Sussex 1894-1908, Hampshire 1909-21, scoring 30,886 runs in first class cricket including 94 centuries. Athletics blue 1892-3-4-5 (president in 1894), winning the long jump 1892-3-4 and the 100 yards in 1893. In 1893 beat the World long jump record with a jump of 23 feet 6½ inches which record he held for some years. Played rugby for Blackheath, Barbarians and Surrey and might have obtained a blue at Oxford if he had not been injured. One time master at Charterhouse 1896-8, he had a spell in journalism and was an unsuccessful Liberal candidate for Parliament before taking over the naval training ship, *Mercury,* in 1908 where he remained until 1950

Club Honour: Southampton—F.A. Cup finalists 1902

It cannot be said that Association Football was the principal sport of this great all-round games player; nevertheless he attained high proficiency at the game and was sound and dependable at right-back.

FURNESS, William I. 1933(1)
b New Washington, Co. Durham.
Career: Usworth Colliery, Leeds United August 1928, Norwich City June 1937 retired 1947 and became assistant trainer and later trainer until May 1955

An aggressive inside-forward with a good turn of speed and a redoubtable shot which he liked to bring into service on every possible occasion.

GALLEY, Thomas 1937(2)
b Hednesford, Staffs 4 August 1917.
Career: Hednesford Schools, Cannock Town (Notts County amateur), Wolverhampton Wanderers April 1934, Grimsby Town November 1947, Kidderminster Harriers cs 1949, Clacton Town player coach May 1950
Club Honours: Wolverhampton Wanderers—F.A. Cup finalists 1939, F.L. Cup winners 1942

A real all-rounder—right-half and inside-right chiefly, centre-half and centre-forward on other occasions. Tall and rangy in build, Galley had ball command and an attacking flair.

GARDNER, Thomas 1934-5(2)
b Huyton, Lancs.
Career: Orrell F.C. (Liverpool), Liverpool amateur 1928, Grimsby Town cs 1931, Hull City cs 1932, Aston Villa February 1934, Burnley April 1938, Wrexham December 1945, Wellington Town August 1947, Oswestry Town player manager thence player coach January 1952, Chester assistant trainer

cs 1954 to May 1967 when he became steward of a Chester Social Club

Club Honours: Hull City—Third Division North Champions 1933, Blackpool—F.L. North Cup winners 1943 (as a guest)

Played a buoyant and enthusiastic game at right-half and became widely known for his long throws, at which accomplishment he vied with the famous Weaver. His post-War League days were spent as Wrexham's outside-right.

GARFIELD, Ben 1898(1)
b 1873 d
Career: Burton Wanderers 1894, West Bromwich Albion cs 1896, Brighton & Hove Albion cs 1902 to 1905

A rare bundle of energy at outside-left and one to whom the game meant total involvement. Enormously popular at West Bromwich and a colourful personality.

GARRATTY, William 1903(1)
b Saltley, Birmingham 6 October 1878 ; d 6 May 1931.
Career: St Saviours School Birmingham, Highfield Villa, Aston Shakespeare, Aston Villa cs 1897, Leicester Fosse September 1908, West Bromwich Albion mid 1908-9, Lincoln City cs 1910 retired cs 1911. A driver with a Birmingham brewery firm for some years up to his death.
Club Honours: Aston Villa—F.L. Champions 1900, F.A. Cup winners 1905

Industrious, never-say-die inside-right or centre-forward. Not polished but invaluable for his scoring proclivities.

GARRETT, Thomas 1952-4(3)
b Whiteless, Co. Durham 28 February 1927.
Career: Horden Colliery, Blackpool amateur 1942, professional 1946, Millwall May 1961, Fleet-

wood August 1962, Mayfield United—Newcastle, Australia cs 1963
Club Honours: Blackpool—F.A. Cup finalists 1951, winners 1953
A back of classic ability able to play in either position. Was dashing, firm and excellent at keeping the opposing winger immobilised on the touch-line.

GAY, Leslie Hewitt   1893-4(3)
b Brighton 24 March 1871; d 2 November 1949.
Career: Marlborough College; Brighton College (XI 1889); Clare College Cambridge (Blue 1892); Old Brightonians; Corinthians 1891-4. An England Test cricketer v Australia in 1894-5 as a wicketkeeper he won his cricket blue at Cambridge in 1892-3 and played for Hampshire 1888-93 and for Somerset in 1894. A land agent in the West country he later played golf for Devon.
A goalkeeper both alert and skilful. Used to take the ball quickly and was utterly fearless.

GEARY, Fred   1890-1(2)
b Hyson Green, Notts 23 January 1868; d 8 January 1955.
Career: Hyson Green Church School, Balmoral, Notts Rangers, Grimsby Town briefly in 1887, Notts Rangers, Notts County, Notts Rangers, Everton cs 1889, Liverpool cs 1895 until 1899. After retirement was a licensee in Liverpool for many pears until 1946
Club Honours: Everton—F.L. Champions 1891, Liverpool—Second Division Champions 1896
The outstanding trait of his game was dash although he was sometimes too hasty. At his best in a closely fought match, a splendid marksman and, altogether, a most lively centre-forward.

GEAVES, Richard Lyon   1875(1)
b Mexico 1854; d 21 March 1935.

Career: Harrow School (XI 1872); Caius College Cambridge (Blue 1874); Clapham Rovers; Old Harrovians. Joined 14th Prince of Wales Yorkshire Regiment in 1875 retiring with the rank of Captain in 1881
Tireless winger with the qualities of mobility, industry and good dribbling. Difficult to knock off the ball.

GEE, Charles W.   1932-7(3)
b Stockport.
Career: Reddish Green Wesleyans, Stockport County mid 1928-9, Everton July 1930 retired May 1940
Club Honours: Everton—F.L. Champions 1932, Second Division Champions 1931
Strong pivot always in good heart and without any hint of temperament. A constructive performer good at plying his attack with ground passes.

GELDARD, Albert   1933-8(4)
b Bradford 11 April 1914.
Career: Whetley Lane School Bradford (England Schools v Scotland Wales 1927-8 v Ireland 1928), Manningham Mills, Bradford amateur cs 1928, professional 1930, Everton November 1932, Bolton Wanderers July 1938, retired cs 1947. Came out of retirement in November 1949 to join Darwen
Club Honour: Everton—F.A. Cup winners 1933
A class outside-right from a very early age, slippery to hold and possessing an exceptional turn of speed. Reputed to be the youngest player to play in the Football League when he played for Bradford in September 1929 at the age of 15 years 156 days.

GEORGE, William   1902(3)
b Woolwich 29 June 1874; d 4 December 1933.
Career: Woolwich Ramblers,

Royal Artillery (Trowbridge), Trowbridge Town, Aston Villa October 1897, Birmingham trainer July 1911. After leaving football worked at the Austin Motor Works at Longbridge. Played cricket for Warwickshire 1901-2 and 1907 and also for Wiltshire and Shropshire

Club Honours: Aston Villa—F.L. Champions 1899-1900, F.A. Cup winners 1905

A goalkeeper particularly agile for a man of his size. Had a keen eye and disposed of the ball to the best advantage.

GIBBINS, W. Vivian T. 1924-5(2) b Forest Gate 7 January 1903.

Career: Clapton, West Ham United December 1923, Clapton January 1932, Brentford February 1932, Bristol Rovers cs 1932, Southampton September 1933, Leyton mid 1933-4. Made twelve England amateur international appearances between 1925-32. A schoolmaster by profession he was until quite recently Headmaster of a school in the West Ham area

Club Honours: Clapton—F.A. Amateur Cup winners 1924 and 1925, Leyton—F.A. Amateur Cup finalists 1934

Talented amateur inside-right or centre-forward. After adjustment to the greater demands of the Football League he scored regularly and fitted in well with his professional colleagues.

GILLIAT, Walter Evelyn 1893(1) b 22 July 1869; d 2 January 1963.

Career: Charterhouse School (XI 1887-8); Magdalen College Oxford (Blue 1892); Old Carthusians; Woking. Played cricket on occasion for Bucks. Ordained in 1895, curate at Woking and Tunbridge Wells, Vicar of Iver 1901-21, Rector of Sevenoaks 1921-9 thence lived in retirement at Woking.

Rated second only to the great Cobbold as the finest dribbler of

the era. Of slight physique he suffered several injuries but, when fit, was a forward good enough for any side.

GOODALL, Frederick Roy
1926-34(25)
b Dronfield, Yorks 31 December 1902.

Career: Dronfield Grammar School, Dronfield Woodhouse, Huddersfield Town 1921, Nottingham Forest training staff May 1937, Mansfield Town manager 1945, Huddersfield Town trainer August 1949 retiring to take charge of the club Youth team in October 1964 leaving the club in July 1965

Club Honours: Huddersfield Town—F.L. Champions 1924-5-6, F.A. Cup finalists 1928, 30

Never overawed by a big occasion this great right-back was an England regular for a long time. He was fast, believed in the shoulder charge and his first-time tackling was masterly.

GOODALL, John 1888-98(14) b London 19 June 1863; d 20 May 1942.

Career: Great Lever 1883, Preston North End 1886, Derby County May 1889, New Brighton Tower cs 1899, Glossop cs 1900, Watford cs 1903 later finished his playing career with Mardy in 1913. Born in London of Scottish parents his brother, Archibald, was born in Ireland and played for that country. Played cricket for Derbyshire and Herts on occasion. For some years from February 1925 he was groundsman at the West Herts Club, Watford

Club Honours: Preston North End —F.A. Cup finalists 1888, winners and F.L. Champions 1889, Derby County—F.A. Cup finalists 1898

Inside-right or centre-forward of unsurpassed excellence. Brilliant in keeping his forwards together and dangerous anywhere near goal being a telling marksman.

GOODHART, Harry Chester
1883(3)

b Wimbledon 17 July 1858; d 21 April 1895.
Career: Eton College (XI 1877); Trinity College, Cambridge (No blue); Old Etonians: Lecturer at Cambridge 1884-90, Professor of Humanities at Edinburgh University 1890-5
Club Honours: Old Etonians— F.A. Cup finalists 1881, 3, winners 1882
A persevering forward who got through a lot of hard work which was marred a little by his lack of pace.

GOODWYN, Alfred George
1873(1)

d 14 March 1874.
Career: Royal Military Academy, Woolwich 1870; Royal Engineers 1871; died whilst on service in the East Indies
Club Honour: Royal Engineers— F.A. Cup finalists 1872
Performed finely at both back and half-back. Had a sure kick and generally very skilful. Seldom passed by an opposing forward.

GOODYER, Arthur Copeland
1879(1)

b Nottingham; d 8 January 1932.
Career: Nottingham Forest November 1878 to March 1880. Was engaged in the lace trade and went to U.S.A. in 1888 and remained there until his death which was as a result of a car accident
He possessed a good shot and was an all-round useful winger but prone to get stranded upfield. A noted middle-distance runner.

GOSLING, Robert Cunliffe
1892-5(5)

b Farnham, Surrey 15 June 1868; d 18 April 1922.
Career: Eton College (XI captain 1887); Trinity College Cambridge (Blue 1890); Old Etonians; Corinthians 1889-1900: Donor of the Arthur Dunn Cup, the well known "Old Boys" trophy. Cambridge cricket blue 1888-9-90, also played for Essex from 1888-96 and scored 101 for Eton v Harrow in 1887. Was High Sheriff of Essex in 1902
An inside forward of great talent; tall, strong, fast and a dangerous marksman. He made one international appearance at outside-right.

GOSNELL, Albert Arthur
1906(1)

b Colchester February 1880.
Career: The Albion (Colchester) cs 1898, Colchester Town, Essex County, New Brompton cs 1901, Chatham cs 1902, Newcastle United May 1904, Tottenham Hotspur cs 1910, Darlington cs 1911, Port Vale circa 1912. During the 1914-18 War worked in Newcastle and ran a very successful works side, helped with Newcastle United after the War until his appointment as Norwich City manager January 1921 which post he held until March 1926.
Club Honours: Newcastle United —F.A. Cup finalists 1905, 6, F.L. Champions 1905, 7
A sparkling outside-left at his peak when enjoying the service provided by his great Newcastle colleagues. Was lively, clever and possessor of a flashing shot.

GOUGH, Harold
1921(1)

b Chesterfield circa 1892.
Career: Spital Olympic, Bradford cs 1910, Castleford Town August 1911, Sheffield United cs 1913, suspended cs 1924 to 31 December 1924 for becoming a licensee at Castleford against Sheffield United rules, Castleford Town January 1925, Harrogate October 1926, Oldham Athletic February 1927, Bolton Wanderers December 1927, Torquay United June 1928 retiring owing to injury 1930

Club Honour: Sheffield United—
F.A. Cup winners 1915
A quite fearless goalkeeper whose
daring was a byword. He had no
hesitation in running out to take
the ball off the toe of an onrush-
ing forward.

GOULDEN, Leonard Arthur
1937-9(14)
b Homerton 16 July 1912.
Career: Holborn Street School
West Ham (England Schools v
Scotland and Wales 1926),
Chelmsford, Leyton cs 1932, West
Ham United professional April
1933, Chelsea August 1945, club
coach cs 1950, Watford manager
November 1952 to July 1956
(general manager October 1955 to
February 1956), Watford coach
July 1959 to cs 1962 after coaching in Libya, Banbury secretary
manager mid 1965-6 to March
1967. Oxford United trainer coach
January 1969
Club Honours: West Ham United
—F.L. War Cup winners 1940,
Chelsea—F.L. South Cup winners
(as a guest) 1945
Quick witted dexterity carried this
attractive inside-left past many a
lunging opponent. The best England player in his position in the
two years prior to the last War.

GRAHAM, Leonard 1925(2)
b Leyton 20 August 1901.
Career: Capworth United, Leytonstone, Millwall October 1923 retired injury cs 1934. F.A. Coach
1934-6. Coach at The Hague
1936-9. After his return to England became a licensee. At one
time on the Essex County Cricket
Club staff he later coached Merchant Taylors School. Later a
business executive.
Club Honour: Millwall—Third
Division South Champions 1928
An intelligent ball player quick to
size up a situation. A stylish and
constructive left-half.

GRAHAM, Thomas 1931-2(2)
b Hamsterley, Co. Durham 5
March 1907.
Career: Hamsterley Swifts, Con-
sett Celtic, Nottingham Forest
May 1927, retired 1944, Forest
trainer to January 1961 thence
scout retiring as a full time scout
in March 1969 and finally retiring
July 1970
Won a deserved and great reputation at centre-half despite being
comparatively small. Relied on
cultured ball play, stylishly combining attack with defence. Figured at wing-half sometimes.

GRAINGER, Colin 1956-7(7)
b Havercroft, Yorks 10 June 1933.
Career: Rye Hill Junior and
South Hindley Secondary School,
South Elmsall, Wrexham ground
staff 1949, professional February
1951, Sheffield United June 1953,
Sunderland February 1957, Leeds
United July 1960, Port Vale October 1961, Doncaster Rovers August 1964, Macclesfield cs 1966 but
released November 1966 to take
up employment in Harrogate.
Uncle of E. Holliday. Also a professional singer
Favoured more clubs with his
talents than most England players,
Grainger was a sprightly outside-
left, mobile and aggressive.

GREAVES, James Peter 1959-67(57)
b Poplar 20 February 1940.
Career: Dagenham Schools, Lake-
side Manor Boys Club, Chelsea
amateur 1955, professional May
1957 (England Youth 1957), A.C.
Milan June 1961, Tottenham Hotspur November 1961, West Ham
United March 1970 retired 1971
Club Honours: Chelsea—F.A.
Youth Cup finalists 1958, Tottenham Hotspur—F.A. Cup winners
1962, 7, European Cup Winners
Cup winners 1963
There has seldom been an opportunist to equal this famous little
inside-forward. For long periods

in a game he would seem innocuous, even anonymous and then strike to fashion a goal where one appeared impossible.

GREEN, Frederick Thomas 1876(1)
b 21 June 1851; d 6 July 1928.
Career: Winchester College; New College Oxford (prior to the University match); Wanderers; Middlesex. Became a Barrister in 1877 but from 1880 was an Inspector of Schools
Club Honours: Oxford University —F.A. Cup winners 1874, Wanderers—F.A. Cup winners 1877, 8
Sure-footed half who was always reliable and determined.

GREEN, George Henry 1925-8(8)
b Leamington.
Career: Leamington Town, Nuneaton Borough, Sheffield United May 1923, Leamington Town July 1934
Club Honour: Sheffield United—F.A. Cup winners 1925
Believed in a vigorous approach though by no means a mere spoiler. Rewarding to watch for the sheer "Englishness" of his style. Made his name at left-half, moving to left-back in the 1930s.

GREENHALGH, Ernest Harwood
1873(2)
d 11 July 1922 aged 73.
Career: Notts County 1867 to 1883, thence secretary of Greenhalgh's F.C. of Mansfield where he was proprietor of Field Mill. This team played on a ground at the rear of Field Mill which is now the home of Mansfield Town. A robust full-back and a great servant of Notts County in their early days. Originally an individualistic player he adapted himself to the team game with some measure of success.

GREENWOOD, Doctor Haydock
1882(2)
b Blackburn 1860; d 3 November 1951.

Career: Malvern College (XI 1878-9); Blackburn Rovers; Corinthians (an original committee member of the club on its formation in 1882)
Played full-back with vigour and a powerful kick but was a thought slow and uncertain. Missed the 1882 Cup Final owing to injury.

GRIMSDELL, Arthur 1920-3(6)
b Watford 23 March 1894; d 12 March 1963.
Career: Field School Watford (England v Wales schools 1908), Watford St Stephen's, Watford 1909, Tottenham Hotspur March 1912, Clapton Orient player manager cs 1929 but his registration as a player was not accepted until October. Watford director 1945-51. Sports outfitter in Watford. Hertfordshire cricket 1922-47
Club Honours: Tottenham Hotspur—Second Division Champions 1920, F.A. Cup winners 1921
One of the great left-halves of all time; determined, aggressive, dominating and an inspiring captain. Was also a sixth forward, loving to burst through and score with a pile-driving shot.

GROSVENOR, Albert Thomas
1934(3)
b Netherton near Dudley, Worcestershire.
Career: Tippity Green Vics, Vono Works, Stourbridge, Birmingham March 1928, Sheffield Wednesday February 1936, Bolton Wanderers May 1937 retired during the War. Hardly a prolific scorer but a useful inside-right to have around. Though standing over 6 feet (so could be commanding in the air) he carried no excess weight and was excellent at providing openings.

GUNN, William 1884(2)
b Nottingham 4 December 1858; d 29 January 1921.

England's World Cup winning team 1966: H. Shepherdson, N. P. Stiles, R. Hunt, G. Banks, J. Charlton, G. R. Cohen, R. Wilson, A. E. Ramsey, (front) M. S. Peters, G. C. Hurst, R. F. Moore, A. J. Ball and R. Charlton

England v Scotland 1893: W. McGregor, R. C. Gosling, J. J. Bentley,
J. Holt, J. C. Clegg, G. Kinsey, R. Holmes, J. Goodall, (middle) W. I. Bassett,
J. Reynolds, G. H. Cotterill, L. H. Gay, A. H. Harrison, (front) F. Spiksley
and E. Chadwick

Career: Nottingham Forest November 1881 (once only), Notts County 1881-90. Reinstated as an amateur September 1890 and played in local amateur football. Later a director of Notts County and Vice-President at the date of his death. Notts County cricket 1880-1904, he played 9 Tests v Australia 1888-99 and scored over 25,840 runs in first class cricket including 48 centuries. Helped Notts to win the County championship 1880-2-3-4-5-6. A sports outfitter for some time in Richard Daft's shop and later on his own account with Gunn & Moore founded in 1885

Uncommonly tall—6 foot 4½ inches—and a brilliant forward usually to be found on the left wing. Could move with great speed although he could be faulted at times for keeping the ball too long.

GURNEY, Robert   1935(1)
b Silksworth, Co. Durham 13 October 1906.
Career: Hetton Juniors, Seaham Harbour, Bishop Auckland, Sunderland May 1925 retired during the War. Later manager of Horden Colliery for 2½ years, manager Peterborough United February 1950, manager Darlington March 1952 to October 1957, Leeds United scout, Horden Colliery manager 1960-3, Hartlepools United manager April 1963 to January 1964. Now travelling for a wine and spirit firm
Club Honours: Sunderland—F.L. Champions 1936, F.A. Cup winners 1937
In spite of bad injuries—both legs were broken during his playing career—Gurney was a consistently scoring centre. Had infinite resource in getting the ball and had the habit of roaming to the wing and making a quick cross. Played at inside-left sometimes.

I

HACKING, John   1929(3)
b Blackburn 1902; d 1 June 1955.
Career: Blackpool Co-op, Blackpool December 1919, Fleetwood cs 1925, Oldham Athletic cs 1926, Manchester United March 1934, Accrington Stanley player manager May 1935 retiring as a player October 1935 and resigning as manager May 1949, Barrow manager May 1949 until his death
Among the safest of goalkeepers his work always being sound and workmanlike.

HADLEY, Harry   1903(1)
b West Bromwich 1878; d
Career: Halesowen, West Bromwich Albion 1897, Aston Villa February 1905, Nottingham Forest April 1906, Southampton cs 1907 to 1908. Merthyr Town manager May 1919 to October 1921 and re-appointed later October 1921 to April 1922, Chesterfield manager April 1922 to August 1922. Subsequently had three more spells as Merthyr Town manager, one spell as Aberdare Athletic manager November 1927 to April 1929 and was Bangor City manager in July 1935
Club Honour: West Bromwich—Second Division Champions 1902
Very useful wing-half energetic and sporting on the field. Occasionally inclined to give the ball too much air.

HAGAN, James   1949(1)
b Washington, Co. Durham 21 January 1917.
Career: Usworth Colliery Intermediate School Washington (England Schools v Scotland and Wales 1932), Liverpool amateur January 1932, Derby County amateur cs 1933, professional cs 1936, Sheffield United November 1938, retired March 1958. Peterborough United manager August 1958 to October 1962, West Bromwich Albion manager April 1963

to May 1967, Manchester City scout 1967-8. Then out of football until joining Benfica as manager trainer March 1970
Club Honour: Sheffield United—Second Division Champions 1953
An inside-forward for the discerning spectator. Quiet, unobstrusive and unselfish but a master craftsman in deep thinking tactical play.

HAINES, John T. W.   1949(1)
b Wickhamford, near Evesham, Worcester 24 April 1920.
Career: Evesham Grammar School, Evesham Town, Cheltenham Town, Liverpool mid 1937-8, Swansea Town cs 1939, Leicester City June 1947, West Bromwich Albion March 1948, Bradford December 1949, Rochdale September 1953, Chester July 1955, Wellington Town cs 1957, Kidderminster Harriers cs 1958, Evesham Town October 1958
In a dream England debut Haines notched two goals. Unfortunately injury affected him subsequently and his skilful ball play and shooting power at inside forward never seemed to reach such heights again.

HALL, Albert Edward   1910(1)
b Wordsley 1882; d 17 October 1957.
Career: Stourbridge, Aston Villa cs 1903, Millwall Athletic mid 1913-14 retiring during the 1914-18 War. He was for some years in business as an enamel ware manufacturer at Stourbridge until ill health caused his retirement
Club Honours: Aston Villa—F.A. Cup winners 1905, F.L. Champions 1910
Owed much to the promptings of his famous partner, Joe Bache, but was a fine left-winger in his own right. Lively, elusive and dangerous in front of goal.

HALL, George William 1934-9(10)
b Newark 12 March 1912; d 23

May 1967.
Career: Nottingham Schools, Ransome & Marles, Notts County November 1930, Tottenham Hotspur December 1932 retired injury 1944. Clapton Orient coach and manager from October to December 1945 when he resigned owing to ill health and eventually had to have both legs amputated. Was then a licensee apart from a short spell as manager of Chingford Town from December 1949
An inside-forward with complete mastery over the ball and an elusive dribbler. Scored 5 goals for England v Ireland in 1938 but was not a high scorer with either Notts County or the Spurs where his role was rather that of a provider.

HALL, Jeffrey James   1956-7(17)
b Scunthorpe, Lincs 7 September 1929; d 4 April 1959.
Career: Wilsden Council School, Bingley Secondary Modern School, Bingley Technical College St Anne's (Keighley), Wilsden, Bank Top, Birmingham City May 1950 until his early death from polio
Club Honours: Birmingham City—Second Division Champions 1955, F.A. Cup finalists 1956
On the small side but was as perky a right-back as could be. Defended sturdily and strongly and was always game.

HALSE, Harold James   1909(1)
b Leytonstone January 1886; d April 1951.
Career: Park Road School Wanstead, Newportians (Leyton), Wanstead, Barking Town, Clapton Orient, Southend United cs 1906, Manchester United cs 1907, Aston Villa July 1912, Chelsea May 1913, Charlton Athletic July 1921 retired cs 1923
Club Honours: Manchester United—F.A. Cup winners 1909, F.L. Champions 1911, Aston Villa—F.A. Cup winners 1913, Chelsea—

F.A. Cup finalists 1915
Mercurial inside-right (and sometimes centre-forward). A small
and frail build did not militate
against his goal scoring for he was
a rare opportunist.

**HAMMOND, Henry Edward
Denison** 1889(1)
b Priston, Somerset 26 November
1866; d 16 June 1910.
Career: St Edwards School Oxford; Lancing College (XI 1883-5
captain in 1885); Corpus Christi
College Oxford (Blue 1888-9);
Corinthians 1889-90: Athletics
Blue 1886-7-9. Master at Blair
Lodge School 1889, Edinburgh
Academy 1890-99, Superintendent
of British Education Section at
the Paris Exhibition 1899, Director General of Education in
Rhodesia from 1900. Cricket for
Somerset 1889.
A half-back whose athletic prowess stood him in good stead. His
style was mainly remarkable for
its consistent power.

HAMPSON, James 1931-3(3)
b Little Hulton, Lancs 1908; d 10
January 1938.
Career: Walkden Park, Little Hulton St Johns, Nelson cs 1925,
Blackpool October 1927 until his
death. Drowned in a fishing accident off Fleetwood
Club Honour: Blackpool—Second
Division Champions 1930
A deadly right foot and fine headwork made him a feared marksman at centre and inside forward.
He was not just a scoring machine
but an all-round footballer with
ball control and a natural swerve.

HAMPTON, Harry 1913-4(4)
b Wellington, Salop 21 April
1885; d 15 March 1963.
Career: Shifnal Juniors, Wellington Town, Aston Villa May 1904,
Birmingham February 1920, Newport County September 1922 to cs

1923, Wellington Town January
1924, Preston North End coach
June 1925 to January 1926. Later
spent many years at Rhyl where
he had catering interests
Club Honours: Aston Villa—F.L.
Champions 1910, F.A. Cup winners 1905 and 1913, Birmingham
—Second Division Champions
1921
A terror of a centre-forward—
devil-may-care, robust and absolutely and utterly fearless. It was
remarkable that he did not suffer
more serious injuries than he did.
Towards the end of his career
played at right-half also.

HANCOCKS, John 1949-51(3)
b Oakengates, Salop 1920.
Career: Oakengates Town, Walsall August 1938, Wolverhampton
Wanderers May 1946, Wellington
Town as player manager July 1957
relinquished managership early
1959-60 and released as a player
December 1959, Cambridge
United January 1960, Oswestry cs
1960, Sankeys December 1960
Club Honours: Wolverhampton
Wanderers—F.A. Cup winners
1949, F.L. Champions 1954
Generally looked upon as an outside-right although he could take
the other flank. Only small but
brave and his size 2 boot carried
a fantastic bullet-like shot.

HAPGOOD, Edris Albert 1933-9(30)
b Bristol 27 September 1908.
Career: St Philips Adult School
juniors, Bristol Rovers trial May
1927, Kettering Town cs 1927,
Arsenal October 1927, Blackburn
Rovers manager June 1946 to February 1947, Shrewsbury Town
player coach August 1947, Watford manager February 1948 to
March 1950, Bath City manager
March 1950 to February 1956
when he finally left the game. On
staff of Y.M.C.A.
Club Honours: Arsenal—F.L.
Champions 1931-3-4-5-8, F.A. Cup

winners 1930, 6, finalists 1932, F.L. War Cup finalists 1941 Universally ranked among the greatest of left-backs. In style not unlike his great England predecessor, Blenkinsop—polished, measured clearances and masterly in timing tackles.

HARDINGE, Harold Thomas Walter　　　　　　1910(1)
b Greenwich 25 February 1886; d 8 May 1965.
Career: Maidstone United, Newcastle United cs 1905, Sheffield United December 1907, Arsenal May 1913 retired cs 1921. Also a Test cricketer for England v Australia in 1921 and played for Kent from 1902-33 scoring over 33,000 runs in first class cricket including 75 centuries. He was on the staff of John Wisden Ltd, the sports outfitters, for many years
Subtle, scheming inside-left with pronounced leanings towards individualism. Highly skilled in drawing the opposing defence.

HARDMAN, Harold Payne
1905-8(4)
b Kirkmanshulme, Manchester 4 April 1882; d 9 June 1965.
Career: Blackpool High School, Northern Nomads, Worsley Wanderers, Chorlton cum Hardy, South Shore Choristers, Blackpool late 1900, Everton cs 1903, Manchester United cs 1908, Bradford City January 1909, Stoke cs 1910 to cs 1913. 10 England amateur international appearances 1907-9. Elected a director of Manchester United in November 1912 and, apart from a short period, remained a director for the rest of his life being Chairman from 1950. He was admitted a solicitor in December 1907 and practised in Manchester
Club Honours: Everton—F.A. Cup winners 1906, finalists 1907
Not considered strong enough to play games as a boy, Hardman became one of the most distin-

guished amateurs of the 1900s. His smallness proved no great handicap at outside-left where he was fast and elusive.

HARDWICK, George Francis M.
1947-8(13)
b Saltburn, Yorks 2 February 1920.
Career: Lingdale School, Cleveland, South Bank East End 1934, Middlesbrough professional May 1937, Oldham Athletic player manager November 1950 resigning and retiring as a player April 1956, coach to U.S. Army team in Germany August 1956, coach to Eindhoven June 1957 to cs 1959. Joined coaching staff of Middlesbrough and the local education authority August 1961 to November 1963. Sunderland manager November 1964 to May 1965. Gateshead manager 1968 until February 1970. Later Chairman of a structural steel firm and lived in Saltburn
Club Honours: Chelsea—F.L. South Cup finalists 1944, winners 1945 (as a guest), Oldham Athletic —Third Division North Champions 1953
First choice as England's left-back immediately after the War through his cultured, composed and solid style. First choice, too, with the fair sex, his good looks making him the George Best of the 'forties.

HARDY, Henry　　　　　　1925(1)
b Stockport 1895.
Career: Stockport Sunday Schools League football, Stockport County mid 1919-20, Everton October 1925, Bury cs 1929 to 1931. Later a professional oboe player for some years and then became a caretaker in Stockport
Club Honour: Stockport County —Third Division North Champions 1922
In the early 1920s was recognised as being one of the best goal-

keepers in the country. He was deft in handling, and had judgment and coolness.

HARDY, Samuel   1907-20(21)
b Newbold, Derbyshire 26 August 1883; d 24 October 1966.
Career: Newbold White Star, Chesterfield April 1903, Liverpool cs 1905, Aston Villa May 1912, Nottingham Forest August 1921 retired cs 1925, thence a hotelier in Chesterfield
Club Honours: Liverpool—F.L. Champions 1906, Aston Villa—F.A. Cup winners 1913, 20, Nottingham Forest—Second Division Champions 1922
Until the emergence of Hibbs was universally regarded as the nonpareil of England goalkeepers. His anticipation was so masterly it made the art of custodianship look easy. Would have been considered a classic performer in any era.

HARGREAVES, Frederick William
1880-2(3)
b Blackburn 1859; d 5 April 1897.
Career: Malvern College (XI 1877) ; Blackburn Rovers ; Lancashire. Brother of John. Lancashire cricket in 1881
Club Honour: Blackburn Rovers —F.A. Cup finalists 1882
Altogether a fine half-back, mobile, industrious, shrewd and a good tackler.

HARGREAVES, John   1881(2)
b Blackburn 1860; d 15 January 1903.
Career: Malvern College (XI 1878-9); Blackburn Rovers 1878-84; Lancashire. Admitted a solicitor in 1884 he practised in Blackburn up to his death
Club Honours: Blackburn Rovers —F.A. Cup finalists 1882, winners 1884
A skilful outside-left having a turn of speed and a capacity for sagacious passing.

HARPER, Edward Cashfield
1926(1)
b Sheerness, Kent 22 August 1902; d 22 July 1959.
Career: Sheppey United, Blackburn Rovers May 1923, Sheffield Wednesday November 1927, Tottenham Hotspur March 1929, Preston North End December 1931, Blackburn Rovers November 1933 retired cs 1935 and was on the Rovers training staff until May 1948. Subsequently worked for English Electric Co. until his death
With all four of his first-class clubs wonderfully consistent in goal scoring. Big, strong and fast, by any yardstick a centre-forward to be reckoned with.

HARRIS, Gordon   1966(1)
b Worksop, Notts 2 June 1940.
Career: Worksop Schools, Firbeck Colliery, Burnley professional January 1958, Sunderland January 1968, South Shields July 1972
Club Honour: Burnley—F.A. Cup finalists 1962
Became known in the first place as a volatile left-winger, his speed and liveliness demanding opponents' attention. He has played inside-left and left-half just as successfully since then.

HARRIS, Peter Philip   1950-4(2)
b Portsmouth 19 December 1925.
Career: Milton Junior School and Meon Road Senior School Portsmouth, de Havillands Works team, Gosport Borough, Portsmouth November 1944, retired ill health December 1959. After retiring from the game opened a restaurant and club at Hayling Island
Club Honours: Portsmouth—F.L. Champions 1949 and 1950
Excellent club man and an excellent outside-right. Was fast and had a grand scoring record for a

winger.

HARRIS, Stanley Schute 1904-6(6)
b Clifton 19 July 1881; d 4 May
1926.
Career: Westminster School (XI
1900-1); Pembroke College Cambridge (Blue 1902-3-4 captain
1904); Old Westminsters; Casuals;
Worthing; Portsmouth; Surrey;
Corinthians 1904-10. England
amateur international 1907. Played
cricket for Cambridge University
(12th man at Lords in 1904),
Gloucestershire, Surrey and Sussex. Head of St Ronans Preparatory School, Worthing from 1904-
26
Crafty ball-playing inside-left,
splendid at dribbling, shooting
and distributing the ball with
either the inside or the outside
of the foot.

HARRISON, Alban Hugh 1893(2)
b Bredhurst, Kent 30 November
1869 ; d 15 August 1943.
Career: Westminster School (XI
1887-8); Trinity College Cambridge (Blue 1889-91 captain
1891) ; Old Westminsters ; Corinthians 1891-4
Unlike many of the 'nineties full-
backs he was not a bustler. Clever
and accurate in his kicking and a
master of the half-volley.

HARRISON, George 1921-2(2)
b Church Gresley, Leics 1891; d
March 1939.
Career: Gresley Rovers, Leicester
Fosse cs 1910, Everton April 1913,
Preston North End November
1923, Blackpool November 1931
retired cs 1932. Later a licensee in
Preston
Club Honour: Everton—F.L.
Champions 1915
Stocky outside-left, fast and direct
in style and one difficult to dispossess because of his strength
backed by 12½ stones weight. One
of the hardest shots and a noted
penalty expert.

HARROW, Jack Harry 1923(2)
b Beddington, Surrey 8 October
1888; d 19 July 1958.
Career: Mill Green Rovers, Croydon Common, Chelsea April 1911
retired cs 1926 and remained on
the Chelsea training staff until
1938. Then worked for Mitcham
Council retiring in 1956
Club Honour: Chelsea—F.A. Cup
finalists 1915
Began as a centre-forward then
becoming a half before finding his
true position at left-back. Appeared casual because of waiting
until the last vital moment to
tackle, his dash being calculated
with precision.

HART, Ernest Arthur 1929-34(8)
b Overseal, Derbyshire 3 January
1902; d 21 July 1954.
Career: Overseal Schools and
Juniors, Woodlands F.C. (Doncaster), Leeds United 1920, Mansfield Town August 1936, Coventry City scout cs 1937, Tunbridge
Wells Rangers player manager
July 1938. After leaving football
he was in business in Doncaster
Club Honour: Leeds United—
Second Division Champions 1924
A great centre-half particularly
noted for his attacking game. Brilliantly constructive and a master
of ball control.

HARTLEY, Frederick 1923(1)
b Shipton under Wychwood, Oxon
1896; d 20 October 1965.
Career: Oxford City ; Corinthians
1924-8; Tottenham Hotspur amateur November 1922, professional
February 1928. 7 England amateur international appearances
1923-6. Played for Oxfordshire at
cricket (also for the Minor Coun-
ties representative team) and at
hockey at which he appeared in
Divisional trials. A member of a
prominent farming family in the
Cotswolds
The amateur game saw the best
part of him. A fine inside-forward

adept at close-dribbling, difficult to knock off the ball and capable of a stinging shot.

HARVEY, A. 1881(1)
Career: Wednesbury Strollers; Staffordshire
An elusive performer—a quality a little uncommon in the backs of his day—who was also dexterous and hard-working.

HARVEY, James Colin 1971(1)
b Liverpool 16 November 1945.
Career: Cardinal Allen Grammar School Liverpool, Liverpool junior football, Everton amateur 1961 then an apprentice professional, full professional October 1962
Club Honours: Everton—F.A. Cup winners 1966, finalists 1968, F.L. Champions 1970
An excellent midfield link at left-half. Has a purposeful tackle and his distribution is astute.

HASSALL, Harold William
1951-4(5)
b Tyldesley, Lancs 4 March 1929.
Career: Leigh Grammar School, Astley and Tyldesley Collieries, Huddersfield Town September 1946, Bolton Wanderers January 1952 retired injury December 1955. Has a notable record in coaching being an F.A. staff coach, a member of the F.I.F.A. panel of coaches since 1966, one time manager of England Youth team, Lecturer at Padgate College of Education, Lancs 1962 being appointed Senior Lecturer in 1965
Club Honour: Bolton Wanderers—F.A. Cup finalists 1953
Sharp-shooting inside-left who had a long striding running action. Tall, powerful and a constant menace to his opponents' citadel.

HAWKES, Robert Murray 1907-8(5)
b Breachwood Green, Herts 18 October 1880; d 12 September 1945.
Career: Luton Higher Grade School, Luton Stanley, Luton Victoria, Luton Clarence, Herts County, Luton Town cs 1901, turning professional 1911 and retiring early 1919-20. Played for Bedford Town for the remainder of the 1919-20 season then retired. Worked in Luton and remained a close follower of the affairs of Luton Town until his death. Made 22 England amateur international appearances between 1907-11
A left-half. Being frail and deficient in heading power as well, he had to rely wholly on judgment and remarkably skilful footwork.

HAWORTH, George 1887-90(5)
b Accrington.
Career: Accrington to 1892; Blackburn Rovers. His association with Blackburn Rovers seems to have been limited to the F.A. Cup Final of 1885.
Club Honour: Blackburn Rovers—F.A. Cup winners 1885
In 1906 the great Crabtree bracketed Haworth and Forrest as the best tacklers and most judicious players he had ever seen—praise indeed! Haworth performed tirelessly at right and centre-half.

HAWTREY, John Purvis 1881(2)
b Eton, Bucks 19 July 1850; d 17 August 1925.
Career: Eton College until 1864 thence at Clifton College. Did not play soccer at school but later played for Old Etonians; Remnants and Berks and Bucks. After leaving school he taught for several years at his father's school, Aldin House, Slough and thence was an actor and producer and finally ran the paper, *Sporting World*
Club Honour: Old Etonians—F.A. Cup winners 1879
A good goalkeeper usually and one who could be at times brilliant and at times ordinary. Too variable to be counted among the very best.

HAYGARTH, Edward Brownlow
1875(1)
b Cirencester 26 April 1854; d 14 April 1915.
Career: Lancing College; Wanderers; Swifts; Reading; Berks. Played cricket for Hants 1875, Gloucestershire 1883 and Berkshire. Admitted a solicitor in August 1876 he practised in Cirencester
Heavily built and courageous, Haygarth kicked powerfully and was altogether a splendid back.

HAYNES, John Norman
1955-62(56)
b Kentish Town 17 October 1934.
Career: Latymer Grammar School Edmonton (England Schools v Ireland 1949 v Wales Scotland (2) Eire 1950), Fulham ground staff July 1950 playing in turn for Feltham United, Wimbledon and Woodford Town until becoming a professional May 1952 (England Youth international 1952), Fulham player manager November 1968 briefly, reverting to player until his retirement cs 1970. Joined Durban City August 1970.
This great inside-forward will be remembered for several things—strategy, ball control and leadership—but chiefly for his outstanding passing ability. He could spray passes from any angle and for any distance and find his man with consummate accuracy.

HEALLESS, Henry
1925-8(2)
b Blackburn 1893; d 11 January 1972.
Career: Blackburn Athletic, Victoria Cross, Blackburn Trinity, Blackburn Rovers amateur mid 1914-15, professional May 1919 retired April 1933. Coach in Holland September 1935 to October 1937 when he returned to England and was reinstated as an amateur. In 1948, at the age of 54, was partnering his son at full-back in local junior football

Club Honour: Blackburn Rovers —F.A. Cup winners 1928
Dour performer in any half-back position and the owner of a relentless tackle. Was a valuable captain of his club over several years because of his generalship.

HEDLEY, George A.
1901(1)
b South Bank, Yorks 1876; d 16 August 1942.
Career: South Bank, Sheffield United amateur mid 1897-8, professional May 1898, Southampton May 1903, Wolverhampton Wanderers May 1906, Bristol City manager April 1913 up to the first World War following which he was a licensee in Bristol until 1941. He then returned to Wolverhampton to take a boarding house.
Club Honours: Sheffield United— F.A. Cup winners 1899, 1902, finalists 1901, Southampton—Southern League Champions 1904, Wolverhampton Wanderers—F.A. Cup winners 1908
Robust, opportunist centre-forward very much an advocate of the open game (a belief he even pleaded in a newspaper article in 1909). Gloried in cup-tie football, as will be gathered from his record above.

HEGAN, Kenneth Edward 1923-4(4)
b Coventry 24 January 1901.
Career: Bablake School; R.M.C. Sandhurst; Army (1st Dublin Fusiliers and Royal Army Service Corps); Corinthians from 1920; 23 England amateur international appearances 1921-33. Retired from the Army with the rank of Lt.-Col. in July 1949. Won O.B.E. during 1939-45 War.
Slight but extremely fast winger (he played on both flanks equally well). Expert in control, able to centre accurately and second to none in courage.

HELLAWELL, Michael S. 1963(2)
b Keighley, Yorks 30 June 1938.
Career: Salts (Huddersfield Town amateur), Queens Park Rangers 1955, Birmingham City May 1957, Sunderland January 1965, Huddersfield Town September 1966, Peterborough United November 1968 to cs 1969, Bromsgrove Rovers August 1969. Played cricket for Warwickshire 1962
Club Honour: Birmingham City— F.L. Cup winners 1963
Red-haired right-winger of lively bent. His chief asset was tremendous speed which posed a continuous threat to the opposition.

HENFREY, Arthur George
1891-6(5)
b Wellingborough, Northants 1868; d 17 October 1929.
Career: Wellingborough Grammar School; Jesus College Cambridge (Blue 1890-1); Finedon; Corinthians 1890-1903; Northamptonshire: Played cricket for Cambridge University in 1890 without getting a blue and for Northamptonshire from 1886-97 (captain 1893-4). Associated with local government in Northamptonshire
Took the roles of half-back and forward with equal facility. Strong and judicious in his passing, he was perhaps seen to best advantage in defence.

HENRY, Ronald Patrick 1963(1)
b London September 1935
Career: Manland Secondary Modern School Harpenden, Harpenden Town, Redbourne F.C. (Luton Town amateur), Tottenham Hotspur January 1955 retired cs 1969. After retirement has been a nurseryman in Hertfordshire and has coached Spurs Colts team
Club Honours: Tottenham Hotspur—F.L. Champions 1961, F.A.

Cup winners 1961 and 1962, European Cup Winners Cup winners 1963
A left-winger originally, Henry moved to left-half on turning professional and, finally, left-back. In the latter berth his steadiness, positioning and all-pervading consistency made him a valued member of the Spurs great early 1960s team.

HERON, Frank 1876(1)
b circa 1850; d
Career: Mill Hill School (briefly in 1864); Uxbridge; Swifts; Wanderers ; Windsor
Club Honour: Wanderers—F.A. Cup winners 1876
Expert in dribbling and in general a useful forward, he had the disadvantage of being lightly built.

HERON, George Hubert Hugh
1873-8(5)
b 30 January 1852; d 5 June 1914.
Career: Mill Hill School; Uxbridge; Wanderers; Swifts; Middlesex ; F.A. Committee 1873-6. Later a wine merchant in Bournemouth, Brother of F.
Club Honours: Wanderers—F.A. Cup winners 1876-7-8
An occasionally brilliant winger, fast and deft in his dribbling. Had an unfortunate tendency to selfishness, which fault he combated with variable success.

HIBBERT, William 1910(1)
b Golborne near Wigan, Lancs 1884; d 6 March 1949.
Career: Golborne School, Golborne juniors, Newton le Willows, Brynn Central, Bury May 1906, Newcastle United October 1911, Bradford City cs 1920, Oldham Athletic May 1922. Went to U.S.A. cs 1923 and in 1925-6 was manager of Coats F.C., Rhode Island. Went to Spain as a coach in June 1927 and joined Wigan Borough as trainer in 1930. He went to live and work in Black-

pool in 1938 and remained there until his death

Not the biggest of attackers (he played at inside-right), Hibbert more than made up with his uncommon dash and enthusiasm. Also he was not one to neglect scoring opportunities.

HIBBS, Henry E.   1930-6(25)
b Wilnecote, Staffs 27 May 1905.
Career: Wilnecote Holy Trinity, Tamworth Castle, Birmingham May 1924 retired May 1940. Walsall manager August 1944 to June 1951. Permit player for de Havillands February 1953 to cs 1954 thence out of football until August 1960 when he returned for a brief spell as manager coach to Ware Town after which he finally retired from the game
Club Honour: Birmingham—F.A. Cup finalists 1931
A great name among goalkeepers. Extraordinary for his gift of anticipation which enabled him to get his body behind the ball when saving the hardest shot. In the 1930's his name was bracketed with that of the earlier maestro, Sam Hardy—there can be no greater praise.

HILL, Frederick   1963(2)
b Sheffield 17 January 1940.
Career: Sheffield Schools, Bolton Wanderers March 1957, Halifax Town July 1969, Manchester City May 1970
Brainy, skilful, ball manipulating inside-forward always apparently with plenty of time to manoeuvre. Can shoot significantly with both feet.

HILL, John Henry   1925-9(11)
b Hetton-le-Hole, Co. Durham 2 March 1899; d April 1972.
Career: Durham junior football, Durham City professional mid 1919-20, Plymouth Argyle September 1920, Burnley May 1923, Newcastle United October 1928,

Bradford City June 1931, Hull City November 1931, retired and became Club manager April 1934 to January 1936 thence in business. Hull City scout 1948-55 and in charge of Scarborough Town Pools Scheme until August 1963. Then lived in retirement for a time in Hull and thence at Blackpool
Club Honour: Hull City—Third Division North Champions 1933
Conspicuous on the field because of his red hair and height. A brainy and constructive right or centre-half whose long legs helped him to become a rare spoiler.

HILL, Richard Henry   1926(1)
b Mapperley, Notts 26 November 1893; d April 1971.
Career: Grenadier Guards, Millwall Athletic cs 1919, Torquay United July 1930 to cs 1931, Mansfield Town trainer August 1932, Coventry City trainer cs 1935, Torquay United trainer July 1950
Club Honour: Millwall—Third Division South Champions 1928
For around a decade had a noted association at full-back with Jack Fort at Millwall. Hill played on the left, his speed and clean kicking, coupled with a rangy build proving an admirable foil to his stolid partner.

HILLMAN, John   1899(1)
b Tavistock, Devon 1871; d
Career: Local junior football, Burnley late 1891, Everton February 1895, Dundee cs 1896, Burnley March 1898, Manchester City January 1902, Millwall January 1907 briefly. Was later trainer of Burnley and in 1952 was reputed to be still living in the town and keeping a sweet shop there
Club Honours: Manchester City—Second Division Champions 1903, F.A. Cup winners 1904
Possessor of a fine physique and

natural agility, Hillman had mastered every phase of the goal keeping art. An impeccable performer.

HILLS, Arnold Frank   1879(1)
b 1875; d 7 March 1927.
Career: Harrow School (XI 1875-6 captain 1876); University College Oxford (Blue 1877-8); Old Harrovians: Athletics blue 1877-8-9-80 (President 1880) and was A.A.A. Mile Champion 1878. Later managing director of Thames Ironworks and founder of the club of that name later, of course, West Ham United
Club Honour: Oxford University —F.A. Cup finalists 1877
Extremely fast but variable winger with an inclination to run the ball over the goal-line when on the attack.

HILSDON, George Richard
                             1907-9(8)
b Bow, East London 10 August 1885; d 7 September 1941.
Career: East Ham Schools, South West Ham, Clapton Orient, Luton Town cs 1902, West Ham United 1903, Chelsea May 1906, West Ham United cs 1912, Chatham cs 1919
Scored goals with grand regularity throughout his first-class career. Strong in shoulder and leg, Hilsdon could unleash bullet shots with either foot and he had brilliant positional sense. A centre-forward to savour.

HINE, Ernest William   1929-32(6)
b Barnsley 9 April 1900.
Career: Staincross Station, Barnsley amateur April 1921, professional January 1922, Leicester City January 1926, Huddersfield Town May 1932, Manchester United February 1933, Barnsley December 1934, club coach May 1939
An unassuming character but an inside-forward with stamina, speed, tremendous shooting power and opportunism. Appeared at centre-forward, too, with Barnsley.

HINTON, Alan Thomas   1963-5(3)
b Wednesbury, Staffs 6 October 1942.
Career: South East Staffs Schools, Wolverhampton W a n d e r e r s ground staff 1958, professional October 1959 (England Youth international 1959), Nottingham Forest January 1964, Derby County September 1967
Club Honours: Derby County— Second Division Champions 1969, F.L. Champions 1972
Would have been at home in earlier times with his fine orthodox play at outside-left. Fast, able to centre in pinpoint fashion when going full tilt and to unleash a rocket shot at will.

HITCHENS, Gerald Archibald
                             1961-2(7)
b Rawnsley, Staffs.
Career: Highley County School, Highley Youth Club, Kidderminster Harriers, Cardiff City January 1955, Aston Villa December 1957, Internazionale Milan June 1961, Torino November 1962, Atlanto of Bergamo June 1965, Cagliari (Sardinia) cs 1967, Worcester City November 1969
Club Honours: Aston Villa— Second Division Champions 1960, Cardiff City—Welsh Cup winners 1956
Dashing, goal scoring centre-forward, one of few British players able to gear his game to differing Italian demands. The first part of his Villa period was at inside-right, in which position he was also fluent.

HOBBIS, Harold Henry Frank
                             1936(2)
b Dartford 9 March 1913.
Career: Brent School Dartford, Brent School Old Boys, Bromley, Charlton Athletic amateur Feb-

ruary 1931, professional March 1931, left cs 1948, Tonbridge player manager November 1948. Later a scout for Crystal Palace and Wolverhampton Wanderers and a licensee at Charlton
Club Honour: Charlton Athletic— Third Division South Champions 1935
Lively outside-left who had a distinctive gait when running down the wing. Often figured on the score sheet for he had a powerful, accurate shot.

HODGETTS, Dennis 1888-94(6)
b 28 November 1863; d 26 March 1945.
Career: Birmingham St. George's, briefly with Great Lever returning to St. George's, Aston Villa 1886, Small Heath 1896 retired cs 1898. Following his retirement he was a licensee. In June 1930 was elected a Vice President of Aston Villa
Club Honours: Aston Villa—F.L. Champions 1894 and 1896, F.A. Cup winners 1887-95, finalists 1892
Inside or outside-left, difficult to dispossess because he was both big and weighty. Distributed the ball with sagacity and altogether an uncommonly fine forward.

HODGKINSON, Alan 1957-61(5)
b Laughton, Rotherham 16 October 1936.
Career: Laughton Council School and Dinnington Secondary Modern School, Thurscroft Youth Club, Worksop Town, Sheffield United amateur January 1953 professional September 1953, retired cs 1971 and became assistant trainer and coach
Guarded the Sheffield United goal for a prodigious period, maintaining a high standard throughout. Heavy in build, sound and courageous in performance.

HODGSON, Gordon 1931(3)
b Johannesburg 16 April 1904; d 14 June 1951.
Career: Transvaal (toured U.K. with the South African team in 1924-5 playing in amateur international matches against each of the four Home countries), Liverpool December 1925, Aston Villa January 1936, Leeds United March 1937 retiring during the War to become coach. Port Vale manager October 1946 until his death. Played cricket for Lancashire 1928-32 and for Forfarshire 1934-6
Powerfully built inside-right or centre-forward, thrustful and a good marksman.

HODKINSON, Joseph 1913-20(3)
b Lancaster 1889; d 18 June 1954.
Career: Lancaster Town, Glossop cs 1909, Blackburn Rovers January 1913, Lancaster Town April 1923 retired January 1925. Later a licensee in Lancaster
Club Honour: Blackburn Rovers —F.L. Champions 1914
Resourceful and full of tricks at outside-left. His main asset, perhaps, was his speed, which was exceptional.

HOGG, William 1902(3)
b Newcastle-upon-Tyne 1879; d 30 January 1937.
Career: Willington Athletic, Sunderland mid 1899-1900, Rangers May 1909, Dundee May 1913, appointed player manager Raith Rovers cs 1914 but on the outbreak of War returned to Sunderland to work in an engineering works, post-War licensee at Earlsdon, West Stanley and Sunderland with some part time football for Montrose. Sunderland coach from October 1927 to 1934. From 1934 to his death was licensee of Old Mill Inn, Southwick near Sunderland
Club Honours: Sunderland—F.L. Champions 1902, Rangers—Scot-

tish League Champions 1911-2-3
Dribbled adequately and centred
expertly but this outside-right's
main characteristic was his dazzling speed.

HOLDCROFT, George Henry
1937(2)
b Norton-le-Moor near Stoke 23
January 1909.
Career: Biddulph, Norton Druids,
Whitfield Colliery, Port Vale cs
1926, Darlington cs 1928, Everton
cs 1931, Preston North End December 1932, Barnsley November
1945, retired owing to injury but
later played for Leyland Motors,
Morecambe and Chorley
Club Honour: Preston North End
—F.A. Cup winners 1938. Missed
1937 Cup final owing to injury.
Cool and agile goalkeeper of resource. Had acute anticipation
and was especially good in dealing
with lofted balls.

HOLDEN, Albert Douglas 1959(5)
b Manchester 1932.
Career: Princess Road School
Manchester, Manchester Y.M.C.A.
and England Youth international
1949 whilst on Bolton Wanderers
books as an amateur, Bolton Wanderers professional May 1949,
Preston North End November
1962, emigrated to Australia cs
1965 and played for Hakoah (Sydney) until 1968 when he became
their coach. Coach to Auburn of
Sydney 1969-70 returning to England November 1970. Grimsby
Town trainer coach January 1971
Club Honours: Bolton Wanderers
—F.A. Cup finalists 1953, winners
1958, Preston North End—F.A.
Cup finalists 1964
A winger at home on the right or
the left. Fast, tricky and a fine
ball player.

HOLDEN, George H. 1881-4(4)
Career: St John's School Wednes-
bury, Wednesbury Old Athletic,
Staffordshire

Small and swift, this outside-right
was a beautiful dribbler.

HOLDEN-WHITE, Charles Henry
1888(2)
b 1869; d 14 July 1948.
Career: Swifts; Clapham Rovers;
Corinthians 1882-91 (original committee and first captain 1882);
F.A. Committee 1883-5. In business in the City of London
A quick-moving half-back with a
sure and determined tackle.

HOLFORD, Thomas 1903(1)
b Hanley 1878; d 6 April 1964.
Career: Granvilles Night School,
Colbridge, Stoke cs 1898, Manchester City April 1908, Stoke cs
1914, Port Vale player manager
cs 1919 to cs 1924 being appointed
trainer as well July 1923. He remained with Port Vale as trainer,
from time to time team manager
and latterly as scout until retiring
in 1950
Club Honour: Manchester City—
Second Division Champions 1910
Generally regarded as a centre-
half though versatile enough to
play anywhere. Excelled at distribution and was a hard worker.
Liable to loft the ball unduly.

HOLLEY, George H. 1909-13(10)
b Seaham Harbour, Co. Durham
25 November 1885; d 27 August
1942.
Career: Seaham Athletic, Seaham
Villa, Seaham White Star mid
1903-4, Sunderland November
1904, Brighton & Hove Albion
July 1919 retired cs 1920. Sunderland coach 1920, Wolverhampton
Wanderers trainer 1922-32, Barnsley trainer from August 1932
Club Honours: Sunderland—F.L.
Champions and F.A. Cup finalists
1913
Held spectators enthralled with
his consummate ball artistry—
and his opponents bewildered. At

the same time he was no flash-in-the-pan performer but completely consistent. A wonderful inside-forward.

HOLLIDAY, Edwin   1960(3)
b Royston near Barnsley June 1939.
Career: Royston Modern School, Middlesbrough amateur 1955, professional June 1956, Sheffield Wednesday March 1962, Middlesbrough June 1965, Hereford United July 1966, Workington February 1968, Peterborough United 1969. Broke a leg November 1970. A nephew of Colin Grainger
Strong, thrustful left-winger. Had a variety of tricks and a dangerous hard shot in either foot.

HOLLINS, John William   1967(1)
b Guildford 16 July 1946.
Career: Guildford Schools, Guildford junior football, Chelsea amateur July 1961 professional July 1963 (England Youth international 1964) Brother of David Hollins, Welsh international goalkeeper
Club Honours: Chelsea—F.L. Cup winners 1965, F.A. Cup finalists 1967, winners 1970, European Cup Winners Cup winners 1971, F.L. Cup finalists 1972
Energetic little right-half always busy and always purposeful. Is crisp in tackling and not averse to seizing a scoring chance himself.

HOLMES, Robert   1888-95(7)
b Preston 23 June 1867; d 17 November 1955.
Career: Preston Olympic, Preston North End 1884-1901, reinstated as an amateur May 1901 and put on the F.L. referees list. Was Bradford City trainer from May 1904 to 1905 and then Blackburn Rovers trainer until November 1913. Also coached at a number of Public Schools
Club Honours: Preston North End—F.L. Champions 1889-90,

F.A. Cup finalists 1888, winners 1889
Equally good on both flanks as a full-back. Active, brave and able to kick from any angle.

HOLT, John   1890-1900(10)
b Blackburn 1865; d
Career: Kings Own Blackburn, Blackpool St John's, Church, Bootle (for three years), Everton, Reading October 1898. Elected a director of Reading in 1902 but was unable to take up the directorship as his application for re-instatement as an amateur was turned down. He later returned to the Liverpool area and just before the 1914-18 War he was scouting for Reading in that area
Club Honours: Everton—F.L. Champions 1891, F.A. Cup finalists 1893-7
Had none of a centre-half's usual physical advantage being only 5 feet $4\frac{1}{2}$ inches tall and a little over 10 stones in weight during his playing career, but a leading pivot of the nineties. Tireless, elusive and with no superior at placing the ball.

HOPKINSON, Edward 1958-60(14)
b Wheatley Hill, Co. Durham 19 October 1935.
Career: Byron Street School Royton and Royton Secondary Modern School, Haggate Lads Club, Oldham Athletic amateur to cs 1952, Bolton Wanderers amateur cs 1952 professional November 1952 retired cs 1970 and joined club coaching staff
Club Honour: Bolton Wanderers —F.A. Cup winners 1958
Could almost be bracketed with Teddy Davison in the matter of lack of inches. Like Davison, too, this did not adversely affect his goalkeeping which had brilliance, daring and remarkable consistency.

HOSSACK, Anthony Henry
1892-4(2)
b Walsall 2 May 1867; d 24 January 1926.
Career: Chigwell School (XI 1882-3-4-5 captain 1885); Jesus College Cambridge (Blue 1890); Corinthians 1891-4. Played cricket for Cambridge University but did not win a blue. Admitted a solicitor in 1897 he practised at Dawlish, Devon
Accomplished in both wing-half berths and notable for his great speed.

HOUGHTON, William Eric
1931-3(7)
b Billingborough, Lincs 29 June 1910.
Career: Donnington G.S., Boston Town, Billingborough, Aston Villa amateur August 1927, professional August 1928, Notts County December 1946, manager April 1949 to August 1953, Aston Villa manager September 1953 to November 1958, Nottingham Forest chief scout July 1959 to November 1960, Rugby Town manager February 1961 to March 1964, Walsall scout late 1965. Later a Walsall Club director which he still is. Played cricket for Lincolnshire and Warwickshire Club and ground
Club Honours: Aston Villa—Second Division Champions 1938, F.L. North Cup winners 1944
Speedy outside-left famed for thunderbolt shooting with both feet and as a successful penalty taker. Perhaps the hardest shot with a dead ball of his generation.

HOULKER, Albert Edward
("Kelly") 1902-6(5)
b Blackburn 27 April 1872; d 27 May 1962.
Career: Blackburn Hornets, Oswaldtwistle Rovers, Cob Wall, Park Road Blackburn, Blackburn Rovers 1894, Portsmouth May 1902, Southampton May

1903, Blackburn Rovers cs 1906 retired cs 1907. Signed for Colne cs 1909. Played once for Blackburn Rovers in emergency in January 1918. After retiring from football he worked in Blackburn for some years as an overlooker at Garden Street Mill and then ran a coal and haulage business in the town until 1947
Club Honour: Southampton—Southern League Champions 1904
Small, enthusiastic left-half who never gave up. A favourite wherever he went because of his pluck and tenacity.

HOWARTH, Robert Henry
1887-94(5)
b Preston, Lancs 1865; d 20 August 1938.
Career: Preston North End, Everton November 1891, Preston North End cs 1894. Admitted a solicitor in January 1908 he practised in Preston
Club Honours: Preston North End—F.A. Cup finalists 1888, winners 1889, F.L. Champions 1889 and 1890, Everton—F.A. Cup finalists 1893
An immaculate right-back always cool and collected and owner of a remarkably sure tackle.

HOWE, Donald
1958-60(23)
b Wolverhampton 12 October 1935.
Career: St Peters School Wolverhampton, West Bromwich Albion amateur 1951 professional November 1952, Arsenal April 1964. Broke a leg March 1966 and this injury ended his playing career. Remained on Arsenal staff, chief coach November 1967, assistant manager March 1969, West Bromwich Albion manager July 1971
Deft positioning, reliability and strength in tackling and kicking and acumen generally were the hall-marks of his play at right-back.

HOWE, John Robert   1948-9(3)
b West Hartlepool 7 October 1913.
Career: Hartlepool junior football, Hartlepools United June 1934, Derby County March 1936, Huddersfield Town October 1949, King's Lynn player manager July 1951, Long Sutton player manager August 1955 and also played for Wisbech Town
Club Honour: Derby County—F.A. Cup winners 1946
A back who played on the left mostly. He was unhesitating and fearless while generous physical proportions provided a measure of dominance.

HOWELL, Leonard Sidgwick
1873(1)
b Dulwich 6 August 1848; d 7 September 1895.
Career: Winchester College; Wanderers; Surrey. Also played cricket for Surrey. A Malt factor by profession
Club Honour: Wanderers—F.A. Cup winners 1873
Appeared as both a back and a half-back and excelled at both. His kicking won much admiration.

HOWELL, Rabbi   1895-9(2)
b Wincobank, Sheffield 12 October 1869; d
Career: Ecclesfield, Rotherham Swifts, Sheffield United cs 1890, Liverpool April 1898, Preston North End cs 1901 retired injury late 1903
Club Honour: Sheffield United—F.L. Champions 1898
Half-back originally a pivot but converted to the right-flank on joining Sheffield United. Despite being small he played tirelessly and was commendably fast.

HUDSON, John   1883(1)
Career: Sheffield Heeley; Sheffield Wednesday 1880-3 (secretary for a period); Blackburn Olympic
A prominent half-back of the 1880's. Very strong defensively because of his resilience and dogged tackling.

HUDSPETH, Francis Carr   1926(1)
b Percy Main, Northumberland April 1890; d 8 February 1963.
Career: Scotswood, Newburn, Clare Vale, North Shields Athletic, Newcastle United March 1910, Stockport County January 1929 retired cs 1930. Rochdale trainer, Burnley assistant trainer 1934-45 when he left football but continued to reside in Burnley
Club Honours: Newcastle United—F.A. Cup winners 1924, F.L. Champions 1927
Had a long first class career for an outfield player. A stalwart left-back and very sound, Hudspeth exploited a forcible kick.

HUFTON, Arthur Edward
1924-9(6)
b Southwell, Notts 25 November 1893; d 2 February 1967.
Career: Atlas & Norfolk Works, Sheffield United mid 1912-13, West Ham United cs 1919, Watford June 1932. Later in the car trade.
Club Honour: West Ham United—F.A. Cup finalists 1923
A real crowd pleaser being a goalkeeper of the spectacular sort. Suffered several bad injuries through taking risks but could not be faulted for courage.

HUGHES, Emlyn Walter   1970-2(18)
b Barrow-in-Furness 1947.
Career: Roose F.C. (Blackpool), Blackpool 1964, Liverpool February 1967. Son of Fred Hughes, a Great Britain Rugby League international
Club Honours: Liverpool—F.A. Cup finalists 1971
A biggish bundle of dynamic energy at left-half, whose attacking instincts have brought him some spectacular goals. Has appeared at full-back also.

C. W. Alcock – the man who started
international football

N. C. Bailey

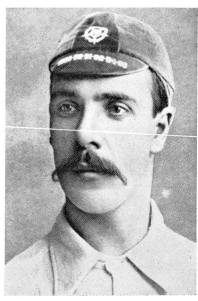

E. C. Bambridge

J. Goodall

W. I. Bassett

J. W. Crabtree

G. O. Smith

S. Bloomer

HUGHES, Lawrence 1950(3)
b Waterloo, Lancs 1926.
Career: Tranmere Rovers amateur 1942, Liverpool February 1943 retired May 1960
Club Honours: Liverpool—F.A. Cup finalists 1950, F.L. Champions 1947
Perfectly built for his pivotal role and a magnificent header of the ball. Preferred the ground pass aimed with constructive intent.

HULME, Joseph Harold
  Anthony 1927-33(9)
b Stafford 26 August 1904.
Career: Stafford Y.M.C.A., York City 1923, Blackburn Rovers February 1924, Arsenal February 1926, Huddersfield Town January 1938, retired cs 1938, Tottenham Hotspur assistant secretary February 1944, team manager October 1945 to May 1949 thence a sports journalist retiring in 1969. Middlesex county cricket 1929-39 scoring 8,103 runs in first class cricket including 12 centuries
Club Honours: Arsenal—F.L. Champions 1931, 3, 5, F.A. Cup winners 1930-6, finalists 1927-32, Huddersfield Town—F.A. Cup finalists 1938
Few outside-rights had his fleetness of foot though speed was not his only quality. He had numerous tricks for beating a back and could centre and shoot with accuracy.

HUMPHREYS, Percy 1903(1)
b Cambridge 1881.
Career: Cambridge St Marys, Queens Park Rangers, Notts County cs 1901, Leicester Fosse June 1907, Chelsea February 1908, Tottenham Hotspur December 1909, Leicester Fosse October 1911, Hartlepools United player manager cs 1912
Probing and thrustful, Humphreys was an inside-right of value, capable of a dexterous dribble and dangerous marksmanship.

K

HUNT, George Samuel 1933(3)
b Barnsley 22 February 1910.
Career: Regent Street Congregationals (Barnsley), Chesterfield, Tottenham Hotspur June 1930, Arsenal October 1937, Bolton Wanderers March 1938, Sheffield Wednesday November 1946, Bolton Wanderers assistant trainer May 1948 remaining on the Club staff until September 1968
Club Honours: Arsenal—F.L. Champions 1938, Bolton Wanderers—F.L. North Cup winners 1945
No giant physically but a consistent goal scorer whether at centre-forward or inside-right. A persistent forager and quite fearless.

HUNT, Kenneth Reginald
  Gunnery 1911(2)
b Oxford 24 February 1884; d 28 April 1949.
Career: Trent College (XI 1901-4 captain 1903-4); Queens College Oxford (Blue 1905-6-7-8); Corinthians 1906-7 and 1920-3; Leyton; Crystal Palace; Wolverhampton Wanderers; Oxford City: F.A. Council 1946-9. Made 20 England amateur international appearances 1907-21. Ordained in 1909, he was a master at Highgate School 1908-45
Club Honours: Wolverhampton Wanderers—F.A. Cup winners 1908; Oxford City—F.A. Amateur Cup finalists 1913
The personification of the muscular Christian, Kenneth Hunt was a wing-half who believed in speed and was absolutely without fear. A striking personality.

HUNT, Roger 1962-9(34)
b Golborne, Lancs 20 July 1938.
Career: Culcheth Secondary Modern School, Leigh Grammar School, Croft Youth Club, Stockton Heath, Liverpool July 1959, Bolton Wanderers December 1969 retired cs 1972. A member of England's World Cup winning

team 1966
Club Honours: Liverpool—Second
Division Champions 1962, F.L.
Champions 1964 and 1966, F.A.
Cup winners 1965, European Cup
Winners Cup finalists 1966
The archetypal honest journey-
man. A sterling inside-right,
utterly reliable, playing with a
dogged resolution and no little
skill for the full ninety minutes.

HUNTER, John   1878-82(7)
b Crookes, Sheffield 1852; d 10
April 1903.
Career: Sheffield Heeley 1870;
Providence; Sheffield Albion;
Sheffield Wednesday and played
on occasion for a number of other
Sheffield teams until going to
Blackburn to play for Blackburn
Olympic in 1882, Blackburn
Rovers 1887 remaining with the
club as assistant trainer and
groundsman. Was also a licensee
in Blackburn. He was a noted
runner in his young days
Club Honour: Blackburn Olympic
—F.A. Cup winners 1883
Reputed to be one of the finest
half-backs of his time, his power-
ful and clean kicking being specially praised. Also played full-back
but was not so good in this position.

HUNTER, Norman   1966-72(20)
b Eighton Banks near Newcastle
29 October 1943.
Career: Birtley Juniors, Leeds
United November 1960
Club Honours: Leeds United—
Second Division Champions 1964,
F.A. Cup finalists 1965, 70, winners 1972, Fairs Cup finalists
1967, F.L. Cup winners 1968, F.L.
Champions 1969, Fairs Cup winners 1968 and 1971
Well built, fierce tackling left-half
who plays as hard a game for
Leeds as Wilf Copping used to
do. Seems to do most things with
his left foot although, by no
means, one-footed.

HURST, Geoffrey Charles
                        1966-72(49)
b Ashton-under-Lyne, Lancs 8
December 1941.
Career: Chelmsford Schools, West
Ham United ground staff 1958,
professional April 1959 (England
Youth international 1959); Stoke
City June 1972. A member of the
England World Cup winning team
of 1966 scoring a hat-trick in the
final v West Germany. Played
cricket for Essex in 1962.
Club Honours: West Ham United
—F.A. Cup winners 1964, European Cup Winners Cup winners
1965, F.L. Cup finalists 1966, F.A.
Youth Cup finalists 1959
Became a household name after
his 1966 World Cup exploits. A
big incisive striker (centre-forward
or inside-left), full of heart and
thoroughly unselfish.

IREMONGER, James   1901-2(2)
b Norton, Yorks 5 March 1876;
d 25 March 1956.
Career: Wilford, Nottingham Jardine, Nottingham Forest early
1896 retiring cs 1910. Trainer
Notts County cs 1919 to cs 1927.
Played cricket for Notts from
1897 to 1914 scoring 16,622 runs
in first class cricket including 31
centuries and took 619 wickets.
He was later on the Notts coaching staff for some years
Heftily built and able to play in
both fullback positions as he was
equally strong in both feet. Although a powerful defender his
rather uncontrolled lunges could
prove costly to his side.

JACK, David Bone Nightingale
                        1924-33(9)
b Bolton 3 April 1899; d 10 September 1958.
Career: Leigh Road School Southend, Plymouth Presbyterians,
Royal Navy, Plymouth Argyle cs
1919, Bolton Wanderers December 1920, Arsenal October 1928,
Southend United manager May
1934 to August 1940. Middles-

brough manager September 1944 to April 1952, Shelbourne manager August 1953 to April 1955. He then served with Inland Revenue as he had done during the early part of his career

Club Honours: Bolton Wanderers —F.A. Cup winners 1923-6, Arsenal—F.A. Cup winners 1930, finalists 1932, F.L. Champions 1931, 3, 4

A cool brain, brilliant close dribbling and deadly finishing distinguished this inside-right, who also on occasion appeared in the centre. A famous name and a great footballer.

JACKSON, Elphinstone　1891(1)
b Calcutta 9 October 1868; d December 1945.

Career: Lancing College (XI 1886-7 captain 1887); Oriel College Oxford (Blue 1890-1); Corinthians 1889-90: Son of a High Court Judge in Calcutta he returned to India on leaving Oxford and was a founder member of the Indian F.A. in 1893

His main attribute as a full-back was a reliable kick and also he was adequate in the tackle. On the debit side was his inability to head the ball.

JARRETT, Beaumont Griffith
1876-8(3)
b London 18 July 1855; d 11 April 1905.

Career: Harrow School; Christ's College Cambridge (Blue 1876-7-8 captain 1877); Old Harrovians; Grantham; F.A. Council 1876-8. Ordained in 1878 he spent the rest of his life in the Ministry in Lincolnshire

Tireless, quick and brave half-back possessing perfect ball control. Could be brilliant but, against this, was apt to be a little too showy.

JEFFERIS, Frank　1912(2)
b Fordingbridge, Hants 1888; d 21 May 1938.

Career: Fordingbridge Turks, Southampton circa 1905, Everton March 1911, Preston North End January 1920, player coach cs 1922, Southport player coach June 1923 to cs 1925, trainer coach May 1926 playing twice in emergency in 1927, Millwall trainer from May 1936 until his death after collapsing at the New Cross ground

Club Honours: Everton—F.L. Champions 1915, Preston North End—F.A. Cup finalists 1922

Had a long career, markedly so for a forward (he was an inside-right throughout). His style was graceful and neat and he brought the best out of the other attackers.

JEZZARD, Bedford A. G.
1954-6(2)
b Clerkenwell 19 October 1926.

Career: Croxley Green School, Croxley Green Juniors, Fulham professional October 1948, retired August 1957 following injury but remained on the Club staff being appointed team manager June 1958, general manager October 1964 but resigned December 1964. After leaving the game became a licensee in the Hammersmith area where he still is

Club Honour: Fulham—Second Division Champions 1949

Speedy centre or inside-forward not easily moved off the ball. He displayed a degree of thrust and was a frequent goal scorer.

JOHNSON, Edward　1880-4(2)
b 1862; d 30 June 1901.

Career: Saltley College 1880-1; Stoke from 1880; Birmingham F.A. and Staffordshire; retired from the game owing to injuries sustained when he fell out of a trap. After his retiral he was closely associated with the running of the Stoke St. Peters Club and was a member of the Staffordshire F.A. until ill-health caused him to give up in 1898.

Fast, dashing winger, a remarkable dribbler and marksman. Occasionally flawed his performance by keeping the ball too long.

JOHNSON, Joseph Arthur 1937(5)
b Grimsby circa 1912.
Career: Grimsby junior football, Scunthorpe United, Bristol City May 1931, Stoke City April 1932, West Bromwich Albion November 1937, Northwich Victoria August 1946
Club Honour: Stoke City—Second Division Champions 1933
An excellent little player who achieved a good scoring record for a left winger. Possibly the highlight of his career was the 1937 Scotland match when his skilful, swerving runs bemused the Scots defence.

JOHNSON, Thomas Clark Fisher
1926-33(5)
b Dalton-in-Furnace, Lancs 19 August 1900.
Career: Dalton Casuals, Manchester City February 1919, Everton March 1930 Liverpool March 1934, Darwen August 1936
Club Honours: Manchester City—F.A. Cup finalists 1926, Second Division Champions 1928, Everton—Second Division Champions 1931, F.L. Champions 1932, F.A. Cup winners 1933
Powerful player often on target in the centre and inside-left. Played mostly in the latter position where his long and short passes were models of judgment.

JOHNSON, William Harold
1900-3(6)
b Ecclesfield mid 1870s; d
Career: Atlas & Norfolk Works, Ecclesfield Church, Sheffield United circa 1897, retired through injury cs 1909 and remained on the club training staff until about 1935
Club Honours: Sheffield United—F.A. Cup winners 1899-1902, finalists 1901

Tireless right-half with an attacking bent, having a good shot and the ability to centre well. This was not at the expense of defence for he was an all-round half.

JOHNSTON, Harry 1947-54(10)
b Droylsden, Lancs 1919.
Career: Fairfield Road School Droylsden, Droylsden Athletic, Blackpool ground staff June 1935 professional 1936 retired November 1955 to become Reading manager until January 1963. Rejoined Blackpool as chief scout in April 1967 and has since had two spells as caretaker manager. Has a newsagency business in Blackpool
Club Honours: Blackpool—F.L. North Cup winners 1943, finalists 1944, F.A. Cup winners 1953, finalists 1948-51
Played with distinction and consistency in all three half-back positions. Was a first-rate strategist and notably constructive.

JONES, Alfred 1882-3(3)
Career: Walsall Town Swifts, Great Lever 1882, Walsall Town Swifts cs 1883, Aston Villa mid 1885-6
A sterling right or left-back. Had many qualities: steady in application, a good tackler and thoughtful throughout.

JONES, Harry 1923(1)
b Blackwell, Derbyshire May 1891.
Career: Blackwell Boys Brigade, Wesley Guild, Blackwell Colliery, Nottingham Forest cs 1911 retired injury cs 1924 but joined Sutton Town December 1924
Club Honour: Nottingham Forest—Second Division Champions 1922
A quite fearless left-back unsurpassed for dash and determination when at his peak. Kept a high standard of performance throughout his Forest period.

JONES, Herbert 1927-8(6)
b Blackpool 1897.
Career: South Shore Strollers, Fleetwood 1920, Blackpool cs 1922, Blackburn Rovers December 1925, Brighton & Hove Albion cs 1934, Fleetwood cs 1935
Club Honour: Blackburn Rovers —F.A. Cup winners 1928
Dauntless, fleet footed left-back. A lot of thought went into his play which showed mastery in positioning.

JONES, Michael David 1965-70(3)
b Worksop 24 April 1945.
Career: Sheffield junior football, Sheffield United apprentice April 1961, professional November 1962, Leeds United September 1967
Club Honours: Leeds United— Fairs Cup winners 1968 and 1971, F.L. Champions 1969, F.A. Cup finalists 1970, F.A. Cup winners 1972
Has the traditional virtues of a burly centre-forward, aggressive, hard to dispossess and a good marksman. In the Leeds attack he acts as the bludgeon, admirably complementing the rapier of Allan Clarke.

JONES, William 1901(1)
b Brighton 1876; d
Career: Bristol Rovers, Willington Athletic (Sussex), Loughborough Town 1896, Bristol City cs 1897, Tottenham Hotspur May 1906, Swindon Town May 1907
Club Honour: Bristol City— Second Division Champions 1906
Was a successful inside-left until joining Bristol City who made him a right-half. It was in the latter position that he achieved international recognition and where he exhibited qualities of interception and distribution.

JONES, William H. 1950(2)
b Whaley Bridge, Derbyshire.
Career: Hayfield St Matthews,

Liverpool September 1938, Ellesmere Port Town player manager May 1954
Club Honours: Liverpool—F.L. Champions 1947, F.A. Cup finalists 1950
Joined Liverpool as an inside-forward and gave his splendid versatility wide rein after the War at right-back and all three half-back berths. Perhaps best as a pivot but boundlessly stylish and showing an innate positional sense anywhere.

JOY, Bernard 1936(1)
b Fulham 29 October 1911.
Career: London University; Casuals; Corinthians; Southend United amateur Fulham amateur 1934; Arsenal amateur May 1935 to cs 1947, when he returned to Casuals, retired cs 1948. Won 12 England amateur caps between 1934-47 and played in the Olympic Games in 1936. Originally a schoolmaster, after retiring from the playing side of the game he became a journalist first with *The Star* and latterly with the *Evening Standard*. Author of *Forward, Arsenal!*, a complete history of the Arsenal club
Club Honours: Casuals—F.A. Amateur Cup winners 1936, Arsenal—F.L. Champions 1938, F.L. War Cup finalists 1941, F.L. South Cup winners 1943
Developed a similar "third back" style to his predecessor as Arsenal's centre-half, Herbert Roberts. Big and powerfully built, Joy was one of the few amateurs in modern times to hold his own in First Division football and was the last amateur to win a full Cap.

KAIL, Edgar Isaac L. 1929(3)
b 26 November 1900.
Career: Goodrich Road School South London (England v Wales and Scotland Schools 1915), Dulwich Hamlet 1915-34, Surrey County. 21 England amateur inter-

national appearances 1921-33. He was a representative of a wine and spirit firm until his retirement in 1966
Club Honours: Dulwich Hamlet— F.A. Amateur Cup winners 1920 and 1932
Between the Wars a famous figure in the amateur game and a very fine inside-right indeed. Excelled in all the skills necessary to an inside-forward and if on the odd occasion he attempted to do too much it was a case of being a little over-confident in his own great ability.

KAY, Anthony Herbert   1963(1)
b Attercliffe, Sheffield May 1937.
Career: Sheffield junior football, Sheffield Wednesday professional May 1954, Everton December 1962 until his suspension April 1965. Now living in Spain
Club Honours: Sheffield Wednesday—Second Division Champions 1959, Everton—F.L. Champions 1963
His fiery play matched his flame hair. A left-half relentless in tackling, forcible in attack and defence.

KEAN, Frederick William
1923-9(9)
b Sheffield 3 April 1897.
Career: Hallam, Portsmouth cs 1919, Sheffield Wednesday cs 1920, Bolton Wanderers September 1928, Luton Town June 1931, Sutton Town player coach November 1935
Club Honours: Sheffield Wednesday—Second Division Champions 1926, Bolton Wanderers—F.A. Cup winners 1929
Noticeable on the field for his upright, Guardsmanlike carriage. This was symptomatic of his play, whether at right or centre-half, which was very efficient. Good with his head and a dour tackler.

KEEN, Errington Ridley Liddell
1933-7(4)
b Walker-on-Tyne 1910.
Career: Newcastle Schools, Nun's Moor, Newcastle United ground staff 1926, professional mid 1927-8 season, Derby County December 1930, Chelmsford City May 1938, Hereford United player manager July 1939, Leeds United December 1945, Bacup Borough July 1946, later a coach in Hong Kong. Prominent on the field for stylishness as well as his very blonde thatch. Keen was a capital left-half—quick to the tackle and in getting his attack moving, and very sure-footed.

KELLY, Robert   1920-8(14)
b Ashton-in-Makerfield, Lancs 16 November 1893; d 22 September 1969.
Career: Ashton White Star, Ashton Central, Earlestown 1912, St Helens Town August 1913, Burnley November 1913, Sunderland December 1925, Huddersfield Town February 1927, Preston North End July 1932, Carlisle United player manager March 1935 retiring as a player mid 1935-6, Stockport County manager November 1936 to March 1939, S C de Portugal trainer August 1946 later Barry Town manager December 1960
Club Honours: Burnley—F.L. Champions 1921, Huddersfield Town—F.A. Cup finalists 1928-30
One of the greatest names between the Wars. A right-wing forward mostly in the inside position, he had wonderful ball control, remarkable acceleration over a short distance, fine distribution and was neat in everything he did.

KENYON-SLANEY, William Slaney   1873(1)
b Rajkote, India 24 August 1847; d 24 April 1908.
Career: Eton College; Christ Church Oxford (prior to the Uni-

versity soccer match); Old Etonians; Wanderers: Served in the Grenadier Guards 1867-88. M.P. for Newport, Shrops 1886-1908 being elected a Privy Councillor in 1904
Club Honours: Wanderers—F.A. Cup winners 1873, Old Etonians—F.A. Cup finalists 1875-6
Regarded as one of the most successful and effective forwards of the mid 1870s. Played with *élan* and dash.

KEVAN, Derek T. 1957-61(14)
b Ripon, Yorks 6 March 1935.
Career: Ripon Secondary Modern School, Ripon Y.M.C.A., Bradford late 1952, West Bromwich Albion July 1953, Chelsea March 1963, Manchester City August 1963, Crystal Palace July 1965, Peterborough United March 1966, Luton Town December 1966, Stockport County March 1967, Macclesfield August 1968, Boston United October 1968, Stourbridge mid 1968-9 to cs 1969. Became a licensee in the latter stages of his career and has remained in that business since his retirement.
Big, rugged, hard shooting centre or inside-forward. His bustling tactics were not viewed with unalloyed approval by some critics, but no one could deny he made his presence felt.

KIDD, Brian 1970(2)
b Manchester 29 May 1949.
Career: St Patricks School (Collyhurst, Manchester), Manchester United apprentice cs 1964, professional June 1966
Club Honour: Manchester United —European Cup winners 1968
Splendidly mobile young inside-forward. Has persistence, attacking flair and is highly dangerous with both head and feet.

KING, Robert Stuart 1882(1)
b Leigh-on-Sea, Essex 1862; d 5 March 1950.
Career: Felsted School (XI 1878-9-80); Hertford College, Oxford (Blue 1882-3-4-5 captain 1885); Upton Park; Grimsby Town; Essex. Ordained in 1887 he was Rector of Leigh-on-Sea from 1892 until his death
A pioneer in one aspect of half-back play—heading, where he was as accurate as with his feet. Was, in addition, composed, reliable and hard.

KINGSFORD, Robert Kennett
1874(1)
b Sydenham Hill 23 December 1849; d 14 October 1895.
Career: Marlborough College; Wanderers (of which club he was at one time secretary); Surrey. Also played cricket for Surrey. At one time a law student he later went to Australia
Club Honours: Wanderers—F.A. Cup winners 1873
Mobile and worthy forward with a penchant for goalscoring. Headed the country's list of scorers in 1873-4 season.

KINGSLEY, Matthew 1901(1)
b Turton, Lancs 1876; d
Career: Turton, Darwen, Newcastle United late 1897-8, West Ham United May 1904, Queens Park Rangers cs 1905 to cs 1906. Rochdale October 1907
A most efficient goalkeeper able to meet most demands. Perhaps his most noticeable trait was in fisting the ball powerfully and effectively.

KINSEY, George 1892-6(4)
b 1867; d early 1911.
Career: Burton Crusaders, Burton Swifts, Mitchell's St George's, Wolverhampton Wanderers cs 1891, Aston Villa cs 1894, Derby County cs 1895, Notts County March 1897, Eastville Rovers cs 1897 reinstated as an amateur August 1904

Club Honours: Wolverhampton
Wanderers—F.A. Cup winners
1893
An able left-half extremely resolute and a really hard worker.

KIRCHEN, Alfred John   1937(3)
b Shouldham, Norfolk 26 April
1913.
Career: Kings Lynn Schools,
Shouldham, Norwich City November 1933, Arsenal March 1935 retiring owing to injury 1943. Norwich City trainer 1946 for a spell
but then became a farmer and
later a director of Norwich City
Club Honours: Arsenal—F.L.
Champions 1938, F.L. War Cup
finalists 1941, F.L. South Cup
winners 1943
An outside-right of the speedy,
dashing variety. Difficult to relieve
of the ball because of his hefty
build and a consistent goal scorer.

KIRTON, William John   1922(1)
b Newcastle-upon-Tyne 2 December 1896.
Career: Todds Nook School North
Shields, Pandon Temperance 1917,
Leeds City May 1919, Aston Villa
October 1919, Coventry City September 1928
Club Honours: Aston Villa—F.A.
Cup winners 1920, finalists 1924
A fine little inside-right. He had a
creditable, though not large, goal
tally, but his main value was a
splendid capacity to link up with
his partner.

KNIGHT, Arthur Egerton   1920(1)
b Godalming, Surrey 7 September
1887; d 10 March 1956.
Career: King Edward VI Grammar School Guildford; Portsmouth 1909-22; Corinthians 1921-
31; Surrey: 30 England amateur
international appearances 1910-
23. Played cricket for Hampshire
occasionally from 1912-23.
Club Honour: Portsmouth—
Southern League Champions 1920
A left-back of sterling worth. Any

deficiency in pace was counter-
acted by clever positioning and
he was also blessed with tackling
and heading skills.

KNOWLES, Cyril Barry   1968(4)
b Fitzwilliam, Yorks 13 July 1944.
Career: Kinsley Council School,
Monckton Colliery (Manchester
United and Wolverhampton Wanderers trials), Middlesbrough professional October 1962, Tottenham Hotspur May 1964
Club Honours: Tottenham Hotspur—F.A. Cup winners 1967,
F.L. Cup winners 1971, UEFA
Cup winners 1972
Right or left-back. Tall and long-
legged, Knowles has a biting
tackle and attacking ideas, being
able to float over a centre from
one of his overlap sorties as well
as an old-time winger.

LABONE, Brian Leslie
                           1963-70(26)
b Liverpool 23 January 1940.
Career: Liverpool   Collegiate
School, Everton July 1957, retired
June 1972
Club Honours: Everton—F.L.
Champions 1963, 70, F.A. Cup
winners 1966, F.A. Cup finalists
1968
There is nothing flamboyant about
this excellent centre-half and he
is none the worse for that. Calm
and reliable in defence, especially
in headwork, and a thorough
sportsman.

LANGLEY, Ernest James   1958(3)
b Kilburn, London 7 February
1929.
Career: Evelyns Senior School
Kilburn,   Yiewsley,   Hounslow
Town, Uxbridge, Hayes (Brentford amateur), Guildford City
1947, Leeds United June 1952,
Brighton & Hove Albion July
1953,   Fulham   February   1957,
Queens Park Rangers June 1965,
Hillingdon Borough player manager September 1967 to May 1971
when he retired, Crystal Palace

trainer coach August 1971
Club Honours: Queens Park
Rangers—F.L. Cup winners and
Third Division Champions 1967
A nimble left-back who had a
long career. An instinct for attack
could be indulged because he had
the speed to get back in position
after an upfield dash.

LANGTON, Robert   1947-51(11)
b Burscough, Lancs 1919.
Career: Burscough Victoria,
Blackburn Rovers September
1938, Preston North End August
1948, Bolton Wanderers 1949,
Blackburn Rovers September 1953,
Ards June 1956, Wisbech Town
July 1957, Kidderminster Harriers
cs 1959, Wisbech Town October
1959 to December 1959, Colwyn
Bay October 1960. Became a licensee in Wisbech late in 1961. Kings
Lynn trainer coach July 1962,
Wisbech Town coach cs 1963 and
later became Burscough Rangers
manager cs 1968
Club Honours Blackburn Rovers
—Second Division Champions
1939, Bolton Wanderers—F.A.
Cup finalists 1953, Glentoran—
Irish Cup finalists 1945 (as a
guest)
A flying outside-left famed for
speed and cleverness. Crossed a
ball with pinpoint accuracy and
his left foot shot could be devastating.

LATHERON, Edwin Gladstone
1913-14(2)
b Grangetown, Yorks; d 14 October 1917.
Career: Grangetown, Blackburn
Rovers March 1906. Killed in
action whilst serving as a Gunner,
Royal Field Artillery
Club Honours: Blackburn Rovers
—F.L. Champions 1912 and 1914
Just before the 1914-18 War was
considered by many critics to be
the finest inside-left in the country.
Certainly he had dazzling footwork and could work openings

for colleagues as well as scoring
himself. Equally effective at inside-right.

LAWLER, Christopher   1971-2(4)
b Liverpool 20 October 1943.
Career: St Teresa's Roman Catholic School Liverpool (England
Schools v Scotland Wales Ireland
Eire and West Germany (2) 1959),
Liverpool amateur May 1959, professional October 1960
Club Honours: Liverpool—F.A.
Cup winners 1965, F.L. Champions 1966, European Cup Winners Cup finalists 1966, F.A. Cup
finalists 1971
First appeared at centre-half and
then attained regular first team
status at right-back. A quick
mover, commandingly tall, with a
penchant for attack. Has a
remarkable number of goals to
his credit for a defender.

LAWTON, Thomas   1939-49(23)
b Bolton 6 October 1919.
Career: Tonge Moor and Castle
Hill Schools, Folds Road Central
School Bolton, Rossendale United,
Burnley amateur May 1935 professional October 1936, Everton
January 1937, Chelsea November
1945, Notts County November
1947, Brentford March 1952,
player manager January 1953 to
September 1953, Arsenal September 1953, Kettering Town player
manager February 1956 to April
1957, Notts County manager May
1957 (signing as a player but not
on Football League forms December 1957 to July 1958). Kettering Town manager November
1963 to April 1964 and later a
Club director. Notts County coach
October 1968 until April 1970
since when he has been out of
football
Club Honours: Everton—F.L.
Champions 1939, Notts County—
Third Division South Champions
1950
A young prodigy who handsomely

realised his early promise to become a great centre-forward. Brilliant on the ground, absolutely supreme in the air and a constant threat to defences throughout a longish career.

LEACH, Thomas   1931(2)
b Wincobank, near Sheffield 23 September 1903.
Career: Wath Athletic cs 1924, Sheffield Wednesday 1926, Newcastle United, June 1934, Stockport County cs 1936, Carlisle United February 1937, Lincoln City November 1938 retired cs 1939
Club Honours: Sheffield Wednesday—F.L. Champions 1929 and 1930, Stockport County—Third Division North Champions 1937
Like his club and country contemporaries, Strange and Marsden, he graduated from the attack to the intermediate line. Leach became an excellent pivot, particularly so in defence, his lithe physique being a distinct asset.

LEAKE, Alexander   1904-5(5)
b Small Heath 11 July 1872; d 29 March 1938.
Career: Green Lane School, Hoskin & Sewell, Kings Heath, Old Hill Wanderers, Small Heath cs 1894, Aston Villa June 1902, Burnley December 1907 to cs 1910, Wednesday Old Athletic cs 1910, Crystal Palace trainer cs 1912 to cs 1915, Merthyr Town trainer October 1919 to cs 1920 when he left football apart from part-time coaching
Club Honour: Aston Villa—F.A. Cup winners 1905
A confirmed humorist on and off the field and his sunny disposition showed in his play. His positions were centre and left-half where he was safe and able in defence, had tremendous stamina and never played to the gallery.

LEE, Ernest Albert   1904(1)
b Bridport, Dorset 1879; d 14 January 1958.
Career: Poole, Southampton cs 1900, Dundee May 1906, Southampton cs 1911 retired during the 1914-18 War and appointed club trainer 1919 retiring in 1935. Later helped with his son's radio business as a salesman.
Club Honours: Southampton—F.A. Cup finalists 1902, Southern League Champions 1901, 3, 4, Dundee—Scottish Cup winners 1910
Swarthy complexioned right-half whose style was a mixture of dash and sagacity. His placing of the ball was praiseworthy and invariably found a team-mate.

LEE, Francis Henry   1969-72(27)
b Westhoughton, Lancs 29 April 1944.
Career: Westhoughton Secondary Modern School, Horwich Technical School, Bolton Wanderers July 1959, Manchester City October 1967
Club Honours: Manchester City—F.L. Champions 1968, F.A. Cup winners 1969, F.L. Cup winners and European Cup Winners Cup winners 1970
Aggressive little forward who made his reputation at outside-right and centre-forward. Extremely sturdy and difficult to move off the ball he can bore his way through with great persistence.

LEE, John   1951(1)
b Sileby, Leicestershire.
Career: Quorn Methodists, Leicester City December 1940, Derby County June 1950, Coventry City November 1954 to cs 1955. Played county cricket for Leicestershire
Club Honour: Leicester City—F.A. Cup finalists 1949
Free scoring, clever centre-forward with perfect ball control and fine two-footed marksmanship from any angle or distance.

Serious injuries denied him greater prominence and probably shortened his playing career.

LEIGHTON, John Edward 1886(1)
b Nottingham 1864 ; d 15 April 1944.
Career: Nottingham schools football; Nottingham Forest 1884-8; Corinthians 1885-9. After finishing playing he remained an ardent follower of Nottingham Forest for the rest of his life rarely missing a match at the Forest ground and he died there watching a match. By profession a wholesale stationer and paper merchant in Nottingham
A leading outside-left of the 1880s his slightness of physique being counterbalanced by speed and industry.

LILLEY, Harry E. 1892(1)
Career: Staveley, Sheffield United cs 1890, Gainsborough Trinity cs 1894
Deservedly a favourite figure at Bramall Lane this left-back possessed a good kick and played with immense vitality.

LINACRE, James Henry 1905(2)
b Aston-on-Trent 1881; d 11 May 1957.
Career: Loughborough Grammar School, Aston-on-Trent, Draycott Mills, Derby County, Nottingham Forest cs 1899 to cs 1909. A brother-in-law of the Formans he was subsequently in business in partnership with Frank Forman as building contractors at West Bridgford
Club Honour: Nottingham Forest —Second Division Champions 1907
A goalkeeper aided by a long reach and an instinctive reflex action. On his day was unsurpassed by any contemporary.

LINDLEY, Tinsley 1886-91(13)
b Nottingham 27 October 1865; d 31 March 1940.
Career: Notingham High School; Leys School Cambridge (where he was in the rugger XV); Caius College Cambridge (Blue 1885-6-7-8 captain 1888); Corinthians 1885-94; Casuals; Notts County; Crusaders; Swifts; Preston North End once in February 1892); Nottingham Forest 1883-92: Played county cricket for Notts in 1888 and also played for Cambridge without getting a blue. Played rugby on occasion for Old Leysians. Called to the Bar in 1889, he practised on the Midland circuit and was a Law Lecturer at Nottingham University. O.B.E. 1918 for his work as Chief Officer, Nottingham Special Constabulary
One of the greatest centre-forwards of the nineteenth century, clever, accurate in passing and shooting and an excellent team man holding his line together admirably.

LINDSAY, William 1877(1)
b India 3 August 1847 ; d 15 February 1923.
Career: Winchester College; Old Wykehamists; Wanderers; Surrey: Surrey country cricket 1876-82. Served in the India Office from 1865 to 1900
Club Honours: Wanderers—F.A. Cup winners 1876, 7, 8
Versatile player who played at back, half back and forward. Noteworthy for his sureness in kicking ; a good team man and plucky.

LINTOTT, Evelyn Henry 1908-9(7)
b Godalming, Surrey 2 November 1883; d 1 July 1916.
Career: King Edward VI Grammar School, Guildford; St Lukes Training College Exeter 1905; Woking; Surrey County; Plymouth Argyle; Queens Park Rangers September 1907, profes-

sional May 1908 (Five England amateur international appearances 1908), Bradford City November 1908, Leeds City cs 1912. A schoolteacher by profession. He was for a time Chairman of the Players Union resigning in January 1911. Killed in action whilst serving on the Somme with the 1st Yorkshire Regiment
Club Honour: Queens Park Rangers—Southern League Champions 1908
In the grand tradition of England left-halves and worthy to follow in the wake of Needham and Forrest—vigorous and clever, tackling and passing with fine judgment.

LIPSHAM, Herbert B.   1902(1)
b Chester.
Career: Chester, Crewe Alexandra cs 1898, Sheffield United February 1900, Fulham mid 1907-8, Millwall cs 1910 player manager cs 1913, West Norwood coach August 1921, Northfleet manager cs 1922. Went to Canada early 1923.
Club Honours: Sheffield United— F.A. Cup finalists 1901, winners 1902.
An enthusiastic wholly dedicated player, Lipsham was a grand outside-left. He was speedy and had a redoubtable shot although his centres were apt to be too strong. He never reproduced his club form in representative matches.

LLOYD, Laurence Valentine
1971-2(3)
b Bristol 6 October 1948.
Career: Bristol School and junior football, Bristol Rovers professional 1966 (England Youth international 1967), Liverpool April 1969
Club Honour: Liverpool—F.A. Cup finalists 1971
A real bulwark at centre-half thanks in good measure to a formidable physique. Primarily a defender, somewhat heavy footed but noticeably sure in headwork.

LOCKETT, Arthur   1903(1)
b Alsagers Bank near Stoke 1875; d
Career: Crewe Alexandra, Stoke May 1900, Aston Villa April 1903, Preston North End September 1905, Watford cs 1908 to 1912
Very swift, very talented outside-left. Not, however, a good team man on the whole, having too great a liking for trying to beat the same player twice and often being too selfish.

LODGE, Lewis Vaughan 1894-6(5)
b 21 December 1872; d 21 November 1916.
Career: Durham School (where he was in the rugger XV); Magdalene College Cambridge (Blue 1893-4-5 acting captain 1895); Casuals; Corinthians 1894-8: Played cricket for Durham and Hampshire. On leaving Cambridge became a master at Horris Hill School, Newbury where he remained until his death
Club Honour: Casuals—F.A. Amateur Cup finalists 1894
Powerful back reliable in kicking and tackling. Prone to rashness at times but had much energy and, in general, made few mistakes.

LOFTHOUSE, Joseph Morris
1885-90(7)
b Bank Top, Witton, Blackburn 14 April 1865; d 10 June 1919.
Career: St Lukes School Witton, Blackburn Grammar School, Kings Own (Blackburn), Blackburn Rovers 1882, Accrington, Blackburn Rovers cs 1889, Darwen cs 1892, Walsall December 1893. He was appointed coach to Magyar Athletic Club, Budapest February 1902 but did not stay long and returned to this country as trainer to New Brompton (now Gillingham, of course) mid 1902-3, thence assistant trainer of Everton in August 1903
Club Honours: Blackburn Rovers

—F.A. Cup winners 1884-5-90-1 A distinguished outside-right combining masterly ball control with uncommon speed.

LOFTHOUSE, Nathaniel 1951-9(33) b Bolton 27 August 1925.
Career: Brentwood and Castle Hill Schools Bolton, Lomax's XI, Bolton Wanderers September 1939, professional 1942 retired injury January 1960 assistant coach March 1960, re-signed as a player July 1960 but finally retired July 1961. Remained on coaching staff, chief coach June 1967, acting manager August 1968, manager December 1968, general manager November 1970, team manager April 1971, chief scout August 1971 to June 1972
Club Honours: Bolton Wanderers —F.L. North Cup winners 1945, F.A. Cup finalists 1953, winners 1958
His dashing, determined, never-say-die play cost him many injuries. A peak in a great career at centre-forward was the game against Austria in 1952 when bravery earned him the journalistic tag "Lion of Vienna," which was much used subsequently by admiring commentators.

LONGWORTH, Ephraim 1920-3(5) b Halliwell, Lancs 1888; d 7 January 1968.
Career: Bolton St Lukes, Halliwell Rovers, Hyde St George, Hyde, Bolton Wanderers cs 1907, Leyton late 1908, Liverpool May 1910 retired cs 1928. After his retirement from the playing side he was a Liverpool coach for some years and after that was a member of the Club's general staff
Club Honours: Liverpool—F.A. Cup finalists 1914, F.L. Champions 1922-3
Had two things in common with his Everton contemporary, Dicky Downs—he occupied the same position (right-back) and was be-

loved of the cartoonists for his bowed legs. Longworth maintained a high standard over a long career and was fine tactically.

LOWDER, Arthur 1889(1) b Wolverhampton 1864; d 4 January 1926.
Career: St Luke's School Blakenhall, Wolverhampton Wanderers early 1880's to late 1891. Later coached in Europe until shortly before his death
Club Honour: Wolverhampton Wanderers—F.A. Cup finalists 1889
Unlike his Wolves' intermediate line colleagues, Fletcher and Harry Allen, Lowder was a lightweight. Nonetheless he played at left-half with a fine pertinacity and judgment.

LOWE, Edmund 1947(3) b Halesowen July 1925.
Career: Napier Aircraft Co (Millwall amateur), Finchley, Kynoch's (Birmingham), Aston Villa May 1945, Fulham May 1950, Notts County manager July 1963 to April 1965. Left football and is purchasing manager of an international Boiler and Central Heating Co.
Commanding left-half, tall, long legged and a hard worker. Was notable in defence yet found time to assist his forwards.

LUCAS, Thomas 1922-6(3) b St Helens, Lancs 1895; d 11 December 1953.
Career: Sherdley Villa, Sutton Commercial, Heywood United, Peasley Cross, Eccles Borough, Liverpool cs 1916, Clapton Orient July 1933 retired cs 1934 and had brief period in charge of Ashford, Kent. On leaving Ashford he became a licensee at Stoke Mandeville where he remained until his death
Club Honour: Liverpool—F.L. Champions 1922

Stockily built right or left-back. Employed a beautifully judged volley and was strong in covering and positioning.

LUNLTEY, Edwin   1880(2)
b Croydon, Surrey 1856; d 1 August 1921.
Career: Nottingham Castle F.C., Nottingham Forest November 1878 to January 1883. Useful cricketer, an early player of lacrosse with Radcliffe and a founder member of Chilwell Manor Golf Club. A lace manufacturer by profession
Revealed assets of courage and quickness in his play. A useful right-back.

LYTTELTON, Hon. Alfred 1877(1)
b Hagley, Worcs 7 February 1857; d 4 July 1913.
Career: Eton College (XI captain 1875); Trinity College Cambridge (Blue 1876-7-8); Old Etonians; Hagley. Played cricket for England v Australia four times between 1880-4 and won his cricket blue at Cambridge 1876-7-8-9 (captain in 1879). Also played for Worcestershire and Middlesex and was President of M.C.C. 1898. Athletics blue 1876, Rackets blue 1876-7, Real Tennis blue 1877-8-9. Called to the Bar in 1881 he became a K.C. M.P. for Warwick 1895-1906 and thence for St George's Hanover Square until his death. Secretary of State for the Colonies 1902-5. Brother of Hon. Edward Lyttelton
Club Honour Old Etonians—F.A. Cup finalists 1876
Made full use of his weight and speed and was a difficult forward to dispossess. A little deficient in ball control.

LYTTELTON, Hon. Edward
1878(1)
b London 23 July 1855; d 26 January 1942.
Career: Eton College; Trinity College Cambridge (no blue); Old Etonians; Hagley. Cricket Blue 1875-8, captain in 1878 and also played for Worcestershire and Middlesex. Master at Wellington College 1880-2, Eton 1882-9, Headmaster of Haileybury 1890-1905 and of Eton from 1905-16. Curate at St Martins in the Fields 1916-18, Rector of Sidestrand, Norfolk 1918-20, Dean of Whitelands College, Chelsea 1920-9 thence an officiate of the diocese of Norwich until his death
Club Honour: Old Etonians—F.A. Cup finalists 1876
Redoubtable at back and a difficult man for opposing attackers to pass. Could kick impressively.

MACAULAY, Reginald Heber
1881(1)
b Hodnet, Shropshire 24 August 1858; d 15 December 1937.
Career: Eton College (XI 1878); Kings College Cambridge (Blue 1881-2); Old Etonians. An Athletics blue 1879-82 winning the high jump in 1879-80 and the quarter-mile in 1880-1-2. In 1879 he was the A.A.A. high jump champion. He was in India from 1884-1901 and was later an East India merchant in the City of London with Wallace & Co.
Club Honours: Old Etonians—F.A. Cup winners 1882, finalists 1881, 3
A quick-moving leader of the attack who had a prodigious appetite for hard graft.

McCALL, Joseph   1913-21(5)
b Kirkham, Lancs 20 July 1886; d 3 February 1965.
Career: Kirkham F.C., Preston North End July 1906 retired cs 1925 thence a smallholder and poultry farmer at Wrea Green where he died
Club Honours: Preston North End—Second Division Champions 1913, F.A. Cup finalists 1922
Only of average size McCall be-

came a centre-half fit to be numbered among the greatest. He was superb in defence with both head and feet, cleverly switching to attack with raking, accurate passes to either wing.

McDONALD, Colin Agnew
1958-9(8)
b Summerseat, Lancs 15 October 1930.
Career: Bury Technical College, Hawkshaw St Mary's, Burnley amateur August 1948, part time professional October 1948 (on loan to Headington United 1950-1 whilst on National Service), full professional July 1952, retired injury cs 1961, Wycombe Wanderers coach August to September 1961, Bury chief scout October 1961 to January 1965, Altrincham as a player January 1965 to cs 1967, Bury chief scout May 1967 to October 1968, Bolton Wanderers chief scout October 1968 to August 1969, Bury administrative manager August 1969, general manager from May 1970
His safe and supple goalkeeping performances were marked by certainty and brilliance

MACDONALD, Malcolm 1972(3)
b Fulham 7 January 1950.
Career: Sloane Grammar School, Tonbridge, Fulham August 1968, Luton Town July 1969, Newcastle United May 1971
Converted by Fulham from fullback to centre-forward, and his form in this position when at Luton made him much sought after. He is stocky and heavily built, playing an aggressive game and being especially dangerous with head and left foot.

McFARLAND, Roy Leslie
1971-2(10)
b Liverpool 5 April 1948.
Career: Edge Hill Boys Club, Tranmere Rovers, Derby County

August 1967
Club Honours: Derby County—Second Division Champions 1969, F.L. Champions 1972
Seems to have acceded as England's regular centre-half after being the most prominent heir-apparent for some little while. He is a powerful, shrewd player, fine defensively.

McGARRY, William Harry
1954-6(4)
b Stoke 10 June 1927.
Career: Northwood Mission, Port Vale 1945, Huddersfield Town March 1951, Bournemouth & Boscombe Athletic as player manager March 1961, Watford manager July 1963, Ipswich Town manager October 1964, Wolverhampton Wanderers manager November 1968
An inside-right originally, finding his true milieu as a right-half. Far from spectacular but thoroughly sound, his tackling solid and passing effective.

McGUINNESS, Wilfred 1959(2)
b Manchester 25 October 1937.
Career: Mount Carmel School Blackley (England Schools v Ireland 1952 v Wales (2) Scotland Eire 1953), Manchester United ground staff cs 1953, professional October 1954 (England Youth 1954-8) retired injury December 1961 and remained on club staff as assistant trainer until his appointment as chief coach June 1969, team manager August 1970 reverting to assistant trainer December 1970 until cs 1971 when he left the Club. Trainer coach of England Youth team for a time from 1963. Became manager-coach to Aris Salonika (Greece) July 1971
Club Honours: Manchester United—F.A. Youth Cup winners 1954-5-6
Stocky, thrusting left-half whose intelligent play had a notable

attacking flavour. It was very much the game's loss when he was compelled to retire so early.

McINROY, Albert 1927(1)
b Walton-le-dale, Lancs 23 April 1901.
Career: St Thomas High School Preston, Upper Walton F.C., Coppull Central (Preston North End amateur during 1921-2), Leyland cs 1922, Sunderland May 1923, Newcastle United October 1929, Sunderland cs 1934, Leeds United May 1935, Gateshead June 1937 retiring during the War. After retirement became a licensee in the North East.
Club Honour: Newcastle United —F.A. Cup winners 1932
His remarkable consistency was exemplified by being the regular 'keeper for each of his League clubs—a period of 16 years. Sound and extremely agile, leaping for the ball with a cat-like action.

McNAB, Robert 1969(4)
b Huddersfield 20 July 1943.
Career: Rawthorne School Huddersfield, Moldgreen Civic Youth Club, Huddersfield Town amateur 1961, professional 1963, Arsenal October 1966
Club Honours: Arsenal—F.L. Cup finalists 1968 and 1969, Fairs Cup winners 1970, F.L. Champions and F.A. Cup winners 1971, F.A. Cup finalists 1972
Soon established himself in the top flight after Second Division experience at Huddersfield. A competent left-back, quick in tackling and able in starting an attack from a defensive position.

McNEAL, Robert 1914(2)
b Hobson, C. Durham 1891 ; d 15 May 1956.
Career: Hobson Wanderers, West Bromwich Albion cs 1910 retired cs 1925. Remained in West Bromwich as a licensee until his death being for a time a part time coach

to Albion
Club Honours: West Bromwich Albion—Second Division Champions 1911, F.A. Cup finalists 1912, F.L. Champions 1920
Although small—around 5 foot 6 inches—McNeal was the regular left-half for the Albion for over a decade which saw some of their greatest triumphs. Pertinacious and confident he gave memorable service to the several left wings he played behind.

McNEIL, Michael 1961-2(9)
b Middlesbrough 7 February 1940.
Career: Middlesbrough Technical College, Cargo Fleet juniors, Middlesbrough amateur June 1954, professional February 1957, Cambridge City June 1972, Ipswich Town June 1964. Also has a sports outfitting business in Ipswich.
Won an England place at left-back but lately Ipswich have played him at left-half. Well favoured physically, McNeil has a stern tackle and is capable of dominating in the air.

MACRAE, Stuart 1883-4(5)
b Port Bannatyne, Bute, Scotland 1857; d 27 January 1927.
Career: Edinburgh Academy (where he was in the Rugby XV 1872-3 captain in 1873); Notts County; Newark; Corinthians 1883-90. A Maltster in Newark with Grilstrap, Earp & Co.
Performed cleverly and well at wing-half where he found scope for the employment of his powerful kicking.

MADDISON, Frederick Brunning
1873(1)
(née Frederick Patey Chappell but assumed the above names in 1873)
b 1850; d 25 September 1907.
Career: Marlborough Grammar School; Brasenose College Oxford (no blue); Wanderers; Crystal Palace. Called to the Bar in 1876

but disbarred October 1884 at his own request to become a solicitor and admitted as such December 1884

Club Honours: Oxford University —F.A. Cup finalists 1873, winners 1874, Wanderers—F.A. Cup winners 1876

Could give a good account of himself at both back and forward. Lively, fearless, a worker and not averse to using his weight.

MADELEY, Paul Edward 1971-2(8)
b Leeds 20 September 1944.
Career: Farsley Celtic, Leeds United May 1962.
Club Honours: Leeds United— F.L. Cup winners and Fairs Cup winners 1968, F.L. Champions 1969, F.A. Cup finalists 1970, winners 1972, Fairs Cup winners 1971
The ultimate in versatility being a player who can and does literally shine anywhere. Beautifully built with an athletic carriage, Madeley's fluent talents have been used by Leeds at back, wing and centre-half and all over the attack.

MAGEE, Thomas Patrick 1923-5(5)
b Widnes, Lancs 12 May 1899.
Career: St Mary's School Widnes, Appleton Hornets, St Helens Recreation (Rugby League), Widnes Athletic, West Bromwich Albion cs 1919, Crystal Palace May 1934, Runcorn as player manager June 1935 to cs 1937. After the War was at one time manager coach of Runcorn
Club Honours: West Bromwich Albion—F.L. Champions 1920, F.A. Cup winners 1931
Played as a forward before finding his true position at right-half. Often called " a pocket Hercules " —he was only 5 feet 3 inches tall —he tackled strongly and gave splendid service to the attack.

MAKEPEACE, Harry 1906-12(4)
b Middlesbrough 22 August 1882; d 19 December 1952.
Career: Liverpool Schools, Liver-

pool junior football, Everton 1903 retired during the 1914-18 War. Lancashire county cricket 1906-30 scoring 25,745 runs including 45 centuries in first class cricket and played in 4 Tests v Australia in 1920-1. Later the Lancashire coach for many years until his retirement in 1951
Club Honours: Everton—F.A. Cup winners 1906, finalists 1907, F.L. Champions 1915
In the first years of the century was a vital cog in the Everton machine. An assertive left-half well suited to attack and often a scorer on his own account.

MALE, Charles George 1935-9(19)
b West Ham 9 May 1910.
Career: West Ham Schools, Clapton, Arsenal May 1930 retired cs 1948 and joined the Club coaching staff of which he is still a member
Club Honours: Arsenal—F.L. Champions 1933-4-5-8, F.A. Cup finalists 1932, winners 1936, F.L. South Cup winners 1943
Converted by his manager, the astute Herbert Chapman, from a half-back to an international ranking right-back. Well-built and distinguished for fine positional play, Male proved a near perfect complement to his partner, Hapgood, at both club and country level.

MANNION, Wilfred J. 1947-52(26)
b South Bank, Yorks 16 May 1918.
Career: St Peters Secondary School South Bank, South Bank juniors, South Bank St Peters, Middlesbrough September 1936 retired June 1954. Returned to play for Hull City December 1954 to May 1955. Poole Town September 1955 to March 1956, Cambridge United August 1956, Kings Lynn May 1958, Haverhill Rovers October 1958 to cs 1959, thence worked at Vauxhall Motors Luton for a time returning to the game

as Earlestown player manager October 1960 to October 1962. After leaving Earlestown he returned to Tees-side where he still lives

An entrancing inside-forward talent for the purist. Mannion played the orthodox game with a quite exceptional facility, killing the ball and making a perfectly executed pass exquisitely placed just as a text book would lay down.

MARSDEN, Joseph Thomas 1891(1)
b Darwen 1868; d 18 January 1897.
Career: Darwen, Everton cs 1891 but only played in the first match of the 1891-2 season
Lightly built but astonishingly dexterous right-back whose judgment was of a high order.

MARSDEN, William 1930(3)
b Silksworth, Co. Durham 1903.
Career: Durham junior football, Sunderland mid 1921-2, Sheffield Wednesday cs 1924 retired owing to injury received whilst playing for England v Germany May 1930. Had a short spell as Gateshead trainer from cs 1934 and was then coaching on the continent until the War including a spell as coach to the Dutch F.A., Be Quick F.C. Holland and from 1938 of Hermes D.W.S. Doncaster Rovers manager April 1944 to January 1946 having previously been a licensee in Sheffield. Also had a spell as Worksop manager from May 1953
Club Honours: Sheffield Wednesday—Second Division Champions 1926, F.L. Champions 1929 and 1930.
Right-footed inside-forward who, by assiduous practice with the other foot became a left-half of international ranking. A shrewd tackler and excellent at prompting his attack.

MARSH, Rodney William 1972(6)
b Hatfield, Herts 11 October 1944.
Career: Hackneys Schools, Alexander Boys Club, West Ham United amateur, Fulham October 1962, Queens Park Rangers March 1966, Manchester City March 1972
Club Honours: Queens Park Rangers—Third Division Champions 1967, F.L. Cup winners 1967
This jaunty inside-forward would have been considered a character in any era. He is tall with long legs, exceptionally skilled in ball play and marvellously entertaining.

MARSHALL, Thomas 1880-1(2)
b Withnell, Lancs 1859; d 29 April 1917.
Career: Darwen 1878, Blackburn Olympic once or twice in 1886 after which he retired
A speedy and capable outside-right able to pass the ball with accuracy and judgment.

MARTIN, Henry 1914(1)
b Selston, Notts 5 December 1891.
Career: Sutton Junction 1909, Sunderland January 1912, Nottingham Forest May 1922, Rochdale June 1925 club trainer cs 1929, Mansfield Town manager December 1933 to March 1935, Swindon Town trainer cs 1936
Club Honours: Sunderland—F.L. Champions and F.A. Cup finalists 1913
He was unusually tall for an outside left and this, together with a great raking stride, made him a daunting adversary for any defender. Could centre when going at high speed brilliantly.

MASKREY, Harry Mart 1908(1)
b Dronfield, Derbyshire 8 October 1883; d 21 April 1927.
Career: Ripley Athletic, Derby County 1903, Bradford City October 1909, Ripley Town cs 1911,

Burton All Saints, Derby Couny mid 1920-1 briefly thence Burton All Saints until his retirement in December 1922

Heavily built custodian, absolutely courageous and quick in clearing his lines. Had the tremendous asset of dependability.

MASON, Charles 1887-90(3)
b April 1863; d
Career: St Luke's School Blakenhall, Wolverhampton Wanderers founder member 1877 retired cs 1892
Club Honour: Wolverhampton Wanderers—F.A. Cup finalists 1889

A lithe and indomitable left-back. Knew no fear and the first of many Wolves to play for his country.

MATTHEWS, Reginald D.
1956-7(5)
b Coventry 1933.
Career: Barkers Butts School Coventry (where he was captain of the rugby XV), Modern Machines Coventry, Coventry City ground staff 1947, professional May 1950, Chelsea November 1956, Derby County October 1961, Rugby Town player manager August 1968

His goalkeeping won early attention, critics correctly forecasting high honours. He was brilliant in anticipation and lacked nothing in courage.

MATTHEWS, Sir Stanley
1935-57(54)
b Hanley 1 February 1915.
Career: Wellington Road School Hanley (England v Wales Schools 1929), Stoke St Peters, Stoke City amateur September 1930, professional February 1932, Blackpool May 1947, Stoke City October 1961, Port Vale general manager July 1965, honorary manager July 1968 resigned 1969 and went to live in Malta. He became manager

of Hibernian F.C. there in April 1970. Created C.B.E. in January 1956 and Knighted in January 1965
Club Honours: Stoke City—Second Division Champions 1933 and 1963, Blackpool—F.A. Cup winners 1953, finalists 1948 and 1951—also F.L. North Cup winners 1943 and finalists 1944 whilst assisting the Club as a guest

Football's first knight and a name of unsurpassed lustre. Stanley Matthews was an outside-right of genius whose swerving, side stepping, dribbling wizardry enchanted football followers for a generation. Obviously a unique talent right from the start.

MATTHEWS, Vincent 1928(2)
b Aylesbury 1896; d 15 November 1950.
Career: St Frideswide F.C., Oxford City, Bournemouth & Boscombe Athletic, Bolton Wanderers January 1923, Tranmere Rovers cs 1925, Sheffield United cs 1927, Shamrock Rovers May 1931, Shrewsbury Town, Oswestry Town player manager. Returned to Oxford in 1944 and worked for Morris Motors at Cowley until his death being coach to the Works F.C. from 1948

Something of a later developer Matthews was rated around 1928 one of the best pivots in the country. He made full use of his height and weight (6 feet and 13 stones) and was essentially a rugged performer.

MAYNARD, W. J. 1873-6(2)
Career: 1st Surrey Rifles; Wanderers ; Surrey
Was a swift moving, diligent winger who was faulted at times for delaying his centres.

MEADOWS, James 1955(1)
b Bolton 21 July 1931.
Career: Bolton Y.M.C.A., Southport October 1948, Manchester

City March 1951 retired injury October 1957, appointed to the training staff late 1959, trainer coach August 1960 to April 1965. Stockport County trainer coach January 1966, team manager October 1966 to April 1969, Bury assistant manager July 1969 to September 1969, Blackpool training staff September 1969, acting manager October 1970, assistant manager December 1970, Bolton Wanderers team manager January to April 1971, Southport manager May 1971
Club Honour: Manchester City—F.A. Cup finalists 1955
First came to notice as a direct, thrustful right winger, his zest, speed and weight later being employed at centre-forward and full-back. He was grievously unfortunate in the matter of injury.

MEDLEY, Leslie D.   1951-2(6)
b Lower Edmonton 3 Sept. 1920. Career: Silver Street Schools, Latymer Grammar School (England Schools v Scotland 1935), Northfleet, Tottenham Hotspur amateur cs 1935, professional February 1939. Left for Canada November 1946 playing for Greenbacks and Ulster United Toronto. Returned to Tottenham Hotspur January 1948 finally retiring May 1953 when he again went to Canada. Later went to South Africa where he was player coach of Randfontein F.C., Johannesburg. Returned to England in spring of 1961
Club Honours: Tottenham Hotspur—Second Division Champions 1950, F.L. Champions 1951
Compactly built outside-left having speed, trickery and the knack of turning up unexpectedly. Packed a good shot which he liked to exercise frequently.

MEEHAN, Thomas   1924(1)
b Manchester 1896; d 18 August 1924.
Career: Newtown, Walkden Central, Rochdale 1916-17, Manchester United 1917-18, Chelsea December 1920. Died of polio whilst at the peak of his career
Pertinacious left-half unimpaired by a slight frame—he stood 5 feet 5 inches and weighed under 9½ stones. Always purposeful and seemingly tireless.

MELIA, James   1963(2)
b Liverpool 1 November 1937.
Career: Liverpool Schools (England v Eire Schools 1953), Liverpool amateur 1953, professional November 1954 (England Youth international 1958), Wolverhampton Wanderers March 1964, Southampton December 1964, Aldershot player coach November 1968, player team manager April 1969 to January 1972, Crewe Alexandra player coach February 1972, manager May 1972
Club Honours: Liverpool—Second Division Champions 1962, F.L. Champions 1964
Quite a rarity, encompassing in his inside-forward play both scheming and scoring abilities in lavish measure. This occurred in his heyday—lately he has adopted a midfield role.

MERCER, David William   1923(2)
b St Helens, Lancs 1893; d 4 June 1950.
Career: Prescot Athletic, Skelmersdale, Hull City January 1914, Sheffield United December 1920, Shirebrook cs 1928, Torquay United June 1929 retired cs 1930. Continued to live and work in Torquay
Club Honour: Sheffield United—F.A. Cup winners 1925
Quick moving outside-right with a degree of craft and cleverness. Knew where the goal lay although his scoring feats for Hull City in Wartime football were not repeated in the 'twenties.

MERCER, Joseph 1939(5)
b Ellesmere Port, Cheshire 9 August 1914.
Career: Cambridge Road School and John Street School Ellesmere Port, Elton Green, Shell Mex, Chester (trial), Runcorn, Blackburn Rovers (trial), Ellesmere Port Town, Everton September 1932, Arsenal November 1946 retired cs 1955 owing to injury, Sheffield United manager August 1955, Aston Villa manager December 1958 to July 1964, Manchester City manager from July 1965 general manager October 1971, Coventry City general manager June 1972
Club Honours: Everton—F.L. Champions 1939, Arsenal—F.L. Champions 1948, 53, F.A. Cup winners 1950, finalists 1952
A leading soccer personality these many years. As a player at wing-half his spindly but cultured legs became legendary. Would take the ball through to the forwards, parting with a disconcerting suddenness. Strong in defence with a trenchant tackle.

MERRICK, Gilbert Harold
1952-4(23)
b Sparkhill, Birmingham 26 January 1922.
Career: Acocks Green School, Fenton Rovers, Shirley Juniors, Olton Sports, Shirley Juniors, Birmingham City amateur, Solihull Town amateur August 1939, Birmingham City professional August 1939, manager June 1960 to April 1964 thence out of football until becoming manager of Bromsgrove Rovers cs 1967. Now Personnel Manager of a Midland Stores Group
Club Honours: Birmingham City —Second Division Champions 1948 and 1955, F.A. Cup finalists 1956
Said to have copied the style of Hibbs, his illustrious predecessor in the Birmingham goal. Certainly

there were similarities for Merrick was calm, unspectacular and had the capacity for making the job look simple.

METCALFE, Victor 1951(2)
b Barrow 3 February 1922.
Career: Wheelbright Grammar School Dewsbury, Ravensthorpe Albion, Huddersfield Town amateur January 1940, professional December 1945, Hull City June 1958 retired February 1960. Huddersfield Town staff 1961 to October 1964, Halifax Town staff December 1964 thence manager June 1966 to November 1967
Served Huddersfield well at outside-left for a long time. He was a clever player with a full repertoire of tricks and fine control.

MEW, John W. 1921(1)
b Sunderland.
Career: Hendon School Sunderland, Blaydon United, Marley Hill Colliery, Manchester United October 1912 after a month's trial, Barrow September 1926 to cs 1927. Later coached in Belgium, Peru and South America and worked in a factory in Manchester
Had studied the art of goalkeeping to some purpose and was skilled in narrowing angles. Sound in handling and the fortunate possessor of abnormally strong wrists.

MIDDLEDITCH, Bernard 1897(1)
b Highgate 1871; d 3 Oct. 1949.
Career: Educated privately and at Jesus College, Cambridge (Blue 1895); Corinthians 1895-1905. Master at University School, Hastings 1895-1900, at Malvern 1900-3 and at Harrow from 1903 until his retirement in 1932
Hardly a Crabtree but a right-half with several manifest virtues: clever, industrious and astute in the feeding of his forwards.

MILBURN, John Edward
Thompson 1949-56(13)
b Ashington 11 May 1924.

Career: Ashington, Newcastle United August 1943, Linfield player manager June 1957, Yiewsley November 1960 player manager December 1960, Ipswich Town manager April 1963 to September 1964 when he became a journalist in Newcastle. Had a spell as Gateshead manager from November 1965
Club Honours: Newcastle United —F.A. Cup winners 1951, 1952 and 1955, Linfield—Irish Cup finalists 1958 winners 1960
A name to conjure with in the early post-war years. Milburn was an outside-right or centre-forward, fleet, graceful as a gazelle and a dangerous shot.

MILLER, Brian G. 1961(1)
b Hapton near Burnley.
Career: St Mary's College Blackburn, Burnley 1954, retired injury April 1968 and joined coaching staff. Now first team trainer
Club Honours: Burnley—F.L. Champions 1960, F.A. Cup finalists 1962
Was no stranger to any of the half-back positions, mostly being at left-half. He played a hard, skilful game, uncompromising in the tackle and resolute in attacking support.

MILLER, Harold Sidney 1923(1)
b St Albans 1904.
Career: St Albans City, Charlton Athletic amateur January 1922, professional December 1922, Chelsea June 1923, Northampton Town cs 1939, retired during the War
Only twice in a League career which stretched 16 seasons did Miller's goal tally reach double figures but he was, nevertheless, a valuable inside-left. Thoughtful, neat and a provider of chances he latterly appeared at left-half too.

MILLS, George Robert 1938(3)
b Deptford 29 December 1908.
Career: Arthur Street School Peckham, Emerald Athletic, Bromley, Chelsea amateur November 1929, professional February 1930, retired during the War
Well built centre-forward or inside-right. A refreshingly direct player with no pretentions towards embroidery and a consistent goal scorer.

MILNE, Gordon 1963-5(14)
b Preston March 1937.
Career: Preston amateurs, Morecambe, Preston North end 1956, Liverpool August 1960, Blackpool May 1967, Wigan Athletic player manager January 1970, Coventry City team manager June 1972. Appointed to look after the England Youth team late 1971
Club Honours: Liverpool—Second Division Champions 1962, F.L. Champions 1964 and 1966, European Cup Winners Cup finalists 1966. Missed the F.A. Cup Final of 1965 owing to injury
Muscular right-half of compact build. Enthusiastic in approach and tireless in action, Milne's name was no stranger to the score sheet.

MILTON, Clement Arthur 1952(1)
b Bristol 10 March 1928.
Career: Cotham Grammar School Bristol, Arsenal July 1946, Bristol City February 1955 retired July 1955. England Test cricketer 1958-9 playing 6 Tests. Scored 104 not out in his first Test innings v New Zealand 1958. Has played for Gloucestershire from 1948 being captain in 1969. Has scored 30,969 runs in first class cricket including 55 centuries
Club Honour: Arsenal—F.L. Champions 1953
Exhibited a fine persistence and speed in his raids from the right wing. One felt that his footballing

retiral, at the age of 27, was premature.

MILWARD, Alfred 1891-7(4)
b Great Marlow, Bucks 1870.
Career: Sir William Borlase's Grammar School, Old Borlasians, Marlow, Everton 1888, New Brighton Tower cs 1897, Southampton cs 1899, New Brompton cs 1901 to 1903
Club Honours: Everton—F.L. Champions 1891, F.A. Cup winners 1893, 7, Southampton—F.A. Cup finalists 1900, Southern League Champions 1901
Of medium height but weighty, at 12 stones, for an outside-left. Quick and plucky with an appetite for work, his partnership at Everton with Edgar Chadwick became famous.

MITCHELL, Clement 1880-5(5)
b Cambridge 20 February 1862; d 6 October 1937.
Career: Felsted School (XI 1877-8-9 captain 1879); Upton Park; Essex ; Corinthians. Played cricket on occasion for Kent in 1890-2. He spent some years in India
Positional sense and fine marksmanship made this centre-forward a prolific goal-scorer. In addition had ball control and passing ability.

MITCHELL, James Frederick
1925(1)
b Manchester 1897.
Career: Arnold Grammar School Blackpool, Blackpool 1915, Northern Nomads, Manchester University, Preston North End October 1920, Manchester City May 1922, Leicester City October 1926. Six England Amateur international appearances 1920-5. For a time a master at Arnold Grammar School he later was on the staff of Stead & Simpson and was secretary of the firm's Sports Club
Club Honour: Preston North End —F.A. finalists 1922

Hefty amateur goalkeeper brisk in action and known for his huge clearance kicks. A rarity in that he played in glasses.

MOFFAT, Hugh 1913(1)
b Congleton circa 1890.
Career: Burnley, Oldham Athletic late 1910, Chesterfield Municipal player manager cs 1919
Achieved prominence in the years leading up to the first World War. Moffat was a well built right-half, highly competent rather than brilliant in defensive and attacking moves.

MOLYNEUX, George 1902-3(4)
b Liverpool 1875; d
Career: Third Grenadiers, South Shore, Wigan County, Everton cs 1898, Southampton cs 1900, Portsmouth cs 1905, Southend United cs 1906 later Colchester Town
Club Honours: Southampton— F.A. Cup finalists 1902, Southern League Champions 1901-3-4
Stalwart left-back of all round ability. Exceptionally good at heading and indeed one of the best exponents of this art at the turn of the century.

MOON, William Robert 1888-91(7)
b 27 June 1868 ; d 9 January 1943.
Career: Westminster School (XI 1884-5) ; Old Westminsters, Corinthians 1886-1901. Played cricket for Middlesex twice in 1891. Admitted a solicitor in 1891 he practised with Moon, Gilks & Moon in Bloomsbury
Resourceful goalkeeper possessing any amount of courage. Alert and quick to avert danger with both hands and feet.

MOORE, Henry Thomas 1883-5(2)
b Nottingham 1861; d 24 September 1939.
Career: Notts County 1881 to 1888. At one time ran an off licence in Nottingham and later lived in retirement at Sudbury,

Middlesex, where he died
A stalwart full-back who could always be relied upon. Sure in his kicking and an excellent tactician.

MOORE, James 1923(1)
b Birmingham circa 1891.
Career: Quebec Albion (Handsworth), Glossop cs 1911, Derby County October 1913, Chesterfield March 1926 retired cs 1927 but played for Mansfield Town from November 1927 to cs 1928
Club Honour: Derby County—Second Division Champions 1915
Had no physical advantages and made up for it with cleverness. He was an inside-left who had speed and delightful ball control and who headed his club's scoring list on more than one occasion.

MOORE, Robert Frederick
1962-72(96)
b Barking 12 April 1941.
Career: Barking and Leyton Schools, Woodford Youth Club, West Ham United professional June 1958 (England Youth international 1958-9). Awarded O.B.E. January 1967 following his captaincy of the England World Cup winning team in 1966
Club Honours: West Ham United —F.A. Youth Cup finalists 1959, F.A. Cup winners 1964, European Cup Winners Cup winners 1965, F.L. Cup finalists 1966
In recent years has been recognised as one of the finest defensive players in the world. Captains West Ham and England from left-half, is always ice-cool, a master strategist and a natural leader.

MOORE, William Gray B. 1923(1)
b Newcastle-upon-Tyne 6 October 1894; d October 1968.
Career: Seaton Delaval, Sunderland 1913 (4 England amateur international appearances in 1914), West Ham United May 1922 retired cs 1929. Joined West

Ham training staff and was chief trainer from 1932 to his retirement in May 1960
Club Honour: West Ham United —F.A. Cup finalists 1923
A light build did not affect unduly this inside-left's ball skills. His subtle promptings were a major contribution to the success of his famous partner, Ruffell.

MORDUE, John 1912-13(2)
b Edmondsley, Co. Durham.
Career: Sacriston, Spennymoor, Barnsley, Woolwich Arsenal April 1907, Sunderland May 1908, Middlesbrough May 1920, Hartlepools United cs 1922, Durham City player manager February 1923 to February 1924
Club Honours: Sunderland—F.L. Champions and F.A. Cup finalists 1913
An England selection on both wings. Mainly, however, an outside-right where he won lasting fame at Sunderland as part of their renowned right wing triangle, his incisive speed and passing skills being outstanding. A penalty specialist, too.

MORICE, Charles John 1873(1)
b 27 May 1850; d 17 June 1932.
Career: Harrow School; Harrow Chequers; Barnes. F.A. Committee 1873-7. Later a member of the Stock Exchange
His forward play won golden opinions, being fast and skilful in moving the ball, although he had the handicap of being of light weight.

MORLEY, Herbert 1910(1)
b Kiveton Park, Sheffield 1884.
Career: Kiveton Park, Grimsby Town, Notts County March 1907 retired during the 1914-18 War
Club Honour: Notts County—Second Division Champions 1914
Tall and hefty right-back dashing and uninhibited. Had magnificent heading ability. Said to have been

the innovator of the offside manoeuvre later made notorious by
McCracken of Newcastle United.

MORREN, Thomas   1898(1)
b Middlesbrough 1875 ; d 31 January 1929.
Career: Middlesbrough Victoria,
Middlesbrough Ironopolis, Middlesbrough, Barnsley St Peters,
Sheffield United early 1896 to cs
1904. After retiring from the game
was a newsagent in the Hunters
Bar area of Sheffield until his
death
Club Honours: Middlesbrough—
F.A. Amateur Cup winners 1895,
Sheffield United—F.L. Champions
1898, F.A. Cup winners 1899,
finalists 1901
Diminutive but effective centre-
half. Attracted some criticism because of a tendency to stray out
of position although it could not
be gainsaid that he was a rare
worrier.

MORRIS, Frederick   1920-1(2)
b Tipton, Staffs 27 August 1893;
d 4 July 1962.
Career: Redditch, West Bromwich
Albion May 1911, Coventry City
August 1924, Oakengates Town
cs 1925. Later worked in Tipton.
Club Honour: West Bromwich
Albion—F.L. Champions 1920
Unusually prolific scorer for an
inside-left—he headed the Football League list with 37 goals in
1919-20. A highly skilled player
with an extremely hard shot.

MORRIS, John   1949-50(3)
b Radcliffe, Lancs 27 September
1924.
Career: Radcliffe, Manchester
United August 1939, Derby
County March 1949, Leicester City
October 1952, Corby Town player
manager May 1958, Kettering
Town cs 1961, Great Harwood
manager cs 1964, Oswestry Town
manager October 1967. Now a
tyre salesman in Lancashire

Club Honours: Manchester United
—F.A. Cup winners 1948, Leicester City—Second Division Champions 1954 and 1957
An inside-right expert in dribbling
and not easily dispossessed because, although small, he was
hard. Opened up the game well
and played a fair portion of
his Leicester sojourn at right-
half.

MORRIS, William Walker 1939(3)
b Handsworth 1915.
Career: Handsworth Schools,
Handsworth Old Boys, West
Bromwich Albion colts, Halesowen Town, Wolverhampton
Wanderers May 1933 retired cs
1947
Club Honour: Wolverhampton
Wanderers—F.A. Cup finalists
1939
Intrinsically a natural player
able to play, and play well, in
almost any position. As a senior
was usually at centre-half for
Wolves until Cullis's arrival, then
moving to right-back where he
became a grandly mobile defender
and in which position he earned
his honours.

MORSE, Harold   1879(1)
Career: Derby Wanderers (rugby);
Notts County ; Notts Rangers
Strong and quick moving back
but with an inclination to over-
kick his forwards.

MORT, Thomas   1924-6(3)
b Kearsley, Lancs December 1897.
Career: St Stephens Sunday
School Bolton, Newton Lads, Altrincham mid 1918-19, Rochdale
cs 1921, Aston Villa April 1922
retired cs 1935
Club Honour: Aston Villa—F.A.
Cup final 1924
The left flank of a famous club
full-back partnership, his more
mobile play providing an ideal
complement to Smart's ponder-
ousness. Mort believed in safety

first tactics and had a singularly effective sliding tackle.

MORTEN, Alexander   1873(1)
Believed to have died in New York 16 September 1916.
Career: Crystal Palace, Middlesex. F.A. Committee 1874. A useful club cricketer with the Crystal Palace club
Distinguished himself as a goalkeeper over several seasons, the Football Annual of 1873 describing him as being without a rival. Had a fine temperament remaining cool in the heaviest of attacks.

MORTENSEN, Stanley Harding
                         1947-54(25)
b South Shields 26 May 1921.
Career: St Mary's School South Shields, South Shields ex Schools, Blackpool April 1937, Hull City November 1955, Southport February 1957, Bath City July 1958 retired May 1959. Came out of retirement to join Lancaster City November 1960 finally retiring March 1962. Blackpool manager February 1967 to April 1969. Since retiring from football has many business interests in Blackpool. Played as a substitute for Wales v England in a war-time international in 1944
Club Honours: Blackpool—F.A. Cup finalists 1948, 51, winners 1953. Scored a hat-trick in Blackpool's win in 1953
An electrifying performer at centre and inside-forward. Had a tremendous burst of speed, the ability to rise surprisingly high to head and fine markmanship.

MORTON, John R.   1938(1)
b Sheffield 1914.
Career: Sheffield Schools, Woodhouse Alliance F.C. (Sheffield), Gainsborough Trinity cs 1931, West Ham United December 1931 retired during the War. Later a bookmaker in the West Ham area
Deceptively frail looking winger

found usually on the left. Fast, possessed a multitude of tricks and a good shot.

MOSFORTH, William   1877-82(9)
b Sheffield early 1858; d 11 July 1929.
Career: Ecclesfield; Sheffield Wednesday; Sheffield Albion; Hallam; Heeley; Providence; Sheffield United
Wily, fast-moving outside-left versed in the arts of dribbling and centring. A great favourite with spectators not least because of his wonderful screw kick.

MOSS, Frank   1922-4(5)
b Aston 17 April 1895; d 15 September 1965.
Career: Burlington Street School Aston, Walsall, Aston Villa February 1914, Cardiff City January 1929, Bromsgrove Rovers player manager cs 1929 thence Worcester City. Licensee of the Grosvenor Arms, Worcester for 35 years up to his death
Club Honours: Aston Villa—F.A. Cup winners 1920, finalists 1924
Master of wing-half play in attack and defence. Noticeable on the field with his fair hair and athletic build.

MOSS, Frank   1934-5(4)
b Leyland, Lancs 5 November 1909; d February 1970.
Career: Leyland Motors, Preston North End cs 1927 professional February 1928, Oldham Athletic cs 1929, Arsenal November 1931 retired cs 1936 through injury, Hearts manager March 1937 until 1940 when he was called up as an engineer for war service. Later a licensee in Chorley
Club Honours: Arsenal—F.L. Champions 1933-4-5, F.A. Cup finalists 1932
Custodian of keenness and exceptional agility. The fact his playing career was plagued by a recurring shoulder injury never affected his courage.

MOSSCROP, Edwin   1914(2)
b Southport 16 June 1892.
Career: Blowick, Shepherds Bush, Middlesex County, Southport Y.M.C.A., Southport Central, Burnley September 1912, retired illness November 1922. A schoolmaster in Lancashire for many years he lives at Southport in retirement.
Club Honours: Burnley—F.A. Cup winners 1914, F.L. Champions 1921
Small and slight but a noteworthy left-winger. His guile, set off by a degree of polish, added spice to any game in which he appeared.

MOZLEY, Bertram   1950(3)
b Derby 21 September 1926.
Career: Derby Schools, Shelton United (Nottingham Forest amateur early 1944), Derby County March 1945 until he emigrated to Canada in January 1955
Displayed unusual coolness and steadiness at right-back and his distribution was well nigh perfect. Almost as fast a back as Laurie Scott.

MULLEN, James   1947-54(12)
b Newcastle-upon-Tyne 6 January 1923.
Career: St Mary's Junior School, St Aloysius R.C. School Newcastle (England Schools v Ireland 1937), Wolverhampton Wanderers ground staff July 1937, professional January 1940 retired cs 1960
Club Honours: Wolverhampton Wanderers—F.A. Cup winners 1949, F.L. Cup winners 1942, F.L. Champions 1954-8-9. Played in F.A. Cup semi-final in 1939 when only 16.
Handsomely realised his schoolboy promise and became a considerable outside-left. He was fast moving and, when cutting in, exercised a deadly shot.

MULLERY, Alan Patrick
     1965-72(35)
b Notting Hill 23 November 1941.
Career: St John's Secondary School Notting Hill, Fulham groundstaff June 1957, professional December 1958, Tottenham Hotspur March 1964, Fulham on loan March 1972, returned to Tottenham Hotspur April 1972, Fulham July 1972
Club Honours: Tottenham Hotspur—F.A. Cup winners 1967, F.L. Cup winners 1971, UEFA Cup winners 1972
Very much a player's player besides, of course, appearing as an accomplished right-half to the eye of a sentient onlooker. Has a football brain, attacking flair, a most purposeful tackle and generalship.

NEEDHAM, Ernest (" Nudger ")
     1894-1902(16)
b Whittington Moor near Chesterfield 21 January 1873; d 8 March 1936.
Career: Waverley F.C. (Staveley), Staveley 1889, Sheffield United April 1891, retired cs 1913. Played cricket for Derbyshire 1901-12 scoring 6,375 runs in first class cricket including seven centuries
Club Honours: Sheffield United—F.L. Champions 1898, F.A. Cup winners 1899, 1902, finalists 1901
Called a prince of half-backs and certainly this left-half deserved the accolade for he must be numbered amongst the very greatest in his position. Of short and solid build he was determined, fast and brave and had great endurance.

NEWTON, Keith Robert
     1966-70(27)
b Manchester 23 June 1941.
Career: Didsbury Grammar School, Spurley Hey Youth Club (Bolton Wanderers amateur), Blackburn Rovers amateur, professional October 1958, Everton December 1969, Burnley June 1972
Club Honour: Blackburn Rovers—F.A. Youth Cup winners 1959
Can play in both back positions (usually latterly on the left) and

wing-half. Is tall, astute and his thoughtful clearances are, as often as not, measured passes.

NICHOLLS, John   1954(2)
b Wolverhampton 3 April 1931.
Career: Prestwood Road, Holy Trinity and Springfield Road Schools (Wolverhampton), Heath Town United (Wolverhampton Wanderers amateur), West Bromwich Albion August 1951, Cardiff City May 1957, Exeter City November 1957, Worcester City June 1959, Wellington Town February 1961, Oswestry cs 1961, Sankeys mid 1961-2
Club Honour: West Bromwich Albion—F.A. Cup winners 1954
Had a meteoric rise but his stay at the top was comparatively short. Then he was a thrustful, enterprising inside-right who made a reputation for goal poaching.

NICHOLSON, William Edward
1951(1)
b Scarborough 26 January 1919.
Career: Scarborough Working Men's Club, Tottenham Hotspur amateur March 1936, sent to Northfleet to develop, professional August 1938, assistant manager August 1957, manager October 1958
Club Honours: Tottenham Hotspur—Second Division Champions 1950, F.L. Champions 1951
Made a few League appearances at left-back just before the War but built his playing reputation at right-half after it, occasionally deputising at centre-half. No frills, rugged, strong tackling and completely dedicated.

NORMAN, Maurice   1962-5(23)
b Mulbarton, Norfolk 8 May 1934.
Career: Mulbarton and Wymondham Secondary Modern School, Wymondham Minors F.C., Mulbarton, Norwich City ground staff

1951, professional 1953, Tottenham Hotspur November 1955 finally retiring December 1967 as a result of broken leg sustained in November 1965. Following his retirement from the game he was for a time assistant manager of a garage in North London and was later a shop-keeper at Frinton-on-Sea
Club Honours: Tottenham Hotspur—F.L. Champions 1961, F.A. Cup winners 1961 and 1962, European Cup Winners Cup winners 1963
Had a goodly spell at right-back but was best at centre-half, where his commanding height and heading skill were immensely valuable. Liked to join in an attack whenever possible.

NUTTALL, Henry   1928-9(3)
b Bolton 9 November 1897; d April 1969.
Career: Bolton St Marks, Fleetwood, Bolton Wanderers December 1920, Rochdale May 1932, Nelson August 1933, Bolton Wanderers staff 1935 assistant trainer July 1946 later being general factotum until his retirement in 1964. Was actually born in a cottage within the confines of Bolton Wanderers' ground, Burnden Park where his father was groundsman
Club Honours: Bolton Wanderers—F.A. Cup winners 1923, 6, 9
Studious wing-half with a fine attacking flair. Prompted his forwards subtly and was invariably in the right position at the right time.

OAKLEY, William John
1895-1901(16)
b 27 April 1873; d 20 September 1934.
Career: Shrewsbury School (XI 1887-92 captain 1892); Christ Church Oxford (Blue 1893-4-5-6); Corinthians 1894-1903 (joint secretary with G. O. Smith 1898-1902);

A Ludgrove schoolmaster he became joint headmaster with G. O. Smith in 1902 following the death of A. T. B. Dunn and shortly after retired from football. Athletics Blue 1893-4-5-6 (President of the Oxford University Athletic Club 1895) winning the hurdles in 1894 and 1895. A.A.A. long jump champion 1894 and jumped and hurdled for England v U.S.A. 1895. Rowed in the Oxford trial eights 1894. Died from the effects of a car accident

One of the swiftest backs of his day. Equally efficient with both feet—he performed on either flank—Oakley was something of an acrobatic kicker.

O'DOWD, James Peter 1932-3(3)
b Halifax 22 February 1908; d 8 May 1964.
Career: St Bees G.S. Bradford, Apperley Bridge, Selby Town, Blackburn Rovers amateur early 1926-7 professional December 1926, Burnley March 1930, Chelsea November 1931, Valenciennes (France) September 1935, Torquay United March 1937 but retired after breaking a leg in a trial match

Best as a pivot although he appeared at wing-half quite a lot. Always unruffled, adept at opening up a game and wholly reliant on his own skill and endurance.

OGILVIE, Robert Andrew Muter Macindoe 1874(1)
b circa 1853; d 5 March 1938.
Career: Brentwood School; Clapham Rovers; F.A. Committee 1874-81 and 1884-6. Member of Lloyds (Chairman of the Institute of Lloyds Underwriters 1910-11), Underwriter to Alliance Assurance Co. up to 1914. With the War Risks Department from 1914-19
Club Honours: Clapham Rovers —F.A. Cup finalists 1879, winners 1880

Back who played half-back occasionally also. He was always hard-working but at times his displays were marred by a degree of uncertainty.

O'GRADY, Michael 1963-9(2)
b Leeds 11 October 1942.
Career: Corpus Christi School Leeds, Huddersfield Town amateur, professional November 1959, Leeds United October 1965, Wolverhampton Wanderers September 1969
Club Honours: Leeds United— Fairs Cup finalists 1967 winners 1968, F.L. Champions 1969
Rose to the top rapidly in the early 'sixties by reason of his speed and incisiveness on the left wing. Has since appeared at outside-right and (at Wolverhampton) inside-forward.

OLIVER, Leonard Frederick 1929(1)
b Fulham 1905; d August 1967.
Career: Fulham Schools, Alma Athletic, Tufnell Park early 1920, Fulham cs 1924 retired cs 1935, later coach to Cliftonville up to the War. Lived in Hertfordshire after the War up to his death.
Club Honour: Fulham—Third Division South Champions 1932
A right-half efficient in attack and defence Oliver's gifts of leadership were given full scope at Fulham; he was captain for seven seasons of his decade as a professional there. Played at centre-half also on occasion.

OLNEY, Benjamin Albert 1928(2)
b Holborn, London 1899.
Career: Fairleys Athletic, Aston Park Rangers, Stourbridge, Derby County April 1921, Aston Villa December 1927, Bilston United July 1931 appointed player manager May 1931 but later cs 1931 joined Walsall, Shrewsbury Town August 1932 to cs 1933

Goalkeeper of sterling worth. Powerfully built, clever in anticipation and highly consistent.

OSBORNE, Frank Raymond
                          1923-6(4)
b Wynberg, South Africa 14 October 1896.
Career: Gymnasium School, South Africa, coming to England in 1911, Bromley 1919, Fulham November 1921, Tottenham Hotspur January 1924, Southampton June 1931 retired cs 1933. Out of football 1933-5 he became a Fulham director in March 1935, manager September 1948, general manager 1950 retiring in October 1964. Brother of R.
In essence a graceful and stylish performer whether at outside-right or centre-forward. His move to the Spurs was unusually salutary to both club and player because their respective styles were complementary.

OSBORNE, Reginald   1928(1)
b Wynberg, South Africa 23 July 1899.
Career: Joined Army as a boy transferring later to Royal Army Medical Corps (2 England amateur international appearances 1922), Watling Street Boot Co. (Leicester), Leicester City February 1923, retired cs 1933 but joined Folkestone November 1933 Club Honour: Leicester City—Second Division Champions 1925
An excellent left-back; fast to recover, quite fearless in tackling and the owner of a reliable kick.

OSGOOD, Peter Leslie   1970(3)
b Windsor, Berks 20 February 1947.
Career: Spital School Windsor, Spital Old Boys, Windsor Corinthians, Chelsea amateur March 1964, professional August 1964 (England Youth international 1965)
Club Honours: Chelsea—F.A.

Cup winners 1970, European Cup Winners Cup winners 1971, F.L. Cup finalists 1972
Few present-day players are better endowed physically or in natural footballing gifts than this centre-forward. Roams to advantage, is excellent in control and two footed power shooting, the only question-mark concerns constant application.

OTTAWAY, Cuthbert John
                          1873-4(2)
b Dover 20 July 1850; d 2 April 1878.
Career: Eton College; Brasenose College Oxford (Blue 1874 when he was captain); Old Etonians; F.A. Committee 1872-3 ; Cricket Blue 1870-1-2-3 captain 1873. Played Kent cricket 1869-70 and for Middlesex 1874-6. Also scored 108 for Eton v Harrow 1869. Rackets blue 1870-1-2-3, also winning the Public Schools doubles rackets championship in 1868 and 1869. Athletics blue 1873. Real Tennis blue 1870-1-2. Despite his athletic achievements at Oxford he found time to obtain a First in moderations and a Third in classics. Called to the Bar 1876
Club Honours: Oxford University—F.A. Cup finalists 1873, winners 1874, Old Etonians—F.A. Cup finalists 1875
A forward of distinction, elegant in style with a great ability for dribbling. He achieved an incredible amount in his tragically short life.

OWEN, John Robert Blayney
                          1874(1)
b 1849; d 13 June 1921.
Career: Queens College, Oxford (prior to the University soccer match); Sheffield F.C.; Sheffield F.A.; Nottinghamshire; Maldon; Essex. Second Master of Trent College 1872-81, Master in charge

Hawkshead Grammar School 1881-3, Headmaster of Trent College 1883-90. Ordained in 1876 he was Vicar of Toftrees 1890-1905 and Rector of Bradwell-on-Sea, Essex 1905-21
Speedy forward with a useful tally of goals, but who required a rather undue measure of " spoon feeding " from his team-mates.

OWEN, Sidney William   1954(3)
b Birmingham 29 September 1922.
Career: Birmingham junior football, Birmingham City October 1945, Luton Town June 1947, manager May 1959 to April 1960, Leeds United chief coach from May 1960
Club Honour: Luton Town—F.A. Cup finalists 1959
Originally a left-half of moderate attainments, Owen's career took an upward turn on moving to pivot. There, his thoughtful play, aided by a commanding height, acquired a degree of polish.

PAGE, Louis Antonia   1927-8(7)
b Kirkdale, Lancs 1899; d 12 October 1959.
Career: South Liverpool, Stoke cs 1919, Northampton Town cs 1922, Burnley May 1925, Manchester United March 1932, Port Vale October 1932, Yeovil Town player manager cs 1933 to cs 1935, Newport County manager June 1935 to September 1937, Glentoran trainer coach December 1938, Swindon Town manager July 1945 to May 1953, Chester manager June 1953 to June 1956
Made his name at outside-left but could turn in a useful performance at inside-left or centre-forward too (as witnessed by his scoring six goals for Burnley v Birmingham from this position in October 1926). Elusive, a powerful marksman and fast.

PAINE, Terence Lionel 1963-6(19)
b Winchester 23 March 1939.

Career: Winchester Schools, Winchester Corinthians, Winchester City, Southampton February 1957. Has varied business interests in Southampton and has been a Southampton Borough Councillor
Club Honour: Southampton—Third Division Champions 1960.
Imbued with a keen competitive spirit while playing a shrewd, scheming game at outside or inside-right. Is two-footed and exploits a telling turn of speed.

PANTLING, Harry Harold
                                1924(1)
b Leighton Buzzard, Beds 1891; d 22 December 1952.
Career: Watford amateur 1908, professional cs 1911, Sheffield United March 1914, Rotherham United cs 1926, Heanor Town November 1927. Later a licensee in Sheffield until his death
Club Honour: Sheffield United—F.A. Cup winners 1925
Sturdily built and capable right-half. He excelled in distribution, both long and short balls being placed with fine accuracy.

PARAVICINI, Percy John de
                                1883(3)
b London 15 July 1862; d 12 October 1921.
Career: Aldin House School, Slough; Eton College (XI 1880-1); Trinity College, Cambridge (Blue 1883); Old Etonians; Windsor; Berks and Bucks ; Corinthians 1885 ; F.A. Committee 1885. Cambridge cricket blue 1882-3-4-5 and also played cricket for Middlesex and Bucks at times. He was created M.V.O. in 1908 and C.V.O. in 1921
Club Honours: Old Etonians—F.A. Cup winners 1882, finalists 1883
Regarded as a leading exponent of full-back play in the 80s. Possessed great speed and kicked splendidly with both feet.

PARKER, Thomas Robert 1925(1)
b Woolston, Hants 19 November
1897.
Career: St Marks Woolston, Shotley Rangers, Shotley Athletic,
Southampton mid 1918-19, Arsenal
March 1926, Norwich City manager March 1933, Southampton
manager February 1937 to May
1943. After leaving Southampton
F.C. he continued to live and
work in the town apart from a
second spell as Norwich City
manager May 1955 to March
1957. He scouted for Southampton
Club Honours: Southampton—
Third Division South Champions
1922, Arsenal—F.A. Cup finalists
1927, 32, winners 1930, F.L.
Champions 1931
Right-back who played a robust
game with speed. An expert taker
of penalties.

PARKINSON, John 1910(2)
b Bootle 1883; d 13 September
1942.
Career: Hertford Albion, Valkyrie, Liverpool amateur mid
1901-2, professional 1903, Bury cs
1914 retired during the 1914-18
War after which he was a newsagent and tobacconist in Liverpool
Club Honour: Liverpool—Second
Division Champions 1905
Was a centre-forward whose effervescent style was laced with
vigour and dash. Had a good eye
for a scoring opportunity.

PARR, Percival Chase 1882(1)
b Bromley 2 December 1859; d
3 September 1912.
Career: Winchester College (XI
1877); New College Oxford (Blue
1880-1-2 captain 1882); West
Kent; F.A. Committee 1881. Barrister 1885. Partner in W. H.
Allen & Co., publishers and later
Editor of the *National Observer*
and *Ladies Field*

Club Honour: Oxford University
—F.A. Cup finalists 1880
Displayed splendid goalkeeping
qualities, brave and unruffled. Was
also a centre-forward of note.

PARRY, Edward Hagarty
1879-82(3)
b Toronto 24 April 1855; d 19
July 1931.
Career: Charterhouse School (XI
1872-3-4 captain 1873-4; Exeter
College Oxford (Blue 1875-6-7
captain 1877); Old Carthusians;
Swifts; Remnants; Stoke Poges;
Windsor; Berks and Bucks; F.A.
Committee 1881. Schoolmaster at
Felsted 1879-80, at Stoke House
School, Slough from 1881 to 1892
thence Headmaster of the latter
school until his retirement in 1918
Club Honours: Oxford University
—F.A. Cup finalists 1877, Old
Carthusians—F.A. Cup winners
1881
Persistent, close-dribbling centreforward with a turn of speed and
a useful shot. Did not, however,
relish the charging which was a
feature of soccer in the 'seventies
and 'eighties.

PARRY, Raymond Alan 1960(2)
b Derby 16 January 1936.
Career: Derwent Secondary
School Derby (England Schools
v Wales Ireland Scotland (2) Eire
1950 v Wales (2) Scotland Eire
1951), Bolton Wanderers amateur
September 1950, professional January 1953, Blackpool October
1960, Bury October 1964, player
coach September 1970
Club Honour: Bolton Wanderers
—F.A. Cup winners 1958
Groomed for the highest class
from his promising schoolboy
days, becoming an accomplished
inside or outside left. Was thrustful, a penalty specialist and had
a left foot deceptively powerful
for a slight man.

PATCHETT, Basil Clement Alderson 1923(2)
b 12 August 1900.
Career: Charterhouse School (XI 1917-18-19 captain 1919) ; Trinity College Cambridge (Blue 1922); Corinthians 1922-3; Castleford Town late 1923. Later was a resident in Johannesburg
Almost the most recent of the several Carthusians to win " full " England recognition. He was sound defensively and had the additional asset of versatility—he appeared at back in the 1922 'Varsity match and at centre and wing-half subsequently.

PAWSON, Francis William 1883-5(2)
b Sheffield 6 April 1861; d 4 July 1921.
Career: Sheffield Collegiate School; Caius College Cambridge (Blue 1882-3-4 captain 1884); Swifts; Sheffield F.C.; Casuals; Surrey; Corinthians 1885-9; F.A. Committee 1882-3. Ordained in 1886 he was curate of Battersea 1886-90, of Bexhill 1890-9, Rector of Lewes 1900-3 and Vicar of Ecclesfield, Sheffield 1903-21
Outside-right or centre-forward. Passed with precision, mobile and a good marksman.

PAYNE, Joseph 1937(1)
b Brinington Common near Chesterfield 17 January 1914.
Career: Bolsover Colliery, Biggleswade Town, Luton Town cs 1934, Chelsea March 1938, West Ham United December 1946, Millwall September 1947 retired injury 1947-8. Made a comeback in October 1952 when he joined Worcester City but his sojourn was brief. Played cricket for Bedfordshire in 1937
Club Honours: Luton Town—Third Division South Champions 1937, Chelsea—F.L. South Cup finalists 1944, winners 1945
There has never been a more sen-

M

sational centre-forward debut than Payne's ten goal spectacular in 1936 (having previously played only in the half-back line he played centre-forward v Bristol Rovers for Luton Town on 13 April 1936 and scored 10 goals). He went on to develop his excellent headwork, two foot strength and eye for the ball, and to play at inside-right as well.

PEACOCK, Alan 1962(6)
b Middlesbrough 29 October 1937.
Career: Lawson Secondary Modern School Middlesbrough, Middlesbrough amateur, professional November 1954 (England Youth international 1956), Leeds United February 1964, Plymouth Argyle November 1967, retired injury March 1968. Is now a newsagent in Middlesbrough
Club Honours: Leeds United—Second Division Champions 1964, F.A. Cup finalists 1965
At Middlesbrough he played at inside-left originally. When Clough went to Sunderland he moved to centre-forward and his clever play and intelligent running became more obvious.

PEACOCK, Joseph 1929(3)
b Wigan 1900.
Career: Atherton, Everton cs 1919, Middlesbrough cs 1927, Sheffield Wednesday cs 1930, Clapton Orient June 1931, coach in Sweden March 1933. Appointed Wrexham trainer July 1939
Club Honour: Middlesbrough—Second Division Champions 1929
A wing-half notable for fine ball control. At Everton appeared also in both right-wing and centre positions in the attack where his natural elusiveness was of more value.

PEARSON, Harold Frederick 1932(1)
b Tamworth, Staffs 7 May 1908.

Career: Tamworth Schools, Glascote United Methodists, Belgrave Working Men's Club, Tamworth Castle, West Bromwich Albion amateur 1925, professional May 1927, Millwall August 1937 retired during the War. His father was also a West Bromwich Albion goalkeeper (he was chosen to play for England but was unable to play) and Harry Hibbs was a cousin

Club Honours: West Bromwich Albion—F.A. Cup winners 1931, finalists 1935, Millwall—Third Division South Champions 1938

Being of goalkeeping stock it was natural he would take a place as a talented practitioner. Sound rather than showy and difficult to beat.

PEARSON, John Hargreaves
1892(1)
b Crewe 25 January 1868; d 22 June 1931.

Career: Crewe Alexandra 1882 playing for the reserve team when only 13½, retired owing to injury and became a referee in 1893. Referee of the F.A. Cup final in 1911. On the staff of the London & North Western (later London Midland & Scottish) Railway for many years until his retirement in December 1930

Speedy inside-right who played with a degree of skill. His performance suffered somewhat, though, from too great a reliance on individualism.

PEARSON, Stanley C.　1948-52(8)
b Salford, Lancs 15 January 1919.

Career: Frederick Road School Salford, Adelphi Lads Club, Manchester United May 1936, Bury February 1954, Chester October 1957, manager April 1959 retiring as a player in May 1959 and resigning as manager November 1961. After leaving the game he became a newsagent in Prestbury, Cheshire and has managed and

coached the local East Cheshire League club

Club Honours: Manchester United—F.A. Cup winners 1948, F.L. Champions 1952, Chester—Welsh Cup finalists 1958

Unspectacular but an inside-forward of comprehensive talent: crafty, a lethal shot, meticulous in control and fine in combination.

PEASE, William Harold　1927(1)
b Leeds 30 September 1899; d 2 October 1955.

Career: Played rugby at school and took up soccer when serving with Royal Northumberland Fusiliers during 1914-18 War, Leeds City amateur mid 1918-19, Northampton Town professional October 1919, Middlesbrough May 1926, Luton Town June 1933 retired injury January 1935. Following his retirement he was a licensee in the Middlesbrough area

Club Honours: Middlesbrough—Second Division Champions 1927, 9

Direct and very fast outside-right able to open up defences by his fine crosses when on the run. Had a most creditable goal tally for his position, in particular scoring over 20 goals in each of Middlesbrough's promotion seasons.

PEGG, David　1957(1)
b Doncaster 20 September 1935; d 6 February 1958.

Career: Highfields Secondary Modern School Doncaster (England Schools v Ireland 1950 v Wales (2) Eire Scotland 1951), Manchester United as an amateur on leaving school 1951, professional September 1952. Killed in the Munich air crash

Club Honours: Manchester United—F.A. Youth Cup winners 1953-4, F.L. Champions 1956-7, F.A. Cup finalists 1957

Like several of the other Munich crash victims had probably not reached his full potential. He was a sparkling outside-left, however, deft in footwork and elusive.

PELLY, Frederick Raymond
1893-4(3)
b Upminster, Essex 11 August 1869; d 16 October 1940.
Career: Forest School (XI 1882-6); Old Foresters; Essex; Casuals; Corinthians 1891-8. He became senior partner in the commercial firm, Mann George & Co. Endowed with formidable physique—a six footer and tipping the scales at 15 stones—this left-back nevertheless was quite fast. Possessed a good kick and, at his best, very dependable.

PENNINGTON, Jesse 1907-20(25)
b West Bromwich 23 August 1884; d September 1970.
Career: Summit Star, Smethwick Centaur, Langley Villa (Aston Villa amateur), Dudley, West Bromwich Albion April 1903 retired August 1922 (briefly with Kidderminster Harriers August 1910 following a pay dispute). Later a poultry farmer
Club Honours: West Bromwich Albion—Second Division Champions 1911, F.A. Cup finalists 1912, F.L. Champions 1920
The doyen of England left-backs and with Sam Hardy and Crompton made up that celebrated defensive triumvirate. Not showy and not very conspicuous, Pennington was immensely effective, timing his tackles to perfection, kicking accurately and masterly in his positional play.

PENTLAND, Frederick Beaconsfield 1909(5)
b Small Heath 1883; d 16 March 1962.
Career: Small Heath junior football, Small Heath August 1900, Blackpool cs 1903, Blackburn Rovers mid 1903-4, Brentford May 1906, Queens Park Rangers May 1907, Middlesbrough cs 1908, Halifax Town cs 1912, Stoke later 1912, coach in Europe at the commencement of the 1914-18 War and was interned. Coach in France in 1920 and in Spain from 1921-36, thence Brentford staff, Barrow manager January 1938 up to the War.
Club Honour: Queens Park Rangers—Southern League Champions 1908
Pentland was a fast outside-right and could centre with precision. He was also dextrous in ball play though guilty at times of over elaboration.

PERRY, Charles 1890-3(3)
b January 1866; 2 July 1927.
Career: West Bromwich Albion late 1882 retired in 1896 and became a director of the Club. Also became a director of the brewery firm, Arnold & Bates, for which he worked
Club Honours: West Bromwich Albion—F.A. Cup winners 1888, 92, finalists 1886, 7. Missed 1895 final owing to injury which finally ended his career
Fine defensive centre-half skilled in holding his side together and feeding his forwards. Was notably courageous too. Brother of T.

PERRY, Thomas 1898(1)
b West Bromwich 1871; d 18 July 1927.
Career: Christchurch West Bromwich, Stourbridge, West Bromwich Albion 1891, Aston Villa October 1901 retired 1903
Club Honour: West Bromwich—F.A. Cup finalists 1895
A most capable and efficient half-back and something of a utility man. Had an enthusiastic and hardworking approach.

PERRY, William 1956(3)
b Johannesburg 10 September 1930.
Career: Johannesburg Rangers,

Blackpool October 1949, Southport June 1962, Hereford United July 1963, South Coast United (Australia) July 1964 but returned to England later 1964. Holyhead Town April 1966. A director of Fleetwood cs 1967 to February 1970
Club Honours: Blackpool—F.A. Cup winners 1953, finalists 1951
Sturdy, persevering outside-left always looking for the ball and a dangerous opportunist.

PETERS, Martin Stanford
1966-72(54)
b Plaistow, East London 8 November 1943.
Career: Fanshawe School Dagenham (England Schools v Scotland Wales Eire Ireland and Germany (2) 1959), West Ham United apprentice May 1959, professional November 1960 (England Youth international 1960-62), Tottenham Hotspur March 1970. A member of England's World Cup winning team of 1966
Club Honours: West Ham United —European Cup Winners Cup winners 1965, F.L. Cup finalists 1966, Tottenham Hotspur—F.L. Cup winners 1971, UEFA Cup winners 1972
A prime example of the modern all-purpose player who can be categorised as a wing-half, inside or outside-left. Very intelligent with a wonderful knack of coming up on the blind side and scorby stealth, as it were.

PHILLIPS, Leonard H. 1952-5(3)
b Hackney, London 1922.
Career: Royal Marines football, Hillside Youth Club, Portsmouth amateur 1944, professional 1946 retired injury May 1956 but joined Poole Town August 1956, Chelmsford City June 1959, Bath City May 1963. Since 1959 has worked with a Portsmouth Engineering firm as a machine operator
Club Honours: Portsmouth—F.L.

Champions 1949 and 1950
Brought speed and incisiveness from his earlier senior days at inside-left to bear on moving to right-half. Was an intelligent player placing his passes to the greatest advantage.

PICKERING, Frederick 1964-5(3)
b Blackburn January 1941.
Career: Blackburn amateur football, Blackburn Rovers professional January 1958, Everton March 1964, Birmingham City August 1967, Blackpool June 1969, Blackburn Rovers March 1971 to February 1972, Brighton & Hove Albion trial February 1972
Club Honours: Blackburn Rovers —F.A. Youth Cup winners 1959. Missed the F.A. Cup Final of 1966 whilst with Everton owing to injury
Blossomed into a centre-forward following an apprenticeship at full-back. He has proved a powerful attacker, quick running and having an eye for openings.

PICKERING, John 1933(1)
b Mortomley, Yorks 18 December 1908.
Career: Barnsley Grammar School, Mortomley St Saviours, Sheffield United May 1925 retired cs 1948. Poole Town manager coach cs 1948
Club Honour: Sheffield United— F.A. Cup finalists 1936
Lithe inside-left whose lengthy stride was deceptively fast. He relied entirely on craft, shot strongly with both feet and gave his club outstandingly long service.

PIKE, Thelwell Mather 1886(1)
b 17 November 1865; d 21 July 1957.
Career: Malvern School (XI 1884-5); Clare College Cambridge (Blue 1886 and 1888); Old Malvernians; Crusaders; Brentwood; Swifts; Thanet Wanderers; Corinthians 1886-91 ; Worcestershire cricket

1886-95. Became a schoolmaster on leaving Cambridge becoming Headmaster of Weybridge Preparatory School 1897-1906 thence of Thanet School, Margate until his retirement

A right wing forward of some merit he was extremely fast and his centres were models of judgment and accuracy.

PILKINGTON, Brian   1955(1)
b Farringdon, Lancs early 1933.
Career: Leyland Motors, Burnley April 1951, Bolton Wanderers March 1961, Bury February 1964, Barrow January 1965, Chorley late 1967 retired injury January 1968 but came out of retirement to sign for Leyland Motors August 1969, manager in 1970

Club   Honour: Burnley—F.L. Champions 1960

An outside-left of the direct type, fast in action and always potentially a goal scorer.

PLANT, John   1900(1)
b Bollington, Cheshire 1872; d
Career: Denton, Bollington, Bury April 1890, Reading cs 1898, Bury cs 1899 to cs 1907

Club   Honours: Bury—Second Division Champions 1895, F.A. Cup winners 1900 and 1903

Kept his incisiveness on the left wing over a goodly period of years, a fact well demonstarted in the 1903 Cup Final. Noted, too, as a deadly shot.

PLUM, Seth Lewis   1923(1)
b Edmonton 15 July 1899; d December 1969.
Career: Page Green School Tottenham, Mildway Athletic 1912-13, Tottenham Park Avondale, Barnet, Charlton Athletic cs 1922, Chelsea March 1924, Southend United cs 1927. Later lived and worked in the Tottenham area up to his death

Good all-round wing-half although slight physically. From his earliest days clever in interception, he later improved his distribution to a like high standard.

POINTER, Raymond   1962(3)
b Cramlington, Co. Durham 10 October 1936.
Career: Cramlington Modern School, Dudley Welfare Juniors, Burnley August 1957, Bury August 1965, Coventry City December 1965, Portsmouth January 1967

Club Honours: Burnley—F.L. Champions 1960, F.A. Cup finalists 1962

When at Burnley at the height of his powers was a goal getting centre-forward, dynamic and apparently tireless. Has since appeared at inside-forward and on the wing, his experience being a considerable asset.

PORTEOUS, Thomas S.   1891(1)
b in England.
Career: Hearts, Kilmarnock, Sunderland cs 1889, Rotherham Town cs 1894, Manchester City cs 1895 for one season only

Club Honours: Sunderland—F.L. Champions 1892 and 1893

A right-back whose peak was membership of the Sunderland "Team of all the talents". Was not the most publicised member but played with proficiency and great steadiness.

PRIEST, Alfred Ernest   1900(1)
b Darlington 1875; d 5 May 1922.
Career: South Bank, Sheffield United cs 1896, Middlesbrough cs 1906 as player assistant trainer, Hartlepools United manager 1908. Later a licensee in Hartlepools

Club Honours: Sheffield United —F.L. Champions 1898, F.A. Cup winners 1899, 1902, finalists 1901

Made his name on the left wing later moving inside on the arrival of Lipsham. He had not a little to do with the latter's success being able to bring out the best in colleagues with his clever, thoughtful prompting.

PRINSEP, James Frederick McLeod 1879(1)
b 27 July 1861; d 22 November 1895.
Career: Charterhouse School (XI 1877-8); Clapham Rovers; Surrey; Old Carthusians. Joined Essex Regiment 1882, served in Egyptian Army 1885-90 when he transferred to the Egyptian Coastguard Service
Club Honours: Clapham Rovers —F.A. Cup finalists 1879, Old Carthusians—F.A. Cup winners 1881
A safe constructive half-back, able to kick the ball from any angle.

PUDDEFOOT, Sydney Charles 1926(2)
b West Ham 17 October 1894.
Career: Park School West Ham, Conder Athletic, Limehouse Town, West Ham United mid 1912-13, Falkirk February 1922, Blackburn Rovers February 1925, West May United February 1932, coach to Fenerbahce (Istanbul) 1933-4, to Galata Seray 1934-5, Northampton Town March 1935 to March 1937, coach in Istanbul 1937-40. After returning from Istanbul he was briefly with Blackpool Borough Police then joined the Civil Service retiring in 1963 when he took a post on the Southend United staff. Essex County cricket 1922-3
Club Honour: Blackburn Rovers —F.A. Cup winners 1928
Between the Wars Puddefoot was a famous figure. A delightfully unorthodox leader or inside-right he played with dash and brought the best out of his attack.

PYE, Jesse 1950(1)
b Treeton, Yorks 22 December 1921.
Career: Catliffe, Treeton, Sheffield United cs 1939, Notts County September 1945, Wolver-

hampton Wanderers May 1946, Luton Town July 1952, Derby County October 1954, Wisbech Town July 1957, player manager March 1960 resigned 1966. Now a hotelier in Blackpool
Club Honour: Wolverhampton Wanderers—F.A. Cup winners 1949
Admirably built for duties at centre and inside-forward where his style was a fine amalgam of subtlety and penetration.

PYM, Richard Henry 1925-6(3)
b Topsham, Devon 2 February 1893.
Career: Topsham St Margarets, Exeter City mid 1911-12, Bolton Wanderers June 1921, Yeovil Town May 1931. Appointed Exeter City assistant trainer August 1937 he later lived and fished in his native Topsham where he still lives
Club Honours: Bolton Wanderers —F.A. Cup winners 1923-6-9
Made goalkeeping look deceptively simple by his excellent anticipation. Calm and unruffled under the severest pressure.

QUANTRILL, Alfred Edward 1920-1(4)
b Punjab 22 January 1897.
Career: Boston Town, Derby County mid 1914-15, Preston North End June 1921, Chorley August 1924, Bradford September 1924, Nottingham Forest May 1930 retiring cs 1932. Later a successful insurance broker. Son-in-law of Steve Bloomer
Club Honour: Bradford—Third Division North Champions 1928
Generally regarded as an outside-left though he appeared on the right-wing too. He had speed, a useful shot and required little space in which to beat an opponent.

QUIXALL, Albert 1954-5(5)
b Sheffield 9 August 1933.
Career: Meynell Road Secondary

Modern School Sheffield (England Schools v Wales and Scotland 1948), Meynell Youth Club, Sheffield Wednesday amateur cs 1948, professional 1950, Manchester United September 1958, Oldham Athletic September 1964, Stockport County cs 1966 retired injury March 1967 but joined Altrincham late 1967. Since retiring has been in business in Manchester as a scrap metal merchant
Club Honours: Sheffield Wednesday—Second Division Champions 1952 and 1956, Manchester United—F.A. Cup winners 1963
Very boyish looking even when a mature player, and wore brief shorts years before they became *à la mode*. An inside-forward of the creative kind, possessor of a clever body swerve and masterly at long passing.

RADFORD, John   1969-72(2)
b Hemsworth, Yorks 22 February 1947.
Career: Hemsworth Schools, Hemsworth Youth Club, Arsenal apprentice October 1962, professional February 1964
Club Honours: Arsenal—F.A. Youth Cup finalists 1965, F.L. Cup finalists 1968 and 1969, Fairs Cup winners 1970, FL. Champions and F.A. Cup winners 1971, F.A. Cup finalists 1972
Performs at centre-forward with a hostile directness when the ball is at his feet once described as intimidating. Very much, too, a threat in the air because he is big and powerful.

RAIKES, George Berkeley
                         1895-6(4)
b Wymondham, Norfolk 14 March 1873 d 18 December 1966.
Career: Shrewsbury School (XI 1890-2); Magdalen College Oxford (Blue 1893-4-5-6); Wymondham ; Norfolk ; Corinthians 1893-6. Retired from first class football on leaving Oxford. Cricket blue 1894-5 and played for Norfolk

in 1890-7 and 1904 and for Hampshire from 1900-2. Ordained in 1897 he was curate of Portsea to 1903, Chaplain to Duke of Portland 1905-20 and Rector of Bergh Apton, Norfolk from 1920 until his retirement in 1936
His admirable goalkeeping was aided by his height—6 foot 2 inches. Alert in performance and very quick with both hands and feet.

RAMSEY, Sir Alfred Ernest
                         1949-54(32)
b Dagenham 22 January 1920.
Career: Becontree Heath School Dagenham, Five Elms (Portsmouth amateur but did not play for the club), Southampton mid 1943-4, professional August 1944, Tottenham Hotspur May 1949, Ipswich Town manager August 1955, England team manager April 1963. Knighted January 1967 for his part in the winning of the World Cup in 1966
Club Honours: Tottenham Hotspur—F.L. Champions 1951, Second Division Champions 1950
Played a cool, highly intelligent game at right-back and his clearances were perfectly judged. He was slow on the turn, particularly latterly, but this vulnerability to a fast winger was not often exposed because of an acute positioning sense.

RAWLINGS, Archibald   1921(1)
b Leicester circa 1890.
Career: Wombwell, Shirebrook, Northampton Town early 1908, Barnsley 1911, left cs 1913, Rochdale cs 1914, Shirebrook, Dundee, Preston North End June 1920, Liverpool March 1924, Walsall June 1926, Bradford February 1927, Southport cs 1928, Dick Kerr's December 1928, Burton Town cs 1931. Later assistant trainer of Preston North End
Club Honour: Preston North End—F.A. Cup finalists 1922

Standing nearly 6 foot was tall for an outside-right. Had no great invention but when in the mood was extremely dangerous with his great pace and shooting power.

RAWLINGS, William Ernest
1922(2)
b Andover, Hants 1896.
Career: Andover, Southampton amateur 1918, professional cs 1919, Manchester United March 1928, Port Vale November 1929
Club Honour: Southampton—Third Division South Champions 1922
Lively centre-forward of the individualist type. Was ideally built for the position and a deadly marksman.

RAWLINSON, John Frederick Peel
1882(1)
b Alresford, Hants 21 December 1860; d 14 January 1926.
Career: Eton College; Trinity College Cambridge (Blue 1882-33; Old Etonians; Corinthians (original committee 1882); F.A. Committee 1885-6. Barrister 1884, Q.C. 1897, Recorder of Cambridge 1898-1926. M.P. for Cambridge University 1906-26
Club Honours: Old Etonians—F.A. Cup finalists 1881, 3, winners 1882
Perhaps not quite as skilful a goalkeeper as his contemporaries, Arthur and Roberts but, nonetheless, a good one even if his coolness at times did border on the casual.

RAWSON, Herbert Edward 1875(1)
b Mauritius 3 September 1852; d 18 October 1924.
Career: Wallace's School Cheltenham; Westminster School (XI 1869-71 captain 1871); Royal Engineers; Royal Military Academy Woolwich; Kent. Joined Royal Engineers 1872 and retired in 1909 with the rank of Col. Brother of W.S. Played cricket for Kent on one occasion
Club Honours: Royal Engineers—

F.A. Cup finalists 1874, winners 1875
Adroit dribbler, accurate marksman, industrious and altogether one of the best centres of the 'seventies.

RAWSON, William Stepney
1875-7(2)
b 14 October 1854; d 4 November 1932.
Career: Westminster School (XI 1872-3 captain 1873); Christ Church Oxford (Blue 1874-5-6-7 captain 1876); Old Westminsters; Wanderers; F.A. Committee 1876-7 and 1879. F.A. Cup Final referee 1876
Club Honours: Oxford University—F.A. Cup winners 1874, finalists 1877
Short, strong and often brilliant half. Used both feet effectively and with judgment, always cool and sure.

READ, A. 1921(1)
b Ealing.
Career: Tufnell Park, Queens Park Rangers May 1921, Reading July 1922 probably retired injury cs 1923. 2 England amateur international appearances 1921
Club Honour: Tufnell Park—F.A. Amateur Cup finalists 1920
Unobtrusive yet effective right or centre-half having no particular preference for attack or defence. His passes were usually on the ground and astutely placed.

READER, Joseph 1894(1)
b West Bromwich 27 February 1866; d 8 March 1954
Career: West Bromwich junior football, West Bromwich Albion 1885 retired illness cs 1901 but retaining an active interest in the club until shortly before his death as a steward and in other capacities, a total of 69 years' service
Club Honours: West Bromwich Albion—F.A. Cup winners 1892, finalists 1895

Reader's extraordinary span of service with the Albion was initiated by sixteen years as their goalkeeper. Here proficiency was enhanced by fine consistency and his courage was noteworthy (he was reputed to have once played with an arm in a sling).

REANEY, Paul 1969-71(3)
b Fulham 22 October 1944.
Career: Gross Green Secondary School Leeds, Middleton Parkside Juniors, Leeds United ground staff when he played for South Leeds, Leeds United professional October 1961
Club Honours: Leeds United—Second Division Champions 1964, F.A. Cup finalists 1965, winners 1972, Fairs Cup finalists 1967, F.L. Cup winners 1968, Fairs Cup winners 1968, 71, F.L. Champions 1969. Missed 1970 Cup Final owing to injury
Like his Leeds partner, Terry Cooper, Reaney likes to work the overlap ploy, which he does admirably being fast for a right-back. In defence is quick to tackle and good at positioning.

REVIE, Donald George 1955-7(6)
b Middlesbrough 10 July 1927.
Career: Archibald School Middlesbrough, Newport Boys Club, Middlesbrough Swifts, Leicester City August 1944, Hull City November 1949, Manchester City October 1951, Sunderland November 1956, Leeds United November 1958, player manager March 1961 retiring as a player cs 1963. Awarded O.B.E. January 1970
Club Honours: Manchester City—F.A. Cup finalists 1955, winners 1956. Missed the F.A. Cup final 1949 whilst with Leicester City owing to injury
Inside-forward or wing-half who became a deep lying centre-forward for Manchester City's much publicised "Revie Plan". A thoughtful, deliberate player with excellent ball control and passing ability.

REYNOLDS, John 1892-7(8)
b Blackburn 1869; d 12 March 1917.
Career: Park Road, Witton, Blackburn Rovers Reserves, Park road. Although born in Blackburn he had spent his youth in Ireland returning to Blackburn in 1884. In 1886 he joined the East Lancashire Regiment and was posted to Ireland where he played for the Regimental team and then joined Distillery, Ulster cs 1890, West Bromwich Albion May 1891, Aston Villa May 1893, Celtic cs 1897, Southampton mid 1897-8, Bristol St George cs 1898. Later coached in New Zealand in 1902 but returned to England to join Stockport County in cs 1903. Played little after this. Whilst playing in Ireland he had played for Ireland 5 times in 1890 and 1891 before his English birth was discovered. He worked as a collier in the Sheffield area after leaving game right up to his death
Club Honours: Ulster—Irish Cup finalists 1891, West Bromwich Albion—F.A. Cup winners 1892, Aston Villa—F.A. Cup winners 1895, 7, F.L. Champions 1894-6-7
A right-half of infinite variety—fast, able with both feet, skilled in heading, a sure shot and presenting a difficult obstacle to his opponents. One of the great names of the 'nineties.

RICHARDS, Charles H. 1898(1)
b Burton 1873; d
Career: Gresley Rovers, Nottingham Forest January 1896, Grimsby Town January 1899, Leicester Fosse cs 1901, Newton Heath mid 1901-2 to 1903
Club Honours: Nottingham Forest—F.A. Cup winners 1898, Grimsby Town—Second Division Champions 1901
Inside-right. Hardly a rip-roaring

character but invaluable for his foraging and ability to fit into a side. Possessed an eye for a goal.

RICHARDS, George Henry 1909(1)
b Castle Donington 1879; d
Career: Whitwick White Cross, Derby County April 1902 retired during the 1914-18 War
Club Honours: Derby County— F.A. Cup finalists 1903, Second Division Champions 1912
At left-half or inside-forward he had several attributes. Chief among them were perseverance, cleverness, outstanding consistency and unqualified sportsmanship.

RICHARDSON, James Robert
1933(2)
b Ashington 8 February 1911; d 28 August 1964.
Career: Hirst East School (Northumberland), (England v Scotland and Wales Schools 1925), Blyth Spartans, Newcastle United April 1928, Huddersfield Town October 1934, Newcastle United October 1937, Millwall March 1938, Leyton Orient player trainer coach January 1948, later assistant trainer and full trainer from June 1951 to June 1955. Worked in a Millwall Engineering firm from June 1955 to November 1956 when he became Millwall assistant trainer from which post he had to retire owing to ill health
Club Honour: Newcastle United —FA. Cup winners 1932
A hard working inside-forward (mostly inside-right). He was tenacious in dribbling (a prime example being the notorious goal in the 1932 Cup Final) and had a useful, if not prodigious, scoring record.

RICHARDSON, William
" Ginger "   1935(1)
b Framwellgate Moor 29 May 1909 ; d 29 March 1959.

Career: Framwellgate Moor School, Easington Colilery School, Horden Wednesday, United Bus Co., Hartlepools United professional mid 1928-9, West Bromwich Albion June 1929, Shrewsbury Town cs 1946 thence on the Albion training staff. He died after collapsing whilst playing in a charity game. Always called W. G. Richardson to distinguish him from another William Richardson who was on West Bromwich Albion's books at the same time
Club Honours: West Bromwich Albion—F.A. Cup winners 1931, finalists 1935
In the 1930s was one of the most feared centre-forwards. Quickness off the mark and accurate shooting brought him many goals.

RICKABY, Stanley   1954(1)
b Stockton 1922.
Career: Middlesbrough 1942, West Bromwich Albion February 1950, Poole Town player manager July 1955, retiring as manager January 1959 but continuing as a player until cs 1960, Weymouth cs 1960 to cs 1961. Did not play 1961-3 but joined Newton Abbot Spurs August 1963. Since leaving football has been manager of a life assurance firm at Hagley in Worcestershire. Missed F.A. Cup Final 1954 owing to injury
Found a powerful build useful to a right-back. Usually reliable in kicking his special excellence was in the art of positioning.

RIGBY, Arthur   1927-8(5)
b Manchester 7 June 1900 ; d 25 March 1960.
Career: Manchester and Salford junior football, Stockport County, Crewe Alexandra 1919, Bradford City February 1921, Blackburn Rovers April 1925, Everton November 1929, Middlesbrough May 1932, Clapton Orient August 1933, Crewe Alexandra August

1935 retired cs 1937
Club Honours: Blackburn Rovers
—F.A. Cup winners 1928, Everton—Second Division Champions
1931, Crewe Alexandra—Welsh
Cup winners 1936
A cunning outside-left possessed
of ball mastery and an unerring
shot. When at Blackburn had a
long run at inside-left.

RIMMER, Ellis James   1930-2(4)
b Birkenhead 2 January 1907 ; d
16 March 1965.
Career: Brassey Street School
Birkenhead, Parkside F.C., Northern Nomads (Everton amateur),
Whitchurch September 1923,
Tranmere Rovers 1924, Sheffield
Wednesday February 1928, Ipswich Town August 1938 to February 1939. Later a licensee
Club Honours: Sheffield Wednesday—F.L. Champions 1929 and
1930, F.A. Cup winners 1935
Had the attributes of speed,
trickiness, centring ability and
on-the-mark shooting. Big physically for a left-winger.

ROBB, George   1954(1)
b Finsbury Park 1 June 1926.
Career: Holloway School, Finchley 1942 (19 England amateur
international appearances 1949-
53), Tottenham Hotspur amateur
December 1951, professional June
1953 retired injury May 1960.
Sports master at Christ's College
Finchley 1952-64 and from 1964
at Ardingly College where he also
teaches English
Outstanding in the amateur world,
Robb became a professional at a
late stage. He was a direct,
straight-for-goal left winger who
packed a hard shot.

ROBERTS, Charles   1905(3)
b Rise Carr, Darlington 6 April
1883 ; d 7 August 1939.
Career: Darlington St Augustines,
Bishop Auckland, Grimsby Town
cs 1903, Manchester United April

1904, Oldham Athletic August
1913 retired during the 1914-18
War. Oldham Athletic manager
July 1921 to December 1922.
Founder member of the Players'
Union and Chairman for a time
up to September 1921. Later a
tobacconist, newsagent and stationer in the Manchester area
Club   Honours: Manchester
United—F.L. Champions 1908, 11,
F.A. Cup winners 1909
A keen footballing brain brought
him to the front rank of centrehalves. Could read a game to a
nicety and his skill in attack and
defence was such that he had no
necessity to resort to vigorous
methods.

ROBERTS, Frank   1925(4)
b Sandbach, Cheshire 3 April
1894 d 23 May 1961
Career: Sandbach Villa, Sandbach
Ramblers, Crewe Alexandra, Bolton Wanderers August 1914,
Manchester City October 1922,
Manchester Central June 1929,
Horwich R.M.I. August 1930. A
licensee after his retirement
Club Honours: Manchester City
—F.A. Cup finalists 1926, Second
Division Champions 1928
Hardly a ball artist but immensely
valuable because of his goal scoring propensities. Was a marksman
of rare accuracy and a great
opportunist at both centre-forward and inside-right.

ROBERTS, Henry   1931(1)
b Barrow-in-Furness, Lancs.
Career: Barrow schools football,
Barrow Wireworks, Barrow December 1925, Chesterfield June
1926, Lincoln City August 1928,
Port Vale June 1930, Millwall
April 1931, Sheffield Wednesday
October 1935 on trial and apparently not retained. Now living in
Devon
Thickset inside-right whose bustle
was troublesome to opponents.
Had clever individual tricks, too,

and would possibly have become better known had he been with more prominent clubs.

ROBERTS, Herbert 1931(1)
b Oswestry 1905; d 19 June 1944.
Career: Oswestry Town, Arsenal December 1926, retired injury mid 1937-8, briefly Margate trainer until cs 1938 when he joined the Arsenal training staff. Died of erysipelas whilst serving as a Lieutenant in the Royal Fusiliers
Club Honours: Arsenal—F.A. Cup winners 1936, finalists 1932, F.L. Champions 1931-3-4-5. Missed the F.A. Cup Final of 1930 owing to injury
The first of the "third-back" centre-halves; a device to combat the new offside law of 1925. Roberts was never drawn upfield, remaining between his backs ably defending with head and feet. Far from being a stylish player but effective.

ROBERTS, Robert 1887-90(3)
b circa 1859; d 28 October 1929.
Career: Christ Church School West Bromwich, West Bromwich Albion December 1879, Sunderland Albion May 1890, West Bromwich Albion cs 1891, Aston Villa 1893, West Bromwich Albion 1894, Sunderland Albion briefly then retired. Worked as a plasterer in Sunderland
Club Honours: West Bromwich Albion—F.A. Cup finalists 1886, 7, winners 1888
Usually a sound and competent executant in all aspects of the goalkeeper's craft although sometimes showing undue agitation.

ROBERTS, William Thomas
1924(2)
b Handsworth 29 November 1899.
Career: Kentish Rovers, Boyce Engineers (Smethwick), Lord

Street, Soho Villa, Leicester Fosse, Southport Vulcan, Preston North End May 1919, Burnley October 1924, Preston North End July 1926, Tottenham Hotspur May 1928, Dick Kerr's cs 1929, Chorley October 1930. Later a licensee in Preston
Club Honour: Preston North End—F.A. Cup final 1922
His dash and scoring power made him one of the most dangerous centre-forwards in the 1920s. Was exceptionally clever in headwork.

ROBINSON, John 1937-9(4)
b Shiremoor, Northumberland 1918.
Career: Shiremoor, Sheffield Wednesday early 1935, Sunderland October 1946, Lincoln City October 1949. Broke a leg soon after joining Lincoln City and had to retire
Club Honour: Sheffield Wednesday—F.L. Cup finalists 1943
Graceful, eye-catching inside-right of much talent. Could dribble, shoot and pass well, was a schemer and always willing to assist his defence.

ROBINSON, John William
1897-1901(11)
b Derby 1870; d 28 October 1931.
Career: Derby Midland, Lincoln City, Derby County mid 1890-1, New Brighton Tower May 1897, Southampton cs 1898, Plymouth Argyle May 1903, Exeter City late 1905, Green Waves (Plymouth) cs 1907, Exeter City September 1908, Stoke May 1909. Went to U.S.A. October 1912 but later returned to England where he died
Club Honours: Southampton—F.A. Cup finalists 1900, 2, Southern League Champions 1899-1901-3
Spectacular goalkeeper of unquestioned brilliance. Fast and agile, he made crowds gasp with his

daring. In the front rank of England custodians.

ROBSON, Robert William
1958-62(20)
b Sacriston, Co. Durham 18 February 1933.
Career: Langley Park, Fulham May 1950, West Bromwich Albion March 1956, Fulham August 1962, Vancouver Royals as player manager May 1967, Fulham manager January 1968 to November 1968, Ipswich Town manager January 1969
Early, at inside-right, made up a famous Fulham inside-forward trio with Jezzard and Haynes, then became equally considerable at right-half when with the Albion. He was an effective player, robust and full of running.

ROSE, William Crispin 1884-91(5)
b 1861 ; d 4 February 1937.
Career: Small Heath, Swifts, Preston North End February 1885, Stoke, Wolverhampton Wanderers mid 1888-9, Loughborough Town cs 1894, Wolverhampton Wanderers cs 1895 retired cs 1896.
After retirement he was in turn a licensee in Birmingham and Wolverhampton and a shop keeper at Bordesley
Club Honour: Wolverhampton Wanderers—F.A. Cup winners 1893
Rightly regarded as one of the best 'keepers of his time. The fact that he was something of a psychologist respecting opposing forwards doubtless contributed to his brilliance.

ROSTRON, "Tot" 1881(2)
b Darwen, Lancs.
Career: Darwen, Great Lever during 1883-4 returning to Darwen in 1885 in which season he also played for Blackburn Rovers
Small but skilful inside-right, zealous and quick. Adept at the " screw " kick.

ROWE, Arthur Sydney 1934(1)
b Tottenham 1 September 1906.
Career: Parkhurst School Cheshunt, Northfleet, Tottenham Hotspur professional May 1929, retired injury 1939 when he became a coach in Hungary. Chelmsford City manager July 1945, Tottenham Hotspur team manager May 1949, retired ill health May 1955. West Bromwich Albion staff August 1957, Crystal Palace staff October 1958, manager April 1960, general manager March 1963. Later assistant manager until he resigned in May 1971 to become secretary of Football's Hall of Fame, until its disbandment in December 1971, general adviser to Orient January 1972
Lavished a lot of thought on the game at centre-half and was clever at turning defence into attack. He tried always, never to waste a ball and to place clearances.

ROWLEY, John Frederick
1949-52(6)
b Wolverhampton January 1918.
Career: Wolverhampton Wanderers November 1935 (on loan first to Cradley Heath and from February 1937 to Bournemouth & Boscombe Athletic), Manchester United October 1937, Plymouth Argyle player manager February 1955 retiring as a player cs 1957 and continuing as manager until March 1960, Oldham Athletic manager July 1960 to July 1963, Ajax (Amsterdam) coach August 1963 to July 1964, Wrexham manager January 1965, Bradford manager April 1967, Oldham Athletic manager October 1968 to December 1969
Club Honours: Wolverhampton Wanderers—F.L. War Cup winners 1942 (as a guest), Manchester United—F.A. Cup winners 1948, F.L. Champions 1952
Aggressive, powerful forward who played in four positions in the

England attack (the exception was outside-right). Dubbed " the Gunner " by the more fanciful critics because of his ubiquitous, searing shooting.

ROWLEY, William   1889-92(2)
b Hanley.
Career: Hanley Orion (as a centre-forward), Stoke reserves 1883-4, Burslem Port Vale, Stoke cs 1887, secretary cs 1896 and as such transferred himself to Leicester Fosse in August 1898 but the registration was not accepted and he was suspended in connection with the matter in October 1898. He was later a licensee in the Potteries and then emigrated to the United States
Had few if any superiors as a custodian when at his peak. Safe, smart and agile.

ROYLE, Joseph   1971(1)
b Liverpool 8 April 1949.
Career: Liverpool Schools, Everton ground staff July 1964, professional August 1966 (England Youth international 1967)
Club Honours: Everton—F.A. Cup finalists 1968, F.L. Champions 1970
Has played elsewhere in the attack but is generally regarded as a centre-forward, where his physique, thrust and, above all, superb headwork, serve Everton well.

RUDDLESDIN, Herod   1904-5(3)
b Birdwell, Yorks 1876; d 26 March 1910.
Career: Birdwell, Sheffield Wednesday cs 1898 retired illness December 1906. Tried a come-back with Northampton Town cs 1908 but was never able to play in a match
Club Honours: Sheffield Wednesday—Second Division Champions 1900, F.L. Champions 1903 and 1904
A wing-half without affectation or showiness Ruddlesdin was clever, adroit and absolutely fair. Indifferent health doubtless cost him more honours.

RUFFELL, James William
    1926-30(6)
b Doncaster 8 August 1900.
Career: Fullers F.C., Chadwell Heath United, Manor Park Albion, East Ham, Wall End United, West Ham United March 1920, Aldershot June 1938 retired injury mid 1938-9. Worked as a Brewery representative and as a licensee in Essex until his retirement early in 1966
Club Honour: West Ham United —F.A. Cup finalists 1923
Opponents learned to pay Ruffell the compliment of close marking —it was fatal to let him give full rein to his exceptional speed and flashing shots. A grand left-winger.

RUSSELL, Bruce Bremner   1883(1)
b 25 August 1859 ; d 13 May 1942.
Career: Cheltenham College (where he played rugby); Royal Military Academy, Woolwich; Royal Engineers. Joined Royal Engineers in 1878 and retired in 1907 with the rank of Colonel but returned for service 1914-18
An estimable left-back precise and judicious in kicking, his chief asset was dependability.

RUTHERFORD, John ("Jock")
    1904-8(11)
b Percy Main, Northumberland 12 October 1884; d 21 April 1963.
Career: Percy Main School, Willington Athletic, Newcastle United cs 1901, Arsenal October 1913, Stoke manager March 1923 re-signed August 1923, rejoined Arsenal as a player September 1923, retired cs 1925 but re-signed again in January 1926, Clapton Orient August 1926 finally retiring cs 1927. A licensee after his retirement from the game

Club Honours: Newcastle United —F.L. Champions 1905-7-9, F.A. Cup winners 1910, finalists 1905-6-8-11

Maintained a high standard over an unusually lengthy first-class career. An outside-right with tremendous speed, clever ball control and a liking for cutting in to score.

SADLER, David   1968-71(4)
b Yalding, Kent 5 February 1946.
Career: Oldborough Manor Secondary Modern School, Maidstone Technical High School, Maidstone United (England amateur international 1963), Manchester United November 1962 professional February 1963
Club Honours: Manchester United —F.A. Youth Cup winners 1964, F.L. Champions 1967, European Cup winners 1968
A neat, judicious and very versatile player. Plays left-half for his club, has played centre-half for England and, in earlier senior days was looked upon as a centre or inside-forward.

SAGAR, Charles   1900-2(2)
b Turton, Lancs 1878; d 5 December 1919.
Career: Edgworth Rovers, Turton, Bury cs 1898, Manchester United cs 1905 until 1907. Joined Haslingden early 1909
Club Honours: Bury—F.A. Cup winners 1900, 3
Could be variable but, when in form, a shrewd forward craftsman, employing good footwork. Divided his allegiance between the centre and inside-left berths.

SAGAR, Edward   1936(4)
b Moorends, Yorks 7 February 1910.
Career: Thorne Colliery, Everton March 1929 retired May 1953
Club Honours: Everton—F.L. Champions 1932, 9, F.A. Cup winners 1933
Undemonstrative but most proficient goalkeeper. Outstanding in anticipation and particularly good in dealing with high balls.

SANDFORD, Edward A.   1933(1)
b Handsworth 22 October 1910.
Career: Wattville Road School Handsworth, Tantany Athletic, Overend Wesley, Birmingham Carriage Works, Smethwick Highfield, West Bromwich Albion amateur October 1929, professional May 1930, Sheffield United March 1939, retired during the War. Later owned a café near the Hawthorns ground and was also at one time on Albion's coaching staff
Club Honours: West Bromwich Albion—F.A. Cup winners 1931, finalists 1935
A player of the quiet type and never flashy, Sandford was nevertheless, an excellent inside-left of subtlety and good marksmanship. Played centre-half in the latter part of his first-class career.

SANDILANDS, Rupert Renorden
                                     1892-6(5)
b 7 August 1868; d 20 April 1946.
Career: Westminster School (XI 1885-6-7); Old Westminsters; Corinthians 1889-97. Was on the staff of the Bank of England
Outside-left whose inclination was to take the direct path to his opponent's goal. Fast, dexterous dribbler, courageous and unselfish to a fault.

SANDS, John   1880(1)
b 1859; d 29 February 1924.
Career: Nottingham Forest 1878 to 1883
One of the early England goalkeepers and a good one, having agility and a soundness in every aspect.

SAUNDERS, Frank Etheridge
1888(1)
b Brighton 26 August 1864; d
14 May 1905.
Career: Repton School (XI 1882-
3); Caius College Cambridge
(Blue 1885-6-7); Swifts; Corinthians 1885-91; St Thomas Hospital; Sussex. A Licentiate of the
Society of Apothecaries he lived
in South Africa for some years up
to his death there
Came into his own when the three
half-back system was invented.
He took the pivotal berth and,
there, with his physical advantages, played a tough and unre-
lenting game.

SAVAGE, A. H.
1876(1)
Career: Crystal Palace; Surrey
A good goalkeeper. His extremely
powerful kicking was not always
employed effectively because of
a tendency to balloon the ball.

SAYER, James
1887(1)
b Mexborough, Yorks 1862; d 1
February 1922
Career: Mexborough; Heeley;
Sheffield Wednesday; Sheffield
F.A.; Stoke. Secretary and later
became a Director of Fielding
Limited, makers of Devon Pot-
tery at Stoke
An outside-right of all round
ability, Sayer's outstanding virtue
was remarkable speed, so much so
he was usually referred to by the
Stoke supporters as " the grey-
hound ".

SCATTERGOOD, Ernald
1913(1)
b Riddings, Derbyshire 1887; d
2 July 1932.
Career: Alfreton junior football,
Ripley Athletic, Derby County,
Bradford late 1914 retired cs
1925.
Club Honour: Derby County—
Second Division Champions 1912
Competent goalkeeper who had
quickness, judgment and a safe
pair of hands. His powerful

punching of the ball was exceptional.

SCHOFIELD, Joseph Alfred
1892-5(3)
b Hanley 1 January 1871; d 28
September 1929.
Career: Stoke junior football,
Stoke 1891 retired injury cs 1899.
Subsequently in turn a schoolmaster, Poor Law official, Stoke
F.C. secretary and, from February 1920 until his death, secretary manager of Port Vale
Had few peers at outside-left in
the 'nineties—lightly built but
swift and very clever.

SCOTT, Lawrence
1947-9(17)
b Sheffield 24 April 1917.
Career: Bradford City amateur
1931, professional 1934, Arsenal
February 1937, Crystal Palace
player manager October 1951, retired as a player August 1953 continuing as manager until September 1954, Hendon manager late
1954 to cs 1957, Hitchin Town
manager August 1957. Now a
sales representative
Club Honours: Arsenal—F.L.
War Cup finalists 1941, F.L.
South Cup winners 1943, F.L.
Champions 1948, F.A. Cup winners 1950
Resilient strong tackling right-
back whose immaculate placing
and positioning won many
friends. Generally regarded as the
fastest back of his era.

SCOTT, William Reed
1937(1)
b Willington Quay, Northumber-
land 6 December 1907; d 18 Octo-
ber 1969.
Career: Howden Bridge British
Legion, Middlesbrough cs 1927,
Brentford May 1932, Aldershot
August 1947, Dover August 1948
Club Honours: Brentford—Third
Division South Champions 1933,
Second Division Champions 1935
At inside-right the architect

behind the fine Brentford attack in the 1930s, his brainy play bringing out the considerable best of Dave McCulloch and others, while he was no sluggard at scoring himself.

SEDDON, James 1923-9(6)
b Bolton 20 May 1895; d 21 October 1971.
Career: Trinity School Bolton, Hamilton Central, Bolton Wanderers amateur mid 1912-13, professional June 1919, Dordrecht (Holland) coach cs 1932, Altrincham trainer June 1935, Southport trainer cs 1936. Post-war was on the Liverpool training staff for a time and later was assistant manager of a hotel in Southport
Club Honours: Bolton Wanderers —F.A. Cup winners 1923-6-9
There were no frills in his play, being a centre-half who believed in the direct approach. A physical player but extremely fair.

SEED, James Marshall 1921-5(5)
b Blackhill, Co. Durham 25 March 1895; d 16 July 1966.
Career: Whitburn, Sunderland April 1914, Mid Rhondda 1919, Tottenham Hotspur February 1920, Sheffield Wednesday August 1927, Clapton Orient manager April 1931, Charlton Athletic manager May 1933 to September 1956, Bristol City adviser January 1957 (acting manager 8 to 25 January 1958), Millwall manager January 1958 to July 1959 remaining as adviser and appointed a director January 1960
Club Honours: Tottenham Hotspur—F.A. Cup winners 1921, Sheffield Wednesday—F.L. Champions 1929-30
A tireless, probing inside-right. Was a grand strategist and a capital shot.

SETTLE, James 1899-1903(6)
b Bolton 1876; d
Career: Bolton junior football, Bolton Wanderers cs 1894, Halli-

well cs 1895, Bury January 1897, Everton April 1899, Stockport County May 1908 to cs 1909
Club Honours: Everton—F.A. Cup winners 1906, finalists 1907
Played inside or outside-left and required little space in which to execute his trickery. Was a dead shot too but had the faults of being lethargic and selfish sometimes.

SEWELL, John 1952-4(6)
b Kells, Cumberland 24 January 1927.
Career: Kells Centre, Whitehaven Town, Notts County October 1944, Sheffield Wednesday March 1951, Aston Villa December 1955, Hull City October 1959, Lusaka City (Rhodesia) coach September 1961
Club Honours: Notts County— Third Division South Champions 1950, Sheffield Wednesday— Second Division Champions 1952, 6, Aston Villa—F.A. Cup winners 1957
A prominent inside-forward in the years following the last War. Had a useful turn of speed, good marksmanship and, above all, a footballing prescience.

SEWELL, William Ronald 1924(1)
b Middlesbrough; d
Career: Wingate Albion, Gainsborough Trinity cs 1911, Burnley February 1913, Blackburn Rovers February 1920, retired cs 1927. Later a licensee in Lincoln
Club Honour: Burnley—F.A. Cup winners 1914
Had an ideal physique for a goalkeeper and he added qualities of daring and coolness to this. His usefulness was not confined to the field because a humorous disposition gave a dressing-room fillip to the rest of the team.

SHACKLETON, Leonard Francis
1949-55(5)
b Bradford 3 May 1922.
Career: Carlton High School

N

Bradford (England Schools v Scotland Wales and Ireland 1936), Kippax United, Arsenal ground staff August 1938 being loaned to London Paper Mills and Enfield. Returned to Bradford on the outbreak of War and signed professional forms for Bradford December 1940, Newcastle United October 1946, Sunderland February 1948 retired injury September 1957. Became a journalist on retirement. Played cricket on occasion for Northumberland

Some wag entitled him "the Clown Prince of Soccer" which was so apt it stuck, for his tricks at inside-forward had a quite personal, impish ingenuity. For all that, however, Shackleton was a fine footballer, brilliant in ball control and perhaps too brilliant in conception for his more pedestrian colleagues.

SHARP, John   1903-5(2)
b Hereford 15 February 1878; d 27 January 1938.
Career: Hereford Thistle, Aston Villa cs 1897, Everton cs 1899 retired cs 1910. Everton director from 1923. Played cricket for England in three Tests v Australia in 1909 scoring 105 at The Oval. Also played for Herefordshire and for Lancashire from 1899 to 1925 being captain for some years. Scored over 22,000 runs in first class cricket including 38 centuries. A well-known sports outfitter in Liverpool
Club Honours: Everton—F.A. Cupwinners 1906, finalists 1907
Prominent outside-right for over a decade, playing with speed and cleverness and also a degree of hardness unusual in a winger.

SHAW, George Edward   1932(1)
b Swinton, Yorks 13 October 1900.
Career: Gillingham, Rossington Main Colliery, Doncaster Rovers, Huddersfield Town February

1924, West Bromwich Albion November 1926, Stalybridge Celtic player manager cs 1938, Worcester City player manager March 1939, retired during the War. After the War was manager coach to Floriana, Malta
Club Honours: West Bromwich Albion—F.A. Cup winners 1931, finalists 1935
Won his club and representative honours when playing at right-back although, being two footed, he could and did play on the left at times. Rangy in build and strong kicking in performance.

SHAW, Graham L.   1959-63(5)
b Sheffield 1932.
Career: Southey Green Secondary School Sheffield, Oaks Fold, Sheffield United 1951, Doncaster Rovers September 1967, Scarborough player manager March 1968 to January 1969
Club Honour: Sheffield United—Second Division Champions 1953
Left-back of pronounced footballing outlook. Used the ball to advantage, was firm in tackling and quite dependable.

SHEA, Daniel   1914(2)
b Wapping 6 November 1887; d 25 December 1960.
Career: Manor Park Albion, West Ham United November 1907, Blackburn Rovers January 1913, West Ham United May 1920, Fulham November 1920, Coventry City cs 1923, Clapton Orient March 1925, Sheppey United October 1926. After his retirement from football he worked as a docker in East London
Club Honour: Blackburn Rovers—F.L. Champions 1914
An artful schemer and a delicate dribbler at inside-right for many seasons. Had the knack of wheeling suddenly when near goal and unleasing a thunderbolt shot.

SHELLITO, Kenneth J.   1963(1)
b East Ham 18 April 1940.
Career: Sutton School Horn-
church, Chelsea May 1956, professional April 1957 retired injury
January 1969. Coach to Chelsea
youth team from cs 1969
Club   Honour: Chelsea—F.A.
Youth Cup finalists 1958
Was a right-back renowned for
boldness and, despite being
weighty, speed—there could have
been few faster backs in his day.
His enforced retirement at an
early age was very regrettable.

SHELTON, Alfred   1889-92(6)
b Nottingham 1866 ; d 24 July
1923.
Career: Notts Rangers, Notts
County cs 1888, Loughborough
Town cs 1896, Ilkeston cs 1897,
reinstated as an amateur cs 1898.
Brother of Charles. Elected a
director of Notts County October
1908 until 1911. Later worked at
Cammell Laird works in Nottingham and was killed when a crane
collapsed
Club Honours: Notts County—
F.A. Cup finalists 1891, winners
1894
His performances at left-half were
notable for hard work and calm-
ness of execution.

SHELTON, Charles   1888(1)
b 22 January 1864; d
Career: Notts Rangers, Notts
County cs 1888
In some respects a typical half-
back of his day—robust and ubiquitous. His solitary England out-
ing was at left-half but he played
many games for Notts County in
the pivotal position.

SHEPHERD, Albert   1906-11(2)
b Great Lever, Lancs 10 December 1885; d 8 November 1929.
Career: Bolton Schools, St Marks
Sunday School, Bolton Temperance, Bolton Wanderers, Blackburn Rovers, Bolton Wanderers

cs 1902, Bolton St Lukes mid
1902-3, Bolton Wanderers professional cs 1904, Newcastle United
mid 1908-9, Bradford City cs
1914 retired during the 1914-18
War.
Club Honours: Newcastle United
—F.L. Champions 1909, F.A. Cup
winners 1910. Missed 1911 Cup
Final owing to injury
A centre-forward who became
famous for his dashing raids
down the middle. Fed his wingers
judiciously and thrived on the
scoring opportunities provided by
ball playing inside partners.

SHILTON, Peter Leslie   1971-2(4)
b Leicester 18 September 1949.
Career: Leicester Schools (England Schools v Eire Scotland (2)
and Ireland 1965), Leicester City
ground staff June 1965, professional June 1966
Club Honours: Leicester City—
F.A. Cup finalists 1969, Second
Division Champions 1971
Recognised as a major goalkeeping talent from the start, as evi-
denced by Leicester's release of
the great Banks when Shilton was
only 17. Has superb anticipation
and can punch a ball an extraordinarily long way.

SHIMWELL, Edmund   1949(1)
b Wirksworth, Derbyshire 27
February 1920
Career: Wirksworth, Sheffield
United 1939, Blackpool December
1946, Oldham Athletic May 1957,
Burton Albion July 1958, retired
December 1958. A licensee at
Matlock
Club Honours: Blackpool—F.A.
Cup finalists 1948, 51, winners
1953
A stalwart physique, resolutely
used, was the distinguishing trait
of his right-back play, and he
kicked strongly and with equal
facility with either foot.

SHUTT, George 1886(1)
Career: Stoke up to 1889. Was a Football League referee in 1891
Presented a difficult barrier at centre-half. Reliable and sure in tackling although, on occasion, not too certain in his kicking.

SILCOCK, John 1921-3(3)
b Wigan 15 January 1897; d 28 June 1966.
Career: Aspull Juniors, Atherton, Manchester United as an amateur April 1916, professional September 1917, Oldham Athletic on trial May 1934 but not retained and retired later in 1934. Was subsequently a licensee in Manchester
Left-back of classic ability, no one in his day surpassing his kicking. In this regard particular mention should be made of the volleyed clearance placed exactly to the feet of the forward intended.

SILLETT, Richard Peter 1955(3)
b Southampton 1933.
Career: Nomansland, Southampton June 1950, Chelsea May 1953, Guildford City June 1962, Ashford player manager July 1965
Club Honour: Chelsea—F.L. Champions 1955
As the Chelsea handbook was wont to put it ". . . in all ways a powerful defender ". Sillett was a right-back, tall, stern tackling and capable of kicking the ball a phenomenal distance.

SIMMS, Ernest 1922(1)
b South Shields 23 June 1892.
Career: Murton Colliery, Barnsley, Luton Town cs 1913, South Shields March 1922, Stockport County January 1924, Scunthorpe United cs 1926
Made a reputation as a goal-scoring centre-forward at Luton, when his opportunism and aptitude for seizing openings attracted attention.

SIMPSON, John 1911-14(8)
b Pendelton, Lancs 25 December 1885; d 4 January 1959.
Career: Scottish schoolboy football, Laurieston Juniors, Falkirk mid 1906-7, Blackburn Rovers January 1911, retired owing to injury during the 1914-18 War. He was later a licensee in Falkirk
Club Honours: Blackburn Rovers —F.L. Champions 1912 and 1914
An outside-right celebrity. Beat opponents by extraordinary acceleration and centred from any position at the precise height and speed required. Needed only the minimum amount of space in which to work.

SLATER, William John 1955-60(12)
b Clitheroe, Lancs 29 April 1927.
Career: Clitheroe Grammar School, Lancashire junior football, Blackpool amateur 1944 (also playing for Yorkshire Amateurs and Leeds University), Brentford amateur December 1951, Wolverhampton Wanderers amateur August 1952, professional February 1954, Brentford May 1963 to cs 1964. Northern Nomads later 1964. 21 England amateur international appearances 1950-4. Deputy Director of Crystal Palace Sports Centre, from November 1964 Director of Physical Education at Liverpool University and now Director of Physical Education at Birmingham University
Club Honours: Blackpool—F.A. Cup finalists 1951, Wolverhampton Wanderers—F.L. Champions 1954-8-9, F.A. Cup winners 1960
A notability as an amateur and more so as a professional. First, an inside-left, then left-half and finally centre-half, always elegant, composed and fine in control.

SMALLEY, Tom 1937(1)
b Kinsley, Yorks 1913.
Career: South Kirkby Colliery, Wolverhampton Wanderers May

1931, Norwich City August 1938, Northampton Town October 1945 to cs 1951.

Smalley was originally an inside-forward and converted to the right-half berth by the Wolves where he made his England appearance. A reliable player and a great worker.

SMART, Thomas   1921-30(5)
b Blackheath, Staffs 20 September 1897 ; d June 1968.
Career: Blackheath Town, Army soccer, Halesowen October 1919, Aston Villa January 1920 retired cs 1934 but later played with Brierley Hill Alliance
Club Honours: Aston Villa—F.A. Cup winners 1920, finalists 1924
His sheer size was said to cause apprehension to the more timid winger. Smart, however, was not deliberately rough and brought brilliant kicking, heading and positional qualities to his play at right-back.

SMITH, Albert   1891-3(3)
b 1869; d 18 April 1921.
Career: Notts County mid 1889-90, Nottingham Forest late 1890, Blackburn Rovers November 1891, Nottingham Forest cs 1892 retired February 1894. Always played as an amateur. Later a boot factor in Nottingham
Plucky, indefatigable right-half possessing forcefulness and a fair tackle. Rather amiss in the service he gave to his forwards.

SMITH, Arnold Kirke   1873(1)
b Ecclesfield, Yorks 23 April 1850; d 8 October 1927.
Career: Cheltenham College ; University College Oxford prior to the University match, captain in 1872; Sheffield F.C. and F.A. Ordained in 1875 he spent the rest of his life in the Ministry in the East Midlands being Vicar of Boxworth 1889-1927
Club Honour: Oxford University —F.A. Cup finalists 1873
Strong and vivacious forward. His liking for being in the thick of things was perhaps too pronounced as he was inclined to get out of position.

SMITH, Bert   1921-2(2)
b Higham, Kent 7 March 1892; d September 1969.
Career: Vanbrugh Park, Crawford United, Metrogas, Huddersfield Town cs 1913, Tottenham Hotspur cs 1919, Northfleet coach May 1930, Sheppey United October 1931 briefly, Young Boys (Switzerland) player coach November 1931 to 1934, Harwich & Parkeston manager coach 1934, Stevenage Town, Hitchin Town groundsman and trainer coach 1937 retired late 1966
Club Honours: Tottenham Hotspur—Second Division Champions 1920, F.A. Cup winners 1921
Tottenham converted him from a forward to a virile right-half. Certain in his tackle, energetic and robust.

SMITH, Charles Eastlake   1876(1)
b Colombo, Ceylon 1850 ; d 10 January 1917.
Career: Rossall School (XI 1869-70 captain 1870); Crystal Palace; Wanderers; Surrey; F.A. Committee 1875-6. Cousin of G. O. Smith. A more than useful club cricketer
A forward with a good eye for the open space and an ability for the art without which no attacker in the early days was complete—dribbling.

SMITH, Gilbert Oswald
                    1893-1901(20)
b Croydon 25 November 1872; d 6 December 1943.
Career: Charterhouse School (XI 1889-92 captain 1890-2); Keble College Oxford (Blue 1893-4-5-6 captain 1896): Old Carthusians ; Corinthians 1892-1903 (being joint secretary with W. J. Oakley 1898-1902). Cricket Blue 1895-6 (scoring 132 v Cambridge in 1896) and

played once for Surrey that year
and on occasions for Herts.
Schoolmaster at Ludgrove from
1896 he gave up playing shortly
after becoming joint Headmaster
of the school following the death
of A. T. B. Dunn. He was later
Headmaster of Sunningdale
School
Club Honours: Old Carthusians—
F.A. Amateur Cup finalists 1895,
winners 1897
Justifiably regarded as the greatest centre-forward in the country
for a decade and in the first flight
of centre-forwards of any era. Not
of particularly robust physique he
was, however, an inspiring leader
with an accurate shot and extraordinarily gifted in the collection
and distribution of passes.

SMITH, Herbert   1905-6(4)
b Witney, Oxon 22 November
1897; d 7 January 1951.
Career: Oxford County School;
Beccles School; Reading; Oxford
City; Witney; Richmond; Stoke;
Derby County; Oxfordshire. 17
England amateur international ap-
pearances 1907-10. President of
Oxfordshire F.A. from 1919
Club Honour: Oxford City—F.A.
Amateur Cup finalists 1903
Burly left-back whose dexterous
left foot was almost legendary. A
brilliant defender and, in spite of
his physique, scrupulously fair.

SMITH, Joseph   1913-20(5)
b Dudley Port, Staffs 25 June
1889; d 12 August 1971.
Career: Newcastle St Luke's, Bolton Wanderers May 1908, Stockport County March 1927, Darwen
cs 1929, Manchester Central cs
1930, Reading manager July 1931
to August 1935, Blackpool manager August 1935 retired April
1958
Club Honours: Bolton Wanderers
—F.A. Cup winners 1923, 6
An inside-left with an exceptional
penchant for scoring goals. He

possessed one of the hardest shots
in the history of the game and
could be both bustling and brilliant at the same time.

SMITH, Joseph   1920-3(2)
b Darley End, Worcs circa 1891;
d
Career: Cradley St Lukes, West
Bromwich Albion May 1910, Birmingham May 1926, Worcester
City player manager cs 1929
Club Honours: West Bromwich
Albion—Second Division Champions 1911, F.L. Champions 1920
Stocky little right-back skilfully
dour in style. His remarkably high
level of performance over a long
period is illustrated by League appearances made from 1919-20 to
1924-5: 247 out of 252.

**SMITH, James Christopher
Reginald**   1939(2)
(born Schmidt)
b East London, South Africa.
Career: Hitchin Town (Totten-
ham Hotspur amateur cs 1932),
Millwall September 1935, Dundee
March 1946, Corby Town player
manager 1948, Dundee early 1949
remaining as trainer coach after
retiring as a player, Dundee
United manager September 1954,
Falkirk manager January 1956 to
May 1959, Millwall manager July
1959 to January 1961, Addington
(South Africa) coach March 1961,
Durban City manager 1961, Bed-
ford Town manager late 1961 to
September 1963, Addington
manager coach December 1963.
Later became Cape Town City
manager, manager of Bedford
Town November 1971 to June
1972
Club Honour: Millwall—Third
Division South Champions 1938
The bigger the occasion the better
this strong left-winger liked it.
Incisive, speedy, possessor of a
deadly shot with both feet and
the capability of playing at inside-
left also.

SMITH, John William   1932(3)
b Whitburn, Co. Durham October 1898.
Career: Whitburn, North Shields Athletic, South Shields cs 1919, Portsmouth December 1927, Bournemouth & Boscombe Athletic May 1935, Clapton Orient October 1936 released February 1937. Brother of Septimus.
Club Honours: Portsmouth—F.A. Cup finalists 1929, 34
An inside-right of exceptional cleverness and resource. For much of a League career which stretched nearly 18 seasons he was counted among the game's leading tacticians.

SMITH, Lionel   1951-3(6)
b Mexborough, Yorks circa 1912.
Career: Yorkshire Tar Distillers, Arsenal amateur August 1939, professional November 1939, Watford June 1954, Gravesend and Northfleet May 1955 as player manager resigning April 1960
Club Honours: Arsenal—F.L. Champions 1953, F.A. Cup finalists 1952
Tall, slim left-back commanding in the air and astute in positioning. Was stylish also, playing with a nonchalant authority.

SMITH, Leslie George Frederick
   1939(1)
b Ealing 13 March 1918.
Career: St Johns Grammar School Brentford (now Gunnersbury Catholic G.S.), Petersham 1932, Brentford office staff 1933 being loaned to Wimbledon 1933, Hayes July, 1935, Brentford professional March 1936, Aston Villa October 1945, Brentford June 1952, Kidderminster Harriers player manager August 1953 to cs 1954, Wolverhampton Wanderers scout until cs 1956. Has since concentrated on his radio and television business in Aston. Since 1965 has

been secretary of Aston Villa Old Stars team which plays for charity
Club Honours: Wimbledon—F.A. Amateur Cup finalists 1935 (believed to be the youngest player to play in the Amateur Cup Final), Brentford—London War Cup winners 1942, Chelsea—F.L. South Cup winners 1945 (as a guest)
Made his First Division debut at 18 and revealed a precocious confidence in his own great ability. A fast left-winger able to beat his man and deliver a rasping shot.

SMITH, Robert Alfred   1961-4(15)
b Lingdale, Co. Durham circa 1933.
Career: Lingdale School, Redcar Boys Club, Redcar United, Chelsea ground staff 1949, professional May 1950, Tottenham Hotspur December 1955, Brighton & Hove Albion May 1964 to October 1965, Hastings United October 1965 to March 1967. Since his retirement from the game he has worked as a van driver on the South coast
Club Honours: Tottenham Hotspur—F.L. Champions 1961, F.A. Cup winners 1961 and 1962, European Cup Winners Cup winners 1963, Brighton & Hove Albion—Fourth Division Champions 1965
Ideally suited to be centre-forward of the Spurs 1961 " Double " team, which had players like the late John White to lay on golden chances—burly, robust, brave and a strong shot.

SMITH, Stephen   1895(1)
b Hednesford, Staffs 1874; d 19 May 1935.
Career: Cannock Town, Rugeley, Ceal F.C. (Hednesford), Aston Villa 1893, Portsmouth cs 1901, New Brompton cs 1906, player manager December 1906 to cs 1908. Later lived in Portsmouth for some time until 1932 when

he took over a business, Roke Stores, Benson, Oxfordshire where he remained until his death.
Club Honours: Aston Villa—F.A. Cup winners 1895, F.L. Champions 1894-6-7-9-1900, Portsmouth —Southern League Champions 1902
An accomplished outside-left. Could pass a ball with pinpoint accuracy, had tremendous speed and was a sure marksman.

SMITH, Septimus Charles   1936(1)
b Whitburn, Co. Durham 15 March 1912.
Career: Whitburn Church of England School (England v Scotland schools 1926), Whitburn, Leicester City March 1929 retired cs 1949 remaining on the club coaching staff until cs 1950. After leaving football worked in Leicester as a flitter
Club Honour: Leicester City— Second Division Champions 1937
Reasonably successful at inside-forward he eventually found his best position at right-half. There his forceful game, which featured fine qualities in tackling, ball control and passing, won international recognition.

SMITH, Trevor   1960(2)
b Quarry Bank, Staffs 13 April 1936.
Career: Quarry Bank Secondary Modern School, Brierley Hill Schools (England Schools Shield finalists 1951), Birmingham City ground staff July 1951, professional April 1953, Walsall October 1964, retired injury February 1966. A licensee at Stonnall near Lichfield and a permit player for a local team
Club Honours: Birmingham City —Second Division Champions 1955, F.A. Cup finalists 1956, F.L. Cup winners 1963
Showed much potential as a youngster, playing in senior football with a veteran's assurance. Of strong build, ideal for a bul-

wark centre-half, and finely constructive.

SMITH, Thomas   1971(1)
b Liverpool 4 April 1945.
Career. St John's School and Cardinal Godfrey College Liverpool, Liverpool apprentice 1961, professional April 1962, (England Youth international 1963)
Club Honours: Liverpool—F.A. Youth Cup finalists 1963, F.A. Cup winners 1965, finalists 1971, F.L. Champions and European Cup Winners Cup finalists 1966
Started as a deep-lying inside-forward then moved to right-half, where he received England status. A powerful defender famed for teak-hard tackling.

SMITH, William Henry   1922-8(3)
b Tantobie, Co. Durham 1895 ; d 13 April 1951.
Career: Hobson Wanderers, Huddersfield Town 1913, Rochdale player manager July 1934 remaining as team manager on retiring as a player. Resigned November 1935 and left the game.
Club Honours: Huddersfield Town—F.A. Cup winners 1922, finalists 1928, 30, F.L. Champions 1924-5-6. Missed 1920 Cup Final owing to suspension
Formed a celebrated left-wing partnership with Clem Stephenson. Smith ran with a long-legged loping stride, was elusive and stylish and had a good goalscoring record for a winger.

SORBY, Thomas Heathcote 1879(1)
b 16 February 1856; d 13 December 1930.
Career: Cheltenham College, Thursday Wanderers (a Sheffield Club), Sheffield F.C. and Sheffield F.A. Was in business in Scarborough for many years and lived there until his death
Keen, level headed forward and a leading exponent of the dribbling art unfortunately prone to selfishness.

SOUTHWORTH, John   1889-92(3)
b Blackburn 1867; d 16 October 1956.
Career: Blackburn Olympic, Blackburn Rovers, Everton August 1893 retired in 1895. A professional musician he played for some years with the Halle Orchestra
Club Honours: Blackburn Rovers —F.A. Cup winners 1890-1
A great and talented centre-forward noted for his marksmanship, speed and accuracy in passing and, by no means least, complete unselfishness.

SPARKS, Francis John   1879-80(3)
b 4 July 1855; d 13 February 1934.
Career: Hertfordshire Rangers; Clapham Rovers; Essex County; F.A. Committee 1878-80.
Club Honour: Clapham Rovers— F.A. Cup winners 1880
Somewhat slow but nevertheless a useful forward to have around being hard-working and usually near to the scene of action.

SPENCE, Joseph Walter   1926-7(2)
b Throckley, Northumberland 1898; d 31 December 1966.
Career: Throckley School, Bluchers Juniors, Throckley Celtic, Scotswood cs 1918, Manchester United March 1919, Bradford City June 1933, Chesterfield May 1935 retired cs 1938. Continued to live in Chesterfield and worked for Chesterfield Tube Co. until retiring in 1965. Did part-time scouting for Chesterfield after his retirement from the game. Cousin of George Brown
Club Honour: Chesterfield—Third Division North Champions 1936
A bustling and lion-hearted forward whose endeavours made him a prime Old Trafford favourite, so much so that the crowd's cry "Give it to Joe" became famous. He gave spirited service over a long career at both outside-right and centre-forward.

SPENCE, Richard   1936(2)
b Platts Common near Barnsley 18 July 1911.
Career: Platts Common, Thorpe Colliery, Barnsley February 1933, Chelsea October 1934, retired to club training staff 1950
Club Honour: Barnsley—Third Division North Champions 1934
Possessed two good feet, speed and plenty of tricks—in short a fine little outside-right. Liked to employ his blistering shooting as much as possible.

SPENCER, Charles William
1924-5(2)
b Washington, Co. Durham 1899; d 9 February 1953.
Career: Glebe Rovers, Washington Chemical Works, Newcastle United October 1921, Manchester United July 1928, Tunbridge Wells Rangers player manager May 1930 to cs 1932, Wigan Athletic player manager August 1932, Grimsby Town manager March 1937 to April 1951, York City manager November 1952 until his death
Club Honours: Newcastle United —F.A. Cup winners 1924, F.L. Champions 1927
By no means a mere stopper centre-half but one with creative abilities, always endeavouring to get his attack in motion.

SPENCER, Howard   1897-1905(6)
b Edgbaston 23 August 1875; d 14 January 1940.
Career: Albert Road School Aston, Stamford, Birchfield Trinity, Aston Villa 1894 retired November 1907. Appointed a director June 1909 remaining on the Board until May 1936. Managing director of a coal and coke contracting firm until his retirement owing to ill health.
Club Honours: Aston Villa—F.A. Cup winners 1895, 7, 1905, F.L. Champions 1896-7, 1900
One of the great names of pre-

1914 soccer and one of the greatest of right-backs. A model player, scrupulously fair, full of resource and exquisite judgment.

SPIKSLEY, Frederick　　1893-8(7)
b Gainsborough, Lincs 25 January 1870; d
Career: Gainsborough Trinity 1887, Sheffield Wednesday January 1891, Glossop October 1904, Leeds City 1905, Southend United cs 1905, Watford mid 1905-6 to cs 1906. Coach in Nuremburg being interned in August 1914. After the War after a spell in Mexico was with Fulham as a coach before returning to Nuremburg in 1926
Club Honours: Sheffield Wednesday—F.A. Cup winners 1896, Second Division Champions 1900, F.L. Champions 1903
An outside-left and one of the celebrities of the 'nineties. Extremely fast, a fine dribbler and always on hand when required Spiksley needed a partner as quick-moving as himself to shine at his brilliant best.

SPILSBURY, Benjamin Ward
　　　　　　　　　1885-6(3)
b Findern, Derbyshire 1 August 1864, d 15 August 1938.
Career: Rossall School; Repton School (XI 1881-3 captain 1883); Jesus College Cambridge (Blue 1884-5-6-7 captain 1887); Corinthians 1885-8; Derby County. Went to Vancouver as a Land Agent shortly after leaving Cambridge and remained there until his death.
Played at outside and inside-right. Could centre and shoot effectively, playing with spirit though not always with discernment.

SPOUNCER, William Alfred
　　　　　　　　　1900(1)
b Gainsborough, Lincs 1876; d 31 August 1962.
Career: Gainsborough Trinity mid 1893-4, Nottingham Forest May

1897 to 1910. Was later a coach in Europe
Club Honours: Nottingham Forest—F.A. Cup winners 1898, Second Division Champions 1907
A smart outside-left skilful in manoeuvre and the capability of centring with fine accuracy.

SPRINGETT, Ronald D. G.
　　　　　　　　　1960-6(33)
b Fulham 22 July 1935.
Career: Victoria United, Queens Park Rangers March 1953, Sheffield Wednesday March 1958, Queens Park Rangers May 1967 retired cs 1970, Ashford Town September 1970. Has a sports shop at Shepherds Bush
Club Honours: Sheffield Wednesday—Second Division Champions 1959, F.A. Cup finalists 1966
Kept goal with a mixture of brilliance and dependability. He had cat-like agility and phenomenal anticipation.

SPROSTON, Bert　　1937-9(11)
b Sandbach, Cheshire 22 June 1915.
Career: Sandbach Ramblers, Leeds United cs 1933, Tottenham Hotspur June 1938, Manchester City November 1938, retired cs 1950. Bolton Wanderers trainer July 1951
Club Honours: Manchester City Second Division Champions 1947
Superbly efficient right-back, finely effective in the tackle and extraordinarily quick in recovery.

SQUIRE, Ralph Tyndall　1886(3)
b 10 September 1863; d 22 August 1944.
Career: Westminster School (XI 1880-2); Trinity Hall Cambridge (Blue 1884-6, secretary in 1885 when unfit to play v Oxford); Old Westminsters; Clapham Rovers; Corinthians 1886-92 (Treasurer for many years from 1903). F.A. Committee 1884-7
Fine, versatile player who performed at back and half-back.

Strong, consistent and fast with an admirably reliable kick.

STANBROUGH, Morris Hugh
1895(1)
b Cleobury, Shropshire 2 September 1870; d 15 December 1904.
Career: Charterhouse School (XI 1889); Caius College Cambridge (Blue 1890-1-2 captain 1892); Old Carthusians; Corinthians 1890-1904. Schoolmaster in turn at Elstree, Stanmore, Eastbourne and at the time of his death, St Peters Broadstairs
Club Honours: Old Carthusians—F.A. Amateur Cup winners 1894, 7, finalists 1895
In his heyday regarded as one of the best outside-lefts in the South. A clever and valuable player with a fine turn of speed.

STANIFORTH, Ronald 1954-5(8)
b Newton Heath, Manchester 13 April 1924.
Career: Hague Street School Newton Heath, Manchester Schools 1938, Newton Albion, Stockport County 1946, Huddersfield Town May 1952, Sheffield Wednesday July 1955, Barrow player manager October 1959, retiring as a player 1961 but continuing as manager until July 1964. Sheffield Wednesday assistant coach July 1960, chief coach March 1971
Club Honours: Sheffield Wednesday—Second Division Champions 1956 and 1959
A right-back in the classic tradition, stylish and polished. Unruffled in deportment he had a clean and sure kick.

STARLING, Ronald William
1933-7(2)
b Pelaw, Co. Durham 11 October 1909.
Career: Co. Durham Schools, Washington Colliery, Hull City 1927, Newcastle United May 1930, Sheffield Wednesday June 1932, Aston Villa January 1937

retired cs 1948. Nottingham Forest coach from July 1948 until June 1950. He then left football and has since been a newsagent in Sheffield
Club Honours: Sheffield Wednesday—F.A. Cup winners 1935, Aston Villa—Second Division Champions 1938, F.L. North Cup winners 1944
Ball playing inside-forward and a crafty schemer. His jugglery was so unusual in invention it was labelled as quaint by a writer in the 'thirties.

STEELE, Frederick Charles 1937(6)
b Hanley 6 May 1916.
Career: Downings F.C., Stoke City 1931, Mansfield Town player manager June 1949, Port Vale player manager December 1951 retiring as a player May 1953 continuing as manager until January 1957. Then a licensee until Port Vale manager October 1962 to February 1965
His senior debut at inside-right won praise for craft and then, in 1935-6, he became a centre-forward with which position his name is associated. Good at dribbling and passing, a hard shot and tremendous in stamina.

STEPHENSON, Clement 1924(1)
b New Delaval, Co. Durham 6 February 1891; d 24 October 1961.
Career: West Stanley, Blyth Spartans, New Delaval Villa, West Stanley, Aston Villa March 1910 (loaned to Stourbridge from cs 1910 to February 1911), Huddersfield Town March 1921, retired and became Club manager May 1929 until May 1942. Brother of G. T.
Club Honours: Aston Villa—F.A. Cup winners 1913, 20, Huddersfield Town—F.A. Cup winners 1922, finalists 1928, F.L. Champions 1924-5-6
During his playing career it was

a matter of comment in the press from time to time that he received only one cap. He was an inside-left, methodically constructive and a brilliant strategist.

STEPHENSON, George Ternent
1928-31(3)
b New Delaval, Co. Durham late 1900.
Career: Northumberland Schools, New Delaval Villa, Leeds City August 1919, Aston Villa November 1919 (on loan to Stourbridge until cs 1920), Derby County November 1927, Sheffield Wednesday February 1931, Preston North End July 1933, Charlton Athletic May 1934 retired injury and joined club staff 1937 later becoming assistant manager, Huddersfield Town manager August 1947 to March 1952 when he left football
Club Honour: Charlton Athletic —Third Division South Champions 1935
Had inherited all the family acumen—a brainy, cultured inside-left whose promptings were of immense value to the attacks he played in.

STEPHENSON, Joseph Eric
1938-9(2)
b Bexleyheath, Kent; d 8 September 1944.
Career: Tom Hood School Leytonstone, Harrogate, Leeds United amateur January 1933, professional September 1934. Killed in action whilst serving as a Major in the Gurkha Rifles in Burma
In a truncated career showed admirable qualities at inside-left. He was particularly constructive and had the ability to link cogently with his partners in attack.

STEPNEY, Alex Cyril   1968(1)
b Mitcham 18 September 1944.
Career: Carshalton West Secondary School, Tooting & Mitcham

United, Millwall May 1963, Chelsea May 1966, Manchester United September 1966
Club Honours: Manchester United—F.L. Champions 1967, European Cup winners 1968
On his day ranks among the best goalkeepers in Britain—alert, clean in handling and lithe in action.

STEWART, James   1907-11(3)
b Gateshead 1883; d 23 May 1957.
Career: Gateshead North Eastern Railway, Sheffield Wednesday May 1902, Newcastle United cs 1908, Rangers September 1913 to cs 1914
Club Honours: Sheffield Wednesday—F.A. Cup winners 1907, Newcastle United—F.L. Champions 1909, F.A. Cup finalists 1911
Delighted spectators with his delicate inside-forward play. Combined cleverly with his teammates, a fine header of the ball and a prolific goal scorer.

STILES, Norbert Peter 1965-70(28)
b Manchester 18 May 1942.
Career: St Patricks School Manchester (England Schools v Eire Wales Ireland Scotland Germany 1957, Manchester United amateur September 1957, professional June 1959 (England Youth international 1959), Middlesbrough May 1971. A member of the England World Cup winning team 1966
Club Honours: Manchester United—F.L. Champions 1965, 7, European Cup winners 1968
Became a national figure through the television screenage of the 1966 World Cup, when his deeds at wing-half attracted wide comment. Aggressive, totally committed and possessor of a tackle astonishingly hard for so small a man.

STOKER, Lewis   1933-4(3)
b Wheatley Hill, Co. Durham 31

March 1911.
Career: Bear Park School, Brandon Juniors, Esh Winning Juniors, Bear Park, West Stanley, Birmingham 1930, Nottingham Forest May 1938
A right-half of effectiveness and no little skill in tackling. His fine distribution gave splendid service to the attack.

STORER, Harry 1924-8(2)
b Liverpool 2 February 1898; d 1 September 1967.
Career: Heanor Secondary School, Ripley Town, Eastwood (Notts County amateur), Grimsby Town cs 1919, Derby County March 1921, Burnley February 1929, Coventry City manager May 1931 to May 1945, Birmingham City manager June 1945, Coventry City manager November 1948 to December 1953, Derby County manager June 1955 retiring May 1962. Played cricket for Derbyshire from 1920-36 scoring 13,485 runs including 17 centuries
A tower of strength whether at inside-forward or left-half. In the attack he was brainy, unselfish and a hard shot. In the intermediate line he was equally thoughtful and employed a hard and decisive tackle.

STOREY, Peter Edwin 1971-2(8)
b Farnham, Surrey 7 September 1945.
Career: Aldershot Schools (England v Wales Ireland and Eire Schools 1961), Arsenal apprentice May 1961, professional September 1962
Club Honours: Arsenal—F.L. Cup finalists 1968-9, F.L. Champions and F.A. Cup winners 1971, Fairs Cup winners 1970, F.A. Cup finalists 1972
Spent several seasons as Arsenal's right-back before becoming a spoiling right-half in their 1970-1 "Double" team. His midfield role is to win the ball, which mission is accomplished by way of a granite-hard tackle.

STOREY-MOORE, Ian 1970(1)
b Ipswich 17 May 1945.
Career: Lincoln Gardens Primary and Westcliffe Secondary Modern Schools, Scunthorpe, Ashby juniors, Nottingham Forest amateur August 1961, professional May 1962, Manchester United March 1972
Probably the most dangerous left-winger in British football today. Is fast and his hard shooting produces many goals. In 1964-5 played outside-right with some success.

STRANGE, Alfred Henry
1930-4(20)
b Ripley, Derbyshire 1900.
Career: Marehay, Portsmouth cs 1922, Port Vale October 1924, Sheffield Wednesday February 1927, Bradford cs 1935 retired cs 1936. A poultry farmer at Ripley
Club Honours: Sheffield Wednesday—F.L. Champions 1929 and 1930
After spending the first third of his first-class career as a forward became a great right-half. Swift tackling, a purveyor of fine passes and a long-range marksman.

STRATFORD, Alfred Hugh
1874(1)
b Kensington 5 September 1853; d 2 May 1914.
Career: Malvern College (XI 1871-2-3-4 captain 1874); Wanderers; Swifts; Middlesex. Played cricket for Middlesex from 1877-1880. Later went to America where he died.
Club Honours: Wanderers—F.A. Cup winners 1876-7-8
Played both as a back and a forward being perhaps better in the first-named position. Was a strong tackler and in kicking but thoughtfulness was not in evidence.

STRETEN, Bernard R. 1950(1)
b Gillingham, Norfolk 14 January
1923.
Career: Norfolk junior football,
Notts County (amateur), Shrewsbury Town, Luton Town amateur
1947 (4 England amateur international appearances 1947), professional 1948, King's Lynn July
1957, Wisbech Town cs 1959,
Cambridge City early 1961. In
December 1962 he was playing as
a permit player for North Wal-
sham, Norfolk and is believed to
be still living in Norfolk
Among the most agile of goalkeepers, his leaps and dives being
brisk and well-timed. Was a
friendly character too, and not
averse to a little banter with spectators behind his goal.

STURGESS, Albert 1911-14(2)
b Etruria, Stoke 21 October 1882.
Career: Tunstall Crosswells, Stoke
1903, Sheffield United June 1908,
Norwich City July 1923 retired
cs 1925
Club Honour: Sheffield United—
F.A. Cup winners 1915
Rangy but somewhat light wing-
half who played a hard and industrious game. A valuable utility
man if an emergency occurred
he could be relied upon to fill the
breach efficiently in practically
any position.

SUMMERBEE, Michael George
1968-72(7)
b Preston 15 December 1942.
Career: Naunton Park Secondary
Modern School Gloucester, Baker
Street Youth Club Cheltenham,
Swindon Town ground staff August 1959, professional December
1959, Manchester City August
1965
Club Honours: Manchester City
—Second Division Champions
1966, F.L. Champions 1968, F.A.
Cup winners 1969, F.L. Cup winners 1970
Completely courageous and a forward for the tight situation. His
willingness to receive the ball at
any time in any position has cost
him many injuries. A menace to
the opposing citadel whether at
outside-right or centre-forward.

SUTCLIFFE, John William
1893-1903(5)
b Shibden near Halifax, Yorks 14
April 1868; d 7 July 1947.
Career: Bradford St Thomas
School (where he learnt rugby),
Bradford Rugby Union, Heck-
mondwike Rugby Union remaining with the Club on the formation of the Northern Union now
the Rugby League, Bolton Wanderers September 1889, Millwall
April 1902, Manchester United
May 1903, Plymouth Argyle cs
1904, Southend United mid 1911-
12. Coach at Arnhem 1914, Bradford City trainer cs 1919. Played
rugby for England v New Zealand
1889 and is, thus, one of the three
men to have played rugby and
soccer for England
Club Honour: Bolton Wanderers
—F.A. Cup finalists 1894
Rightly numbered among the very
greatest of English goalkeepers.
Strong in all departments of his
art he had no weakness. Marvellously able in coping with sharp
shots and unsurpassed at picking
up and in dealing with ground
shots.

SWAN, Peter 1960-2(19)
b South Elmsall, Yorks 8 October
1936.
Career: Doncaster Schools, Sheffield Wednesday amateur 1952,
professional December 1953 (England Youth international 1955)
until his suspension May 1965.
Ban lifted June 1972
Club Honour: Sheffield Wednesday—Second Division Champions
1959
Possibly the best stopper centre-
half of his day. Strong, tall,
dominating and hard to beat on
the ground and in the air.

SWEPSTONE, Harry Albemarle
1880-3(6)
b 1859; d 7 May 1907.
Career: Chigwell School; Clapton; Pilgrims; Ramblers; Essex County. Founder member of Corinthians and proposer of the Club name; F.A. Committee 1883-4. Admitted a solicitor in 1881 he practised at Bethnal Green from 1881-92 and thence in Bishopsgate
Rated the best goalkeeper of his day, agile and resourceful in action. Also played at full-back.

SWIFT, Frank Victor   1947-9(19)
b Blackpool 24 December 1914; d 6 February 1958.
Career: Blackpool Schools, Blackpool Gas Works, Fleetwood, Manchester City amateur mid 1931-2 season, professional October 1932 retired cs 1949 but returned to play a few games during the early part of the 1949-50 season. Later a reporter with the *News of the World* he was killed in the Munich air crash
Club Honours: Manchester City —F.A. Cup winners 1934, F.L. Champions 1937, Second Division Champions 1947
A big man and a big talent. Crowds loved his goalkeeping aerobatics, huge hands smothering the ball and his unfailing good humour. A warm personality made him equally popular off the field.

TAIT, George   1881(1)
b 1859; d late 1882.
Career: Birmingham Excelsior
Not really a centre-forward of international rank and this showed in his sole appearance. He was, however, excellent in club matches, leading his line well and dangerous near goal.

TAMBLING, Robert Victor
1963-6(3)
b Storrington, Sussex 18 September 1941.

Career: Storrington School (England Schools v Ireland 1956 v Eire Wales (2) Ireland Scotland Germany 1957), Chelsea ground staff July 1957, professional September 1958, Crystal Palace—briefly on loan January 1970—permanently transferred June 1970
Club Honours: Chelsea—F.A. Youth Cup winners 1960, F.L. Cup winners 1965, F.A. Cup finalists 1967
A versatile forward happy anywhere in the attack. Fast, quick to see an opening and one who has amassed an excellent scoring tally.

TATE, Joseph Thomas   1931-3(3)
b Old Hill, Staffs circa 1906.
Career: Stourbridge Grammar School, Round Oak, Cradley Heath, Aston Villa April 1925, Brierley Hill Alliance as player manager cs 1935. A useful cricketer at one time on the Warwickshire ground staff
Originally an inside-left and successfully made the switch to left-half. Tall and commanding, ideally linking defence and attack, Tate's career was marred by serious injuries.

TAYLOR, Ernest   1954(1)
b Sunderland 2 September 1925.
Career: Hylton Colliery Juniors, Newcastle United 1942, Blackpool October 1951, Manchester United February 1958, Sunderland December 1958, Altrincham cs 1961, Derry City December 1961 retired February 1962. Went to New Zealand February 1964 as coach to New Brighton F.C., Christchurch but in 1965 had left this appointment to work in Auckland. Has now returned to England and is working at Vauxhall Motors, Hooton, Cheshire
Club Honours: Newcastle United —F.A. Cup winners 1951, Blackpool—F.A. Cup winners 1953, Manchester United—F.A. Cup finalists 1958

Surprisingly strong in marksmanship for a small man and an inside-right with several other skills; speed, ball control and an eye for the open space.

TAYLOR, Edward Hallows
                                    1923-6(8)
b Liverpool 7 March 1891.
Career: Marlborough Old Boys (Liverpool), Liverpool Balmoral (England amateur trial 1912), Oldham Athletic February 1912, Huddersfield Town June 1922, Everton February 1927, Ashton National September 1928, Wrexham November 1928 retired cs 1929. Later in the cotton trade in Manchester
Club Honours: Huddersfield Town—F.L. Champions 1924 and 1926, Everton—F.L. Champions 1928
Not the tallest of custodians but a fine one all the same. Was quick thinking without any noticeable weakness and was successful, to a large extent, because of his study of opponents.

TAYLOR, James Guy   1951(2)
b Hillingdon, Middlesex 5 November 1917.
Career: Hillingdon Town, Fulham March 1938, Queens Park Rangers April 1953, Tunbridge Wells Rangers player manager May 1954, Yiewsley manager June 1958 to March 1959, Uxbridge manager cs 1959
Club Honour. Fulham—Second Division Champions 1949
Joined Fulham as an inside-right, became a wing-half after the War and moved to centre-half in 1948-9. He was likened to Franklin by reason of a strong, quick tackle and his constructive use of the ball.

TAYLOR, Philip H.   1948(3)
b Bristol 1917.
Career: Greenbank School Bristol (England Schools v Scotland, Wales 1932), Bristol Rovers

ground staff cs 1932, professional 1935, Liverpool March 1936, retired and became club coach July 1954, acting manager May 1956, manager April 1957 to November 1959. Later a sales representative
Club Honours: Liverpool—F.L. Champions 1947, F.A. Cup finalists 1950
As a youngster was a clever, weaving inside-forward and then in 1946, moved to right-half. There he became a classic exponent, his ground passes being exquisitely placed so that his forwards did not lose momentum.

TAYLOR, Thomas   1953-8(19)
b Smithies near Barnsley 1932; d 6 February 1958.
Career: Smithies United, Barnsley July 1959, Manchester United March 1953, killed in the Munich air crash
Club Honours: Manchester United—F.L. Champions 1956 and 1957, F.A. Cup finalists 1957
Hailed as the finest English centre-forward since Lawton his early death came as an irreparable blow. Taylor was of the opportunist type, a formidable shot and magnificent at heading.

TEMPLE, Derek William   1965(1)
b Liverpool 1939.
Career: Dovecot Secondary Modern School Liverpool (England v Wales Schools 1954), Everton ground staff 1955, professional August 1956 (England Youth international 1958), Preston North End September 1967, Wigan Athletic July 1970. Has a business in Wigan
Club Honour: Everton—F.A. Cup winners 1966, Liverpool Schools—England Schools Shield winners 1954
His great speed, shooting power and intricate footwork could be utilised in both inside and wing forward positions, although he

R. Crompton   W. J. Wedlock

E. Needham   V. J. Woodward

J. Pennington　　　　　　　　S. Hardy

E. Blenkinsop,　　　　　　　　W. R. Dean

was perhaps best at outside-left.

THICKETT, Henry   1899(2)
b Hexthorpe near Doncaster
1873; d 15 November 1920.
Career: Hexthorpe, Sheffield
United 1890, Rotherham Town,
Sheffield United December 1893,
Bristol City May 1904 as player
manager, retiring as a player in
cs 1905 and continuing as manager until 1910. After retirement
was a licensee at Trowbridge until his death
Club Honours: Sheffield United—
F.L. Champions 1898, F.A. Cup
winners 1899, 1902, finalists 1901
Brave and swiftly moving right-
back and owner of a splendid
kick. His blemish was somewhat
indifferent tackling.

THOMPSON, Peter   1964-70(16)
b Carlisle 27 November 1942.
Career: Carlisle Schools (England
Schools v Scotland, Wales, Germany 1958), Preston North End
ground staff August 1958, professional November 1959, Liverpool August 1963
Club Honours: Preston North End
—F.A. Youth Cup finalists 1960,
Liverpool—F.L. Champions 1964,
6, F.A. Cup winners 1965, finalists 1971, European Cup Winners
Cup finalists 1966
Reminds one of the old-time winger by his fine orthodoxy on the
left. Has speed, dazzling footwork and a myriad of tricks.

THOMPSON, Thomas   1952-7(2)
b Fencehouses, Co. Durham 10
November 1929.
Career: Lumley Y.M.C.A., New-
castle United August 1946, Aston
Villa September 1950, Preston
North End June 1955, Stoke City
cs 1961, Barrow March 1963
Keen, thrustful little inside-right.
Speed off the mark led to his
special ploy of the quick break-
through.

o

THOMSON, Robert Anthony
                              1964-5(8)
b Smethwick, Staffs 1944.
Career: Birmingham Schools,
Wolverhampton Wanderers
ground staff cs 1959, professional
July 1961, Birmingham City
March 1969, Walsall November
1971, Luton Town June 1972
Club Honours: Wolverhampton
Wanderers—F.A. Youth Cup
finalists 1962
On graduating to the senior ranks
as a youngster showed unusual
maturity. A good left-back on
his day, polished, quick moving
and clean kicking.

THORNEWELL, George   1923-5(4)
b Romiley, Cheshire.
Career: St James Road School
Derby, local Derby junior clubs
including Rolls Royce, Nottingham Forest as an amateur during
1917-18 season, Derby County cs
1918, professional May 1919,
Blackburn Rovers December
1927, Chesterfield August 1929 to
cs 1932
Club Honours: Blackburn Rovers
—F.A. Cup winners 1928, Chesterfield—Third Division North
Champions 1931
Neatness was the hall-mark of
this tricky little outside-right who
played with some economy, seldom wasting a ball.

THORNLEY, Irvine   1907(1)
b Glossop.
Career: Glossop Villa, Glossop St
James, Glossop, Manchester City
March 1904, South Shields Aug-
ust 1912, Hamilton Academicals
cs 1919, Houghton (North Eastern
League) cs 1920
Club Honour: Manchester City—
Second Division Champions 1910
A centre-forward difficult to con-
tain and a menace to his oppon-
ents goal because of his liveliness
and thrust.

TILSON, Samuel Frederick
                          1934-6(4)
b Barnsley 19 April 1903.
Career: Barnsley Schools, Regent
Street Congregationals (Barnsley),
Barnsley March 1926, Manchester
City March 1928, Northampton
Town March 1938, York City
cs 1939 retired during the War.
Post War coach to Manchester
City thence assistant manager to
July 1965 when he became chief
scout
Club Honours: Manchester City
—F.A. Cup winners 1934, F.L.
Champions 1937. Missed the 1933
Cup Final owing to injury
Unfortunate with injuries but a
prominent forward at inside-left
and, later, at centre-forward. No
giant physically and so, reliant on
quick thinking, a fine body swerve
and sharp shooting.

TITMUSS, Frederick   1922-3(2)
b Pirton, Herts 15 February 1898;
d 2 October 1966.
Career: Pirton United 1914-15,
Hitchin Town, Southampton cs
1919, Plymouth Argyle February
1926 retired cs 1932. From his
retirement until his death he was
a licensee at Plymouth latterly at
The Laira. For a time after leaving Plymouth Argyle played as a
part timer with St Austell
Club Honours: Southampton—
Third Division South Champions
1922, Plymouth Argyle—Third
Division South Champions 1930
A left-back of great merit.
Tackled surely and his clearance
kicks were made constructively
and with measured judgment.

TODD, Colin   1972(1)
b Chester-le-Street, Co. Durham
12 December 1948.
Career: Chester-le-Street Schools,
Sunderland 1965 (England Youth
international 1967), Derby County—February 1971
Club Honours: Sunderland—F.A.

Youth Cup finalists 1966, Derby
County—F.L. Champions 1972
Fine young left-half who can, in
addition, turn in a useful game at
full-back. Has a sure tackle and
passes with thought and discernment.

TOONE, George   1892(2)
b Nottingham 1868; d 1 September 1943.
Career: Nottingham   Jardine,
Notts Rangers, Notts County
1889, Bedminster cs 1899, Bristol
City cs 1900, Notts County 1901
1901 retired 1902. After retirement was a licensee in Nottingham for some years.
Club Honours: Notts County—
F.A. Cup winners 1894, Second
Division Champions 1897. Missed
1891 Cup Final owing to injury.
Earned a great reputation for
goalkeeping. Exceedingly cool,
confident in handling and smart
in clearing his lines.

TOPHAM, Arthur George 1894(1)
b 19 February 1869; d 18 May
1931.
Career: Oswestry School; Keble
College   Oxford   (Blue   1890);
Casuals; Eastbourne; Chiswick
Park; Corinthians 1893-7. Brother
of R. A schoolmaster he was a
partner in Lynchmere School
Eastbourne and thence at Ascham
St Vincents School from 1912
Club Honour: Casuals—F.A.
Amateur Cup finalists 1894
An amateur right-half of stand-
ing, splendidly effective in tack-
ling. Unfortunately his kicking
and distribution were not on a
par with this and could be erratic.

TOPHAM, Robert   1893-4(2)
b Ellesmere, Salop 3 November
1867 d 31 August 1951.
Career: Oswestry School; Keble
College Oxford (no Blue); Oswes-
try F.C.; (selected for Wales v
Scotland 1885 but did not accept);
Casuals; Chiswick Park; Corin-

thians 1894-8: A schoolmaster at Brighton College from 1892-1905 thence a hop grower in Kent
Club Honours: Oswestry—Welsh Cup finalists 1885, Wolverhampton Wanderers—F.A. Cup winners 1893, Casuals—F.A. Amateur Cup finalists 1894
Difficult to contain, this outside-right often burst through by sheer vigour. Had speed, dribbling ability and middled the ball with skill.

TOWNLEY, WILLIAM J.
1889-90(2)
b Blackburn.
Career: Local junior football, Blackburn Rovers, Stockton cs 1892, Darwen cs 1894, Manchester City September 1896 to cs 1897. A schoolmaster by profession during his playing career he went to Germany as a soccer coach in 1909. After a period in Holland, Sweden and Switzerland from 1923-6, he returned to Germany until late 1934
Club Honour: Blackburn Rovers —F.A. Cup winners 1890 and 1891
Outside-left with a reputation for scoring goals. He had a magnificent long-range shot and was good in headwork besides being a useful winger generally.

TOWNROW, John Edward
1925-6(2)
b West Ham 28 March 1901.
Career: Pelly Memorial School West Ham (England Schools v Scotland and Wales 1915), Fairbairn House, Clapton Orient August 1919, Chelsea February 1927, Bristol Rovers May 1932. Later a groundsman and coach to Fairbairn House and he also worked at Becton Gasworks and later for a Brewery Company
A centre-half chiefly notable for coolness and self-possession. Placed his passes with accuracy and was excellent in defence.

TREMELLING, Daniel R. 1928(1)
b Mansfield 12 November 1899.
Career: Langwith Colliery Junction Wagon Works, Shirebrook, Lincoln City, Birmingham June 1919, Bury cs 1933, assistant trainer January 1936, Birmingham assistant trainer June 1936 up to the War
Club Honour: Birmingham—Second Division Champions 1921
A "fixture" in the Birmingham goal for a decade, being wonderfully consistent (he actually made more League appearances for the club than Hibbs). Brilliant at catching and handling the ball.

TRESADERN, John 1923(2)
b Leytonstone 26 September 1892; d 26 December 1959.
Career: Barking Town, West Ham United July 1913, Burnley October 1924, Northampton Town player manager May 1925 retiring as a player in cs 1927 and remaining as manager, Crystal Palace manager October 1930, Tottenham Hotspur manager June 1935, Plymouth Argyle manager April 1938 to November 1947, Aston Villa scout 1948-9, Chelmsford City manager June 1949 to November 1950, Hastings United manager December 1951, Tonbridge manager April 1958 until his death
Club Honour: West Ham United —F.A. Cup finalists 1923
A left-half quietly proficient in attack and defence. Attained a high level of consistency and seldom had an off day.

TUNSTALL, Frederick Edward
1923-5(7)
b Low Valley near Wombwell, Yorks 29 March 1901.
Career: Darfield St George's Scunthorpe United 1920, Sheffield United December 1920, Halifax Town January 1933, Boston United cs 1936 remaining with the Club after his retirement as a

player being at various times manager, trainer and coach
Club Honour: Sheffield United—F.A. Cup winners 1925
A live-wire outside-left of the direct type. Exceptionally speedy and packing a fine shot of abnormal velocity.

TURNBULL, Robert Joseph
                              1920(1)
b South Bank, Yorks 1895; d 18 March 1952.
Career: South Bank Schools, South Bank East End, Bradford January 1918, Leeds United May 1925, Rhyl September 1932 retired 1933. Later worked for Dorman Long in Middlesbrough
First achieved prominence as a goal scoring inside-left in Wartime football and his scoring touch remained when he became an outside-right in the peacetime game. Direct with no undue frills and finely consistent.

TURNER, Arthur   1900-1(2)
b Farnborough, Hants 1877; d 4 April 1925.
Career: Aldershot North End 1892-4; South Farnborough, Camberley St Michael's, Southampton 1899, Derby County May 1902, Newcastle United early 1903, Tottenham Hotspur mid 1903-4, Southampton cs 1904 to cs 1905. He then returned to Farnborough to join his father's business there. A keen club cricketer.
Club Honours: Southampton—F.A. Cup finalists 1900, 2, Southern League Champions 1901
An outside-right quick to seize upon an opening, pounce on the ball and centre to the best advantage. Opportunist type of forward.

TURNER, Hugh   1931(2)
b Wigan.
Career: Felling Colliery (Darlington amateur cs 1924), High Fell cs 1925, Huddersfield Town early

1926, Fulham cs 1937 retired during the War
Club Honour: Huddersfield Town—F.A. Cup finalists 1930
Enjoyed regular first team football nearly all his League career thanks to a splendid consistency, being sound in all goalkeeping facets.

TURNER, James Albert 1893-8(3)
b Black Bull, Staffs 1866; d 9 April 1904.
Career: Black Lane Rovers, Bolton Wanderers early 1889, Stoke cs 1894, Derby County cs 1896, Stoke August 1898 thence worked as a commercial clerk
Club Honour: Derby County—F.A. Cup finalists 1898. Unable to play for Bolton Wanderers in the Cup Final 1894
Serviceable left-half whose main attribute was his utter dependability. This quality plus judgment and fine tackling outweighed any lack of flashy brilliance.

TWEEDY, George Jacob   1937(1)
b Willington, Co. Durham 6 January 1913.
Career: Durham Schools, Willington Town, Grimsby Town August 1931, assistant manager September 1950 but reverted to player late 1951 and finally retired cs 1953. He remained in the Town being associated with a family furnishing business
One wonders if this fine custodian would have received more caps if he had been associated with a "fashionable" club. Adept at dealing with any type of shot, always unruffled and a loyal club man.

UFTON, Derek Gilbert   1954(1)
b Crayford, Kent 31 May 1928.
Career: Dartford Grammar School, Borough United, Dulwich Hamlet, Cardiff City amateur whilst in Forces, Bexleyheath & Welling, Charlton Athletic Sep-

tember 1948 retired cs 1960 owing to injury. Tooting & Mitcham coach January 1962, Plymouth Argyle coach September 1964, caretaker manager May 1965, manager later May 1965 until January 1968. Played cricket for Kent from 1949-62 and in first class cricket scored 3,919 runs and, as a wicket-keeper, made 314 dismissals, 271 caught and 43 stumped, 92 dismissals in 1961. Worked as a photographic model and is now manager of a West End Club

Ufton was a cool, strong and mobile left-half before showing like qualities as a pivot. Always a good tackler, he was unlucky in being plagued by a recurring shoulder injury.

UNDERWOOD, Alfred 1891-2(2)
b Hanley 1867; d 8 October 1928.
Career: Hanley Tabernacle, Etruria, Stoke retired injury cs 1893 but made further isolated appearances. A potter by trade he was chronically ill for 25 years until his death

A hard, formidable left-back who played with much determination. Reliable to a degree.

URWIN, Thomas 1923-6(4)
b Haswell, Co. Durham 5 February 1896.
Career: Monkwearmouth Colliery School, Sunderland Schools (England Schools Shield winners 1910), Fulwell, Lambton Star, Shildon 1913, professional February 1914, Middlesbrough May 1914, Newcastle United August 1924, Sunderland February 1930 retired cs 1936. Later coached Sunderland juniors and worked as a clerk in a Sunderland Hospital until his retirement in February 1962

Club Honour: Newcastle United —F.L. Champions 1927

A crafty midget winger able to function on both flanks. He was fast and justly famed for the consummate accuracy of his centres.

UTLEY, George 1913(1)
b Elsecar, Yorks.
Career: Elsecar, Sheffield Wednesday cs 1906, returned to Elsecar, Barnsley 1908, Sheffield United November 1913, Manchester City September 1922, Bristol City trainer November 1923, Sheffield Wednesday trainer/coach May 1924, Fulham trainer July 1925. He was for many years cricket coach at Rossall School

Club Honours: Barnsley—F.A. Cup finalists 1910, winners 1912, Sheffield United—F.A. Cup winners 1915

A battler imbued with a splendid competitive spirit, Utley was a left-half who also had generalship. Renowned for his long throws.

VAUGHTON, Oliver Howard 1882-4(5)
b Aston 9 January 1861; d 6 January 1937.
Career: Waterloo F.C., Birmingham F.C. (No connection with the present Club), Wednesbury Strollers, Aston Villa 1880. Aston Villa Vice President 1923, President June 1924, Director September 1924 retired owing to illness December 1932, elected a Life member February 1933. A silversmith in Birmingham, his firm were makers of the second F.A. Cup after the original had been stolen from a shop in Birmingham in 1895

Club Honour: Aston Villa—F.A. Cup winners 1887

Fine inside-left and an excellent team man. Had all the attacking skills except in shooting where he was inclined to be erratic.

VEITCH, Colin Campbell McKechnie 1906-9(6)
b Newcastle-upon-Tyne 1882; d 26 August 1938.

Career: Rutherford College, New-castle United amateur 1901, pro-fessional 1903, retired during the 1914-18 War and was later on the club staff, Bradford City manager August 1926 to January 1928, from 1929 a journalist with New-castle *Daily Journal* reporting soccer, cricket and golf. He was training to be a schoolteacher at the time of joining Newcastle United. From 1909-12 he was Chairman of the Players' Union. An amateur actor of merit he became Chairman of Newcastle People's Theatre and was also a producer
Club Honours: Newcastle United —F.A. Cup winners 1910, finalists 1905, 6, 8, 11, F.L. Champions 1905, 7, 9
Perhaps the most versatile player of his day, he could give a com-petent performance in practically any position. He shone most, how-ever, at half-back where he dis-played a flair and polish of the highest order.

VEITCH, John Gould   1894(1)
b Kingston Hill, Surrey 19 July 1869; d 3 October 1914.
Career: Westminster Schools (XI 1887) Trinity College Cambridge (Blue 1888-9-90-1); Old Westmin-sters; Corinthians 1889-98
Could be variable but when on form was fine in both the left-wing forward positions. Tall and strong, an astute dribbler and a most consistent marksman (63 goals in 72 matches for the Corin-thians).

VENABLES, Terence Frederick
1965(2)
b Dagenham 6 January 1943.
Career: Dagenham Schools (Eng-land Schools v Ireland Eire Wales West Germany and Scotland (2) 1958), Chelsea amateur July 1958 (England Amateur and Youth in-ternational 1960), professional August 1960, Tottenham Hotspur

May 1966, Queens Park Rangers June 1969. The only player to be capped by England in five grades —Schools, Youth, Amateur, Un-der 23 and Full
Club Honours: Chelsea—F.A. Youth Cup winers 1960 and 1961, F.L. Cup winners 1965, Totten-ham Hotspur—F.A. Cup winners 1967
A professional approach has coloured his work at right-half and inside-left since the earliest days. Can read a game, is a schemer and able to take chances himself.

VIDAL, Robert Walpole Sealy
(later known as R. W. Sealy)
1873(1)
b Cornborough near Bideford, Devon 3 September 1853; d 5 November 1914.
Career: Westminster School (XI 1870-2 captain 1872); Christ Church Oxford (Blue 1874-5 cap-tain 1875); Wanderers; Old West-minsters; F.A. Committee 1872 and 1874. An Oxford rugby blue in 1873 (prior to the University soccer match) he was ordained in 1877 and was Vicar of Abbots-ham, Devon from 1881 until his death. He also became a fine golfer at the Westward Ho course
Club Honours: Wanderers—F.A. Cup winners 1872 (and so far as is known the only player to win a Cup Winners medal whilst still at school), Oxford University— F.A. Cup finalists 1873, winners 1874
Adroit and mobile forward famed for his dribbling—he was a mas-ter of ball control—and wonder-ful shooting.

VIOLLET, Dennis S.   1960-2(2)
b Manchester 20 September 1933.
Career: St Margarets Central School Whalley (England Schools v Ireland 1948 v Eire Scotland and Wales (2) 1949), Manchester United amateur cs 1949, profes-

sional September 1950, Stoke City January 1962, Baltimore Bays (U.S.A.) May 1967 to September 1968, Witton Albion January 1969, Linfield player coach July 1969, Preston North End coach later 1970, Crewe Alexandra coach February 1971, team manager cs 1971 to November 1971
Club Honours: Manchester United—F.L. Champions 1956-7, F.A. Cup finalists 1958, Stoke City—Second Division Champions 1963, F.L. Cup finalists 1964, Linfield—Irish Cup winners 1970. Missed the 1957 Cup Final owing to injury
A compelling performer at inside and centre-forward, exploiting ball control, a deceptive swerve, cunning and a powerful shot.

VON DONOP, Pelham George
1873-5(2)
b Southsea, Hants 28 April 1851; d 7 November 1921.
Career: Somerset College, Bath; Royal Military Academy Woolwich; Royal Engineers. Joined Royal Engineers in 1871 and retired in 1899 with the rank of Lt.-Col. Inspecting Officer of Railways from 1899 to 1913 and Chief Inspecting Officer from 1913-16
Club Honours: Royal Engineers—F.A. Cup finalists 1874, winners 1875
Had many assets; a fine dribbler, tremendously fast and the capacity for being up with the play. Said to be the best outside-right of his time.

WACE, Henry   1878-9(3)
b Shrewsbury 21 September 1853; d 5 November 1947.
Career: Shrewsbury School; St John's College Cambridge (Blue 1874-5); Wanderers; Clapham Rovers; Shropshire Wanderers: Cambridge Rugby blue 1874-5. Despite his double blue for soccer and rugger he had a notable academic record at Cambridge win-

ning a number of prizes and medals. Son of a Shrewsbury solicitor he was called to the Bar in 1879 and became an acknowledged expert in Bankruptcy
Club Honours: Wanderers—F.A. Cup winners 1877-8
Plucky, tenacious centre possessing speed and shooting ability but apt to station himself too far upfield.

WADSWORTH, Samuel John
1922-7(9)
b Darwen, Lancs 1896; d 1 September 1961.
Career: Darwen, Blackburn Rovers 1914, Nelson May 1919, Huddersfield Town April 1921, Burnley September 1929, Lytham 1931 retired injury, later a coach in Holland (including PSV Eindhoven where he spent the rest of his life apart from the War years).
Club Honours: Huddersfield Town—F.A. Cup winners 1922, F.L. Champions—1924-5-6
A prominent figure in the long line of Huddersfield international backs, Wadsworth performed on the left. He was fast and always constructive, striving to place his clearances to the best advantage.

WAINSCOAT, William Russell
1929(1)
b Maltby, Yorks 28 July 1897.
Career: Maltby Main, Barnsley March 1920, Middlesbrough December 1923, Leeds United March 1925, Hull City October 1931 to cs 1934
Club Honour: Hull City—Third Division North Champions 1933
Big, strong inside-left who also had a deal of experience at centre-forward. Had an aggressive spirit combined with intricate footwork more often found in Scots inside-forwards.

WAITERS, Anthony Keith
1964-5(5)
b Southport 1937.

Career: Farnborough Road School and King George V Grammar School Southport, R.A.F. football (whilst on National service), Loughborough Colleges (England amateur international 1959), Bishop Auckland, Macclesfield, Blackpool amateur July 1959, professional October 1959, retired May 1967 to take up an appointment as F.A. North West regional coach, Liverpool coach January 1969, Burnley player coach July 1970, Coventry City director of coaching December 1971 to March 1972

On his return to the playing side in 1970 proved he had retained much goalkeeping brilliance. Tall, heavily built and with exceptionally quick reflex action when dealing with close range shots.

WALDEN, Frederick Ingram
("Fanny") 1914-22(2)
b Wellingborough 1 March 1888; d 3 May 1949.
Career: Victoria School Wellingborough, Wellingborough White Cross, Wellingborough All Saints, Wellingborough Redwell, Wellingborough Town, Northampton Town cs 1909, Tottenham Hotspur April 1913, Northampton Town May 1926 retired cs 1927. Played cricket for Northamptonshire 1910 to 1929 scoring 7,462 runs including 5 centuries and was later a first class umpire
Club Honour: Tottenham Hotspur—Second Division Champions 1920. Missed the 1921 Cup Final as he had not regained his form following injury.
It is questionable whether there has ever been a more popular player than this diminutive outside right. Standing but a shade over 5 foot 2 inches Walden could wriggle past a defender like an eel and be difficult to catch because of his acceleration.

WALKER, William Henry
1921-33(18)

b Wednesbury, Staffs 29 October 1897; d 28 November 1964.
Career: Kings Hill School, Hednesford Town, Darlaston, Wednesbury Old Park, Aston Villa 1915 professional May 1919, retired to become Sheffield Wednesday manager December 1933 until November 1937. Chelmsford City manager January 1938 to October 1938, Nottingham Forest manager March 1939 to July 1960 when he retired owing to ill-health and was on the Club committee until his death
Club Honours: Aston Villa—F.A. Cup winners 1920, finalists 1924
Started his senior career at centre-forward moving to inside-left later. He played for his country in both positions and, with his strategy, opportunism and ability to bring out the very best in his partners, became one of the most illustrious figures of the '20s.

WALL, George 1907-13(7)
b Boldon Colliery, Co. Durham 20 February 1885.
Career: Boldon Royal Rovers, Whitburn, Jarrow, Barnsley 1902, Manchester United March 1906, Oldham Athletic cs 1919, Hamilton Academicals June 1921, Rochdale cs 1922 retired cs 1923. Later worked for many years in Manchester Docks
Club Honours: Manchester United—F.L. Champions 1908, 11, F.A. Cup winners 1909
Long serving outside-left consummate in ball control and possessor of a terrific shot in his left foot.

WALLACE, Charles William
1913-20(3)
b Sunderland 20 January 1885; d January 1970.
Career: Southwick, Crystal Palace cs 1905, Aston Villa May 1907, Oldham Athletic May 1921 retired cs 1923. After retirement worked in Birmingham as a painter and decorator and was a steward at Villa Park for many

years

Club Honours: Aston Villa—F.A. Cup winners 1913, 20, F.L. Champions 1910

Clever outside-right whose chief merits were great pace, the ability for accurate centring and unselfishness.

WALTERS, Arthur Melmoth
1885-90(9)
b Ewell, Surrey 26 January 1865; d 2 May 1941.
Career: Charterhouse School (XI 1882-3); Trinity College Cambridge (Blue 1884-5-6-7); Old Carthusians; East Sheen; Corinthians 1885-93 ; Surrey. Retired in 1893 owing to the death of his brother H. M. as a result of an accident when playing football although he made the occasional appearance for Old Carthusians. Admitted a solicitor in November 1889 he practised in London with Walters & Co.
Club Honours: Old Carthusians— F.A. Amateur Cup winners 1894, finalists 1895
The right-flank of the famous full-back partnership and brother of P. M. Could kick well with both feet and a swift mover.

WALTERS, Percy Melmoth
1885-90(13)
b Ewell, Surrey 30 September 1863 ; d 6 October 1936.
Career: Charterhouse School (not in XI); Oriel College Oxford (Blue 1885); Old Carthusians; East Sheen; Epsom; Corinthians 1885-92 ; Surrey. Retired in 1893 like his brother, A. M. F.A. Committee 1886, Vice President 1891-2. Called to the Bar at Lincoln's Inn 1888
Club Honour: Old Carthusians— F.A. Amateur Cup finalists 1895
Left-back. There can be no greater praise than to say he was Arthur's equal as a back, although dissimilar in some methods, Strong, courageous, a good judge of pace

and kicking finely from any angle.

WALTON, Nathaniel　　1890(1)
b Preston 1867; d 3 March 1930.
Career: Witton, Blackburn Rovers 1885, Nelson cs 1893, Blackburn Rovers trainer 1898 to 1906. Later a licensee in Blackburn and retained his interest in the Club up to his death
Club Honours: Blackburn Rovers —F.A. Cup winners 1886, 90-1
Among the most versatile of the early leading players his diverse talents enabling him to perform anywhere. Best at inside-forward where his attacking and foraging powers could be fully employed.

WARD, James Thomas　　1885(1)
b Blackburn 28 March 1865 ; d prior to 1900.
Career: Furthergate School Blackburn, Little Harwood 1879, Blackburn Olympic 1881, Blackburn Rovers 1886. Originally an operative in the cotton trade he later became a licensee in Blackburn
Club Honour: Blackburn Olympic —F.A. Cup winners 1883
Quick moving right-back sound and sure in his kicking whom opponents found hard to circumvent.

WARD, Timothy Victor　1948-9(2)
b Cheltenham circa 1917.
Career: Cheltenham schools, Cheltenham Town, Derby County April 1937, Barnsley March 1951, Exeter City manager March 1953 for 14 days only then returned to Barnsley as their manager, Grimsby Town manager February 1960, Derby County manager June 1962 to May 1967, Carlisle United manager June 1967 to September 1968. Lives at Burton-on-Trent and is Midlands representative of a civil engineering firm. Did some scouting for Nottingham Forest from August 1969 Immediately after the War had no superior and few equals at wing-

half. Speedy, a shrewd schemer and strongly biased towards attack.

WARING, Thomas (" Pongo ")
1931-2(5)
b Birkenhead 12 October 1906.
Career: Birkenhead Schools, Tranmere Celtic, Tranmere Rovers early 1926, Aston Villa February 1928, Barnsley November 1935, Wolverhampton Wanderers July 1936, Tranmere Rovers October 1936, Accrington Stanley November 1938, Bath City July 1939. Post War played at various times for Ellesmere Port Town, Graysons F.C., Birkenhead Dockers and Harrowby whilst working in the Merseyside docks
Club Honour: Tranmere Rovers —Third Division North Champions 1938
Tall, long striding, free scoring centre-forward beloved at Villa Park. Supremely self-confident Waring was a colourful character and the stories about him, apocryphal and otherwise, were legion.

WARNER, Conrad   1878(1)
b 1852; d 10 April 1890.
Career: Upton Park. He was a merchant in the City of London and died of pneumonia in New York shortly after his arrival there on a business visit
Looked up as the best goalkeeper of his period. Always calm when under pressure clearing the ball with despatch.

WARREN, Benjamin   1906-11(22)
b Newhall, Derbyshire 1879; d 15 January 1917.
Career: Newhall Town, Newhall Swifts, Derby County 1899, Chelsea cs 1908, retired illness February 1912
Club Honour: Derby County—F.A. Cup finalists 1903
Intuitive right-half who, although a trifle slow, controlled the ball perfectly, tackled cleanly and distributed immaculately.

WATERFIELD, George Smith
1927(1)
b Swinton, Yorks 2 June 1901.
Career: Mexborough, Burnley October 1923 (as an outside-left), Crystal Palace June 1935
Found his earlier experience on the left wing useful when he transferred to left-back. Very fast, remarkably so in recovery, composed and a sure volleyer.

WATSON, Victor M.   1923-30(5)
b Girton, Cambridge 10 November 1898;
Career: Girton, Cambridge Town, Peterborough & Fletton United, Brotherhood Engineering Works, West Ham United March 1920, Southampton June 1935 retired cs 1936. Has been a market gardener at Girton since his retirement from the game
Club Honours: West Ham United —F.A. Cup finalists 1923. Scored 6 goals for West Ham United v Leeds United in a League match, 9 February 1929
Dashing centre-forward whose tactic was to persistently harass the opposing defence. He maintained a fine consistency of good play for West Ham over many seasons.

WATSON, William   1913-20(3)
b Southport 11 September 1890; d 1 September 1955.
Career: All Saints Wennington Road School, Blowick Wesleyans, Southport Central 1907, professional 1908, Burnley March 1909, Accrington Stanley cs 1925. On Blackburn Rovers staff as coach for a time from November 1926 thence an ironmonger and later a decorator in Southport. Had two spells as a Liberal councillor at Southport the second from May 1955 until his death
Club Honours: Burnley—F.A. Cup winners 1914, F.L. Cham-

pions 1921

Thoughtful in distribution and capable in defence Watson was a polished left-half. His main attribute, though, was a remarkably high level of consistency.

WATSON, William 1950-1(4)
b Bolton-on-Dearne 7 March 1920.

Career: Paddock Council School Huddersfield, Local Juniors, Huddersfield Town October 1937, Sunderland April 1946 retired cs 1954. Halifax Town player manager November 1954 to April 1956, re-elected manager September 1964, Bradford City manager April 1966 to January 1968. England Test cricketer 1953-8 (23 Tests) playing for Yorkshire 1939-57 and later captained Leicestershire. Has also acted as a Test selector

Changed from his early days as a progressive and lively outside-left to become, at Sunderland, an accomplished right-half. Adroit at winning the ball and perceptive in feeding his attack.

WEAVER, Samuel 1932-3(3)
b Pilsley, Derbyshire 1909.

Career: Pilsley, Sutton Junction, Sutton Town 1926, Hull City March 1928, Newcastle United November 1929, Chelsea August 1936, Stockport County December 1945 retired cs 1947, Leeds United training staff 1947-9, Millwall trainer coach June 1949 to January 1954, Steward Oxo Sports Club Bromley January 1954, Mansfield Town coach September 1955, manager June 1958 to January 1960 remaining with the Club being at various times coach, assistant trainer and chief scout and, briefly in November 1971, caretaker manager. Played cricket for Derbyshire and, in 1939, Somerset. Has been masseur to Derbyshire County Cricket Club since 1956

Club Honour: Newcastle United —F.A. Cup winners 1932

Left-half or inside-left, better known in the former position because his long throws—over 35 yards—made him a national figure around 1932. Was competent in other directions too with an effective tackle and an aggressive attacking spirit.

WEBB, George W. 1911(2)
b East London circa 1887; d prior to 1931.

Career: Shaftesbury Road School Ilford, Ilford Alliance, Ilford, Wanstead (making odd appearances for West Ham United), West Ham United mid 1908-9, Manchester City cs 1912 retired cs 1913. Made seven England amateur international appearances 1910-12

An amateur centre-forward and a power in the land in the pre 1914 era. He was fast, had a great shot while a hefty physique made him even more redoubtable.

WEBSTER, Maurice 1930(3)
b Blackpool.

Career: Bloomfield Villa, South Shore Wednesday, Fleetwood, Lytham, Stalybridge Celtic October 1921, Middlesbrough April 1922, Carlisle United June 1935, retired cs 1936. Middlesbrough training staff 1936-7, Carlisle United trainer May 1937

Club Honour: Middlesbrough— Second Division Champions 1929

Short of stature for a centre-half but made up for this with his constructive powers—he prompted the forwards well—and exceptional speed of recovery.

WEDLOCK, William John
1907-14(26)
b Bedminster 28 October 1881; d 24 January 1965.

Career: Masonic Rovers, Arlington Rovers (Bristol City amateur), Gloucester County, Aberdare, Bristol City cs 1905 retired cs

1921. After his retirement he was
for many years a licensee near to
the City ground
Club Honours: Aberdare—Welsh
Cup finalists 1904 and 1905,
Bristol City—Second Division
Champions 1906, F.A. Cup finalists 1909
Would appear in any list of great
England centre-halves. Only
around 5 feet 4 inches tall, Wedlock was scintillating both in
attack and defence. Contemporary
critics referred to him as a rubber
man because of his bounding
energy.

WEIR, David   1889(2)
b Aldershot   ; d
Career: Maybole, Glasgow
Thistle, Halliwell, Bolton Wanderers cs 1888, Ardwick May
1890, Bolton Wanderers January
1893 retired and returned to Scotland cs 1895 where he coached
and played on occasion for Maybole. Appointed Glossop manager
late 1909 thence to Stuttgart as
coach in April 1911
A strong attacking player, by
inclination very individualistic.
Extremely versatile, his two England games were played at centre-
half and inside-left, and he
assisted Bolton in a variety of forward positions.

WELCH, Reginald de Courtenay
1873-4(2)
b Kensington late 1851; d 4 June
1939.
Career: Harrow School (XI 1871);
Harrow Chequers; Wanderers;
Remnants; Middlesex; F.A. Com-
mittee 1873-5 and 1879-80. Army
Tutor 1883-95 thence Principal of
the Army College, Heath End,
Farnham, Surrey
Club Honours: Wanderers—F.A.
Cup winners 1872-3   ,
His first England appearance was
at full-back and the other in goal.
A competent back and equally

good between the posts where
he was a notably safe performer.

WELSH, Donald   1938-9(3)
b Manchester 25 February 1911.
Career: Manchester Schools,
Royal Navy, Torquay United
amateur early 1933 professional
July 1934, Charlton Athletic Feb-
ruary 1935, Brighton & Hove
Albion manager November 1947,
Liverpool manager March 1951
to May 1956 thence for a spell a
licensee in Devon. Bournemouth
& Boscombe Athletic manager
July 1958 to February 1961.
Manager of Clubland, Camber-
well Youth Centre May 1961,
Wycombe Wanderers manager
July 1963 to November 1964.
From December 1964 very briefly
on the Charlton Athletic administrative staff
Club Honours: Charlton Athletic
—Third Division South Champions 1935, F.L. South Cup finalists 1943, winners 1944, F.A. Cup
finalists 1946, winners 1947
Well endowed in physique and in
ability for he could fill four positions—centre and left-half, centre-
forward and inside-left—with
equal distinction. He was bold
and strong shooting in attack and
massively resourceful in all phases
of defence.

WEST, Gordon   1969(3)
b Darfield, Barnsley 24 April
1943.
Career: Don and Dearne Schools,
Blackpool amateur 1958 professional April 1960 (England Youth
international 1960-1), Everton
March 1962
Club Honours: Everton—F.L.
Champions 1963, 70, F.A. Cup
winners 1966, finalists 1968
Perhaps not the most composed
of goalkeepers but on his day a
brilliant one, spectacularly hurling
his heavy frame around the area
with effective abandon.

WESTWOOD, Raymond William
1935-7(6)
b Brierley Hill, Staffs 14 April
1912.
Career: Brierley Hill Schools,
Stourbridge, Brierley Hill Alliance, Bolton Wanderers March
1930, Chester December 1947,
Darwen late 1949
Made his debut in senior football
as a teenager and played at outside-left, moving inside when his
physique developed. A swift
mover and a lethal shot he was
noted for direct straight-through
dashes.

WHATELEY, Oliver 1883(2)
b 1861; d October 1926.
Career: Gladstone Unity (Coventry), Aston Villa 1880 to the late
1880s. An artist and designer he
underwent a severe cancer opera-
tion in 1911 but nevertheless, although over military age, worked
from 1914-18 in the Y.M.C.A. Hut
at Rouen. He was in very poor
health for some time until his
death
Variable in performance but at his
best a formidable inside-forward.
Had an aggressive spirit and his
shooting, which would be tried
from any angle, was reputed to be
the hardest of his day.

WHEELER, John E. 1955(1)
b Crosby, Lancs 26 July 1928.
Career: St Leonards School
Bootle, Carlton F.C., Tranmere
Rovers April 1946, Bolton Wan-
derers February 1951, Liverpool
September 1956. Appointed New
Brighton player manager May
1963 but did not take up the
appointment. Bury assistant
trainer cs 1963 to cs 1969, assist-
ant manager trainer September
1969 to September 1970
Club Honour: Bolton Wanderers
—F.A. Cup finalists 1953
A right-half of strong build with

trenchancy in tackling and considerable stamina. Had some
attacking flair, too, playing at inside-right on occasions.

WHELDON, George Frederick
1897-8(4)
b Langley Green 1 November
1871; d 14 January 1924.
Career: Road End White Star,
Langley Green Victoria, Small
Heath 1890, Aston Villa June
1896, West Bromwich Albion cs
1900, Queens Park Rangers December 1901, Portsmouth cs 1902,
Worcester City cs 1904, Coventry
City cs 1905 retired January 1907.
Worcestershire cricket 1899-1906
scoring 4,938 runs including 3
centuries and later played for
Carmarthen
Club Honours: Small Heath—
Second Division Champions 1893,
Aston Villa—F.L. Champions
1897-9-1900, F.A. Cup winners
1897
Demoralised many a defence with
his intricate dribbling. Wheldon
was a brilliant inside-left whose
greatest contribution to the team
was in the laying on of chances
for others.

WHITE, Thomas Angus 1933(1)
b Manchester 1908; d 13 August
1967.
Career: Southport Schools, Trinity Old Boys, Southport September 1925, Everton February 1927,
Northampton Town (trial) October 1937, New Brighton February
1938 retired cs 1938. After leaving
football worked in Liverpool
Docks and died as a result of injuries received whilst working
there
Club Honours: Everton—F.L.
Champions 1932, F.A. Cup winners 1933
Not the biggest of centre-halves
though his discerning distribution
could hardly be bettered. Played
also at centre and inside-forward,

scoring regularly.

WHITEHEAD, James   1893-4(2)
b Church, Lancs.
Career: Peel Bank, Accrington cs 1890, Blackburn Rovers cs 1893, Manchester City October 1897 to 1899
Too lightly built for bustling tactics, Whitehead was a spruce, lively inside-right adroit in evading weightier opponents. An excellent club man.

WHITFELD, Herbert   1879(1)
b Lewes, Sussex 25 November 1858; d 6 May 1909.
Career: Eton College (XI 1877); Trinity College Cambridge (Blue 1879-80-1) ; Old Etonians. Cricket blue 1878-9-80-1 and also played for Sussex 1875-85 (captain in 1884). Athletics blue 1879, Real Tennis blue 1880. A local director of Barclays Bank
Club Honours: Old Etonians— F.A. Cup winners 1879, finalists 1881
A tireless winger of merit despite some lack of speed. Had excellent dribbling technique.

WHITHAM, Michael   1892(1)
b Ecclesfield, Yorks 6 November 1869; d 6 May 1924.
Career: Ecclesfield, Rotherham Swifts, Sheffield United early 1890, Gainsborough Trinity trainer, thence of Rotherham County, Gainsborough Trinity for a second spell, Huddersfield Town and of Brentford up to the time of his death
His solitary appearance for England was at left-half but he mostly played at back for Sheffield United. Height contributed to his great heading ability and resource and zeal were also marked features

WIDDOWSON, Sam Weller 1880(1)
b Hucknall Torkard, Notts 16 April 1851; d 9 May 1927.
Career: Hucknall Torkard School, Peoples College Nottingham, Nottingham Forest 1866, Chairman 1879-1884. F.A. Committee 1888-92 and 1893-4. Patentee of shin-guards 1874
Displayed much prowess at centre-forward being quick off the mark and remarkably sure as a marksman. Notts County cricket twice in 1878-9 and a noted amateur sprinter and hurdler. Was engaged in the lace trade.

WIGNALL, Frank   1965(2)
b Blackrod, Lancs 21 August 1939.
Career: Blackrod,   Horwich R.M.I., Everton amateur May 1958, professional May 1960, Nottingham Forest June 1963, Wolverhampton Wanderers March 1968, Derby County February 1969, Mansfield Town November 1971
Nicely built for leading an attack or for acting as a twin spearhead from inside-forward. His height gives aerial command while his weight provides thrust.

WILKES, Albert   1901-2(5)
b 1875; d 9 December 1936.
Career: Oldbury Town, Walsall, Aston Villa cs 1898, Fulham cs 1907, retired July 1909 in order to concentrate on his business following a fire at his studio. He was a well-known photographer at West Bromwich specialising in team photographs. Elected an Aston Villa director in September 1934
Club Honour: Aston Villa—F.L. Champions 1900
Renowned as a never-say-die wing-half, his capacity for hard work being a byword. Possessed a formidable tackle and a great helpmeet to his full-back.

WILKINSON, Bernard   1904(1)
b Thorpe Hesley, Yorks 1879; d 28 May 1949.
Career: Shiregreen,   Sheffield United July 1899, Rotherham Town cs 1913, later a successful business man in Sheffield

Club Honour: Sheffield United—
F.A. Cup winners 1902
Like several other Sheffield
United and England half-backs of
the period was short in stature.
This one was a pivot, good with
his head and tireless. Had an
attacking bent, being fond of back-
ing up the forwards and shooting.
A good cricketer he might well
have played for Yorkshire had he
been prepared to give the time to
it.

WILKINSON, Leonard Rodwell
1891(1)
b Highgate, 15 October 1868; d
10 February 1913.
Career: Charterhouse School (XI
1887); Christ Church Oxford
(Blue 1889-90-1); Old Carthusians; Corinthians 1890-3. Athletics Blue 1890-1. Called to the
Bar 1893
Club Honours: Old Carthusians—
F.A. Amateur Cup winners 1894,
7, finalists 1895
A capable goalkeeper lithe in
movement. Could rise to brilliant
heights at times.

WILLIAMS, Bert Frederick
1949-56(24)
b Bilston, Staffs 31 January 1922.
Career: Bilston Schools, Thompson's F.C. (Wolverhampton), Walsall April 1937, Wolverhampton
Wanderers September 1945 retired
cs 1957. Since retirement has been
a sports outfitter in Bilston
Club Honours: Wolverhampton
Wanderers—F.A. Cup winners
1949, F.L. Champions 1954
Among the most daring and spectacular of goalkeepers. His leaps
and dives were perfectly timed,
moving with a grace feline almost
in its arched beauty.

WILLIAMS, Owen   1923(2)
b Ryhope, Co. Durham 23 Sep-
tember 1895.
Career: Sunderland Schools (Eng-
lish Schools Shield winners 1910),
Ryhope Colliery (Sunderland
trial), Manchester United cs 1913,
Easington Colliery, Clapton Orient
September 1919, Middlesbrough
February 1924, Southend United
July 1930 retired cs 1931
Club Honours: Middlesbrough—
Second Division Champions 1927
and 1929
Sturdily built and one of the
speediest wingers of his day. Owen
Williams played at outside-left.
He had excellent ball control and
scored consistently.

WILLIAMS, William   1897-9(6)
b Smethwick, Staffs 1875; d 22
January 1929.
Career: Oldbury Road School,
West Smethwick, Old Hill Wanderers, West Bromwich Albion
1893 retired injury mid 1901-2.
After a short spell as West Bromwich Albion trainer he became
a licensee in West Bromwich until his death
Club Honour: West Bromwich
Albion—F.A. Cup finalists 1895
Efficient, reliable full-back. Had
a most effective tackle and
showed a praiseworthy never-say-
die spirit in sticking to an opponent after having been momentar-
ily beaten.

WILLIAMSON, Ernest C. 1923(2)
b Murton Colliery, Co. Durham
1890.
Career: Murton Red Star, Wingate Albion, Croydon Common
June 1913, Arsenal cs 1919, Norwich City June 1923 retired cs
1926. After retirement was a
licensee in Norwich for many
years
Apart from 1913-14—spent in the
Southern League Division 2—
Williamson's participation in
peace time first-class football was
limited to six seasons, his last
League appearance being in 1924-
5. His peak was round 1923 when
his cool, efficient goalkeeping won
representative recognition.

WILLIAMSON, Reginald Garnet ("Tim") 1905-13(7)
b North Ormesby, Yorks 6 June 1884; d 1 August 1943.
Career: Coatham Grammar School, Redcar Crusaders, Middlesbrough 1903 retired cs 1924. Later worked as an Engineer's draughtsman
A man of fine character he became one of the greatest goalkeepers of his time. He was a master in all departments of the craft and played with impressive imperturbability.

WILLINGHAM, Charles Kenneth 1937-9(12)
b Sheffield 1 December 1912.
Career: Yorkshire Schools, Ecclesfield, Worksop Town, Huddersfield Town ground staff 1930, professional November 1931, Sunderland December 1945, Leeds United March 1947 retired May 1948 remaining with the Club for two years on the coaching staff. Following his retirement from the game has been a licensee in Leeds
Club Honour: Huddersfield Town —F.A. Cup finalists 1938
A virilely enthusiastic right-half. A noteworthy facet of his play was the speed with which he took the ball through in attack, a legacy of schoolboy running prowess.

WILLIS, Arthur 1952(1)
b Denaby circa 1921.
Career: Finchley, Tottenham Hotspur amateur 1938, professional January 1944, Swansea Town September 1954, assistant trainer November 1957 continuing as a player to cs 1958 and as assistant trainer to cs 1960, Haverfordwest player manager cs 1960
Club Honours: Tottenham Hotspur—F.L. Champions 1951, Swansea Town—Welsh Cup finalists 1956

Proved a determined efficient right-back in the immediate post-war years and, later in his Tottenham spell, switched to the left flank. Here he developed an excellent understanding with Ramsey, his positioning being first-class.

WILSHAW, Dennis J. 1954-7(12)
b Stoke 11 March 1926.
Career: Hanley High School, Packmoor Boys Club, Wolverhampton Wanderers March 1944, Walsall May 1946 (on loan) returning to Wolverhampton Wanderers September 1948, Stoke City December 1957 retired owing to injury July 1961. A schoolmaster by profession
Club Honour: Wolverhampton Wanderers—F.L. Champions 1954
Performed in the centre and both left wing positions with like facility. Was very thrustful and a frequent goal scorer.

WILSON, Charles Plumpton 1884(2)
b Roydon, Norfolk 12 May 1859; d 9 March 1938.
Career: Uppingham School and Marlborough College (at which schools he played rugger); Trinity College, Cambridge (no soccer blue); Hendon; Casuals; Corinthians. Cambridge rugger blue 1878-9-80-1 being captain in 1881 in which season he played for England v Wales thus being one of the three men to have played for England at rugger and soccer. Also a cricket blue 1880-1 and played for Norfolk 1881-5. Rode in the bicycling race for Cambridge in 1879. Brother of G. P. Master at Elstree School 1881-98, Joint Headmaster of Sandroyd School, Cobham, Surrey 1898-1920
Wing-half of strength and stamina especially good at heading the ball.

E. A. Hapgood

S. Matthews

T. Finney

W. A. Wright

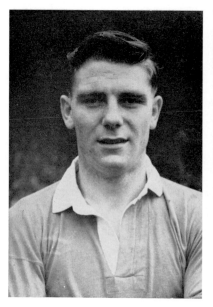

D. Edwards

R. Charlton

R. F. Moore

G. Banks

WILSON, Claude William
1879-81(2)
b 12 May 1858; d 7 June 1881.
Career: Brighton College (XI 1876-7 captain 1877); Exeter College, Oxford (Blue 1879-80-1); Old Brightonians; Sussex. Played cricket for Surrey and was challenging strongly for a cricket blue at the date of his death
Club Honour: Oxford University —F.A. Cup finalists 1880
In a sadly brief career had proved himself to be a fine back. Lively, fast and kicking with power and accuracy.

WILSON, George 1921-4(12)
b Blackpool 1892; d 25 November 1961.
Career: Sacred Heart School Blackpool, Catholic College Preston, Kirkham Sunday School League football, Morecambe, Blackpool February 1912, Sheffield Wednesday March 1920, Nelson July 1925 retired cs 1930.
He became a licensee in 1931 and retired from the Mere Park Hotel at Blackpool in May 1961
Regarded as the best centre-half in the Kingdom immediately after the first World War. Worked prodigiously, fast, wonderful at heading and a stylist.

WILSON, George Plumpton 1900(2)
b 21 February 1878; d 30 July 1934.
Career: Rossall School (XI 1894-5-6 captain 1896); Corinthians 1898 to 1902; Casuals; Southampton; London Hospital. Qualified as a physician and surgeon at London in 1902
Neat in dribbling, a good shot and able in combining with his fellow forwards, this inside-left had, in addition, wonderful ball control.

WILSON, Ramon 1960-8(63)
b Shirebrook 17 December 1934.
Career: Shirebrook Central Secondary Modern School, Langwith

Boys Club, Langwith Junction Imps, Huddersfield Town ground staff May 1952, professional August 1952, Everton June 1964, Oldham Athletic June 1969, Bradford City as player coach August 1970, retired and became assistant manager May 1971, caretaker manager September 1971 but left the club and went into business December 1971. A member of the England World Cup winning team of 1966
Club Honours: Everton—F.A. Cup winners 1966, finalists 1968
In the mid 1960s considered by many to be the best left-back in the World and the claim was not wildly extravagant. He was a stylist, great in the tackle, fast in recovery and a superb kicker.

WILSON, Thomas 1928(1)
b Seaham, Co. Durham April 1896; d 2 February 1948.
Career: Sunderland Schools, Seaham Colliery, Sunderland, Seaham Colliery mid 1918-19, Huddersfield Town June 1919, Blackpool November 1931, Huddersfield Town assistant trainer on retirement June 1932 up to the War. During the War worked for British Dyes and assisted with Huddersfield Town training. Barnsley trainer from 1945 up to his death
Club Honours: Huddersfield Town—F.A. Cup winners 1922, finalists 1920, 8, 30, F.L. Chamions 1924-5-6
A centre-half of the "stopper" type possessing outstanding heading ability. When parting with the ball he preferred the ground pass to the wings or down the centre.

WINCKWORTH, William Norman
1892-3(2)
b 9 February 1870; d 9 November 1941.
Career: Westminster School (XI 1888); Old Westminsters; Corinthians 1890-4. In business in Cal-

P

cutta 1894-1914, his playing
career ended in 1894
Little but good exponent of both
the centre-half and inside-left
berths. Dexterous, diligent, judicious in his passing and adept at
heading.

WINDRIDGE, James Edward
1908-9(8)
b Small Heath 21 October 1883;
d 23 September 1939
Career: Small Heath, Chelsea
April 1905, Middlesbrough November 1911, Birmingham April
1914 retiring during the 1914-18
War. Played cricket for Warwickshire on three occasions between
1909-13.
Artful and skilful inside-forward
strongly individualist in leaning.
Had a good eye for the goal
scoring opening.

**WINGFIELD-STRATFORD, Cecil
Vernon**   1877(1)
b 7 October 1853; d 5 February
1939.
Career: Royal Military Academy
Woolwich; Royal Engineers;
Kent. Served in the Royal Engineers from 1873 to 1910 when he
retired with the rank of Brigadier,
returning for service in 1914-18.
C.M.G. 1916, C.B. 1918.
Club Honour: Royal Engineers—
F.A. Cup winners 1875
A useful winger whose main attribute was his great speed. Unfortunately apt to tire towards the
end of a game.

**WOLLASTON, Charles Henry
Reynolds**   1874-80(4)
b 31 July 1849; d 22 June 1926.
Career: Lancing College (XI 1864-
8 captain 1867-8); Trinity College,
Oxford (prior to the University
match); Clapham Rovers; Lancing Old Boys; Wanderers; Middlesex. Admitted a solicitor in
1875 he was successively assistant
secretary and secretary of the
Union Bank of London 1878-98

Club Honours: Wanderers—F.A.
Cup winners 1872-3, 6-7-8
Had consummate skill in dribbling
and unerring in his shooting.
Without doubt one of the finest
of the early inside-forwards.

WOLSTENHOLME, Samuel
1904-5(3)
b Little Lever, Lancs 1878 ; d
Career: Farnworth Alliance, Horwich, Everton 1897, Blackburn
Rovers May 1904, Croydon Common cs 1908, Norwich City cs
1909 to cs 1913. Coach in Germany at the outbreak of the
1914-18 War and interned.
Brainy and thoughtful right-half.
Placed his passes with precision
and was usually able to counter
the wiles of the most tricky
adversary.

WOOD, Harry   1890-6(3)
b Walsall 1868; d 5 July 1951.
Career: Walsall Town Swifts,
Wolverhampton Wanderers, Walsall cs 1891, Wolverhampton Wanderers mid 1891-2, Southampton
cs 1898, Portsmouth trainer cs
1905 thence a licensee in Portsmouth. Lived in Portsmouth following his retirement until his
death
Club Honours: Wolverhampton
Wanderers—F.A. Cup winners
1893, finalists 1889, 96, Southampton—F.A. Cup finalists 1900, 2,
Southern League Champions
1899, 1901, 3-4
A gentlemanly, model player who
was also a great inside-forward.
Clever in ball manipulation and
staidly exact in distribution.

WOOD, Raymond E.   1955-6(3)
b Hebburn-on-Tyne 11 June 1931.
Career: Newcastle United amateur, Darlington July 1949, Manchester United December 1949,
Huddersfield Town December
1958, Bradford City October 1965,
Barnsley October 1966, Los
Angeles Wolves manager early

1968 later manager of Cyprus National team
Club Honours: Manchester United—F.L. Champions 1956 and 1957, F.A. Cup finalists 1957
An accomplished goalkeeper, ideally built. Was clean in fielding, had anticipation and was very courageous.

WOODGER, George 1911(1)
b Croydon 3 September 1884.
Career: Thornton Heath Wednesday, Croydon Glenrose, Croydon Wanderers, Crystal Palace mid 1905-6 professional cs 1906, Oldham Athletic late 1910, Tottenham Hotspur cs 1914 retired during the 1914-18 War
Was a delicate ball player who could be deceptively dangerous on occasion. His positions were inside and outside-left.

WOODHALL, George (" Spry ")
1888(2)
b 1863; d 29 September 1924.
Career: West Bromwich Albion 1885, Wolverhampton Wanderers October 1892 to 1894. Worked at Salters, the West Bromwich firm so closely associated with Albion history
Club Honours: West Bromwich Albion—F.A. Cup finalists 1886 and 1887, winners 1888
Singularly well nicknamed for he was indeed a sprightly outside-right, centring with great accuracy and combining well in team work.

WOODLEY, Victor Robert
1937-9(19)
b Cippenham, Bucks 26 February 1911.
Career: Cippenham, Windsor and Eton, Chelsea cs 1931, Bath City December 1945, Derby County March 1946, Bath City player manager cs 1947 to December 1949. He is now a licensee in Wiltshire
Club Honours: Chelsea—F.L.

South Cup finalists 1944, Derby County—F.A. Cup winners 1946
A goalkeeper of high calibre. Was not showy or particularly spectacular but obviously a class performer in the ease with which he met all demands.

WOODWARD, Vivian John
1903-11(23)
b Kennington 3 June 1879; d 31 January 1954.
Career: Ascham College Clacton, Clacton, Harwich & Parkeston, Chelmsford, Essex County, Tottenham Hotspur 1901, Chelsea cs 1909 retired during the 1914-18 War. 38 England amateur international appearances 1907-13. Tottenham Hotspur director 1908-9, Chelsea director July 1922 to 1930. Cricket for Essex 2nd XI. An architect by profession.
A celebrated centre or inside-forward ranking among the greatest of amateur players. He relied entirely on his own subtle skills in ground passing, solo dribbling and accurate marksmanship with both foot and head. A fine sportsman.

WOOSNAM, Maxwell 1922(1)
b Liverpool 6 September 1892; d 14 January 1965.
Career: Winchester College (XI 1908-11); Trinity College Cambridge (Blue 1912-13-14 captain 1914); Chelsea 1914; Corinthians 1913-21; Manchester City 1919-25 Northwich Victoria cs 1925.
Played for Wales Amateur F.A. 1913 and for England Amateurs 1922. He was on the staff of I.C.I. for 31 years retiring in 1954 when Personnel Manager
Golf Blue 1912-13, Lawn Tennis Blue 1914-19, Real Tennis Blue 1913-14 and 12th man for the University cricket match 1914. Won Wimbledon doubles with R. Lycett 1921 and reached mixed doubles final that year. Represented Britain in the Olympic

Games of 1920 and 1924 at Lawn Tennis
Dubbed the Admirable Crichton of his day and certainly his appearance and skill at ball games made him one to bracket with C. B. Fry. At soccer played a typically amateur game at centre-half —courageous, hard as nails with a belief in the shoulder charge and the open game.

WORRALL, Frederick 1935-7(2)
b Warrington, Lancs 1911.
Career: Witton Albion, Nantwich, Oldham Athletic December 1928 (after an illegal signing for Bolton Wanderers), Portsmouth October 1931, retired during the War, Chester coach July 1948, Warrington Rugby League Club trainer thence Stockton Heath manager cs 1953
Club Honours: Portsmouth—F.A. Cup finalists 1934, winners 1939
Fast, direct right-winger who always seemed to be in form. Lack of inches did not affect his effectiveness in the air for he was a veritable Jack in the box.

WREFORD-BROWN, Charles
1889-98(4)
b Clifton, Bristol 9 October 1866; d 26 November 1951.
Career: Charterhouse School (XI 1884-5-6); Oriel College Oxford (Blue 1888-9 captain 1889); Old Carthusians; Corinthians 1887-1903 ; F.A. Committee 1892-3, 1895-1902 and 1903-4, F.A. Council 1919-41, Vice President from 1941. Selector for many years. Awarded Oxford cricket blue 1887 but had to withdraw owing to injury. Played for Gloucestershire 1896-8. Admitted a solicitor in 1895 he practised in London with Baker, Jenkins & Co.
Club Honours: Old Carthusians— F.A. Amateur Cup winners 1894-7
A centre-half in the classic mould and ranked among the best ever;

equally strong in either foot, clever in defence and passing the ball with superb judgment. Never played to the gallery.

WRIGHT, Edward Gordon Dundas
1906(1)
b Earlsfield Green, Surrey 3 October 1884; d June 1947.
Career: St Lawrence School, Ramsgate, Queens College, Cambridge (Blue 1904-5-6) ; Royal School of Mines; Worthing; Reigate Priory; Leyton; Portsmouth; Hull City; Corinthians; Sussex; 20 England amateur international appearances 1908-13.
After being a lecturer at Hymers College, Hull he went to South Africa in 1913 as a mining engineer and after being in U.S.A. for a time returned to South Africa until his death
An outside-left notability who could middle the ball from any angle when travelling at high speed. Had excellent ball control and tactical knowledge.

WRIGHT, John Douglas 1939(1)
b near Southend-on-Sea 1917.
Career: Southend junior football, Southend United mid 1936-7, Newcastle United May 1938, Lincoln City December 1948, Blyth Spartans player coach December 1954
Club Honour: Lincoln City— Third Division North Champions 1952
A left-half with an enchanting artistry in ball control which he was prone to exercise near his own goal when safety first tactics might have appeared more appropriate. At Lincoln his captaincy was marked with a fine degree of generalship.

WRIGHT, Thomas James
1968-70(11)
b Liverpool 21 October 1944.
Career: Liverpool Schools, Everton amateur 1961, professional

March 1963
Club Honours: Everton—F.A. Cup winners 1966, finalists 1968, F.L. Champions 1970
As with many modern right-backs he likes to advance with the ball. In addition has a clean kick and his covering is first-rate.

WRIGHT, William Ambrose
1947-59(105)
b Ironbridge, Shropshire 6 February 1924.
Career: Madeley Wood and Madeley Senior Schools, Wolverhampton Wanderers ground staff 1938, professional 1941, retired August 1959. Appointed manager to England Youth team October 1960, Arsenal manager May 1962 to June 1966 since when he has been an Associated Television sports reporter in Birmingham. Awarded C.B.E. June 1959. He was the first player to make 100 international appearances and was made an honorary member of the F.A. He was a member of the Pilkington Commission on Television and Broadcasting
Club Honours: Wolverhampton Wanderers—F.A. Cup winners 1949, F.L. Champions 1954, 1958 and 1959
Captained club and country with distinction for many years. Started as an inside-forward, then became a wing-half of world class and latterly, despite having no height advantage, a more than adequate pivot. Industrious, incisive in tackling and passing and inspiring in leadership.

WYLIE, John George   1878(1)
b 1854; d 30 July 1924.
Career: Shrewsbury School; Wanderers; Sheffield F.C. and F.A.; Doncaster F.C. Admitted a solicitor in 1878 and practised in London
Club Honour: Wanderers—F.A. Cup winners 1878
Fast, strong centre and an effective marksman relying, though, too much on individual effort at the expense of team work.

YATES, John   1889(1)
b Blackburn   ; d prior to 1933.
Career: Accrington 1879, Blackburn Olympic returning to Accrington in February 1886, Burnley cs 1888 to 1894. A cotton weaver by profession
Club Honour: Blackburn Olympic—F.A. Cup winners 1883
Was a well-known left-winger some years before appearing for England—for instance his forceful, positive play had a lot to do with Blackburn Olympic's free scoring and successful F.A. Cup run of 1883.

YORK, Richard Ernest   1922-6(2)
b Birmingham 1899.
Career: Icknield Street School Birmingham (England Schools v Wales and Scotland 1913), King Edward G.S. Birmingham (where he played rugby), thence local junior and Army and R.A.F. football before joining Aston Villa May 1919, Port Vale June 1931, Brierley Hill Alliance cs 1932. Later a plumber and decorator in Birmingham
Club Honour: Aston Villa—F.A. Cup finalists 1924
An outside-right of extraordinary speed adept at accurate passing (possibly a legacy from his early days at right-half) and the placing of centres.

YOUNG, Alfred   1933-9(9)
b Sunderland 4 November 1907.
Career: Durham City 1926, Huddersfield Town January 1927, York City November 1945, coach in Copenhagen 1946-8, Huddersfield Town coach August 1948 to May 1952 later Bradford team manager December 1957 to November 1958, coach to Esbjerg November 1958, Huddersfield

Town coach December 1960, chief scout 1964 leaving the Club July 1965

Club Honour: Huddersfield Town —F.A. Cup finalists 1938

An unflagging worker having confidence in his own great ability— useful attributes in a pivot. Was a grand tackler and liked to go on an occasional attacking sortie.

YOUNG, Gerald Morton 1965(1) b South Shields 1 October 1936.

Career: Croft Terrace School Jarrow, Leslie Juniors (Newcastle United on amateur forms for some time), Sheffield Wednesday July 1955, trainer coach to the reserves from July 1971

Club Honour: Sheffield Wednesday—F.A. Cup finalists 1966

Indefatigable and strong at left-half and noted for resolution in the tackle. Had shown versatility earlier, making his senior debut as an inside-left, later playing in the centre and on the extreme left.

5

Other International Matches

A NUMBER OF international matches have been played which are not recognised as " full " internationals, namely, a match v Canada in 1891, the Victory matches of 1919 and 1946, the war-time matches of 1940 to 1945 and the Test matches played during the tours of South Africa in 1910, 1920, 1929, 1939 and 1956 and of Australia in 1925 and 1951.

The results of these matches were as follows:

1	1891	Dec	19	Canada	The Oval	6-1	Henfrey, Cotterill, Smith 4
2	1910	June	29	South Africa	Durban	3-0	Hibbert 3
3		July	23	South Africa	Johan'burg	6-2	Fleming 2, Woodward 2, Wall, Holley
4		July	30	South Africa	Cape Town	6-3	Holley 2, Woodward 2, Fleming and Berry
5	1919	Apr	26	Scotland	Everton	2-2	Turnbull, Puddefoot
6		May	3	Scotland	Glasgow	4-3	Puddefoot 2, Grimsdell 2
7		Oct	11	Wales	Cardiff	1-2	Puddefoot
8		Oct	18	Wales	Stoke	2-0	Whittingham, Smith
9	1920	June	19	South Africa	Durban	3-1	Turnbull 2, Rogers
10		June	26	South Africa	Johan'burg	3-1	Fazackerley 2, Woodcock
11		July	17	South Africa	Cape Town	9-1	Fazackerley 4, Smith 2, Mercer, Turnbull, Bamber
12	1925	June	27	Australia	Brisbane	5-1	Simms 3, Batten 2
13		July	4	Australia	Sydney	2-1	Elkes, Simms
14		July	11	Australia	Maitland	8-2	Batten 5, Simms 2, Hannaford
15		July	18	Australia	Sydney	5-0	Simms 2, Batten 2, Elkes
16		July	25	Australia	Melbourne	2-0	Charlton, Batten

17	1929	June 15	South Africa	Durban	3-2	Chandler 2, Hart
18		July 13	South Africa	Johan'burg	2-1	Chandler 2
19		July 17	South Africa	Cape Town	3-1	Chandler 2, and an opponent
20	1939	June 17	South Africa	Johan'burg	3-0	Lewis 2, M. Fenton
21		June 24	South Africa	Durban	8-2	M. Fenton 3, Beasley, Finch, Gibbons 2 and Lewis
22		July 1	South Africa	Johan'burg	2-1	Gibbons and Finch
23		Nov 11	Wales	Cardiff	1-1	Goulden
24		Nov 18	Wales	Wrexham	3-2	Balmer, Lawton, Martin
25		Dec 2	Scotland	Newcastle	2-1	Carter, Lawton
26	1940	Apr 13	Wales	Wembley	0-1	
27		May 11	Scotland	Glasgow	1-1	Welsh
28	1941	Feb 8	Scotland	Newcastle	2-3	Lawton, Birkett
29		Apr 26	Wales	Nottingham	4-1	Welsh 4
30		May 3	Scotland	Glasgow	3-1	Welsh 2, Goulden
31		June 7	Wales	Cardiff	3-2	Hagan 2, Welsh
32		Oct 4	Scotland	Wembley	2-0	Welsh, Hagan
33		Oct 25	Wales	Birmingham	2-1	Edelston, Hagan
34	1942	Jan 17	Scotland	Wembley	3-0	Lawton 2, Hagan
35		Apr 18	Scotland	Glasgow	4-5	Lawton 3, Hagan
36		May 9	Wales	Cardiff	0-1	
37		Oct 10	Scotland	Wembley	0-0	
38		Oct 24	Wales	Wolverh'ton	1-2	Lawton
39	1943	Feb 27	Wales	Wembley	5-3	Westcott 3, Carter 2
40		Apr 17	Scotland	Glasgow	4-0	Carter 2, Westcott, D. Compton
41		May 8	Wales	Cardiff	1-1	Westcott
42		Sep 25	Wales	Wembley	8-3	Carter 2, Welsh 3, Hagan 2 and D. Compton
43		Oct 16	Scotland	Manchester	8-0	Lawton 4, Matthews, Carter and Hagan 2
44	1944	Feb 19	Scotland	Wembley	6-2	Mercer, Lawton, Hagan 2, Carter and an opponent
45		Apr 22	Scotland	Glasgow	3-2	Carter, Lawton 2
46		May 6	Wales	Cardiff	2-0	Lawton, Smith
47	1944	Sep 16	Wales	Liverpool	2-2	Carter, Lawton
48		Oct 14	Scotland	Wembley	6-2	Carter, Lawton 3, Goulden, Smith
49	1945	Feb 3	Scotland	Birmingham	3-2	Brown, Mortensen 2
50		Apr 14	Scotland	Glasgow	6-1	Matthews, Carter, Lawton 2, Brown and Smith
51		May 5	Wales	Cardiff	3-2	Carter 3

52		May	26	France	Wembley	2-2 Carter, Lawton
53		Sep	15	Ireland	Belfast	1-0 Mortensen
54		Oct	20	Wales	West Brom.	0-1
55	1946	Jan	19	Belgium	Wembley	2-0 Brown, Pye
56		Apr	13	Scotland	Glasgow	0-1
57		May	11	Switzerland	Chelsea	4-1 Carter 2, Lawton, Brown
58		May	19	France	Paris	1-2 Hagan
59	1951	May	26	Australia	Sydney	4-1 Sewell 2, Clarke, Hurst
60		June	30	Australia	Sydney	17-0 Clarke 4, Sewell 6, Hagan 3, Broome 3, Hurst
61		July	7	Australia	Brisbane	4-1 Clarke 2, Hagan, Langton
62		July	14	Australia	Sydney	6-1 Webster 3, Sewell, Hurst, Clarke
63		July	21	Australia	Newcastle	5-0 Sewell, Smith, Clarke 2, Hurst
64	1956	June	23	South Africa	Johan'burg	4-3 Harris, King, Perry, Robson
65		June	30	South Africa	Durban	4-2 Harris 2, Hitchens, Robson
66		July	9	South Africa	Cape Town	0-0
67		July	14	South Africa	Salisbury	4-1 Hitchens 2, McGarry, Ayre

LIST OF PLAYERS

(Figure in front of player's name indicates number of appearances)

1   G. E. Ainsley (Leeds United) v SA 1939
2   L. Armitage (Stoke City) v SA(2) 1929
1   R. W. Ayre (Charlton Athletic) v SA 1956
13 J. D. Bacuzzi (Fulham) v S 1941(2)-2(3)-3 v W 1940(2)-1(2)-2-3 Fr 1946
1   J. J. Bagshaw (Derby County) v W 1920
1   W. Ball (Birmingham) v W 1920
1   J. Balmer (Liverpool) v W 1940
2   J. Bamber (Liverpool) v SA(2) 1920
5   H. C. Bamford (Bristol Rovers) v Aust(5) 1951
1   H. Barnes (Manchester City) v W 1920
1   M. W. Barrass (Bolton Wanderers) v W 1946
2   A. F. Barrett (Fulham) v SA(2) 1929
6   S. Bartram (Charlton Athletic) v SA 1939 v W 1940-1 v S 1941 v Aust(2) 1951
5   H. G. Batten (Plymouth Argyle) v Aust(5) 1925
2   A. Beasley (Huddersfield Town) v SA(2) 1939
3   R. W. Benson (Sheffield United) v SA(3) 1910
1   A. Berry (Everton) v SA 1910
2   H. A. Betmead (Grimsby Town) v SA(2) 1939
1   R. J. E. Birkett (Newcastle United) v S 1941
1   J. F. Bond (West Ham United) v SA 1956

15   C. S. Britton (Everton) v S 1943(2)-4(2) v W 1941(2)-2-3(3)-4(2)
    v SA(3) 1939

1   A. K. Brook (Casuals) v Ca 1892

2   E. F. Brook (Manchester City) v SA 1939 v W 1940

1   S. Brooks (Wolverhampton Wanderers) v W 1920

3   F. H. Broome (Aston Villa) v S 1940 (Notts County) v Aust(2)
    1951

7   R. A. J. Brown (Charlton Athletic) v SA 1939 v S(2) Fr W 1945
    v Be 1946 (Nottingham Forest) v Swi 1946

1   C. M. Buchan (Sunderland) v W 1920

2   V. F. Buckingham (Tottenham Hotspur) v W(2) 1941

2   J. Bulcock (Crystal Palace) v SA(2) 1910

7   E. Burgin (Sheffield United) v Aust(3) 1951 v SA(4) 1956

1   W. C. Caesar (Dulwich Hamlet) v Aust 1925

17   H. S. Carter (Sunderland) v S 1940-3-4(3)-5(2) v W 1943(2)-4(2)
    -5(2) v Fr 1945 v I 1946 (Derby County) v Fr Swi 1946

3   A. Chandler (Leicester City) v SA(3) 1929

5   S. Charlton (Exeter City) v Aust(5) 1925

5   I. Clarke (Portsmouth) v Aust(5) 1951

1   H. Clifton (Newcastle United) v S 1940

1   J. G. Cock (Huddersfield Town) v W 1920

12   D. C. S. Compton (Arsenal) v S 1941-2(2)-3(2)-4-6 v W 1940-2
    -3(2)-4

5   L. H. Compton (Arsenal) v W 1940-3-4 v S 1943-4

1   W. Copping (Leeds United) v W 1940

1   G. H. Cotterill (Old Brightonians) v Ca 1892

1   W. J. Crayston (Arsenal) v W 1940

1   W. Crook (Blackburn Rovers) v W 1940

20   S. Cullis (Wolverhampton Wanderers) v S 1940-1(2)-2(2)-3(2)-4(3)
    v W 1940(2)-1(2)-2-3(3)-4(2)

3   A. S. Davies (Swindon Town) v SA(3) 1920

2   H. A. Davies (Stoke City) v SA(2) 1929

1   H. Davis (Birmingham St George) v Ca 1892

3   J. E. Davison (Sheffield Wednesday) v Aust(3) 1925

2   E. G. Ditchburn (Tottenham Hotspur) v S W 1944

2   F. Duckworth (Blackburn Rovers) v S(2) 1919

1   R. Duckworth (Manchester United) v SA 1910

5   M. Edelston (Reading) v S 1942-3 v W 1941-2(2)

5   J. W. Elkes (Tottenham Hotspur) v Aust(5) 1925

2   W. B. Elliott (West Bromwich Albion) v W 1944 v S 1946

3   J. R. Elvey (Luton Town) v SA(3) 1920

2   S. N. Fazackerley (Sheffield United) v SA(2) 1920

4   E. B. A. Fenton (West Ham United) v SA(3) 1939 v W 1940

4   M. Fenton (Middlesbrough) v SA(3) 1939 v W 1946

3   L. C. Finch (Barnet) v SA(2) 1939 v W 1941

1   F. W. Fisher (Millwall) v W 1941

2   T. Fleetwood (Everton) v S(2) 1919

2   H. J. Fleming (Swindon Town) v SA(2) 1910

5   R. Flewin (Portsmouth) v W 1945 v Aust(4) 1951

10   C. F. Franklin (Stoke City) v S(2) W Fr 1945 v S W I Fr Be
    Swi 1946

1   C. B. Fry (Oxford University) v Ca 1892

1   K. J. Gadsby (Leeds United) v SA 1939

1   L. H. Gay (Cambridge University) v Ca 1892

3 A. H. Gibbons (Brentford) v SA(2) 1939 (Tottenham Hotspur) v W 1943
4 H. A. Goslin (Bolton Wanderers) v S 1940-1-2 v W 1942
2 H. Gough (Sheffield United) v SA(2) 1920
6 L. A. Goulden (West Ham United) v S 1941(2)-5 v W 1940(2)-1
5 L. Graham (Millwall Athletic) v Aust(5) 1925
1 N. H. Greenhalgh (Everton) v S 1940
1 A. Grenyer (Everton) v W 1920
2 A. Grimsdell (Tottenham Hotspur) v S(2) 1919
19 J. Hagan (Sheffield United) v S 1942(3)-3(2)-4(3)-6 v W 1941(2) -2-3(2)-4 v Fr 1946 v Aust(3) 1951
3 G. W. Hall (Tottenham Hotspur) v W 1940(2)-2
4 J. Hamilton (Crystal Palace) v Aust(4) 1925
3 C. Hannaford (Clapton Orient) v Aust(3) 1925
4 J. H. Hannah (Norwich City) v Aust(4) 1925
1 A. J. Hanson (Chelsea) v S 1941
13 E. A. Hapgood (Arsenal) v S 1940-1-2(3)-3 v W 1940(2)-1-2(2)-3(2)
17 G. F. M. Hardwick (Middlesbrough) v S 1943-4(2)-5(3) v W 1941-3(2)-4-5(2) v Fr 1945 v S Fr Be Swi 1946
2 H. Hardy (Stockport County) v Aust(2) 1925
3 S. Hardy (Aston Villa) v S 1919(2) v W 1920
1 B. Harper (Barnsley) v S 1940
3 P. P. Harris (Portsmouth) v SA(3) 1956
1 A. Harrison (Nottingham Forest) v SA 1929
3 E. A. Hart (Leeds United) v SA(3) 1929
1 E. H. Hendren (Brentford) v W 1920
1 A. G. Henfrey (Corinthians) v Ca 1892
1 W. Hibbert (Bury) v SA 1910
1 H. E. Hibbs (Birmingham) v SA 1929
4 C. G. Hilditch (Manchester United) v W SA(3) 1920
3 G. A. Hitchens (Cardiff City) v SA(2) 1956 and SA(s) 1956
1 J. Hodkinson (Blackburn Rovers) v W 1920
3 G. H. Holley (Sunderland) v SA(3) 1910
1 F. C. Hudspeth (Newcastle United) v W 1920
5 G. Hurst (Charlton Athletic) v Aust(5) 1951
3 G. Jackson (Everton) v SA(3) 1939
2 B. A. G. Jezzard (Fulham) v SA(2) 1956
2 W. H. Johnson (Charlton Athletic) v Fr Swi 1946
2 J. E. Jones (Everton) v SA(2) 1939
1 B. Joy (Arsenal) v S 1945
3 A. E. Keeping (Southampton) v SA(3) 1929
1 L. V. Kieran (Tranmere Rovers) v Aust 1951
3 J. W. King (Stoke City) v SA(3) 1956
2 T. H. Kinsell (West Bromwich Albion) v I W 1946
3 A. J. Kirchen (Arsenal) v W 1941-2 v S 1942
1 A. E. Knight (Portsmouth) v W 1920
1 J. Landells (Millwall) v SA 1929
4 E. J. Langley (Brighton & Hove Albion) v SA(4) 1956
4 R. Langton (Bolton Wanderers) v Aust(4) 1951
23 T. Lawton (Everton) v S 1940-1-2(2)-3-4(3)-5(3) v W 1940-2-3-4-5(2) v Fr 1945 v I 1946 (Chelsea) v S Swi Fr Be 1946
1 J. Leeming (Brighton & Hove Albion) v SA 1910
3 J. W. Lewis (Walthamstow Avenue) v SA(2) 1939 v W(s) 1940
3 J. Lievesley (Sheffield United) v SA(3) 1910

1 F. W. Lock (Charlton Athletic) v Aust 1951
5 E. Longworth (Liverpool) v S(2) 1919 v SA(3) 1920
2 J. McCall (Preston North End) v S(2) 1919
4 J. W. McCue (Stoke City) v Aust(4) 1951
4 W. H. McGarry (Huddersfield Town) v SA(4) 1956
1 J. Mahon (Huddersfield Town) v SA 1939
4 W. J. Mannion (Middlesbrough) v S 1941(2)-2(2)
1 J. Mansell (Portsmouth) v SA 1956
3 J. D. Mapson (Sunderland) v SA(2) 1939 v W 1941
8 G. W. Marks (Arsenal) v S 1942(3)-3 v W 1942(2)-3(2)
2 H. Martin (Sunderland) v S(2) 1919
2 J. R. Martin (Aston Villa) v S W 1940
2 G. W. Mason (Coventry City) v S W 1942
29 S. Matthews (Stoke City) v S 1940(2)-1-2(3)-3(2)-4(3)-5(3) v W 1940(2)-2-3(3)-4-5(2) v Fr 1945 v W I Fr Be Swi 1946
1 D. W. Mercer (Hull City) v SA 1920
27 J. Mercer (Everton) v S 1940(2)-1(2)-2(2)-3(2)-4(3)-5(3) v W 1940-2-3(3)-4-5(2) v Fr 1945 v S W I Be 1946
1 J. W. Mew (Manchester United) v SA 1920
3 S. H. Mortensen (Blackpool) v S W 1945 v I 1946
2 R. H. Morton (Luton Town) v SA(2) 1956
1 R. C. Mountford (Huddersfield Town) v S 1941
3 J. Mullen (Wolverhampton Wanderers) v W 1943-5 v Be 1946
2 John Oakes (Charlton Athletic) v SA 1939 v W 1940
2 B. A. Olney (Aston Villa) v SA(2) 1929
4 S. W. Owen (Luton Town) v Aust(2) 1951 v SA(2) 1956
1 C. W. Parker (Stoke) v W 1920
3 D. Parker (West Ham United) v Aust(3) 1951
1 T. U. Pearson (Newcastle United) v S 1940
2 W. H. Pease (Middlesbrough) v SA (2) 1929
1 F. R. Pelly (Old Foresters) v Ca 1892
4 W. Perry (Blackpool) v SA(4) 1956
3 G. E. Petherbridge (Bristol Rovers) v SA(3) 1956
1 C. Poynton (Tottenham Hotspur) v Aust 1925
1 W. J. Price (Fulham) v SA 1929
3 S. C. Puddefoot (West Ham United) v S(2) 1919 v W 1920
1 J. Pye (Notts County) v Be 1946
4 L. W. Quested (Huddersfield Town) v SA(4) 1956
2 J. E. Raine (Glossop) v SA(2) 1910
2 G. H. Richards (Derby County) v SA(2) 1910
1 J. Richardson (Newcastle United) v S 1940
4 R. W. Robson (West Bromwich Albion) v SA(4) 1956
1 D. Rogers (Swindon Town) v SA 1920
1 R. L. Rooke (Fulham) v W 1943
1 J. F. Rowley (Manchester United) v W 1944
1 A. W. Roxburgh (Blackpool) v W 1944
16 L. Scott (Arsenal) v S 1944(2)-5(3) v W 1942-4(2)-5(2) v Fr 1945 v S W I Be Swi 1946
2 J. M. Seed (Sheffield Wednesday) v SA(2) 1929
5 J. Sewell (Sheffield Wednesday) v Aust(5) 1951
2 G. S. Seymour (Newcastle United) v Aust(2) 1925
1 L. F. Shackleton (Bradford) v S 1946
5 J. Shaw (Sheffield United) v Aust(5) 1951
2 D Shea (Blackburn Rovers) v S(2) 1919

2 F. A. Shelley (Southampton) v SA(2) 1929
1 W. A. Silto (Swindon Town) v SA 1910
5 E. Simms (Stockport County) v Aust(5) 1925
1 G. C. Smith (Charlton Athletic) v W 1945
6 J. Smith (Bolton Wanderers) v S(2) 1919 v W 1920 v SA(3) 1920
1 J. Smith (West Bromwich Albion) v W 1920
3 J. C. R. Smith (Millwall) v S 1940 v W 1940-1
13 L. G. F. Smith (Brentford) v S 1944(2)-5(3) v W 1940-2-4-5 v Fr
   1945 v I Fr Swi 1946
1 W. Smith (Nottingham Forest) v Ca 1892
1 W. H. Smith (Birmingham City) v Aust 1951
9 F. Soo (Stoke City) v W 1942-4 v S 1944-5(3) v Fr 1945 v I 1946
   (Leicester City) v W 1946
5 C. W. Spencer (Newcastle United) v Aust(5) 1925
2 B. Sproston (Manchester City) v S W 1940
1 M. H. Stanbrough (Cambridge University) v Ca 1892
1 A. Stubbins (Newcastle United) v W 1946
2 A. Sturgess (Sheffield United) v SA(2) 1910
14 F. V. Swift (Manchester City) v S 1941-3-4(2)-5(3) v W 1940-3-5
   v S I Swi Be 1946
1 T. A. Swinburne (Newcastle United) v S 1940
1 F. Taylor (Wolverhampton Wanderers) v S 1944
1 F. Thompson (Nottingham Forest) v Ca 1892
2 W. P. Thompson (Nottingham Forest) v SA(2) 1929
1 A. G. Topham (Casuals) v Ca 1892
8 R. J. Turnbull (Bradford) v S 1919(2) v W SA(3) 1920 (Leeds
   United) v SA(2) 1929
4 W. Voisey (Millwall Athletic) v W SA(3) 1920
3 G. Wall (Manchester United) v SA(3) 1910
3 J. A. Walsh (Liverpool) v Aust(3) 1925
1 W. Watson (Burnley) v W 1920
1 W. Watson (Huddersfield Town) v W 1946
1 H. Webster (Bolton Wanderers) v Aust(s) 1951
3 W. J. Wedlock (Bristol City) v SA(3) 1910
9 D. Welsh (Charlton Athletic) v S 1940-1-2(2) v W 1941(2)-2-4-5
4 D. Westcott (Wolverhampton Wanderers) v W 1940-3(2) v S 1943
1 R. Whittingham (Chelsea) v W 1920
4 B. F. Williams (Walsall) v W Fr 1945 (Wolverhampton Wanderers)
   v W Fr 1946
2 J. J. Williams (Stoke City) v SA(2) 1929
2 W. D. Williams (West Ham United) v Aust(2) 1925
1 E. C. Williamson (Arsenal) v W 1920
6 C. K. Willingham (Huddersfield Town) v S 1940-1-2(2) v W
   1940(2)
2 W. Woodcock (Manchester City) v SA(2) 1920
1 J. Woodhouse (Brighton & Hove Albion) v SA 1920
2 V. R. Woodley (Chelsea) v S W 1940
3 V. J. Woodward (Chelsea) v SA(3) 1910
4 W. A. Wright (Wolverhampton Wanderers) v S Fr Be Swi 1946

UNOFFICIAL INTERNATIONAL MATCHES

As related in Chapter One, five unofficial international matches were played before the first official international in November 1872. In previous books on the history of the game a varying number of these matches have been mentioned but never the whole five, and it is felt that it might be a matter of historical interest if these matches were recorded in full.

5 March 1870, at The Oval

England 1 (Baker)   **Scotland 1 (Crawford)**

England 1 (Baker)	Scotland 1 (Crawford)
C. W. Alcock (Old Harrovians) Capt.	R. E. W. Crawford (Harrow Sch.)
A. J. Baker (N.N.)	W. H. Gladstone (Old Etonians)
E. E. Bowen (Wanderers)	G. C. Gordon (N.N.)
W. C. Butler (Barnes)	C. R. B. Hamilton (Civil Service)
W. P. Crake (Harrow School)	W. A. B. Hamilton (Old Harrovians)
E. Freeth (Civil Service)	A. F. Kinnaird (Crusaders)
E. Lubbock (Old Etonians)	J. Kirkpatrick (Civil Service) Capt.
A. Nash (Clapham Rovers)	W. Lindsay (Old Wykehamists)
J. C. Smith (Crusaders)	J. W. Malcolm (London Scottish Rifles)
A. H. Thornton (Old Harrovians)	A. Morten (Crystal Palace)
R. W. S. Vidal (Westminster Sch.)	K. Muir Mackenzie (Old Carthusians)

It will be seen that the Scotland team included both W. Lindsay and A. Morten who subsequently played for England when the official series started.

19 November 1870, at The Oval

England 1 (Walker)	Scotland 0
C. W. Alcock (Wanderers) Capt.	G. F. Congreve (Old Rugbeians)
A. J. Baker (Wanderers)	R. E. Crawford (Harrow School)
T. N. Carter (Eton College)	W. A. B. Hamilton (Old Harrovians)
J. Cockerell (Brixton)	Quintin Hogg (Wanderers)
W. P. Crake (Barnes)	G. G. Kennedy (Wanderers)
T. C. Hooman (Wanderers)	A. F. Kinnaird (Old Etonians)
E. Lubbock (West Kent)	J. Kirkpatrick (Civil Service) Capt.
W. B. Paton (Harrow School)	W. Lindsay (Old Wykehamists)
H. J. Preston (Eton College)	C. E. B. Nepean (Oxford Univer.)
R. W. S. Vidal (Westminster Sch.)	H. W. Primrose (Civil Service)
R. S. F. Walker (Clapham Rovers)	R. Smith (Queens Park)

25 February 1871, at The Oval

England 1 (Walker)   Scotland 1 (Nepean)

M. P. Betts (West Kent)   J. Kirkpatrick (Civil Service)
C. W. Stephenson   W. H. Gladstone (Old Etonians)
    (Westminster School)   Quintin Hogg (Wanderers)
E. Lubbock (West Kent)   A. F. Kinaird (Wanderers)
C. W. Alcock (Pilgrims)   F. B. Maddison (Oxford Univer.)
A. J. Baker (Wanderers)   J. F. Inglis (Charterhouse Sch.)
W. C. Butler (Civil Service)   W. Lindsay (Old Wykehamists)
J. Cockerell (Brixton)   A. K. Smith (Oxford University)
W. P. Crake (Barnes)   C. E. B. Nepean (Oxford Univer.)
T. C. Hooman (Wanderers)   R. Smith (Queens Park)
R. W. S. Vidal (Westminster Sch.)   C. E. Primrose (Civil Service)
R. S. F. Walker (Clapham Rovers)

In this match the teams played one goalkeeper, one back, one half-back and the rest were forwards. The teams are shown in that order. It will be seen that F. B. Maddison and A. K. Smith, who became full English internationals, were in the Scotland team.

18 November 1871, at The Oval

England 2 (Walker 2)   Scotland 1 (Renny-Tailyour)

C. W. Stephenson (Wanderers)   R. Smith (Queens Park)
A. C. Thompson   W. Lindsay (Old Wykehamists)
    (Eton Cambridge Club) C. E. B. Nepean (Oxford Univer.)
E. Lubbock (West Kent)   H. W. Renny-Tailyour
C. W. Alcock (Wanderers) Capt.   (Royal Engineers)
T. S. Baker (Clapham Rovers)   H. E. Mitchell (Royal Engineers)
M. P. Betts (Harrow Chequers)   R. E. W. Crawford
J. Kenrick (Clapham Rovers)   (Old Harrovians)
R. W. S. Vidal (Westminster Sch.)   H. S. Ferguson
R. S. F. Walker (Clapham Rovers)   (R.M.A. Woolwich)
P. Weston (Barnes)   F. H. Crawford (Harrow Cheq'rs)
W. P. Crake (Harrow Chequers)   A. K. Smith (Oxford University)
                           J. Kirkpatrick (Civil Service)
                           E. H. M. Elliot (Harrow Chequers)

24 February 1872 at The Oval

England 1 (Clegg)   Scotland 0

C. W. Stephenson (Wanderers)   C. E. B. Nepean (Oxford Uni.)
E. Lubbock (West Kent)   E. H. M. Elliot (Harrow Chequers)
A. C. Thompson (Wanderers)   W. Lindsay (Civil Service)
C. W. Alcock (Wanderers) Capt.   M. Muir-Mackenzie
A. G. Bonsor (Wanderers)   (Old Carthusians) Capt.

C. J. Chenery (Crystal Palace)   R. E. W. Crawford
J. C. Clegg (Sheffield Wednesday)   (Harrow Chequers)
T. C. Hooman (Wanderers)   H. S. Ferguson (Royal Artillery)
P. Weston (Barnes)   H. E. Mitchell (Royal Engineers)
R. W. S. Vidal (Westminster Sch.)   F. H. Crawford (Harrow Cheq'rs)
C. H. R. Wollaston (Oxford Uni.)   E. V. Ravenshaw
                                                 (Charterhouse School)
                                       H. H. Stewart (Wanderers)
                                       C. M. Thompson
                                                 (Cambridge University)

NOTE: In the last two games the teams, as in the third match, lined
      up with one goalkeeper, one back, one half-back and
      remainder were forwards. In the first two matches the teams
      are listed in alphabetical order and the players' playing
      positions are unknown.

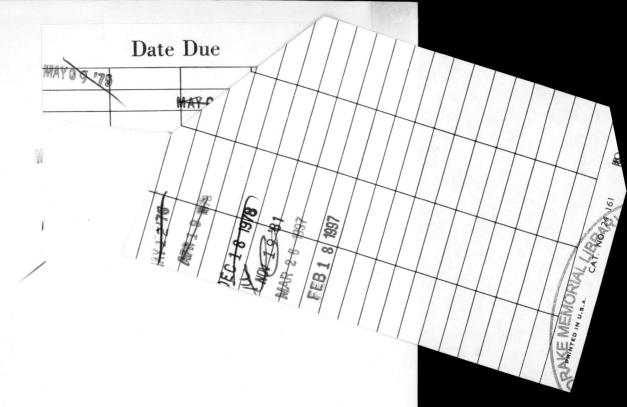